Future-proof CALL: language learning as exploration and encounters

Short papers from EUROCALL 2018

Edited by Peppi Taalas, Juha Jalkanen,
Linda Bradley & Sylvie Thouësny

Research-publishing.net

Research-publishing.net

Published by Research-publishing.net, a not-for-profit association
Contact: info@research-publishing.net

Future-proof CALL: language learning as exploration and encounters – short papers from EUROCALL 2018
Edited by Peppi Taalas, Juha Jalkanen, Linda Bradley, and Sylvie Thouësny

Publication date: 2018/12/08

Typeset by Research-publishing.net
Cover theme by © 2018 Antti Myöhänen (antti.myohanen@gmail.com)
Cover layout by © 2018 Raphaël Savina (raphael@savina.net)
Drawings by © 2018 Linda Saukko-Rauta (linda@redanredan.fi)

ISBN13: 978-2-490057-22-1 (Ebook, PDF, colour)
ISBN13: 978-2-490057-23-8 (Ebook, EPUB, colour)
ISBN13: 978-2-490057-21-4 (Paperback - Print on demand, black and white)
Print on demand technology is a high-quality, innovative and ecological printing method; with which the book is never 'out of stock' or 'out of print'.

British Library Cataloguing-in-Publication Data.
A cataloguing record for this book is available from the British Library.

Legal deposit, UK: British Library.
Legal deposit, France: Bibliothèque Nationale de France - Dépôt légal: Décembre 2018.

Table of contents

JYVÄSKYLÄN YLIOPISTO
UNIVERSITY OF JYVÄSKYLÄ

Programme committee

Programme chairs

- Sake Jager (chair), *University of Groningen*
- John Gillespie (co-chair), *University of Ulster*

Committee members

- Christine Appel, *Universitat Oberta de Catalunya*
- David Barr, *Ulster University*
- Becky Bergman, *Chalmers University of Technology*
- Françoise Blin, *Dublin City University*
- Kate Borthwick, *University of Southampton*
- Alex Boulton, *University of Lorraine*
- Jack Burston, *Cyprus University of Technology*
- Jozef Colpaert, *Universiteit Antwerpen*
- Ana Gimeno, *Universidad Politécnica de Valencia*
- Nicolas Guichon, *Université Lyon 2*
- Mirjam Hauck, *Open University*
- Philip Hubbard, *Stanford University*
- Teppo Jakonen, *University of Jyväskylä*
- Kristi Jauregi, *Utrecht University*
- Carita Kiili, *University of Oslo*
- Leena Kuure, *University of Oulu*
- Teresa MacKinnon, *Warwick University*
- Vera Menezes, *UFMG*
- Liam Murray, *University of Limerick*
- Susanna Nocchi, *Dublin Institute of Technology*
- Luisa Panichi, *University of Pisa*
- Salomi Papadima, *Cyprus University of Technology*
- Hans Paulussen, *KU Leuven KULAK*
- Shannon Sauro, *Malmö University*
- Oranna Speicher, *University of Nottingham*
- Mirja Tarnanen, *University of Jyvaskyla*
- Sylvie Thouësny, *Research-publishing.net*
- Cornelia Tschichold, *Swansea University*

- Julie Van de Vyver, *Université Catholique de Louvain*
- Sylvi Vigmo, *University of Gothenburg*
- Shona Whyte, *Université Côte d'Azur*

Peer-reviewing committee (full articles)

- Kazumi Aizawa, *Tokyo Denki University, Tokyo, Japan*
- Sahar Alzahrani, *Umm AlQura University, Makkah, Saudi Arabia*
- Androulla Athanasiou, *Cyprus University of Technology, Limassol, Cyprus*
- Mike Barcomb, *Concordia University, Montreal, Canada*
- Ana Beaven, *University of Bologna, Bologna, Italy*
- Tita Beaven, *The Open University, Milton Keynes, United Kingdom*
- Branislav Bedi, *University of Iceland, Reykjavík, Iceland*
- Tiago Bione, *Concordia University, Montreal, Canada*
- Alex Boulton, *ATILF (University of Lorraine & CNRS), France*
- Walcir Cardoso, *Concordia University, Montreal, Canada*
- Aparajita Dey-Plissonneau, *Dublin City University, Dublin, Ireland*
- Paul Dickinson, *Meijo University, Nagoya, Japan*
- Marta Fondo, *Universitat Oberta de Catalunya, Barcelona, Spain*
- Andrew Gallacher, *Kyushu Sangyo University, Fukuoka, Japan*
- Ana Gimeno-Sanz, *Universitat Politècnica de València, València, Spain*
- Jennica Grimshaw, *Concordia University, Montreal, Canada*
- Sandra Healy, *Kyoto Institute of Technology, Kyoto, Japan*
- Clinton Hendry, *Concordia University, Montreal, Canada*
- Tatsuo Iso, *Tokyo Denki University, Tokyo, Japan*
- Nasser Jabbari, *University of Reading, Reading, United Kingdom*
- Kristi Jauregi, *Utrecht University, Utrecht, the Netherlands*
- Paul John, *Université du Québec à Trois-Rivières, Trois-Rivières, Canada*
- Regina Kaplan-Rakowski, *Valdosta State University, Valdosta, Georgia, United States*
- Johanna Komppa, *University of Helsinki, Helsinki, Finland*
- Lari Kotilainen, *University of Helsinki, Helsinki, Finland*
- Leena Kuure, *University of Oulu, Oulu, Finland*
- Natallia Liakina, *McGill University, Montreal, Canada*
- Paul Lyddon, *University of Shizuoka, Japan*
- Conchúr Mac Lochlainn, *Dublin City University, Dublin, Ireland*
- Eva Malessa, *University of Jyväskylä, Finland*
- Antonio Martínez-Sáez, *Universidad Politécnica de Madrid, Madrid, Spain*
- Maryam Sadat Mirzaei, *Kyoto University, Kyoto, Japan*
- Mitsuhiro Morita, *Hiroshima University, Higashihiroshima, Japan*

- Anu Muhonen, *University of Toronto, Toronto, Canada*
- Paul Nadasdy, *Tokyo Denki University, Tokyo, Japan*
- Neasa Ní Chiaráin, *Trinity College, Dublin, Ireland*
- Louise Ohashi, *Meiji University, Japan*
- Salomi Papadima-Sophocleous, *Cyprus University of Technology, Limassol, Cyprus*
- Kevin Papin, *McGill University, Montreal, Canada*
- Giouli Pappa, *Cyprus University of Technology, Limassol, Cyprus*
- Bart Pardoel, *Cyprus University of Technology, Limassol, Cyprus*
- Maritta Riekki, *University of Oulu, Oulu, Finland*
- Avery Rueb, *Vanier College, Montreal, Canada*
- June Ruivivar, *Concordia University, Montreal, Canada*
- Anne-Marie Sénécal, *Concordia University, Montréal, Canada*
- Andrew Thompson, *Fukuoka Women's University, Fukuoka, Japan*
- Yasushi Tsubota, *Kyoto Institute of Technology, Kyoto, Japan*
- Margarita Vinagre-Laranjeira, *Universidad Autónoma de Madrid, Madrid, Spain*
- Ruby Vurdien, *White Rose Language School, Valladolid, Spain*
- Tomasz Wojdynski, *The School of Banking and Management, Cracow, Poland*
- Nina Woll, *Université du Québec à Trois-Rivières, Trois-Rivières, Canada*
- Yu-Feng (Diana) Yang, *National Sun Yat-Sen University, Kaohsiung, Taiwan*
- Torsten Zesch, *University Duisburg-Essen, Duisburg, Germany*

JYVÄSKYLÄN YLIOPISTO
UNIVERSITY OF JYVÄSKYLÄ

Preface

Peppi Taalas[1] and Juha Jalkanen[2]

The theme of this year's conference was 'Future-proof CALL: language learning as exploration and encounters', which reflects an attempt to envision language teaching and learning futures in a changing world. What brought us together this year are shared concerns in relation to the sustainability of language learning and teaching in technology-rich contexts that are marked by ever-increasing complexity. The need to redefine our purpose and mission is as important as ever. Technology is affecting learning, teaching, researching – in fact, all aspects of our lives – in so many different ways.

The 26th EuroCALL conference was organised by the University of Jyväskylä (JYU) Language Campus and specifically the Language Centre. The conference gathered together close to 300 participants from 30 different countries for four days to present papers, attend presentations, workshops, symposia, meetings and – most importantly – network and socialise with colleagues and friends from near and far.

Our keynote speakers, who came more or less outside the field of Computer-Assisted Language Learning (CALL), explored and unpacked the notion of future proofing from multiple and thought-provoking angles.

Saku Tuominen started with the question 'why', asking why is it that we need to change education, or do we? One of his key messages was that the essence of education is to help people to flourish in life no matter what happens. The difficult question, however, for us educators to think about is what are the skills that are needed to flourish in life both today and tomorrow?

1. Eurocall conference chair, University of Jyväskylä, Jyväskylä, Finland; peppi.taalas@jyu.fi
2. Eurocall conference co-chair, University of Jyväskylä, Jyväskylä, Finland; juha.k.jalkanen@jyu.fi

How to cite: Taalas, P., & Jalkanen, J. (2018). Preface. In P. Taalas, J. Jalkanen, L. Bradley & S. Thouësny (Eds), *Future-proof CALL: language learning as exploration and encounters – short papers from EUROCALL 2018* (pp. xii-xiv). Research-publishing.net. https://doi.org/10.14705/rpnet.2018.26.802

Claire Kramsch, in turn, took a perspective of an applied linguist. She reminded us that technology is not only assisting language learning but it is transforming what we call a language. Touching upon the notions of identity, equality, and accessibility, Kramsch raised the question of 'what is in our hands' when the technology brings us together? What are the issues we should be talking about and what are the problems that need to be addressed? She also argued that the basic elements of language teaching have mainly remained the same despite the theoretical developments of language and language use. Reflecting on the burning issues in the recent political discussions, she also raised the question of whether language teaching is preparing students for the reality of language use and being a speaker of a certain language.

The Graham Davies keynote speaker, Mark Brown, talked about the future and what it has been considered to be in different times. He emphasised the difficulty of seeing what is relevant in amidst the rapidly changing environment of teaching and learning. The teachers' mindsets play an important role in shaping the ways in which learning is organised. He said that the complexity makes it difficult to control the horizons of expectation and to know who to believe and whose ideas and initiatives to discard. He emphasised the need to establish a culture of vision and trust within which a strategic thinking can actually help us identify the voices we should hear and follow.

More information about the keynote addresses, as well as the full programme, may be found at the conference website: http://jyu.fi/eurocall2018.

The conference themes were organised around the following five main themes:

- Environments for interaction and learning.
- Pedagogies, practices, and cultures.
- CALL for future – beyond SLA.
- CALL and 21st century skills.
- Assessment for learning.

We received 275 submissions of which 184 were accepted to be presented as workshops, symposia, individual oral presentations, or posters. The oral presentations were categorised as research, research and development, reflective practice papers, along with presentations on European projects.

This collection of short papers in this volume is a very thorough view into the conference proper exhibiting the complexity and novelty of the field of CALL.

There are exciting new openings and a more profound exploration of theoretical underpinnings of the contemporary issues in teaching and learning, cross-cultural communication, mobile learning and the like.

We would like to thank all participants, presenters, keynotes, special interest groups (SIGs), and programme committee members who made Eurocall 2018 such a success. We would also like to thank the authors of the papers and the reviewers who put in their time and effort to ensure the high quality of the submissions. A big thank you goes to Sylvie Thouësny and Linda Bradley for their dedication to EuroCALL and its publications.

We hope you will enjoy reading this volume and that the insights into the current research agendas captured in the papers will move forward our thinking about how to futureproof CALL.

We look forward to seeing you at next EuroCALL conferences!

Social media in language learning: a mixed-methods investigation of Saudi students' perceptions

Nouf Aloraini[1] and Walcir Cardoso[2]

Abstract. This study investigates Saudi students' attitudes towards the use of four Social Media (SM) applications for learning English as a Foreign Language (EFL): Instagram, Snapchat, Twitter, and WhatsApp. Ninety-nine adult students participated in this mixed-methods study, which included surveys and interviews to examine their perception of SM as pedagogical tools. A two-way analysis of variance (ANOVAs) revealed that there are differences between beginner and advanced students in their perceptions of the usefulness of SM applications for language learning, but not in their affective feelings towards SM for use outside the classroom, nor their choice of SM application for learning. In addition, groups' choices of SM varied according to language purposes and skills to be learned. Further qualitative analysis revealed that advanced learners are reluctant to use SM for academic purposes, considering them to be their own social (not educational) spaces.

Keywords: social media, language learning, perceptions, attitudes.

1.   Introduction

Previous research has reported students' positive perceptions towards using SM for academic purposes (e.g. Lee & Markey, 2014). However, researchers have also reported a possible variance in perceptions because of students' proficiency level (Gamble & Wilkins, 2014). Interestingly, studies in the context of general education found that students hold negative attitudes towards using SM for educational purposes (Venkatesh et al., 2016). The factors that motivated this study include: the mixed findings reported above, and the lack or scarcity of studies that: (1) focus on Arab users of SM (particularly those from Saudi Arabia),

1. King Saud University, Riyadh, Saudi Arabia; naloraini@ksu.edu.sa
2. Concordia University, Montréal, Canada; walcir.cardoso@concordia.ca

How to cite this article: Aloraini, N., & Cardoso, W. (2018). Social media in language learning: a mixed-methods investigation of Saudi students' perceptions. In P. Taalas, J. Jalkanen, L. Bradley & S. Thouësny (Eds), *Future-proof CALL: language learning as exploration and encounters – short papers from EUROCALL 2018* (pp. 1-5). Research-publishing.net. https://doi.org/10.14705/rpnet.2018.26.803

(2) investigate more recent SM applications (e.g. Snapchat and Instagram), (3) examine SM's pedagogical usefulness (e.g. whether learners' SM choices differ according to the targeted language skill to be learned), and (4) that probe students' affective feelings towards them. As such, the ultimate goal of this study is to inform language teachers who consider adopting SM to extend their classroom practices. Four Research Questions (RQs) guided this study:

- What are students' perceptions of the usefulness of four SM applications (i.e. WhatsApp, Instagram, Snapchat, and Twitter) and their affective feelings towards their pedagogical use? Are these perceptions affected by users' proficiency level in English?

- Are there differences in student use of SM applications for different language purposes?

- Which SM application(s) do students prefer for learning English? Are there differences in students' SM choices according to the targeted language skills?

- What are Saudi students' perceived advantages and disadvantages of learning EFL through SM?

2.   Method

2.1.   Participants

Ninety-nine EFL students from King Saud University in Riyadh (Saudi Arabia) were randomly selected to participate in the study. They were stratified among two proficiency levels determined by their institution: beginners (24 males, 25 females, mean age 21) and advanced (25 males, 25 females, mean age 23).

2.2.   Materials and procedure

An initial online survey was created to determine SM applications used by Saudis. The survey was distributed via SM and yielded around 800 responses revealing that WhatsApp, Snapchat, Instagram, and Twitter were the top most used SM in Saudi Arabia. Based on these results, a six-point Likert scale survey was created and distributed to the participants. This survey was designed to elicit students' perceptions towards the usefulness of SM, students' affective feelings towards SM use for language learning, and SM choices when used for learning EFL. Finally, open-ended semi-structured oral interviews were also conducted with 14 randomly selected participants to obtain qualitative data about their perceptions of their English-learning experience using the four SM applications targeted by this research.

3.   Results

A two-way analysis of variance was run to answer the first RQ and part of the third RQ; consequently, alpha was reduced to $p=0.017$ to account for the number of ANOVAs conducted. The remaining quantitative data were answered through means of frequency counts.

For RQ1, the statistical results indicated that there were differences in the perceived usefulness of SM as a learning tool between beginner and advanced students ($p=0.014$). Advanced participants significantly viewed Twitter more useful than the other three SMs, while Snapchat and Instagram did not differ from each other, and WhatsApp was perceived as the least useful: Twitter>Snapchat=Instagram>WhatsApp; where > indicates more useful/preferred than). For beginner students, only WhatsApp was different from the other three applications, being perceived as less useful, while Snapchat, Instagram, and Twitter were nearly identical in usefulness: Twitter=Snapchat=Instagram>WhatsApp.

However, the two proficiency groups did not differ in their affective feelings towards SM use outside the classroom, nor in their choice of application for learning purposes. As such, students had significantly less affective feelings towards using WhatsApp for learning than Snapchat, Instagram and Twitter. Interestingly, Twitter was the only application viewed positively by both groups for its learning potential.

Regarding RQ2 and 3, data analysis revealed that students' SM preferences varied according to different language purposes and the targeted language skills to be learned: both groups favoured WhatsApp for communication with family and friends, Twitter for reading, and Snapchat for learning aural skills (listening and speaking). As for vocabulary, grammar and writing, advanced students preferred Twitter while beginners chose WhatsApp.

Students also reported that the main advantages of using SM for learning (RQ4) were the availability and affordability of these applications, in addition to offering an opportunity to practise English and immerse themselves in the L2 environment, especially when L2 English use in Saudi Arabia is usually limited and often confined to the classroom. Most participants mentioned that they often pay attention to their grammar and vocabulary before posting in SM. They also reported some disadvantages regarding the use of SM for L2 learning. Advanced learners fear lack of privacy and expressed concerns that the academic use of SM might inhibit their overall enjoyment using them. The two groups also expressed concerns regarding the accuracy of information found on SM, as well as the spelling and grammar errors observed in such platforms, thus questioning its suitability for language learning. Other issues such as the lack of feedback and being distracted by other features in the selected SM platforms were also expressed.

4.   Discussion and conclusion

This study investigated Saudi students' attitudes towards the use of four social media applications for learning EFL. Results indicated that there were differences in the perceived usefulness of SM as a learning tool between beginner and advanced students; however, the groups did not differ in their affective feelings towards SM use outside the classroom, nor in their choice of application for learning. Twitter, on the other hand, was viewed positively by both groups for its learning potential. Thematic analysis of the qualitative data gives us some explanations for such differences in perception between the two groups regarding SM's ability to support learning. For advanced learners, 'supportive' means with minimum teacher involvement (e.g. completed independently), as SM is perceived as their private space. For beginners, 'supportive' denotes learning with additional resources to what is already provided in the classroom, which may also be teacher-guided. Both groups therefore accept SM as pedagogical tools, but differently: one as a complement (advanced) and the other as an extension (beyond).

Favouring Snapchat for listening and speaking can be attributed to the services offered by the application, as it offers instant, but temporary, video chat. Without the ability to review previous videos, learners probably feel less embarrassed if they make mistakes, as the videos disappear within seconds.

Many factors may have contributed to Saudi students' overall preference for Twitter. First, Twitter is quick and easy to use, limits the length of user posts to 280 characters, and is accessed by many users around the world, regardless of age, cultural background, or profession. Secondly, our qualitative results suggest that Twitter is a platform on which students can freely express their thoughts, state their opinions, and engage in discussions – activities which they do not usually engage in in any other SM. Participants also associate Twitter with receiving breaking news, accessing information, and communicating with experts. In addition, students use it for formal practices, and they seem to behave more seriously on Twitter than on other SM applications given that Twitter is associated with intellectual discourse in politics, religion, and culture (see, for example, the current use of Twitter by politicians, royalty, and political figures such as Trump, Trudeau, King Salman, and the Pope). Therefore, Twitter is perceived as an acceptable medium for pedagogical purposes.

The results indicate that there are differences in the perceived usefulness of SM as a learning tool between beginner and advanced students, and that students' preferences for SM vary according to the targeted language skill (e.g. Snapchat for listening and speaking and Twitter for reading). As such, our findings reinforce the prevalence of Twitter among the other SM applications for language learning, and indicate that beginner students are more willing to use SM outside the classroom for pedagogical purposes. Advanced learners, on the other hand, claim SM as their personal space, thus disfavouring its use as it might interfere with their private lives.

References

Gamble, C., & Wilkins, M. (2014). Student attitudes and perceptions of using Facebook for language learning. *Dimension, 3*, 49-72.

Lee, L., & Markey, A. (2014). A study of learners' perceptions of online intercultural exchange through Web 2.0 technologies. *ReCALL, 26*(3), 281-297. https://doi.org/10.1017/S0958344014000111

Venkatesh, V., Rabah, J., Fusaro, M., Couture, A., Varela, W., & Alexander, K. (2016). Factors impacting university instructors' and students' perceptions of course effectiveness and technology integration in the age of Web 2.0. *McGill Journal of Education, 51*(1), 533-561. https://doi.org/10.7202/1037358ar

Practices, challenges, and prospects of e-learning at a Saudi university: English teachers' perspectives

Sahar Alzahrani[1]

Abstract. This research aims to examine the practices of university English Language (EL) teachers in e-learning and to explore perspectives on the challenges and prospects of e-learning. It is an exploratory study which adopts a pragmatic paradigm and a mixed method approach to inquiry. A survey design and a phenomenological design are used in this research to investigate the use of technology by the teachers of EL at Umm AlQura University (UQU) in Saudi Arabia (SA) and to explore their lived experiences as well as their views in relation to the challenges and prospects of e-learning implementation. It uses both quantitative data taken from a closed-ended survey (N=43) and qualitative data taken from a Focus Group (FG) with ten university EL teachers who teach English for Specific Purposes (ESP, i.e. medical purposes) in a country where English is used as a foreign language. The research seeks to examine the university EL teachers' practices of e-learning in their teaching and to explore their perspectives on the challenges and prospects of the implementation of e-learning.

Keywords: e-learning, English language teachers, practices, challenges, prospects.

1. Introduction

With the revolution of technology in the last century, technology is now incorporated in many aspects of our life. The educational field is one of the areas which benefits from the proliferated use of digital technologies. Language teaching and learning is not an exception as technology can be used by teachers and learners for different purposes, e.g. finding information online about language, online interaction, and online consumption of target language via

1. Umm AlQura University, Makkah, Saudi Arabia; saharmatar2@gmail.com

How to cite this article: Alzahrani, S. (2018). Practices, challenges, and prospects of e-learning at a Saudi university: English teachers' perspectives. In P. Taalas, J. Jalkanen, L. Bradley & S. Thouësny (Eds), *Future-proof CALL: language learning as exploration and encounters – short papers from EUROCALL 2018* (pp. 6-10). Research-publishing.net. https://doi.org/10.14705/rpnet.2018.26.804

technological media (Stanley, 2013). In the last decade, e-learning in higher education has seen dramatic development not only in the developed, but also in the developing countries (Mbati & Minnaar, 2015). Policy makers in SA have established the *e-Learning Strategic Plan* and have set the protocols for e-learning use (Alshahrani & Alshehri, 2012). However, the implementation of e-learning in the Saudi universities seems to be not very effective as compared to the massive funds provided to technology by the Ministry of Education (Quadri et al., 2017).

This paper reports on an exploratory study investigating the practices of university EL teachers in e-learning and exploring their perspectives on the challenges and prospects of e-learning in their institution and in SA. Therefore, the study asks three research questions:

- To what extent do university EL teachers *practise* e-learning? And what are their practices?

- What are the teachers' perspectives on the *challenges* for implementing e-learning in their institution and country?

- What are the teachers' perspectives on the *prospects* of implementing e-learning in their institution and country?

2.   Method

2.1.   Study design

This is an exploratory study which exploits a mixed method approach to inquiry and a pragmatic paradigm with survey and phenomenological designs to investigate the practices of e-learning by the teachers of EL at UQU in SA and to explore their views on the use of e-learning. The population is the university EL teachers who teach ESP. The sample in the survey design consists of 43 university EL teachers and the one used in the phenomenological design encompasses ten teachers.

2.2.   Data collection

Two methods are used to answer the research questions. This mixed-method study uses quantitative data. A closed-ended survey (23 items about frequency of technology use) was administered to forty-three volunteering university language teachers to examine their practices of e-learning using a five-point Likert scale ranging from 'never' to 'always'. The response rate was a hundred percent. This quantitative data is integrated with qualitative data from a focus group discussion with ten volunteering teachers to further explore their perspectives regarding their practices, challenges, and the prospects of technology implementation in teaching.

3.   Results and discussion

SPSS was used to carry out descriptive statistics on teachers' responses in the survey about their practices in e-learning. The findings from the two types of data regarding teachers' practices of e-learning were integrated to ensure the validity of the findings in each type. Findings are extracted from the qualitative data in the FG to explore teachers' perspectives on the challenges and prospects of e-learning.

3.1.   Practice

3.1.1.   Quantitative data

It was found that the mean for the university English teachers' technology use in teaching is 3.095, $SD=0.489$. This mean indicates a medium frequency of technology use as demonstrated in the calculated length of the scale cells (2.60 to less than 3.40) (see supplementary materials[2]). The mean for teachers' use of search engines (e.g. Google) is 4.1860 in the range (3.40 to less than 4.20) suggesting that they are often used for teaching. Moreover, the mean for teachers' use of emails is 4.0698, in the range (3.40 to less than 4.20), showing that email is often used.

Nonetheless, the mean for teachers' use of virtual classrooms is 1.814, in the range (1.80 to less than 2.60), indicating a rare use of virtual environments in teaching English. Similarly, the mean for the use of online learning environments (e.g. Jusur, Moodle, Blackboard, D2L) is 1.937, in the range (1.80 to less than 2.60), suggesting a rare use. These findings are not surprising as online learning environments have only recently been adopted by the university and virtual classrooms are being trialled with a small number of teachers.

---

2. https://www.dropbox.com/s/iqsuz13c4xqnlca/EUROCALL2018%20proceedings-%20Appendix.docx?dl=0

3.1.2. Qualitative data

Asking teachers in the FG about their role in e-learning, no one goes with the option 'decision makers', but six chose 'users', and three have gone with 'other' which indicates that three of them do not use technology in teaching. The responses about the progress of their institution in e-learning varied: three were positive (e.g. "progressing very fast"), whereas only one negative response suggests low progress (e.g. "baby steps"). Additionally, four positive responses were given about the progress in e-learning in their country (e.g. "advancing"). More of the teachers identified as users than non-users; and most teachers have reported a progress in e-learning in their institution and country. These findings go in line with medium frequency of practice as demonstrated in the mean of teachers' technology use.

3.2. Challenges

Teachers' responses in the FG about the challenges they face for e-learning varied. Eight responses fall into four categories: equipment ("machines are not provided"), training ("and training of course"), lack of knowledge about how to use technology ("we have to learn how to use it"), and lack of time (e.g. "not enough time"), and one uncategorised response (e.g. "they are all challenges"). The two responses about the expected challenges for e-learning were related to learners: motivating learners ("to motivate students to actually use technology on their own") and controlling independent learners ("it will be difficult [...] to step in and control the independent students").

3.3. Prospects

Teachers have given one positive response about the prospects of e-learning in their institution ("a time will come when e-learning will be the only solution") and one ambitious response ("we have to make technology a strength"). However, the responses about e-learning future in SA were more varied: nine positive, four neutral, and two negative responses. Positive responses are like "it is the future" and "technology is taking over". Examples of the neutral responses are "we need to try to make technology useful for learning" and "the university provided technology and it is up to the teacher if she wants to use it". A teacher with a negative attitude and low knowledge of technology use had two negative responses, e.g. "be realistic ladies". Knowing the existing excessive efforts of the deanship of e-learning and distance education and the huge investments in technology made by the university and the Ministry of Education, it was expected to get positive responses about e-learning prospects.

The question about what is needed to facilitate the implementation of e-learning yielded seven different responses about time, practice, staff members, positive attitudes, technical resources, and training. The authorities in the university are recommended to consider these elements in their ongoing plans.

4.   Conclusions

The findings identified the medium frequency of the university EL teachers' e-learning practice. Teachers often use search engines and emails, but they rarely use virtual classrooms and online learning environments in teaching English. Teachers' roles in technology use is either as user or non-user with a greater number of participants (double) reporting being users than those being non-users. Most teachers' responses are positive about e-learning progress and e-learning prospects in their university and country. Potential challenges are reported to the implementation of e-learning; and teachers are aware of what can facilitate it. These findings can be considered in the university's ongoing plans for successful implementation of e-learning.

5.   Acknowledgements

I would like to thank the administration of the EL Centre at UQU and the teachers for taking part in this study.

References

Alshahrani, K, & Alshehri, S. (2012). Conceptions and responses to e-learning: the case of EFL teachers and students in a Saudi Arabian university. *Monash University Linguistics Papers, 8*(1), 21-31.

Mbati, L., & Minnaar, A. (2015). Guidelines towards the facilitation of interactive online learning programmes in higher education. *International Review of Research in Open and Distributed Learning, 12*(2), 272-287.

Quadri, N. N., Muhammed, A., Sanober, S., Qureshi, M. R. N., & Shah, A. (2017). Barriers effecting successful implementation of e-learning in Saudi Arabian universities. *International Journal of Emerging Technologies in Learning (iJET), 12*(6), 94-107. https://doi.org/10.3991/ijet.v12i06.7003

Stanley, G. (2013). *Language learning with technology: ideas for integrating technology in the classroom*. Cambridge University Press.

JYVÄSKYLÄN YLIOPISTO
UNIVERSITY OF JYVÄSKYLÄ

Instructors as MALL engineers: adapting, modifying, and creating mobile materials for listening practice

Mike Barcomb[1], Jennica Grimshaw[2], and Walcir Cardoso[3]

Abstract. For teachers to utilize Mobile Assisted Language Learning (MALL) resources, they must consider how to balance implementation with their available resources. As it is no longer the case that programming is required to create one's own MALL resources, teachers could benefit from a framework that helps them to match their resources and pedagogical goals with user-friendly and customizable MALL materials. To this end, this paper serves as a proposal for a framework that helps teachers to match their available resources with three levels of customizable MALL materials for listening practice: adaptation, modification, and creation. The possibilities for teacher customized MALL materials at each level will be discussed.

Keywords: mobile-assisted language learning, MALL, design, teacher education.

1. Introduction

In the foreign/second language (L2) context, language practice is often limited to generic homework activities derived from textbooks intended for a wide audience and may therefore not be relevant to every learning context (Howard & Major, 2004). To mitigate this issue, the use of MALL and teacher-friendly applications afford language instructors the opportunity to generate custom-made activities that can increase target language input exposure – an important step when learning a language (e.g. Nation & Newton, 2009) – that is designed specifically for their students.

1. Concordia University, Montreal, Canada; michael.barcomb@mail.concordia.ca
2. Concordia University, Montreal, Canada; jennica.grimshaw@concordia.ca
3. Concordia University, Montreal, Canada; walcir.cardoso@concordia.ca

How to cite this article: Barcomb, M., Grimshaw, J., & Cardoso, W. (2018). Instructors as MALL engineers: adapting, modifying, and creating mobile materials for listening practice. In P. Taalas, J. Jalkanen, L. Bradley & S. Thouësny (Eds), *Future-proof CALL: language learning as exploration and encounters – short papers from EUROCALL 2018* (pp. 11-15). Research-publishing.net. https://doi.org/10.14705/rpnet.2018.26.805

Instructors who have decided to incorporate MALL into their courses need to make pedagogical choices such as the type of application (app), the type of engagement (e.g. aural input, oral output), and between whom the interaction takes place (e.g. student to computer, student to student). With the many options available, including learning how to navigate and use MALL software, it is important that instructors understand how to organize their time and resources to fully benefit from the pool of available MALL resources.

As teachers no longer need to program to make their own materials, this paper proposes a framework that places instructor-friendly customizable MALL resources on a continuum with three distinct levels of involvement (as in Barcomb, Grimshaw, & Cardoso, 2017). It provides an overview of the duties associated with building materials at each level: adaptation, modification, and creation, with the intent of helping instructors to match their abilities, resources, and pedagogical goals to current MALL resources.

Although MALL resources can target many different skills, this paper provides specific examples of how listening practice can be targeted at each level of the framework, as customized listening practice outside the classroom is often difficult to come by. By mobilizing and customizing aural input and practice, the instructor can enhance the learning experience and increase student exposure to the target language without the restrictions of time or space.

2.   Background

When it comes to using technology in the classroom, language instructors often feel limited by restrictions such as budgeting, additional planning time, restricted classroom time, and, most importantly, a lack of training (Godwin-Jones, 2015). Many instructors may also feel overwhelmed by the sheer volume of resources, not knowing where to start or how to critically choose the best programs.

In line with Godwin-Jones's (2015) call for language instructors to develop the programming skills necessary to increase their understanding of how technology can be used to teach languages, the proposed framework is designed to introduce instructors to a pool of MALL materials by taking into account their resources and prior experiences. This process aims to enable teachers to work at a level more likely to lead to successful implementation of MALL, concentrating on adapting, modifying, and creating customizable materials that can increase interaction with the target language input in the mobile setting.

The proposed framework is designed to help instructors begin or reconsider their current use of MALL in their classes to critically select and construct content, tools, and activities, but other frameworks, such as Chapelle's (2001) criteria for computer assisted language learning task appropriateness, should also be considered when designing materials using customizable programs.

3.   Our proposal: the three levels

To alleviate the above issues, we propose three levels of instructor involvement in customizable MALL implementation: adaptation, modification, and creation (Table 1), with a focus on listening practice. The levels reflect the degree of instructor involvement in material creation (e.g. active versus passive roles), and the amount of time and effort required. The levels are not static and share many commonalities, depending on how the instructor engages with the materials.

Table 1.   Three levels of instructor involvement

User role	Level 1	Level 2	Level 3
Choose from pre-made content	Yes	Yes	Yes
Modify pre-made activities		Yes	Yes
Create own content			Yes
Create own activities			Yes
Examples	Duolingo for Schools, Google Translate	Quizlet, TinyCards	Moodle, ARIS

3.1.   Level 1: adaptation as means of entering MALL customization

At the first level, the focus is on *adapting* pre-made MALL materials. This is an important first step that frees instructors of modifying and creating content, and thus enables them to focus on implementing the selected technology to facilitate the development of the L2. For example, *Duolingo for Schools* allows instructors to assign pre-made interactive content, levels, and tasks to their learners, including listening and dictation tasks. Instructors therefore do not have to create any content, activities, or gamified elements on their own; instead they *adapt* pre-made materials by assigning only the relevant ones to their students.

By helping instructors become aware of the way that resources at Level 1 are amenable to adaptation, the use of non-pedagogical apps such as *Google Translate* can be further explored to provide textual and aural input on the go. Here, the instructor could guide learners to use certain features of the app for specific purposes, such as a pronunciation model. Working at this level is best for teachers who may have limited resources or no prior experience using MALL materials, though advanced users are also likely to incorporate skills and/or apps from Level 1 in the following two levels.

3.2.   Level 2: modification as a means of customizing content

As an extension of Level 1, Level 2 focuses on the actual *modification* of pre-made materials, which positions the instructor in a more active role as a designer. This is particularly helpful when generic textbook or MALL activities do not meet the specific learning needs of a group of students. In Level 2, instructors can, for example, customize student listening practice by modifying a set of Text-To-Speech (TTS) enhanced vocabulary cards by replacing the TTS voice with his or her own, adding original images, or editing the text on each card. Instructors who are comfortable with software modification (e.g. TTS vocabulary cards) can advance and use flashcard-building apps such as *Quizlet* to modify aspects of TTS-based cards. They can then make them available in pre-made matching games and multiple choice listening quizzes with gamified elements to motivate students to practice.

Despite the challenges associated with modifying customizable MALL materials (e.g. they require more time and technological expertise), teachers at Level 2 can tailor apps to address the needs of their students, based on their pedagogical and technological know-how and available time.

3.3.   Level 3: creating a complete MALL experience

Finally, instructors engaging at Level 3 have full creative control over adapting, modifying, and creating MALL materials that increase interaction with the target language (Barcomb et al., 2017, p. 2). Not only do instructors have the ability to create their own materials, but they can also determine how these materials are organized and presented to learners. One approach to creation at the third level is through learning management systems, which can lead to the creation of highly effective MALL materials that incorporate modified, adapted, and created materials. For example, through the use of user-generated plugins in *Moodle*, teachers can incorporate videos, quizzes with embedded audio, and student-generated glossary entries. The latter can include video, audio, and/or images that reward points to learners upon the completion of each activity.

Another example of Level 3 creation that highlights mobility is the use of augmented reality app creators such as *ARIS* to create place-based mobile applications. By using GPS markers, *ARIS* allows instructors to mobilize the classroom by taking the learners on a language learning experience of discovery; for example, students can use their mobile devices to scan QR codes around the classroom in an interactive scavenger hunt. As students scan QR codes or reach GPS locations, video and/or audio cues can pop up on the user's screen to enable additional listening practice.

4.   Conclusions

By establishing these three levels of teacher involvement, we hope to help instructors bypass some of the hindrances commonly associated with implementing educational technology and support new and experienced users of MALL in their journey towards becoming creators of their own MALL materials. In this paper, we identify resources and activities that permit instructors to adapt, modify, and/ or create listening activities that are relevant and engaging to their students. By doing so, we hope that the MALL design process becomes more tangible to all instructors, regardless of ability, training, or available resources.

References

Barcomb, M., Grimshaw, J., & Cardoso, W. (2017). I can't program! Customizable mobile language-learning resources for researchers and practitioners. *Languages, 2*(3), 1-15. https://doi.org/10.3390/languages2030008

Chapelle, C. (2001). *Computer applications in second language acquisition.* Cambridge. https://doi.org/10.1017/CBO9781139524681

Godwin-Jones, R. (2015). Emerging technologies the evolving roles of language teachers: trained coders, local researchers, global citizens. *Learning and Technology, 19*(1), 10-22.

Howard, J., & Major, J. (2004). Guidelines for designing effective English language teaching materials. *The TESOLANZ Journal, 12*, 50-58.

Nation, I. S. P., & Newton, J. (2009). *Teaching ESL/EFL listening and speaking. ESL & applied linguistics professional series.* Routledge.

Learning L2 pronunciation
with a text-to-speech synthesizer

Walcir Cardoso[1]

Abstract. The study explored the pedagogical use of Text-To-Speech (TTS) synthesizers by comparing two groups of students learning the pronunciations associated with Regular Past Tense (RPT) marking in English (e.g. talk[t], clean[d], want[id]). While one group received TTS-based instruction, the other was taught RPT with teacher assistance. Our findings indicate that both groups behaved similarly regarding the production of RPT, and that the target allomorphs are acquired in the following order: *id>d>t*.

Keywords: text-to-speech synthesis, L2 pronunciation.

1.   Introduction

TTS are applications that convert written text into spoken voice output. Although the literature on its pedagogical applications in L2 education is still scarce, the few available studies indicate that the technology has potential for the teaching/ learning of L2 pronunciation (Liakin, Cardoso, & Liakina, 2017). Research has also shown that the technology is ready for use in the L2 classroom, as its output is comparable to that of humans on measures such as intelligibility, comprehensibility, and morphophonemic accuracy (Cardoso, Smith, & Garcia-Fuentes, 2015).

We hypothesize that TTS can contribute to the learning of L2 pronunciation because it can enhance the target input in both quantity and quality via features such as speed control (slow/fast speech), multimodal visual presentation (through orthography and the highlighting of words being read/synthesized), word/phrase repetition, and voice selection (e.g. male or female voices for high phonetic

1. Concordia University, Montreal, Canada; walcir.cardoso@concordia.ca

How to cite this article: Cardoso, W. (2018). Learning L2 pronunciation with a text-to-speech synthesizer. In P. Taalas, J. Jalkanen, L. Bradley & S. Thouësny (Eds), *Future-proof CALL: language learning as exploration and encounters – short papers from EUROCALL 2018* (pp. 16-21). Research-publishing.net. https://doi.org/10.14705/rpnet.2018.26.806

variability, as recommended by Logan, Lively, & Pisoni, 1991). These features are shown in Figure 1.

Figure 1. Input enhancement via TTS: features (reproduced with permission from NaturalSoft)

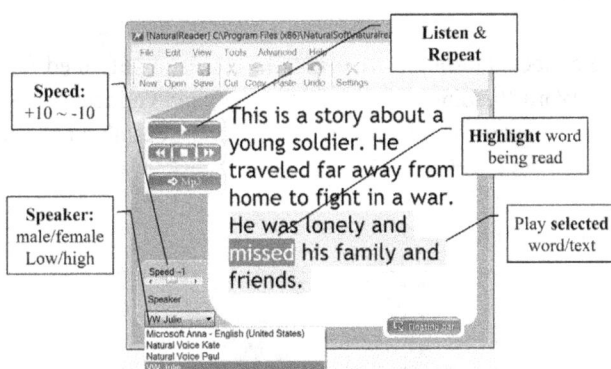

To examine the pedagogical suitability of TTS, this study focused on the acquisition of the allomorphy found in RPT marking in English (i.e. talk[t], clean[d] and want[id]). As suggested in the literature (Collins et al., 2009), the acquisition of RPT and related morphophonemics is difficult because -ed forms are not readily available to L2 learners (an issue of input 'quantity') and they occur in hard-to-perceive phonetic contexts (an issue of input 'quality'). By allowing learners to manipulate the quantity and quality of exposure to the forms being learned, TTS can address the issues of availability and accessibility reported in Collins et al. (2009). This study was guided by the following question:

- Which type of instruction is more effective in the learning of simple past -ed allomorphy: TTS-based instruction or one led by a language teacher?

2. Method

2.1. Participants and experimental groups

Eighteen English-as-a-foreign-language students (proficiency: intermediate; age: 13-22; gender: seven females, 11 males) were stratified among two groups: while the TTS Group was asked to complete learning activities using the TTS application in Figure 1 (thus manipulating the L2 input in quantity and quality), the Non-

TTS Group received the same treatment with the assistance of an English teacher. Over a four-week period, all participants engaged in incidental learning of RPT allomorphy via listening activities that focused on the pronunciation of the target forms (e.g. listen and fill-in the gap, and sound categorization).

2.2. Instruments

The data were collected through two oral tasks consisting of 70 ed-final verbs and 30 distractors: Word Reading (id=10; d=23; t=12) and Guided Task (id=3; d=14; t=8) in which participants were asked to answer questions about the past holidays of fictional characters (see Figure 2 for an illustration).

Figure 2.   Guided oral task

Last July, Lena took a four-week vacation in Japan. What did she do?

	YES	NO
arrive safely?	✓	
work during her vacation?	✓	
call her boss every day?		✓ (week)
stay at a hotel?		✓ (with friends)
wash her clothes every day?	✓	
clean her bedroom?	✓	
dress informally?		✓ (formally)
need guides to travel in Japan?	✓	
love the weather?	✓	
travel with her friends?		✓ (boyfriend)

2.3.   Research design and procedures

The study followed a pretest-posttest design. Participants were pretested using the two instruments described above and tested within one week of completion of the learning activities described above. The posttest was followed by a 20-minute oral interview in which participants were asked about their pedagogical experience. Figure 3 illustrates the research design and procedures adopted.

The data were coded by two research assistants (1=correct, 0=incorrect) and checked for consistency by a third rater (95.56% rater consistency). The interview data were audio-recorded, transcribed, and categorized into pertinent themes (e.g. morphophonemic awareness and perceived pedagogical benefits).

Figure 3.   Research design and procedures

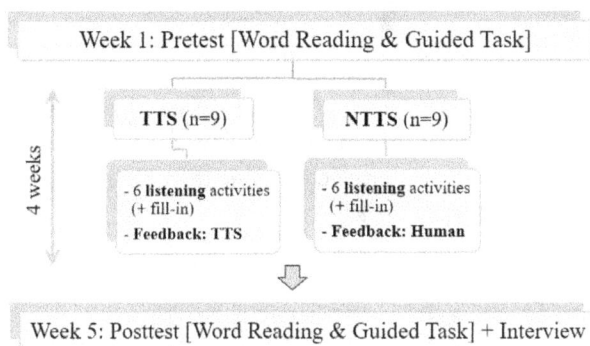

3. **Results**

Due to space limitations, only the final stage of the statistical analysis is reported in detail. Mixed between-within subjects analysis of variance (ANOVA), followed by pairwise comparisons, were conducted with RPT allomorphy (-id, -d, -t) as dependent variable, and Time (pretest, posttest), Group (TTS, Non-TTS), and Task (Word Reading, Guided Task) as independent variables. For both Word Reading and Guided Task, there was no effect for Time or Group, indicating no significant improvement: the RPT allomorphs remained the same from pretest to posttest, across the two groups and tasks. There was, however, a difference for RPT production in the two tasks on the pretests and posttests, attesting that the three allomorphs behaved significantly differently; while -id was unproblematic, -d was relatively less difficult to produce than -t: id>d>t (where > indicates "easier to produce than" or "acquired before"). Finally, additional analysis revealed no significant improvement in Word Reading. Due to the uneven distribution of RPT forms, the results are provided in mean percentages in Table 1.

Table 1.   RTP allomorphs by group (type of instruction), time, and task

Group	Pretest (%)						Posttest (%)					
	Word Reading			Guided Task			Word Reading			Guided Task		
	-id	-d	-t	-id	-d	-t	-id	-d	-t	-id	-d	-t
TTS	100	20	8.9	75	30.6	13.9	100	18.8	7.41	63	42.9	13.9
Non-TTS	97.8	13.3	2.2	66.7	19.4	8.3	95.6	10.1	0	74.1	23	6.9

Because the two groups were statistically similar and no improvement was observed in Word Reading, follow-up Within-Subjects ANOVAs involving Guided Task and the two groups combined were conducted. This revealed an interaction between Time and RTP allomorphy ($F(1,17)$=15.609, p=0.001 (alpha level set at .003), suggesting a performance improvement for -d (shaded in Table 1), but not for -t on the posttest.

To summarize, the TTS and Non-TTS groups behaved similarly regarding the production of RPT: while they both improved in producing [d], there was no significant improvement in their production of -id (participants scored at the ceiling level on the pretest) and [t].

4.   Discussion and concluding remarks

The study examined the effects of two types of instruction in the learning of RPT allomorphy: TTS-based instruction and one led by a language teacher. The results indicate that the TTS and Non-TTS groups behaved similarly regarding the production of RPT. An interesting pattern emerged in the analysis: an improvement of allomorph -d by both groups, suggesting a development sequence in the acquisition of RPT allomorphy. While -ed is acquired first, due to L1 influence (see Cardoso, 2011), the order -d>-t can be explained by the fact that syllabic coda -d is more sonorous than -t (languages favor sonorous codas; Cardoso, 2011).

The lack of major improvements observed can be attributed to at least two factors. Firstly, it is possible that an exclusive focus on perception via the proposed TTS-based listening activities (under the 'perception precedes production' hypothesis – Flege, 1995) was not appropriate to lead learners to transfer the newly-acquired knowledge into production. If these activities had been complemented with speaking activities (e.g. via speech recognition software or even silent practice), learners would have had an opportunity to practice and possibly transfer this novel perceptual knowledge into production. That many learners became aware of RPT allomorphy became evident in the analysis of their interview data, particularly among participants in the TTS Group. When asked what they had learned in the study, most participants reported that they had become aware of the differences in RPT pronunciation: "*if I were to [listen to these stories] again, I wouldn't pronounce as much this "ed" at the end*"; "*I never knew that the {ed} sometimes sounds strong, sometimes weak*". Secondly, it is possible that the four hours allotted for listening practice was not enough, particularly in an experiment in which pronunciation was learned implicitly (see Saito & Lyster, 2012, for the effects of explicit pronunciation teaching).

An important pedagogical implication of these findings is that TTS has the potential to increase and improve the target language input (preferably accompanied by explicit instruction and oral practice), develop better grapheme-to-phoneme associations (there is no clear relationship between orthographic -ed and its allomorphs -id, -d and -t in English), and address some of the time constraints that affect many L2 learning environments (TTS has the potential to foster autonomous and anytime-anywhere learning). Using TTS as an out-of-class pedagogical tool could then increase in-class time so that teachers and students could focus on other important tasks such as providing feedback and engaging in real-life communicative activities.

References

Cardoso, W. (2011). The development of coda perception in second language phonology: a variationist perspective. *Second Language Research, 27*(4), 433-465.

Cardoso, W., Smith, G., & Garcia Fuentes, C. (2015). Evaluating text-to-speech synthesizers. In F. Helm, L. Bradley, M. Guarda, & S. Thouësny (Eds), *Critical CALL – Proceedings of the 2015 EUROCALL Conference, Padova, Italy* (pp.108-113). Research-publishing.net. https://doi.org/10.14705/rpnet.2015.000318

Collins, L., Trofimovich, P., White, J., Cardoso, W., & Horst, M. (2009). Some input on the easy/difficult grammar question. *Modern Language Journal, 93*(3), 336-353. https://doi.org/10.1111/j.1540-4781.2009.00894.x

Flege, J. (1995). Second language speech learning: theory, findings, and problems. In W. Strange (Ed.), *Speech perception and linguistic experience: issues in cross-language research* (pp. 233-72). York Press.

Liakin, D., Cardoso, W., & Liakina, N. (2017). The pedagogical use of mobile speech synthesis: focus on French liaison. *Computer Assisted Language Learning, 30*(3-4), 348-365. https://doi.org/10.1080/09588221.2017.1312463

Logan, J., Lively, S., & Pisoni, D. (1991). Training Japanese listeners to identify English /r/ and /l/: a first report. *Journal of the Acoustical Society of America, 89*(2), 874-886.

Saito, K., & Lyster, R. (2012). Effects of form-focused instruction and corrective feedback on L2 pronunciation development of /r/ by Japanese learners of English. *Language Learning, 62*(2), 595-633. https://doi.org/10.1111/j.1467-9922.2011.00639.x

JYVÄSKYLÄN YLIOPISTO
UNIVERSITY OF JYVÄSKYLÄ

Learners' satisfaction comparison between text and speech dialogue-based computer assisted language learning system

Sung-Kwon Choi[1], Oh-Woog Kwon[2], and Young-Kil Kim[3]

Abstract. This paper is about the learners' satisfaction comparison between text and speech Dialogue-Based Computer-Assisted Language Learning systems (DB-CALL system). A DB-CALL system aims to allow learners to talk to the system in a foreign language as if they were talking with a native speaker and to provide learning feedback that will grammatically correct spoken foreign language or recommend a better expression. The satisfaction analysis of the text DB-CALL system was conducted by 20 learners. The satisfaction analysis of the speech DB-CALL system was conducted by 36 learners. The average satisfaction of the text DB-CALL system was 3.44 points. This system needs to improve the ability to respond appropriately to out-of-topic conversations (2.10 points). The average satisfaction of the speech DB-CALL system was 3.87 points. This system needs to enhance the speech recognition function (3.36 points).

Keywords: satisfaction analysis, computer assisted language learning system, dialogue system, DB-CALL.

1.　Introduction

The DB-CALL system aims to either grammatically correct learners' foreign language utterance or to provide learning feedback that recommends better expressions. The Electronics and Telecommunications Research Institute (ETRI) has developed the DB-CALL system since 2010. The DB-CALL system developed

1. Electronics and Telecommunications Research Institute, Daejeon, Korea; choisk@etri.re.kr
2. Electronics and Telecommunications Research Institute, Daejeon, Korea; ohwoog@etri.re.kr
3. Electronics and Telecommunications Research Institute, Daejeon, Korea; kimyk@etri.re.kr

How to cite this article: Choi, S.-K., Kwon, O.-W., & Kim, Y.-K. (2018). Learners' satisfaction comparison between text and speech dialogue-based computer assisted language learning system. In P. Taalas, J. Jalkanen, L. Bradley & S. Thouësny (Eds), *Future-proof CALL: language learning as exploration and encounters – short papers from EUROCALL 2018* (pp. 22-28). Research-publishing.net. https://doi.org/10.14705/rpnet.2018.26.807

from 2010 to 2015 was text-based and system-oriented, which restricted the learner's dialogue flow and did not allow free conversation beyond the topic (Choi, Kwon, Kim, & Lee, 2016). As a hybrid approach between the DB-CALL system and a chat bot became active (Dingli & Scerri, 2013), the DB-CALL systems evolved from system-oriented to a mixed form between system-oriented and user-oriented. The DB-CALL system developed from 2016 to 2018 was speech-based and a mix of system-oriented and user-oriented, that allowed free conversation outside the topic and feedback on grammar errors without limiting the learner's flow of conversation (Choi, Kwon, & Kim, 2017). In this paper, we describe the learners' satisfaction comparison between the text DB-CALL system and the speech DB-CALL system.

2. Configuration of ETRI's speech DB-CALL system

ETRI's speech DB-CALL system consists of speech recognition, language understanding, computer-assisted language learning, dialogue management, language generation, and speech synthesis. As described in detail in Choi et al. (2017), the speech DB-CALL system's strategy for user utterance is shown in Figure 1.

Figure 1.   Dialogue strategy of ETRI speech DB-CALL system

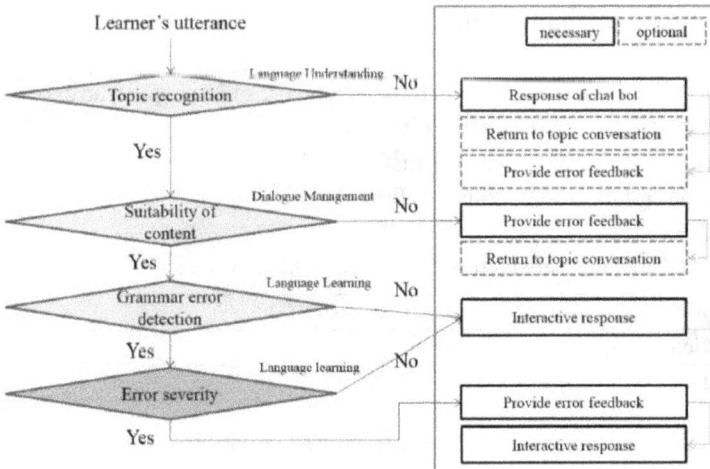

When a learner makes an utterance, ETRI speech DB-CALL system first confirms whether the utterance is topic-oriented. If the utterance is not a topic conversation,

ETRI speech DB-CALL system responds with the chat bot and then returns to the topic conversation. If the learner's utterance is topic-oriented, ETRI speech DB-CALL system in turn processes suitability of content, grammar error detection, and error severity (Choi et al., 2017).

3.   Text DB-CALL system

3.1.   Evaluation

The evaluation of the text DB-CALL system was conducted by 20 testers, whose English level was beginner (ten) and intermediate (ten). Each tester communicated with the system literally about the four topics. Topics for evaluation consist of purchasing tickets for a New York city tour, ordering food, talking about health habits, and thinking about future currency. Participants performed ten missions on four topics, each taking an average of 50 minutes per person. The success rate of dialogue turns on four topics was 80.86% as follows:

> Success rate of dialogue turn (%) = (number of correct system's responses to learner's utterance)/(total number of learners' utterances) × 100.

3.2.   Learners' satisfaction

Satisfaction analysis was based on the questionnaire of 20 people who experimented with the text DB-CALL system. Five-point Likert scales were assigned to each question. One point was 'very unsatisfied' and 5 points were 'very satisfied'. The satisfaction results were as follows (Table 1).

Table 1.   Learners' satisfaction of text DB-CALL system

Questionnaire	Score
1. Questions about system performance	
1.1. Did the system respond appropriately?	2.90
1.2. Do you feel free to talk to the system?	2.90
1.3. Did the system properly point out grammatical errors?	3.15
1.4. Did the system adequately recommend sentences that would help you learn?	3.60
1.5. Did the out-of-topic conversations (ex. chat bots) respond appropriately?	2.10
Average	2.93

2. Questions about system function	
2.1. Do you think the ability to correct grammatical errors is necessary for the conversation system?	4.40
2.2. Do you think the ability to recommend sentences is necessary for the conversation system?	4.55
2.3. Do you think conversations outside of the topic (ex. chat bots) are necessary for the conversation system?	3.60
Average	4.18
3. Questions about system effects	
3.1. After using the system, did the DB-CALL system help you learn English?	3.60
3.2. Do you think this DB-CALL system helps you learn English better than traditional learning methods (such as conversation texts)?	3.55
3.3. Do you think this DB-CALL system will help you motivate your learning?	3.60
3.4. Does this DB-CALL system have fun?	3.35
Average	3.53
4. Questions about future services	
4.1. Would you like to use the online education service of the DB-CALL system?	3.65
4.2. Do you want to use the above service even if it is charged?	2.40
4.3. Are you willing to repeat many times (on average 4-5 times or more) on a topic conversation?	3.30
Average	3.12

Overall, the satisfaction rate of the text DB-CALL system was 3.44 points out of 5 points. A factor that lowers overall satisfaction is the DB-CALL system's inability to respond appropriately to out-of-topic conversations (2.10 points). Therefore, it is expected that the learner's satisfaction with the text DB-CALL system will increase if the topic-oriented chat bot system is improved.

4. Speech DB-CALL system

4.1. Evaluation

The speech DB-CALL system was tested in voice on speech phones. Thirty-six learners whose English level was beginner (18) and intermediate (18) were divided into three groups. Topics to talk with were given differently for each group. Table 2 shows the progress of satisfaction analysis.

Table 2. Evaluation method of speech DB-CALL system

	Group A	Group B	Group C
Participants	12 college students (7 male, 5 female)	12 middle school students (male 1, female 11)	12 middle school students (male 2, female 10)
Topic	• How can we save our environment? • What is your opinion about DIY fashion? • What do you think of Korean food culture? • Which role on the rowing team do you think you'll be good at?	How can we save our environment?	What healthy habit do you have?
Evaluation items	• Usability in class • Content and Services • Speech recognition		
How to proceed	• System introduction and explanation of learning method • Distribution of test equipment • Pre-learning: after learning words, sentences and expression, 3 free conversations with DB-CALL system • Learning • Confirm result • Fill out the questionnaire		

4.2. Learners' satisfaction

Five-point Likert scales were assigned to each question. One point was 'very poor' and 5 points were 'very satisfied'. The satisfaction results were as follows (Table 3).

Satisfaction with speech DB-CALL system was 3.87 out of 5 points. Specifically, the satisfaction of usability in class was 4.11, the content and service satisfaction was 4.14, and the speech recognition satisfaction was 3.36. The speech recognition function should be improved. The satisfaction analysis of the speech DB-CALL system is similar to that of the online survey of speech assisted language learning of Grimshaw, Cardoso, and Collins (2017). If technology of speech recognition improves further, the satisfaction level of Table 3 below will be higher.

Table 3. Learners' satisfaction of speech DB-CALL system

	Group A	Group B	Group C	Total
Usability in class	3.92 very satisfied(0) satisfied(11) moderate(1) unsatisfied(0) very unsatisfied(0)	4.50 very satisfied(6) satisfied(6) moderate(0) unsatisfied(0) very unsatisfied(0)	3.92 very satisfied(1) satisfied(9) moderate(2) unsatisfied(0) very unsatisfied(0)	4.11
Content and Services	3.83 very satisfied(0) satisfied(10) moderate(2) unsatisfied(0) very unsatisfied(0)	4.50 very satisfied(6) satisfied(6) moderate(0) unsatisfied(0) very unsatisfied(0)	4.08 very satisfied(2) satisfied(9) moderate(1) unsatisfied(0) very unsatisfied(0)	4.14
Speech recognition	3.00 very satisfied(1) satisfied(2) moderate(5) unsatisfied(4) very unsatisfied(0)	3.83 very satisfied(1) satisfied(8) moderate(3) unsatisfied(0) very unsatisfied(0)	3.25 very satisfied(1) satisfied(4) moderate(4) unsatisfied(3) very unsatisfied(0)	3.36
Total				**3.87**

5.   Conclusions

In this paper, we described the learners' satisfaction comparison between text and speech DB-CALL system. The average satisfaction rate of the text DB-CALL system was 3.44 points. The average satisfaction rate of the speech DB-CALL system was 3.87 points.

In the future, we will further enhance the performance of the speech DB-CALL system by improving speech recognition and dialogue management modules.

6.   Acknowledgements

This work was supported by the ICT R&D programme of MSIT/IITP. [2015-0-00187, Core technology development of the spontaneous speech dialogue processing for the language learning].

References

Choi, S. K., Kwon, O. W., & Kim, Y. K. (2017). Computer-assisted English learning system based on free conversation by topic. In K. Borthwick, L. Bradley & S. Thouësny (Eds), *CALL in a climate of change: adapting to turbulent global conditions – short papers from EUROCALL 2017* (pp. 79-85). Research-publishing.net. https://doi.org/10.14705/rpnet.2017.eurocall2017.693

Choi, S. K., Kwon, O. W., Kim, Y. K., & Lee, Y. K. (2016). Using a dialogue system based on dialogue maps for computer assisted second language learning. In S. Papadima-Sophocleous, L. Bradley & S. Thouësny (Eds), *CALL communities and culture – short papers from EUROCALL 2016* (pp. 106-112). Research-publishing.net. https://doi.org/10.14705/rpnet.2016.eurocall2016.546

Dingli, A., & Scerri, D. (2013). Building a hybrid: chatterbot-dialog system. *Proceedings of 16th International Conference of Text, Speech, and Dialogue* (pp. 145-152). https://doi.org/10.1007/978-3-642-40585-3_19

Grimshaw, J., Cardoso, W., & Collins, L. (2017). Teacher perspectives on the integration of mobile-assisted language learning. In K. Borthwick, L. Bradley & S. Thouësny (Eds), *CALL in a climate of change: adapting to turbulent global conditions – short papers from EUROCALL 2017* (pp. 135-139). Research-publishing.net. https://doi.org/10.14705/rpnet.2017.eurocall2017.702

JYVÄSKYLÄN YLIOPISTO
UNIVERSITY OF JYVÄSKYLÄ

Can TTS help L2 learners develop their phonological awareness?

Almir Anacleto de Araújo Gomes[1], Walcir Cardoso[2],
and Rubens Marques de Lucena[3]

Abstract. Text-To-Speech synthesizers (TTS) have raised the interest of researchers and teachers for their ability to enhance foreign/second language (L2) learning, particularly with regards to the development of pronunciation skills (Liakin, Cardoso, & Liakina, 2017). Despite some optimistic results, there are no studies that investigate TTS's pedagogical potential to enhance L2 Phonological Awareness (PA), especially in *foreign* language contexts, where access to rich aural input is limited in terms of both quantity and quality. The present study examines TTS's pedagogical potential as a tool to assist English L2 learners develop their PA, focusing on the morphophonological alternations that characterize regular past tense marking in English (past -ed). Results show that TTS contributed positively for the auditory perception and controlled (but not spontaneous) production of the targeted phenomenon.

Keywords: Text-to-speech synthesizers, phonological awareness, L2 pronunciation.

1. Introduction

Research has shown that the pedagogical use of TTS has the potential to contribute to learning in the acquisition of L2 vocabulary and pronunciation (e.g. Liakin et al., 2017; Soler-Urzúa, 2011). Recently, there have been studies that evaluate the voice quality of TTS systems, corroborating previous hypotheses that current synthesized voices are ready for use in L2 education: they are not only perceived as appropriate

1. Universidade Federal da Paraíba, João Pessoa, Brazil; almir@ufcg.edu.br
2. Concordia University, Montreal, Canada; walcir.cardoso@concordia.ca
3. Universidade Federal da Paraíba, João Pessoa, Brazil; rubenslucena@yahoo.com

How to cite this article: De Araújo Gomes, A. A., Cardoso, W., & De Lucena, R. M. (2018). Can TTS help L2 learners develop their phonological awareness? In P. Taalas, J. Jalkanen, L. Bradley & S. Thouësny (Eds), *Future-proof CALL: language learning as exploration and encounters – short papers from EUROCALL 2018* (pp. 29-34). Research-publishing.net.
https://doi.org/10.14705/rpnet.2018.26.808

(or 'good enough') from a sound perspective (Bione, Grimshaw, & Cardoso, 2017; Cardoso, Smith, & Garcia Fuentes, 2015), but they are also more likely to enhance opaque features of the target language (e.g. regular past tense marking in English is often detected with higher accuracy in synthesized speech; Bione et al., 2017; John & Cardoso, 2017). One area that has not received consideration by researchers is TTS' ability to raise L2 learners' PA.

As such, this pilot study attempts to contribute to the literature on CALL-assisted PA. It focused on TTS's ability to provide the type of input necessary to develop learners' ability to become aware that past tense marking (past -ed) in English is characterized by three allomorphs: /t/ in the presence of a preceding voiceless segment (e.g. talk[t]), /Id/ when the targeted morpheme is preceded by homorganic /t/ or /d/ (e.g. add[Id]), and /d/ elsewhere (e.g. play[d]). To assess participants' PA development, we included tasks that evaluated their pre-/post-test awareness of past -ed pronunciation, their auditory perception of the phenomenon, and their controlled/spontaneous oral production. The general question that guided this research was: can English as a Foreign Language (EFL) learners benefit from exposure to synthesized voices for developing their awareness to past -ed allomorphy?

2.   Method

Nine Brazilian Portuguese (BP) native speakers participated in this study. They were EFL students living in João Pessoa (Brazil, with ages ranging from 25 to 35. They had all completed (or were attending) secondary school.

The study consisted of two hour one-shot sessions with the participants. For the treatment, participants were asked to complete a set of learning activities using a popular NeoSpeech synthesized voice, *Julie* (via the NaturalReader software). They consisted of activities that encouraged them to listen and respond to question such as *listen and decide whether the action took place in the present or past.*

For data collection, participants were asked to complete a series of tasks designed to evaluate their PA before and after the use of TTS during the treatment phase. To examine learners' PA, participants completed two questionnaires (pre- and post-tests), in which they were asked to evaluate ten propositions about English pronunciation using an eight point Likert scale, according to Alves's (2012) five levels of PA: L2 phonemes, L2 allophones, identification of non-distinctive sounds in L1 and distinctive sounds in L2, syllabic patterns, and rhymes.

Based on Cardoso et al. (2015) and Bione et al. (2017), participants also performed an auditory identification task, in which they heard 16 sentences, 12 of them in the past (four distractors), but without lexical elements that could identify their tense.

To evaluate the controlled production of past -ed, participants read a list of 26 words aloud (14 were regular past verbs, the others were distractors). To evaluate less controlled (*spontaneous* henceforth) production, participants were asked to answer questions about the past holidays of fictional characters, using a set of regular past verbs. The key difference between these tasks was the amount of cognitive effort to complete them: while the first relied on the participants' ability to produce ed-final words in isolation, the spontaneous task required them to focus on content, allowing us to obtain more natural speech (Gomes, 2015; Ortiz & Ivette, 2005; see Labov, 1972 for a sociolinguistic perspective).

3.   Results

3.1.   Auditory perception

Due to the limited scope of the study and the small number of participants, we report the results using descriptive statistics, in percentages. As Figure 1 indicates, there was a 7% improvement in past tense perception from pre-test to post-test.

Figure 1.   Auditory identification of past -ed: pre-test and post-test

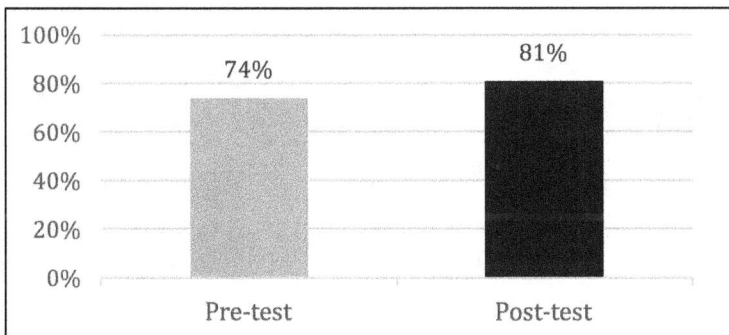

These results suggest that access to synthesized L2 input may contribute to a better perception of sentential verbal tense, as well as the identification of regular past -ed in English.

3.2.   Production

Comparing pre-test to post-test results in controlled production, we observed an overall improvement of 12% in past -ed pronunciation, as shown in Figure 2.

Figure 2.   Controlled production of past -ed: pre-test and post-test

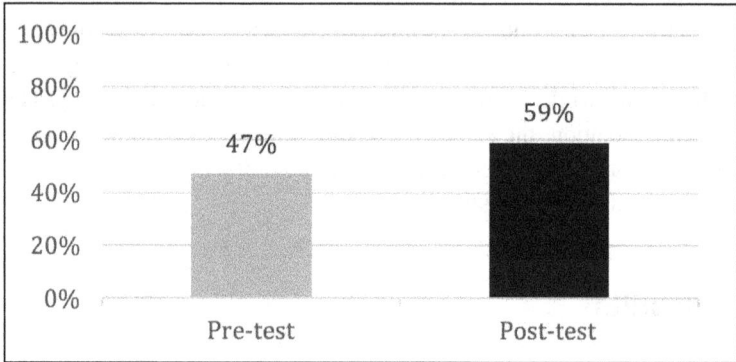

Interestingly, data from spontaneous production yielded a different pattern, showing a reduction in past -ed marking on the post-test, as illustrated in Figure 3.

Figure 3.   Spontaneous production of past -ed: pre-test and post-test

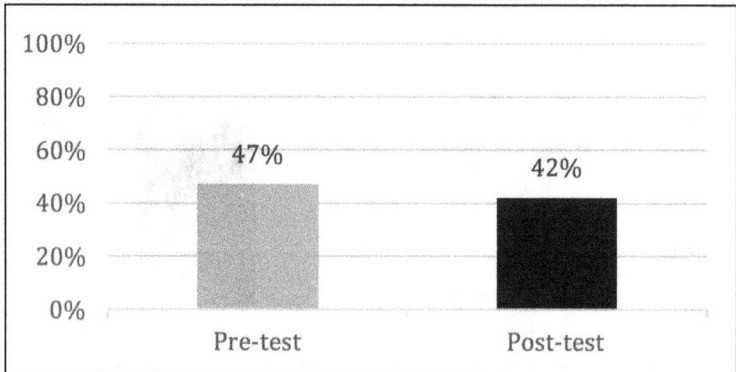

In sum, our findings for oral production yielded mixed results regarding the pedagogical effects of TTS: While an improvement in past -ed pronunciation was observed in controlled production, the reverse was found in spontaneous tasks.

3.3.   PA test

Figure 4 shows an improvement in past -ed PA in three of the five levels of phonological awareness considered: L2 phonemes (from 50% to 88.89%), L2 allophones (from 33.33% to 44.44 %), and identification of non-distinctive sounds in L1 (allophones) and distinctive in L2 (from 44.44% to 55.56%). Regarding the other two levels (syllabic patterns and rhymes), PA decreased from 61.11% to 27.78% and from 72.22% to 50.00%, respectively.

Figure 4.   PA tests: pre-test and post-test

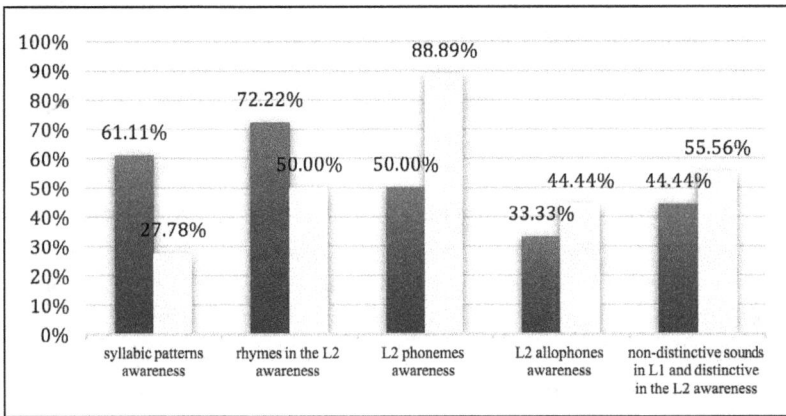

Overall, considering the five levels of PA adopted, the participants' phonological awareness only increased by a mere 1.11% on the post-test (from 52.22% to 53.33%).

4.   Discussions and conclusions

This study aimed to answer whether EFL learners could benefit from exposure to synthesized voices for developing their awareness to past -ed allomorphy. Our findings suggest that the pedagogical use of TTS can be effective in at least two of the measures encompassed by our definition of PA: auditory -ed perception and its controlled production. This can be explained by the fact that these two tasks required a focus on language (e.g. in comparison with spontaneous production). These findings suggest that, considering these two measures, TTS constitutes a good source of aural input (as reported Cardoso et al., 2015 and Bione et al., 2017), and that it may be used to enhance the opaque alternations found in past -ed marking in English (as hypothesized, based on Bione et al., 2017, and John &

Cardoso, 2017). We acknowledge some of the limitations of our study, particularly the limited number of participants and lack of statistical rigour in our analysis. In future research, we would like to mitigate these limitations and verify if, given a larger sample, there will be a more significant improvement at post-test.

5.   Acknowledgements

We would like to thank the participants for their invaluable contributions. We would also like to acknowledge the financial support from CAPES (Brazilian Federal Agency for the Support and Evaluation of Graduate Education, Ministry of Education of Brazil). PDSE - 88881.131607/2016-01.

References

Alves, U. K. (2012). O que é consciência fonológica. In R. Lamprecht, A. P. Blanco-Dutra et al. (Eds), *Consciência dos sons da língua* (pp. 31-46). Edipucrs.

Bione, T., Grimshaw, J., & Cardoso, W. (2017). An evaluation of TTS as a pedagogical tool for pronunciation instruction: the 'foreign' language context. In K. Borthwick, L. Bradley & S. Thouësny (Eds), *CALL in a climate of change: adapting to turbulent global conditions – short papers from EUROCALL 2017* (pp. 56-61). Research-publishing.net. https://doi.org/10.14705/rpnet.2017.eurocall2017.689

Cardoso, W., Smith, G., & Garcia Fuentes, C. (2015). Evaluating text-to-speech synthesizers. In F. Helm, L. Bradley, M. Guarda, & S. Thouësny (Eds), *Critical CALL – Proceedings of the 2015 EUROCALL Conference, Padova, Italy* (pp. 108-113). Research-publishing.net. https://doi.org/10.14705/rpnet.2015.000318

Gomes, A. A. A. (2015). *A epêntese vocálica inicial em clusters sC por aprendentes brasileiros de inglês como LDE*. Edufcg.

John, P., & Cardoso, W. (2017). A comparative study of text-to-speech and native speaker output. In J. Demperio, E. Rosales & S. Springer (Eds), *Proceedings of the meeting on English language teaching* (pp. 78-96). Université du Québec à Montréal Press.

Labov, W. (1972). *Sociolinguistic patterns*. University of Pennsylvania Press.

Liakin, D., Cardoso, W., & Liakina, N. (2017). The pedagogical use of mobile speech synthesis (TTS): focus on French liaison. *Computer Assisted Language Learning, 30*(3-4), 348-365. https://doi.org/10.1080/09588221.2017.1312463

Ortiz, E., & Ivette, C. (2005). *The development of sC onset clusters in Spanish English*. Doctoral dissertation, Concordia University.

Soler-Urzúa, F. (2011). The acquisition of English /ɪ/ by Spanish speakers via text-to-speech synthesizers: a quasi-experimental study. Master's thesis. Concordia University.

Designed and emerging CALL affordances in videoconferencing for language learning and teaching

Aparajita Dey-Plissonneau[1]

Abstract. This study aims to identify a few perception-action relations or affordances enacted in an asymmetrical (tutor-tutee) videoconferencing environment for L2 learning. Following Engeström's (2014) Cultural Historical Activity Theory (CHAT) and an ecological Computer-Assisted Language Learning (CALL) perspective, the study focusses on the interactions between language use, technology use, and the enactment of designed language learning tasks. Master's students of French as a foreign language from a French university interacted online via videoconferencing with undergraduate students of business learning French at an Irish university over a six-week period. The online interactions between tutors and tutees generated a multimodal corpus (ISMAEL). The fifth session plan prepared by the tutors and their online conversations were investigated for four tutor-tutee systems. The findings reveal that the designed and emerging technological and linguistic affordances influence the online interactions at the micro level and the educational affordances at the macro level.

Keywords: CALL affordances, activity theory, asymmetrical, videoconferencing.

1. Introduction

"The affordances of the environment are what it offers the animal, what it provides or furnishes, either for good or ill" (Gibson, 1977, p. 68). Affordance is a relational property that depends not only on the inherent characteristics of the environment

1. Dublin City University, Dublin, Ireland; aparajita.deyplissonneau2@mail.dcu.ie

How to cite this article: Dey-Plissonneau, A. (2018). Designed and emerging CALL affordances in videoconferencing for language learning and teaching. In P. Taalas, J. Jalkanen, L. Bradley & S. Thouësny (Eds), *Future-proof CALL: language learning as exploration and encounters – short papers from EUROCALL 2018* (pp. 35-40). Research-publishing.net. https://doi.org/10.14705/rpnet.2018.26.809

but also on the action capabilities of the organism. CALL affordances manifest themselves as technological, linguistic, social, and educational affordances and the relation between these needs to be further developed.

In the context of videoconferencing between tutors and language learners, numerous studies have looked into micro level (moment-to-moment) interactions (Guichon & Tellier, 2017). This paper proposes to study the emergence of CALL affordances and the relation between them at the macro, meso, and micro levels of the learning ecology by investigating the following research questions:

- What are the designed affordances in the videoconferencing environment?

- What are the emerging affordances at the macro, meso, and micro levels of the interacting activity systems?

- What are the implications for curriculum design and online synchronous interaction?

2.   Method

2.1.   Context

French as a foreign language master's students from University of Lyon 2 tutored online undergraduate business students learning French (target level B2) at Dublin City University via a videoconferencing platform VISU. Weekly conversations took place with one or two students for a period of six weeks. These sessions were recorded and incorporated into a multimodal corpus: ISMAEL (Guichon, Blin, Wigham, & Thouësny, 2014).

The module's project-based learning activity was subdivided into three contiguous sub-activities:

- group work proposing services to a company,

- an individual CV and cover letter writing activity, and

- videoconference conversations to hone learners' interactional skills. The fifth session analysed here proposed a 'food truck for French hipsters' project-pitching role play and negotiation task. Students formulated questions regarding a client's business plan and proposed a marketing strategy.

2.2.   Theoretical framework

Within Engeström's (2014) CHAT, individuals or groups of individuals share an 'object' that becomes an 'outcome' through the mediation of the 'tool/instrument'. That mediation is regulated by implicit or explicit 'rules', 'community', and 'division of labour'. So, the context of the activity system and the interdependence between a network of interacting activity systems is taken into account for a detailed analysis.

2.3.   Unit of analysis

The macro level is the videoconference project that encompasses the six weekly sessions. Each weekly session comprised meso level interactions. Finally, the moment-to-moment interactions within each session compose the micro level interactions. The unit of analysis for this study is the macro level systemic interactions, focussing on the fifth session (meso) for a micro analysis.

3.   Data sets and analysis

3.1.   Macro analysis

Students' reflections and evaluations of their learning experience in the post session phase via oral presentations and an anonymous questionnaire respectively were analysed to get a macro picture of the tensions and contradictions in the online interactions. The tutors' post session reflections were also taken into account to interpret the learning ecosystem's interactional dynamics.

In Dublin's learning ecology, the 'object' of the group work became the 'tools' for the individual activity (see Figure 1 in supplementary materials[2]). The combined 'objects' of these two sub-activities supported the 'object' for the videoconferencing (the last session was a mock job interview). Videoconferencing was integrated in

---

2. https://research-publishing.box.com/s/f6yv6kqyspmgv442qsb6e2os8q87xihh

the learning ecology with the intention of developing students' L2 interactional skills and intercultural competences.

In Lyon, the first sub-activity's 'object' (L2 pedagogy and task design) became the 'tools' for the videoconference sub-activity. The 'object' of the videoconference (develop online pedagogical competence) became the tool for their following activity, i.e. reflection on teaching practice. The contradictions that arose between the interacting Dublin and Lyon activity systems are graphically represented using the CHAT framework (Figure 2 in supplementary materials[3]).

3.2.   Meso and micro analyses

The linguistic affordances designed by the tutors for the fifth session were coded in order to review how and when they were enacted in the course of the online videoconference conversations. The designed technological affordances for synchronous videoconferencing for Visu were also coded as "Information & Communication affordances", "Navigation & Spatial affordances", and "Traceability & Temporal affordances" (Dey-Plissonneau, 2017, pp. 95-96).

The recorded videoconference conversations were annotated on ELAN (transcription and annotation tool for multimodal data) for four tutor-tutee triads (one tutor and two students). It was noted that these online instantiations did not necessarily follow the scripted session design. New linguistic affordances emerged in the course of videoconferencing. The coded transcription was then uploaded on the qualitative analysis tool Atlas.ti to get a network view of the tutor-tutee micro interactions at the meso/session level.

4.   Findings and discussions

At the macro level, the interacting tutor-tutee activity systems had the same tools but different individual 'objects' (Figure 2 in supplementary materials[4]). This triggered a mismatch between the students' business module-oriented expectations and the tutor-designed session plans that differed from the students' module 'objects'. However, the exchanges were largely seen as highly beneficial by students, mostly improving their confidence in speaking. 'Pronunciation' was ranked second, followed by 'understanding/oral comprehension'. 'Overall oral

---

3. https://research-publishing.box.com/s/f6yv6kqyspmgv442qsb6e2os8q87xihh
4. https://research-publishing.box.com/s/f6yv6kqyspmgv442qsb6e2os8q87xihh

fluency', 'vocabulary knowledge', and 'cultural knowledge' were ranked low in the list of knowledge/skills developed during these online interactions.

Indeed, six sessions are not enough to develop 'overall oral fluency'. Student reflections expressed their desire to memorise lexical units or expressions. Videoconferencing following the dictates of oral speech and speed has an ephemeral quality. Additionally, the tutor's or peer's constant gaze added to the pressure. It was difficult to think and speak in L2 simultaneously as students constantly translated from L1 to L2 while conversing.

At a B2 level, students found the project-pitching tasks difficult. Most students were unfamiliar with the concepts of a food truck and French hipsters and were unable to deepen their reflection or formulate probing questions. Two students with higher linguistic abilities and agency adapted themselves well to the teaching design while the others seemed blocked. In order to help students overcome the stress of deciphering unfamiliar interaction themes, cultural contexts, new expressions, and vocabulary under pressure, a flip approach could be used to familiarise students with the theme, expressions, and vocabulary before the online session. Tutors used 'Information & Communication affordances' to help students understand the cultural concepts via images, but this did not necessarily trigger deep reflective expression. 'Traceability & Temporal affordances' (Figure 3 in supplementary materials[5]) were enacted by the tutors at the micro level in order to overcome this communication breakdown.

At the micro level, the linguistic affordances (Figure 4 in supplementary materials[6]) that co-occured with the traceability and temporal affordances reveal that the tutors frequently use text chat to repeat or add on student production to verify student responses and for corrective feedback. This is because very often tutors tried to guess what students would say in their B1 interlanguage with an anglicised pronunciation. Recasts and repetitions were common corrective feedback forms because tutors corrected diplomatically without sounding threatening (emergence of a social affordance).

Furthermore, tutors often 'initiate linguistic help' for negotiation of meaning to overcome communication breakdown. Additionally, tutors reformulate questions from lesson plans because students have problems in understanding the instructions or encourage complexification of responses through hedging or

5. https://research-publishing.box.com/s/f6yv6kqyspmgv442qsb6e2os8q87xihh
6. https://research-publishing.box.com/s/f6yv6kqyspmgv442qsb6e2os8q87xihh

questioning strategies to encourage well-reflected responses rather than simple yes/
no responses, typical of this environment.

5.   Conclusion

In this videoconferencing specific environment, the designed educational (task) and
technological affordances (chat) at the macro and meso levels give rise to emerging
networks of linguistic affordances at the micro level which influence the upper levels.
Interactional skills such as negotiation of meaning etc. are predominant yet students
seem to be inclined towards accretion of linguistic knowledge with module (probably
assessment) objectives in mind. Contradictions at the educational affordance level
(macro) of the interacting activity systems could be resolved at the tool level by
adapting the session design's interaction tasks (meso) to the 'objects' of the
students' learning ecology. Further investigations could look into how the designed
technological affordances are linked with emerging linguistic and social affordances.

6.   Acknowledgements

Special thanks to Professors Françoise Blin and Nicolas Guichon for their insightful
comments. Funded by the Irish Research Council, Ireland.

References

Dey-Plissonneau, A. (2017). Emerging affordances in videoconferencing for language learning
    and teaching. In K. Borthwick, L. Bradley & S. Thouësny (Eds), *CALL in a climate of
    change: adapting to turbulent global conditions – short papers from EUROCALL 2017* (pp.
    92-98). Research-publishing.net. https://doi.org/10.14705/rpnet.2017.eurocall2017.695

Engeström, Y. (2014). *Learning by expanding: an activity-theoretical approach to development
    research* (2nd ed.). Originally published in 1987. Cambridge University Press. https://doi.
    org/10.1017/CBO9781139814744

Gibson, J. J. (1977). The theory of affordances. In R. Shaw & J. Bransford (Eds), *Perceiving,
    acting, and knowing: toward an ecological psychology* (pp. 67-82). Lawrence Erlbaum.

Guichon, N., Blin, F., Wigham, C. R., & Thouësny, S. (2014). *ISMAEL learning and teaching
    corpus.* Dublin, Ireland: Centre for Translation & Textual Studies & Lyon, France:
    Laboratoire Interactions, Corpus, Apprentissages & Représentations.

Guichon, N., & Tellier, M. (2017). *Enseigner l'oral en ligne. Une approche multimodale.*
    Editions Didier.

JYVÄSKYLÄN YLIOPISTO
UNIVERSITY OF JYVÄSKYLÄ

Addressing current and future challenges in EAL writing with Universal Design for Learning

Paul Dickinson[1]

Abstract. Writing is an essential literacy skill that is crucial to meeting various social demands. It is also extremely difficult to master, especially for learners of an additional language who face significant barriers to learning. Universal Design for Learning (UDL), is an instructional framework promoted as an effective means of removing such barriers. The basis of UDL is that learning barriers are best addressed through curricula and lessons that provide multiple means of *engagement*, *representation*, and *action and expression*. This study explores the application of UDL in an English as an Additional Language (EAL) writing course at a Japanese university. The UDL guidelines were used in the design and implementation of goals, instruction, learning tasks, and assessments. Learners' perceptions of the UDL-based instruction were investigated using a questionnaire survey.

Keywords: writing, universal design for learning, inclusive learning.

1.   Introduction

Writing is an essential literacy skill that is extremely difficult to master, especially for language learners who face many barriers to learning (Tillema, 2012). UDL, an instructional framework which often employs the affordances of digital technology, exists to remove such barriers (Rose & Meyer, 2002). Although the success of UDL in enhancing L1 writing instruction has been reported (e.g. in Vue & Hall, 2012), research on its use in EAL writing contexts is scarce. Addressing this gap, the current paper reports on the implementation of UDL-based instruction in an English writing course at a Japanese university. It describes how UDL informed the

1. Meijo University, Nagoya, Japan; paul.dickinson01@gmail.com

How to cite this article: Dickinson, P. (2018). Addressing current and future challenges in EAL writing with Universal Design for Learning. In P. Taalas, J. Jalkanen, L. Bradley & S. Thouësny (Eds), *Future-proof CALL: language learning as exploration and encounters – short papers from EUROCALL 2018* (pp. 41-46). Research-publishing.net. https://doi.org/10.14705/rpnet.2018.26.810

design of learning activities and assessments, and discusses learners' perceptions of the course.

UDL was developed from neuroscience and educational research and is based on three principles linked to the affective, recognition, and strategic learning networks (CAST, 2018). These principles are that learning barriers are best addressed through instruction that provides multiple means of *engagement*, *representation*, and *action and expression*. A set of guidelines (Figure 1) was created to help educators reflect on current practice and assess where learning barriers may exist. This enables the design of inclusive instruction that provides flexible goals, methods, materials, and assessments that optimize accessibility and engagement (Tokuhama-Espinosa, 2011).

2. Method

Participants were 40 first-year nursing students taking a 15-week English writing course. All were Japanese L1 users, aged between 18 and 20 years old. Participants' English proficiency levels equated approximately to an average CEFR[2] level of A2.

Types of writing in the course included descriptive, argumentative, and narrative texts. Activities included both individual and collaborative tasks, with learners creating an individual writing portfolio based on ten texts posted on an online forum and working on three collaborative tasks. The *UDL Guidelines* (CAST, 2018) were used in the design and implementation of the course. For example, to optimize individual choice and autonomy (checkpoint 7.1), choices of topics, tools, and means of expression were provided (e.g. each group assignment had topic choices and the narrative task could, after it was written, be presented in visual, dramatic, or textual formats). Also, to foster collaboration and community (checkpoint 8.3) learners formed small groups to do collaborative writing tasks and give peer support. In addition, an online forum was created for learners to share and respond to each other's writing. Further examples of the use of the UDL guidelines (Figure 1) can be found in the supplementary material[3].

To investigate learners' perceptions of the UDL-based course, a questionnaire survey was administered in the final lesson. The questionnaire included items asking for a preference, a free comment section, and Likert items.

---

2. Common European Framework of Reference for languages
3. https://research-publishing.box.com/s/luuek05xzlokc5bbc0yivolat2qzb95k

---

Figure 1.   UDL guidelines

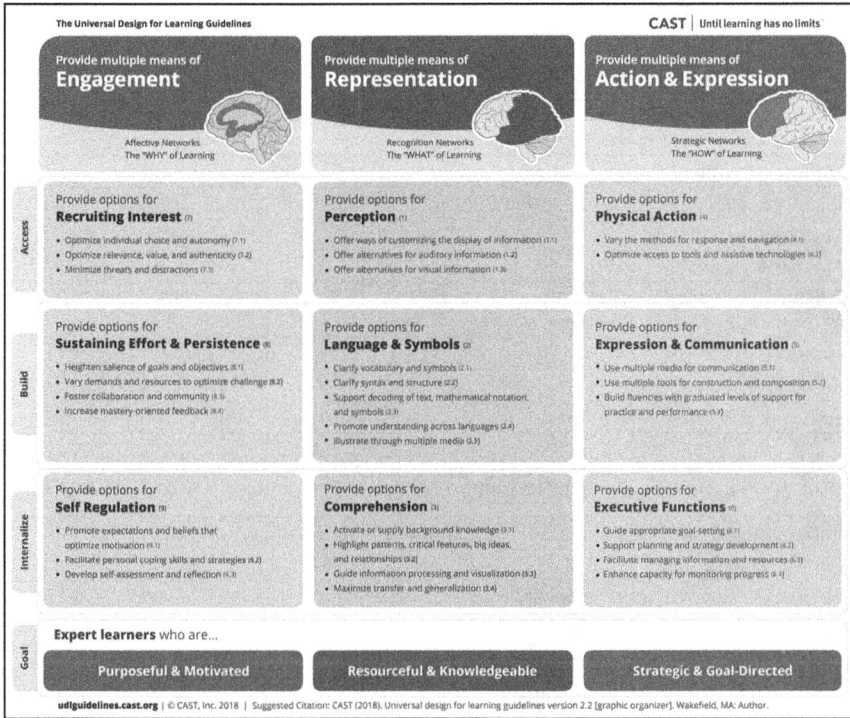

The Universal Design for Learning Guidelines

CAST | Until learning has no limits

Provide multiple means of
Engagement

Affective Networks
The "WHY" of Learning

Provide multiple means of
Representation

Recognition Networks
The "WHAT" of Learning

Provide multiple means of
Action & Expression

Strategic Networks
The "HOW" of Learning

Access

Provide options for
Recruiting Interest (7)
- Optimize individual choice and autonomy (7.1)
- Optimize relevance, value, and authenticity (7.2)
- Minimize threats and distractions (7.3)

Provide options for
Perception (1)
- Offer ways of customizing the display of information (1.1)
- Offer alternatives for auditory information (1.2)
- Offer alternatives for visual information (1.3)

Provide options for
Physical Action (4)
- Vary the methods for response and navigation (4.1)
- Optimize access to tools and assistive technologies (4.2)

Build

Provide options for
Sustaining Effort & Persistence (8)
- Heighten salience of goals and objectives (8.1)
- Vary demands and resources to optimize challenge (8.2)
- Foster collaboration and community (8.3)
- Increase mastery-oriented feedback (8.4)

Provide options for
Language & Symbols (2)
- Clarify vocabulary and symbols (2.1)
- Clarify syntax and structure (2.2)
- Support decoding of text, mathematical notation, and symbols (2.3)
- Promote understanding across languages (2.4)
- Illustrate through multiple media (2.5)

Provide options for
Expression & Communication (5)
- Use multiple media for communication (5.1)
- Use multiple tools for construction and composition (5.2)
- Build fluencies with graduated levels of support for practice and performance (5.3)

Internalize

Provide options for
Self Regulation (9)
- Promote expectations and beliefs that optimize motivation (9.1)
- Facilitate personal coping skills and strategies (9.2)
- Develop self-assessment and reflection (9.3)

Provide options for
Comprehension (3)
- Activate or supply background knowledge (3.1)
- Highlight patterns, critical features, big ideas, and relationships (3.2)
- Guide information processing and visualization (3.3)
- Maximize transfer and generalization (3.4)

Provide options for
Executive Functions (6)
- Guide appropriate goal-setting (6.1)
- Support planning and strategy development (6.2)
- Facilitate managing information and resources (6.3)
- Enhance capacity for monitoring progress (6.4)

Goal

Expert learners who are...

Purposeful & Motivated

Resourceful & Knowledgeable

Strategic & Goal-Directed

udlguidelines.cast.org | © CAST, Inc. 2018 | Suggested Citation: CAST (2018). Universal design for learning guidelines version 2.2 [graphic organizer]. Wakefield, MA: Author.

3.   Results

As discussed above, the questionnaire included several item types. Two questions were designed to elicit preferences regarding topics and expressive formats for assignments. Specifically, learners were asked whether they prefer being assigned a single topic and format for each assignment or to have a selection of topics and formats. The results indicated a clear preference for having options for both, with 80% of learners preferring a choice of topics and 88% preferring a choice of formats. In the free comment section, the most common theme to emerge was that learners considered the group writing tasks the best aspect of the course, with many comments directly praising them.

The results of the analysis of the Likert items data are presented in Table 1 and Table 2. These results also show strong support for group writing (M=4.45), choice of topics (M=4.13), as well as the usefulness of the teacher feedback (M=4.63).

There was also strong support for the statement (*M*=4.28) "Writing and reading posts on Edmodo improved my writing".

Table 1.   Learner evaluation of course and activities (*n*=40)

1. How useful were the following for improving your English writing ability? (1=poor, 5=excellent), α = .82	M	SD
Group Assignments	4.45	0.76
Writing Edmodo posts and comments	3.8	0.84
Textbook activities	3.6	0.74
Teacher feedback	4.63	0.63
2. How interesting were the following activities (1=boring, 5=very interesting), α = .63	**M**	**SD**
Group Assignments	4.45	0.68
Edmodo posts and comments	3.8	0.82
Textbook activities	3.6	0.87

Table 2.   Learner responses to course-related statements (*n* = 40)

Statements (1=strongly disagree, 5=strongly agree), α = .82	M	SD
I prefer to write alone	3.08	1.05
I prefer to write with other students	4.08	0.73
I learn more when I write alone	3.2	0.88
I learn more when I write with other students	4.0	0.78
When I study alone, I am motivated to learn English	3.23	0.89
When I study with other students, I am motivated to learn English	4.13	0.65
I understood the teacher's presentation of information in class	4.05	0.75
Writing and reading posts on Edmodo improved my English writing	4.28	0.72
I enjoyed writing and reading posts on Edmodo	3.73	0.85
The group assignments improved my English writing	4.13	0.69
I enjoyed doing the group assignments	4.5	0.64
The writing portfolio improved my English writing	4.35	0.66
The teacher's comments on my writing portfolio were useful	4.6	0.55
It is better to have a choice of topics for each assignment	4.13	0.85
It is better to have one topic for each assignment	3.35	1.12

4.   Discussion

This study investigated learner perceptions of a UDL-based writing course. One important finding was the learners' favorable response to collaborative writing activities. The inclusion of collaborative writing opportunities was informed by

UDL checkpoints such as foster collaboration and community, build fluencies with graduated levels of support for practice and performance, and enhance capacity for monitoring progress. Although findings on the effects of collaborative writing on language learning gains are mixed (Storch, 2016, p. 395) both socioconstructivist and second language acquisition theories offer strong support for its use (Grosbois, 2016, p. 271). Collaborative writing provides opportunities for learners to learn from more advanced peers and, through the process of writing a common text, learners can notice gaps between their existing linguistic knowledge and the target language, test and receive feedback on new hypotheses about language, and be encouraged to reflect on the language produced, all of which benefit language acquisition.

Another important finding was the strong support for options for both topics and expressive formats. Based on UDL checkpoints related to optimizing individual choice and autonomy and options for expression and communication, the provision of topic choices for each group writing assignment and, where possible, of expressive formats, appeared to make tasks more accessible for learners, enabling them to express themselves in ways suited to their individual strengths and interests.

While it is possible to include the types of activities, assessments, tools, and feedback implemented here without referring to UDL, using the framework enables informed decision making with a source based on extensive research. The UDL framework, which is updated as new knowledge comes to light, has principles, guidelines, and checkpoints which provide a systematic strategy for evaluating our current learning environments and to explore ways to make them more accessible and effective for all learners.

5.   Conclusion

It is hoped that this paper has provided an understanding of UDL and how it might be used to reduce learning barriers not only in EAL writing classrooms, but in all language learning contexts. Although this study did not focus on specific writing outcomes, it found that overall learners considered that the collaborative writing tasks, options for topics and expressive formats, the online forum, and mastery-oriented teacher feedback especially contributed to improving their writing abilities. While this is promising, research investigating the effects of UDL-based learning on specific aspects of learners' writing is a necessary step in further evaluating its efficacy.

References

CAST. (2018). *Universal design for learning guidelines version 2.2* [graphic organizer]. http://udlguidelines.cast.org

Grosbois, M. (2016). Computer supported collaborative writing and language learning. In F. Farr & L. Murray (Eds), *The Routledge handbook of language learning and technology* (pp. 269-280). Routledge.

Rose, D. H., & Meyer, A. (2002). *Teaching every student in the digital age: universal design for learning*. Association for Supervision and Curriculum Development.

Storch, N. (2016). Collaborative writing. In R. M. Manchon & P. K. Matsuda (Eds), *Handbook of second and foreign language writing* (pp. 387-406). De Gruyter Mouton. https://doi.org/10.1515/9781614511335-021

Tillema, M. (2012). *Writing in first and second language. Empirical studies on text quality and writing processes*. University of Utrecht.

Tokuhama-Espinosa, T. (2011). *Mind, brain, and education science: a comprehensive guide to the new brain-based teaching*. Norton.

Vue, G., & Hall, T. E. (2012). Transforming writing instruction with universal design for learning. In T. E. Hall, A. Meyer & D. H. Rose (Eds), *Universal design for learning in the classroom: practical applications* (pp. 38-54). The Guildford Press.

Tracking online learning behaviour in a cross-platform web application for vocabulary learning courses

Kazumichi Enokida[1], Kunihiro Kusanagi[2], Shusaku Kida[3], Mitsuhiro Morita[4], and Tatsuya Sakaue[5]

Abstract. The present study aims to reveal English as a Foreign Language (EFL) learners' online learning behaviour in a cross-platform web application for EFL vocabulary learning courses at a national university in Japan. Students were divided into two groups: those who were provided with the new, cross-platform application for vocabulary learning, and those with the older, PC-based Web-Based Training (WBT) system. The learning contents, learning processes, and the course evaluation systems were almost identical between these two groups. The log data of approximately 850 students over a year was extracted, and the online learning behaviour was statistically compared between the two groups. The comparison results can be summarised as (1) the total learning duration, the outcome, and learning efficiency are almost equivalent across the groups, and (2) the students with the new application exhibited a relatively significant tendency of frequent, steady, and periodical logins than those with the old one. The analyses suggested that the cross-platform, mobile-optimised web application elicited the students' ability to regulate their everyday self-accessed online learning.

Keywords: WBT, vocabulary learning, learning behaviour.

1. Hiroshima University, Higashihiroshima, Japan; kenokida@hiroshima-u.ac.jp
2. Hiroshima University, Higashihiroshima, Japan; kusanagi@hiroshima-u.ac.jp
3. Hiroshima University, Higashihiroshima, Japan; skida@hiroshima-u.ac.jp
4. Hiroshima University, Higashihiroshima, Japan; mmorita@hiroshima-u.ac.jp
5. Hiroshima University, Higashihiroshima, Japan; tsakaue@hiroshima-u.ac.jp

How to cite this article: Enokida, K., Kusanagi, K., Kida, S., Morita, M., & Sakaue, T. (2018). Tracking online learning behaviour in a cross-platform web application for vocabulary learning courses. In P. Taalas, J. Jalkanen, L. Bradley & S. Thouësny (Eds), *Future-proof CALL: language learning as exploration and encounters – short papers from EUROCALL 2018* (pp. 47-53). Research-publishing.net. https://doi.org/10.14705/rpnet.2018.26.811

1.   Introduction

Enokida et al. (2017) reported on the development of the web application to be utilised for EFL vocabulary learning courses at a national university in Japan. The older version of the WBT system, based on Adobe Flash, has long been used since these courses were first implemented in 2011, targeting 1,000 first-year students at the university. In the academic year 2017, the Flash-based system was partially replaced by a new, HTML5-based one: a group of students were provided with the new system, while the rest of them did their coursework on the old one.

This division has provided two data sets with which the online learning behaviour of the two groups can be compared. Although there has been a steady stream of studies that have reported the impacts of two different CALL materials on students' usability feedback (e.g. a questionnaire survey) and learning outcomes (e.g. pre- and post-test scores), relatively few studies have examined students' online learning behaviour itself. Considering the positive effects of mobile English vocabulary learning on the learning performances and interests of learners (Chen & Chung, 2008), it is expected that providing a cross-platform application will positively affect their online learning behaviour as well. The present study extracted online learning log data of approximately 850 students over one year, and statistically compared the students' online learning behaviour between the two groups. The purpose of the present study is to answer the following research question:

- How can users of the new, cross-platform application be compared with those of the older, PC-based WBT system in terms of their learning behaviour, as measured by (1) the frequency (number) of logins, (2) the periodicity (cycle) of logins, (3) the outcome, and (4) the learning efficiency?

2.   Method

2.1.   Participants and instruments

There were 841 participants in this study who took the semester-based online courses, 'Communication Basic I/II' in academic year 2017, which are compulsory courses for first-year students at Hiroshima University. They were required to learn 3,000 words per semester (15 weeks) and 6,000 per year on a self-study basis through the WBT system, the *HiroTan App*. The materials are based on an essential vocabulary list called *The Hirodai Standard 6000 Vocabulary List*, which was specially developed for the courses.

2.1.1. The Hirodai Standard 6000 Vocabulary List

The Hirodai Standard 6000 Vocabulary List consists of two levels (basic and advanced) of words that are used in daily communication as well as in academic and business contexts. The basic list consists of 2,000 words and the advanced 1,000 words – all to be learned within one university semester. Each word comes with its Japanese translation and a sample sentence with its Japanese translation. The students were provided with a printed textbook and downloadable audio podcasts with which they could listen to the pronunciation and sample sentence of each word, as well as the WBT materials.

2.1.2. The HiroTan App (WBT system)

An original WBT system is used for these courses to enable the students to learn the forms, meanings, and pronunciations of the large number of words in small steps (10 words per unit) and review them repeatedly (Enokida et al., 2017). Detailed log data is stored in the server, so that it can be analysed to assess the students' online performance. The latest cross-platform version of the WBT system is called HiroTan (see Figure 1).

Figure 1.   The HiroTan App: learning ten words in a unit

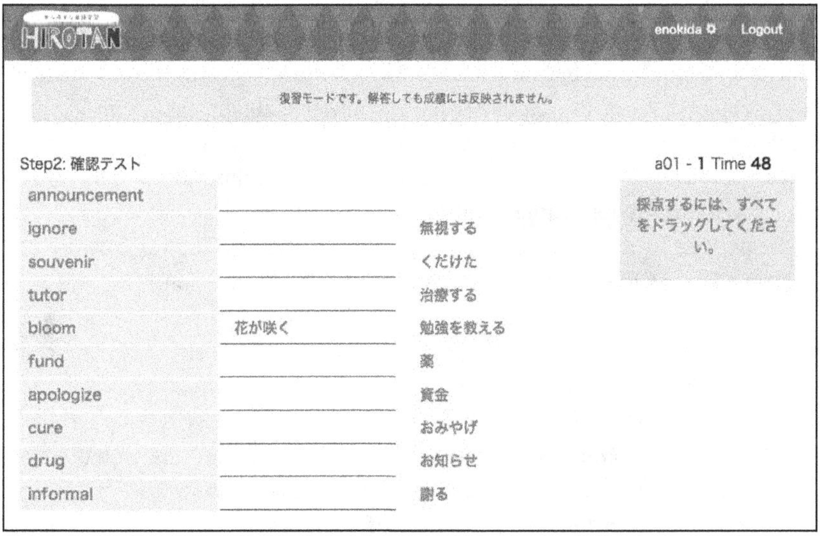

2.2.   Data collection

The participants engaged in a self-access vocabulary list learning for one academic semester, but reflecting the above-mentioned transition from the old to the new system, they were divided into the two groups based on the accessibility conditions: (1) a Flash-based application via PC and PC web browsers, and (2) a newly developed HTML5-based application that is optimised to mobile devices such as smartphones and tablets. The learning contents, learning processes, and the course evaluation systems were almost identical between these two groups.

2.3.   Data analysis

The log data of the students' 120-day-long learning behaviour that was automatically recorded by the implemented function in the two accessibility conditions were then extracted, in order to compare (1) the frequency of logins in a day, (2) the periodicity of logins, and (3) the number of the contents completed during the semester. Since the size of the log data is too big to perform statistical testing, the present study visualised the data and fitted some statistical distributions using the maximum likelihood estimation as appropriate.

3.   Results and discussion

The present study at first compared the frequencies of logins in a day, which are visualised in Figure 2. The number of students in each data set was standardised as density. The figure clearly shows that the new version (left) promoted more frequent logins than the older (right), meeting our expectations. To support this statistically, the present study fitted the exponential distribution using the maximum likelihood estimation, and compared the parameter λ for each group, since the data are, at a glance, extremely skewed. The estimated parameter values are $\lambda=0.039$ for the new HTML5-based application, and $\lambda=0.059$ for the old Flash-based application, and the expected values were calculated by the parameters. The values were 25.64 logins in a day for the new version, and 16.90 for the old version.

Secondly, the present study inspected the periodicity of logins. Figure 3 represents the time series of the cumulative total number of logins in a day for both the conditions. There are higher numbers of daily logins to the new version throughout the 120 days of the online course, which means that the new version has a strong tendency of shorter cycles of logins than the older. This tendency becomes clearer when we break down the data into days of week. As Figure 4 shows, the new version has a statistically steady half-week cycle of logins (Day 1/7 and Day 4) while the older does not exhibit the tendency.

The total numbers of the contents completed during the semester were almost equivalent between the two groups. That makes sense considering that the minimum requirements of the materials to be learned to pass the online course were the same in both groups. Also, against the two previous findings that suggest the new versions' advantages, no striking differences were found in the outcome of the courses, which were measured by the vocabulary tests, and the total learning duration, which can be operationalised by the logout – login time difference. That might imply that the outcome and the learning efficiency themselves were not facilitated by the replacement of the systems.

Figure 2.   Histograms representing the cumulative total number of students' login to the web apps in a day

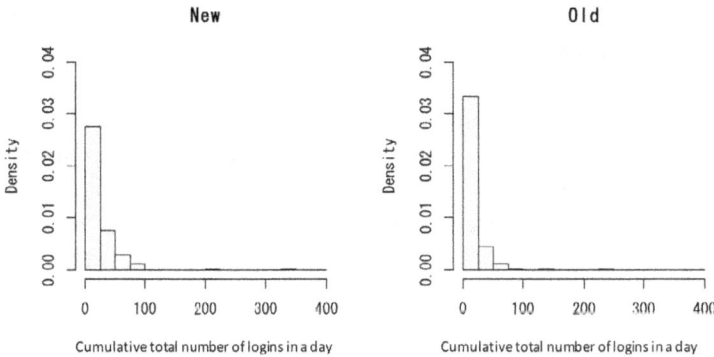

Figure 3.   Time series plots representing the total number of logins in a day

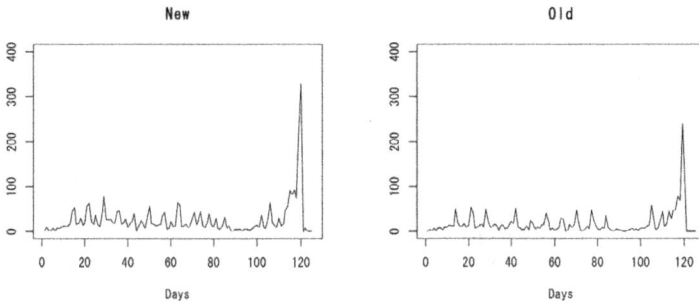

Figure 4.   Plots representing the total numbers of logins in a day, showing the differences of logins by the day of week; Day 1 represents Sunday and Day 7 is Saturday

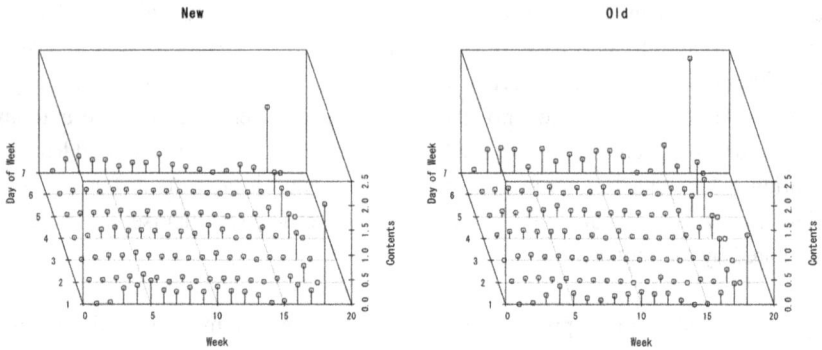

4.   Conclusions

The analyses of the online learning behaviour can be summarised as (1) the total learning durations, the outcome, and learning efficiency are almost equivalent across the groups, and (2) the students with the new, cross-platform application exhibited a relatively significant tendency of frequent, steady and periodical logins than those with the old, PC-only one. The analyses suggested that the cross-platform, mobile-optimised web application elicited the students' ability to regulate their everyday self-accessed online learning.

Since only the new application is currently used in the Communication Basic courses, our future directions will include: (1) comparing the online learning behaviour of successful vocabulary learners with that of unsuccessful learners, and (2) addressing the questions regarding the effectiveness of WBT-based list learning, as given in Enokida et al. (2017).

References

Chen, C. M., & Chung, C. J. (2008). Personalized mobile English vocabulary learning system based on item response theory and learning memory cycle. *Computers & Education, 51*(2), 624-645. https://doi.org/10.1016/j.compedu.2007.06.011

Enokida, K., Sakaue, T., Morita, M., Kida, S., & Ohnishi, A. (2017). Developing a cross-platform web application for online EFL vocabulary learning courses. In K. Borthwick, L. Bradley & S. Thouësny (Eds), *CALL in a climate of change: adapting to turbulent global conditions – short papers from EUROCALL2017* (pp. 99-104). Research-publishing.net. https://doi.org/10.14705/rpnet.2017.eurocall2017.696

Exploring foreign language anxiety and self-disclosure relationships in task design for e-tandem speaking practice

Marta Fondo[1] and Iker Erdocia[2]

Abstract. The emergence of videoconferencing tools in the 1990s provided language learners with opportunities to carry out speaking practice anytime and anywhere. However, the presence of Foreign Language Anxiety (FLA) in this interactional setting can hinder such ubiquitous benefits as FLA inhibits learning and communication in the Foreign Language (FL) (Horwitz, 2001). This article presents a case study developed in a five week e-tandem project in which 12 language learners (six Spanish and six English native speakers) participated via videoconference. Based on a mixed methods approach, the study explores the relationship between four different communicative task types with different levels of required Self-Disclosure (SD), the participants' levels of SD and FLA, and the resulting SD elements present in the conversation. Results showed that the different task types seem to have an effect on participants linking FLA and SD. However, the real trigger for SD events was not the task but the learner's characteristics and familiarity with the partner and topic.

Keywords: FLA, self-disclosure, e-tandem, communicative tasks.

1.   Introduction

With web 2.0 communication tools, new opportunities for language practice were opened up as, for instance, e-tandem, the online equivalent of 'tandem language learning'. E-tandem provides FL learners with online speaking practice with native/near-native speakers of the target language and culture. However, learners

1. Universitat Oberta de Catalunya, Barcelona, Spain; mfondo@uoc.edu
2. Dublin City University, Dublin, Ireland; iker.erdocia@dcu.ie

How to cite this article: Fondo, M., & Erdocia, I. (2018). Exploring foreign language anxiety and self-disclosure relationships in task design for e-tandem speaking practice. In P. Taalas, J. Jalkanen, L. Bradley & S. Thouësny (Eds), *Future-proof CALL: language learning as exploration and encounters – short papers from EUROCALL 2018* (pp. 54-58). Research-publishing.net. https://doi.org/10.14705/rpnet.2018.26.812

usually interact one-on-one with no teacher assistance, so supporting this speaking practice with communicative tasks is recommended to guide the conversation and foster FL skills development. Often, speaking practice activities and tasks invite learners to use themselves as a conversational topic, presenting themselves and sharing personal information. Since FLA is considered more an identity-based than a linguistic construct (Alrabai, 2015), self-consciousness and fear of negative evaluation, two FLA factors (Yon Yim, 2014), can be triggered by SD events increasing learners' FLA levels. As, to our knowledge, SD and FLA have not been jointly explored so far and their study requires a multilevel approach from the individual (learner) to the context (tasks). Analysing not only task compositions and effects, but also participants' profiles and perceptions in order to understand how all the elements interplay. Hence, this study aims to explore to what extent SD and FLA factors are linked in speaking practice and, in more detail, what is the relationship between task types, SD elements, and FLA levels.

2.   Method

The study took place on the *SpeaQ With Me* platform, a free social networking and language exchange service through video conference and text chat. A total of 61 users were contacted on the platform, 14 learners of English and 47 learners of Spanish. The selection was done by the level of English and Spanish, native or near-native, and an intermediate level of the target language. Due to the low activity of users on the platform, a call for participation among colleagues at the Universitat Oberta de Catalunya learning FLs was needed to complete the 12 required participants. The five-week project counted on nine active participants who interacted on the platform carrying out five sessions with four different task types in the spring of 2017. Participants were paired up with different partners weekly.

The present case study is based on a mixed-methods approach. Participants answered two different questionnaires before starting the interactions. The first one measured their FLA levels in an e-tandem setting, the *E-Tandem Foreign Language Anxiety Questionnaire* (ETFLAQ), specially tailored for the study. The second one measured their SD levels (Magno, Cuason, & Figueroa, 2008) in order to explore if FLA and SD could be related as personality traits. After each session, participants answered a Task Evaluation Questionnaire (TEQ) to explore the level of required SD perceived by the learners, the effect of the topic (depth-breadth SD), and the possible effect on their FLA levels. Due to technical problems, the TEQ could not be answered by all the participants after every interaction. Hence, a complementary questionnaire was sent by email at the end of the project aiming to explore the participants' perception of the different task types regarding SD and FLA. As a means to better understand the participants' perception of SD, FLA, speaking practice, and communicative tasks, online semi-structured interviews (N=4) and a focus group (N=4) were carried out by the main researcher. Interactions were audio recorded and shared with the researchers for observation. Interviews and focus group notes taken by the researcher, as well as partial transcription, was done transcribing the pieces of the discourse relevant for the study after two rounds of observation. The same partial transcription process was applied in the observations in which discourse elements regarding FLA and SD were transcribed and categorised for analysis.

3.   Results

3.1.   FLA and SD potential relationship

The first exploration was to measure participants' FLA and SD levels in order to find FLA and SD relationships on an individual level. As the sample was not sufficient to carry out statistical analysis (for statistical results about SD and FLA as personality traits please see Fondo, Jacobetty, & Erdocia, 2018), the levels of each construct were compared (Table 1). Unexpectedly, three out of four anxious participants were also high self-disclosers.

Table 1.   Participants' FLA and SD levels

Participants	ETFLAQ (Anxious > 54)*	SD scale (self-disclosers >150)*
PSE1	24	146
PSE2	24	133
PSS3	73*	167*
PSS3	75*	203*
PSS1	50	157*
PSS5	59*	182*
PSS2	23	163*
PSS7	32	189*
PSE13	93*	139

Results from the qualitative data analysis show a relationship between constructs, as different factors of FLA and SD elements influence each other during the speaking practice (Table 2), which also supports FLA and SD link at individual levels (Table 1).

Table 2. Common factors found between FLA and SD

Statements by participants	Observed in interaction	FLA and SD potential relationship
When I get nervous I talk more about myself.	Pairs who did not know each other talk about themselves.	Anxiety triggers self-disclosure
Talking about familiar topics like my family makes me feel more comfortable.	Participants tend to adapt the topic or aim of the task to their interest and knowledge.	Familiar topics do not trigger FLA.
I can disclose information about what I do or have feeling comfortable.	Participants talk about common and general topics.	Breadth self-disclosure does not trigger FLA.
I do not feel comfortable talking about feelings and relationships.	Participants did not develop deep SD.	Deep SD triggers FLA.

3.2. The tasks

Four different communicative task types (spot the difference, role-play, problem-solving, and opinion-exchange) and a free-talk session (without task) were used for the study. The preferred task by anxious learners to meet a person online for the first time was *spot the difference*, and less anxious learners, on the contrary, liked the free-talk session more. Decision-making and free-talk were marked as most anxiety provoking. In addition, participants in the interviews and focus group agreed on the benefits of having a task as guidance for carrying out the speaking practice. They indicated to feel more comfortable in *role-playing* as they do not act as themselves, and in the *spot the difference* tasks if they know the necessary vocabulary.

4. Discussion

From participants' performance observation, tasks did not seem to have a direct effect on triggering SD besides the opinion exchange tasks. The triggering element in all the cases in this study was the fact that participants were interacting for the first time and, surprisingly, had higher levels of FLA. Participants who knew each other beforehand just carried out the task with no presence of explicit self-disclosure elements. Participants preferred breadth self-disclosure and felt more comfortable talking about topics that were familiar to them. None of the observations found any

SD element regarding feelings, difficult situations, or personal relationships. On the contrary, participants openly shared their opinions and daily life activities. This could be an indicator that tasks with familiar topics in breadth levels of required SD could be positive to reduce anxiety in interaction during FL speaking practice. In summary, the results linking FLA and SD from observation, interviews, and focus group data (Table 2), and the ones expressed by the learners through the TEQs, seem to be consistent.

5.   Conclusion

First hints seem to link FLA and SD at individual levels as anxious non-native speakers expressed that they tend to start 'over talking' about themselves as a means to mitigate FLA. This is supported also by the relation found between FLA and SD participants' levels (three out of four anxious participants were also high self-disclosers). Results also highlight the importance of the topic and partner beyond the effect of different task types. This first exploratory analysis of the relationship between FLA and SD in e-tandem speaking practice sets the starting point for further research on the elements analysed in this study at individual, contextual, and interactional levels. More consistent and valid results are needed to better inform FL teachers and task designers of the effect of SD on FLA in FL speaking practice.

References

Alrabai, F. (2015). The influence of teachers' anxiety-reducing strategies on learners' foreign language anxiety. *Innovation in Language and Teaching, 9*(2), 163-190. https://doi.org/10.1 080/17501229.2014.890203

Fondo, M., Jacobetty, P., & Erdocia, I. (2018). Foreign language anxiety and self-disclosure analysis as personality traits for online synchronous intercultural exchange practice. development. In P. Taalas, J. Jalkanen, L. Bradley & S. Thouësny (Eds), *Future-proof CALL: language learning as exploration and encounters – short papers from EUROCALL 2018* (pp. 59-63). Research-publishing.net. https://doi.org/10.14705/rpnet.2018.26.813

Horwitz, E. K. (2001). Language anxiety and achievement. *Annual Review of Applied Linguistics, 21*, 112-126. https://doi.org/10.1017/S0267190501000071

Magno, C., Cuason, S., & Figueroa, C. (2008). The development of the self-disclosure scale. *SCRIBD*. https://www.scribd.com/doc/7791609/The-Development-of-the-Self-disclosure-Scale

Yon Yim, S. (2014). An anxiety model for EFL young learners: a path analysis. *System, 42*, 344-454. https://doi.org/10.1016/j.system.2013.12.022

EUROCALL

JYVÄSKYLÄN YLIOPISTO
UNIVERSITY OF JYVÄSKYLÄ

Foreign language anxiety and self-disclosure analysis as personality traits for online synchronous intercultural exchange practice

Marta Fondo[1], Pedro Jacobetty[2], and Iker Erdocia[3]

Abstract. Videoconferences are a perfect scenario for autonomous Foreign Language (FL) and intercultural speaking practices. However, it is also a threatening context as learners communicate in an FL, often with a stranger and about personal information and experiences. That may lead to increase Foreign Language Anxiety (FLA) among participants, affecting students' learning experiences and even provoking drop-outs (Bailey, Onwuegbuzie, & Daley, 2003). This study aims to explore the relationship between FLA and Self-Disclosure (SD) as personality traits. The first indicators of the potential relationship between FLA and SD in online speaking practice were found by Fondo and Erdocia (2018) in which anxious learners showed a tendency to self-disclose as a means to manage their discomfort using the FL. Data was gathered in the first stage of a nine-week-synchronous oral Online Intercultural Exchange (OIE) project between undergraduate business students from the United States, Ireland, Mexico, and Spain.

Keywords: foreign language anxiety, self-disclosure, personality trait, online intercultural exchange.

1. Introduction

In the last three decades, the affective dimension of the FL learning process has taken prominence in the field of second language acquisition. In this regard, FLA, or the situational and contextual anxiety experienced by language learners, has

1. Universitat Oberta de Catalunya, Barcelona, Spain; mfondo@uoc.edu
2. Universitat Oberta de Catalunya, Barcelona, Spain; pedro.jacobetty@gmail.com
3. Dublin City University, Dublin, Ireland; iker.erdocia@dcu.ie

How to cite this article: Fondo, M., Jacobetty, P., & Erdocia, I. (2018). Foreign language anxiety and self-disclosure analysis as personality traits for online synchronous intercultural exchange practice. In P. Taalas, J. Jalkanen, L. Bradley & S. Thouësny (Eds), *Future-proof CALL: language learning as exploration and encounters – short papers from EUROCALL 2018* (pp. 59-63). Research-publishing.net. https://doi.org/10.14705/rpnet.2018.26.813

been one of the most studied learning barriers since Horwtiz, Hortwitz, and Cope coined the term in 1986. Approximately half of the students suffer from FLA when using the FL (Atas, 2015), particularly when speaking. Communication in the FL, as in the L1, involves private information exchange, also known as SD. Indeed, many FL teaching practices are based on inviting the students to share personal information. To our knowledge, no study has looked into this private information sharing effect on students' FLA. The present article analyses student profiles of FLA and their relation to SD, considering both constructs as personality traits in order to understand the role played by both constructs and their effects on OIE practices.

2. Method

The project was a nine-week OIE through videoconference for Spanish/English speaking practice and intercultural skills development among Business students. Five universities joined the one-on-one project: Universitat Oberta de Catalunya in Spain, University of Maryland and University of Minnesota from the United States, University of Limerick in Ireland, and Benemérita Universidad Autónoma de Puebla (BUAP) from Mexico. A parallel monolingual intercultural project was run between students from Queens College New York and BUAP. As this project was fully in English, we did not survey New York students for FLA so only the students from Mexico (Spanish speakers) have been included in this study.

One hundred and fourteen students from the five universities mentioned above participated in the project. Every student was provided with a participant code at the beginning of the project in order to assure their anonymity. Participants were paired according to their time compatibility, and had to complete five online sessions in total.

The pre-project questionnaire, which provides the data for this article, was delivered online in the first stage of the project. The questionnaire measures participants' personal levels of FLA using the widely known Foreign Language Classroom Anxiety Scale (FLCAS) (Horwitz, Horwitz, & Cope, 1986) and the FLCAS Spanish version (Pérez-Paredes & Martínez-Sánchez, 2000). In order to assure the reliability of the results, we provided students with a version in their L1: Spanish and English. SD as a personality trait is measured using the General Disclosiveness Scale (GDS) by Wheeless (1978). For this study we translated the GDS into Spanish and validated the translation in dialogue with other experts – to our knowledge this is the first time the GDS has been translated and applied in Spanish. A total of 87 cases were used in data analysis.

3.   Results

We performed a Principal Component Analysis (PCA) of the FLCAS for dimension reduction. This analysis used the varimax rotation and resulted in three components. We named the components as *Negative attitudes towards FL learning* (Neg. att.), *FL classroom participation anxiety* (Class. anx.), and *Confidence in using the FL* (Conf.).

We then performed the k-means clustering technique to the PCA score to create FLA profiles, resulting in a total of six clusters (Table 1). The two most common FLA profiles seem to us, intuitively, to represent the typical profiles of FL students, each gathering about 25% of the sample each. The first, *Reluctant learners*, show very low Class. anx. but moderate levels of Neg. att. and Conf. In turn, *Confidents* have the highest level of Conf. but moderate Class. anx. The confidence in FL use together with moderate negative attitude towards learning seems to us a typical trait in FL students.

Table 1.   FL student profiles (clusters) and FLA – general and by dimension (averages of scale items and PCA scores)

Learners' cluster	N = 87	General FLCA	Negative attitude learning	Classroom participation anxiety	Confidence in using the FL
Reluctant learners	22 (25,3%)	2.3	0.6	-0.8	0.4
Insecure	17 (19,6%)	2.7	-0.6	0	-1.2
Achievers	9 (10,3%)	1.6	-1.2	-1.1	0.46
Confidents	21 (24,1%)	2.6	0.1	0.5	0.7
Anxious partakers	10 (11,5%)	2.7	-0.9	1.5	0.2
Challenged	8 (9,2%)	3.8	1.8	0.5	-1.1

Two categories seem to be related to extremes in FLA. On the least anxious extreme are those we called *Achievers,* characterised by the lowest levels of general FLA, Neg. att., and Class. anx., as well as moderate Conf. The moderate confidence level of the Achievers may be related to a more engaged and knowledgeable FL student profile, resulting in the reduction of overconfidence. On the other side of the FLA spectrum, we identified the *Challenged* profile (highest level of general FLA, Neg. att., moderate Class. anx., and very low Conf.). As expected, the proportion of learners in those categories is marginal (each gathering about 10% of the sample). The *Anxious partakers* profile also contains a similar proportion of the sample, (very low Neg. att. but the highest level of Class. anx.). Finally, the last identified profile is the *Insecure*, with the lowest levels of Conf. and moderately low levels of Neg. att.

A PCA was not performed on the GDS as its dimensions were established by Wheeless (1978) – in contrast with the FLCAS, which does not have defined dimensions. Wheeless (1978) identified five dimensions of SD: *Intent*, *Amount*, *Positiveness*, *Depth*, and *Honesty*. The learners' FLA profiles and SD levels were analysed in their different dimensions (Table 2).

Surprisingly, the *Challenged* group presents medium levels of SD *Amount* and high levels of *Depth*, thus not very different from the *Achievers*. However, these profiles are opposed regarding *Intent*, *Positiveness* and *Honesty*: *Achievers* rank high in these dimensions and *Challenged* low.

The two most common profiles (*Reluctant learners* and *Confidents*) show similar levels of SD in all dimensions (high *Intent*, *Positiveness*, *Depth* and *Honesty* but low *Amount*). The *Insecure* profile presents the lowest SD levels in every dimension.

Table 2.   FLCAS clusters and SD levels (average of Likert scales from 1 to 7) by SD dimensions

| FLCAS profiles | GDS dimensions of SD | | | | |
	Intent	Amount	Positiveness	Depth	Honesty
Reluctant learners	5.4	3.8	5.3	3.8	4.9
Insecure	4.6	3.9	4.6	3.2	4.4
Achievers	5.7	4.7	5.6	3.8	5.1
Confidents	5.3	4	5.3	4.1	4.9
Anxious partakers	5.1	4.2	5.2	4.2	4.9
Challenged	4.7	4.3	4.7	3.9	4.4

4.   Discussion

This study sheds light on how FLA and SD interact. The fact that *Challenged* and *Insecure* profiles have lower levels in SD dimensions point to a connection between low confidence in using the FL and SD, particularly *Intent*, *Honesty* (unobservable in interaction), and *Positiveness*.

In addition, *Anxious partakers* and *Challenged* show relatively high tendency to talk about themselves (*Amount* and *Depth*), as found in the above mentioned case-study (Fondo & Erdocia, 2018), which are observable in speaking practices and could be misinterpreted as a lack of anxiety as in the case of the *Achievers* profile.

5.   Conclusion

The study shows that some characteristics and events that influence interactions in speaking practices are not easily observable without a previous personality trait analysis. FLA and SD have shown to be related at an individual level. However, this first stage of personality trait analysis does not clarify yet if self-disclosing is a strategy used by students for FLA reduction nor the role these profiles play in the context of OIE. The next stages of analysis will try to answer this question, diving into the qualitative and quantitative data collected during the project in order to understand, from an ecolinguistic approach, how these profiles affect interaction and how students perceive it. Students, environment, and outcomes will be explored individually and in interaction in order to fully understand how SD and FLA are related during speaking practices. Our aim is to assess the benefits and/or risks of SD in relation to FLA to inform decision-making by the FL teaching community about learning scenarios and situations.

References

Atas, M. (2015). The reduction of speaking anxiety in EFL learners through drama techniques. *Procedia - Social and Behavioral Sciences, 176*, 961-969. https://doi.org/10.1016/j.sbspro.2015.01.565

Bailey, P., Onwuegbuzie, A., & Daley, C. (2003). Foreign language anxiety and student attrition. *Academic Exchange Quarterly, 7*(2), 304-308.

Fondo, M., & Erdocia, I. (2018). Exploring foreign language anxiety and self-disclosure relationship in task design for e-tandem speaking practice. In P. Taalas, J. Jalkanen, L. Bradley & S. Thouësny (Eds), *Future-proof CALL: language learning as exploration and encounters – short papers from EUROCALL 2018* (pp. 54-58). Research-publishing.net. https://doi.org/10.14705/rpnet.2018.26.812

Horwitz, E. K., Horwitz, M. B., & Cope, J. A. (1986). Foreign language classroom anxiety. *The Modern Language Journal, 70*(2), 125-132. https://doi.org/10.1111/j.1540-4781.1986.tb05256.x

Pérez-Paredes, P. F., & Martínez-Sánchez, F. (2000-2001). A Spanish version of the foreign language classroom anxiety scale: revisiting Aida's factor analysis. *RESLA, 14*, 337-352.

Wheeless, L. R. (1978). A follow-up study of the relationships among trust, disclosure, and interpersonal solidarity. *Human Communication Research, 4*(Winter), 143-157. https://doi.org/10.1111/j.1468-2958.1978.tb00604.x

Design of a MOOC on personal language learning environments for digital language skills development

Marta Fondo[1] and Angelos Konstantinidis[2]

Abstract. There is a mismatch between the availability of learning opportunities on the internet and the optimised use of them by learners. Disruptive technologies have always required time to be integrated into society to fully make use of their benefits. The Massive Open Online Course (MOOC) 'Create your own Personal Language Learning Environment (PLLE)' emerges from the willingness to provide language learners with digital and language skills for autonomous learning while fulfilling the research interests about exploring the learners' needs, how they use the internet, and how they can become more autonomous. Following the Analysis, Design, Development, Implementation, and Evaluation (ADDIE) model for instructional design and connectivism principles, the study presents the design process of a MOOC which aims to integrate data gathering tools into course content in a way that allows iterative formative course evaluations not affecting the learning process.

Keywords: personal language learning environments, connectivism, online course design, MOOC.

1.   Introduction

Over the last decades web technologies have drastically changed the way people live, work, communicate, and study. Nowadays, language students can boost their learning by using a variety of digital tools for language learning while interacting virtually with other learners and speakers of their target language. However, only a few learners go one step further establishing more complex relationships between tools, tasks, and themselves, enriching each other (Buckingham, 2007). In this project, we designed a MOOC on PLLE to support language learners in developing

1. Universitat Oberta de Catalunya, Barcelona, Spain; mfondo@uoc.edu
2. University of Nottingham, Nottingham, United Kingdom; angelos.konstantinidis@nottingham.ac.uk

How to cite this article: Fondo, M., & Konstantinidis, A. (2018). Design of a MOOC on personal language learning environments for digital language skills development. In P. Taalas, J. Jalkanen, L. Bradley & S. Thouësny (Eds), *Future-proof CALL: language learning as exploration and encounters – short papers from EUROCALL 2018* (pp. 64-69). Research-publishing.net. https://doi.org/10.14705/rpnet.2018.26.814

language learning strategies and self-managing their learning. The ADDIE model (Davis, 2013) is employed for the design and development of the MOOC, whereas the theory of connectivism (Siemens, 2005) forms its pedagogical foundation. The article presents the stages of the development process of the MOOC in a pre-pilot phase. The aim of the current study is to present how the ADDIE model and connectivism can be used jointly for MOOC design on PLLE. In addition, we aimed to showcase a method for developing course content which also allows data gathering in order to carry out a less intrusive research.

2. Method

The design and development of the MOOC on PLLE is based on two theoretical cornerstones. It is guided by the stages and processes of the ADDIE model for instructional design, which provides a necessary structure and order for the development of the MOOC. On the other hand, learning in online environments is hardly a straightforward and simple process, making it challenging to be approached by traditional pedagogical theories. Therefore, the theory of connectivism, which perceives learning as a process that is not entirely under the control of the individual and occurs within complex and lacking definite form environments (Siemens, 2005), has been employed.

In the following subsections, the five phases – *Analysis, Design, Development, Implementation*, and *Evaluation* (of the ADDIE model) – of the course design process are explained under the prism of the theory of connectivism.

2.1. Analysis

In this first phase, the objective was identifying the needs of language learners regarding internet use and set the instructional and research goals. Taking into account the underlying rationale for developing the MOOC, its aim was established as: *To support participants in developing their language learning strategies, building their PLLE, cultivating their digital skills, and becoming more autonomous.* The topics established for each week were: (1) PLLE concepts and practice, (2) digital tools for enhancing listening, and speaking skills, (3) digital tools for enhancing reading and writing skills, and (4) revision. In order to assure adequate communication between participants, a B1 level of English was required for participation in the course. Regarding the research goals, it was agreed to explore whether and to what extent participants in the course alter their strategies and ways of using digital tools for language learning.

2.2. Design

In the design phase, the main instructional strategies, the learning activities, and the assessment methods were determined as well as the technologies to be used. The aim of each week was designed to have an affordable workload and with the objective of developing language and digital skills in a holistic manner.

Each week there was a video lecture introducing the content and activities of the week as well as a gamut of different activities. Following the connectivist principles, the activities were directed to share and collaborate, learning and building knowledge in community (see Table 1).

Table 1.   Aims and pedagogical foundations of the activities in the course

Type of task	Type of activity	Aim	Pedagogical foundation (connectivism)
Forum discussion	Collaborative	Collaborative space to share and reflect	Building knowledge from diverse opinions
Online synchronous discussions	Collaborative	Direct communication with peers and tutors	Strengthen connections among participants
Creation of learning material using and reusing open educational resources	Individual	Tailored learning materials adapted to each learner needs	Building participants' capacity to learn
Sharing learning materials created and/or researched by the learners	Individual + Collaborative	Providing self-created and used learning resources	Connecting information sources
Questionnaires and activities of self-reflection	Individual	Self-reflection and awareness of their learning needs	Developing participants' ability to see connections between concepts and ideas

The use of Open Educational Resources (OER) as content served as a starting point for encouraging participants to create and share their own learning outcomes and products. Data gathering tools were included as part of the learning activities proposed in the course in order to minimise their intrusiveness in the learning process (see Table 2).

Table 2.   Study and course aims of the data gathering tools implemented as learning activities

Data type	Data gathering tool	Delivery format	Aim in the course	Aim in the study
Quantitative	SIL Questionnaire (Oxford, 1990)	Online questionnaire	Raising awareness of the learning behaviour and needs among the learners	To gain knowledge about the participants learning behaviours
Quantitative	FLCAS Questionnaire (Horwitz, Horwitz, & Cope, 1986)	Online questionnaire	Awareness of the emotional barriers the learners experience	To find relations between emotional barriers and the use of the internet resources
Qualitative	Forum participation	Forums on Moodle	Self-reflection of learning practices and difficulties	To gain insight into learners' habits and problems
Qualitative	Synchronous online discussion	Recorded video conference	To promote reflection on the topic of the week	Focus group to reach the deeper layers of the participants' behaviour and needs

2.3.   Development

In this phase, the course curriculum was developed on the Moodle platform. The development process required to move back to the design phase quite often, revising activities and materials as the research team gained more knowledge and insight about the web 2.0 tools and to fine-tune activities and materials. Many OERs were used for the course and new ones were created under a creative commons license.

2.4.   Implementation

We conducted a pre-pilot of the MOOC in July 2017 to test the course design in close-to-real settings to spot flaws and weaknesses. We announced the course in social media and 35 people answered the call and registered for the course. The pressure of a real audience and the feedback provided by the participants in combination with observation of their behaviour, materials use, and performance during the pre-pilot was key to complete the course development phase with a more realistic perspective.

2.5.   Evaluation

Course evaluation was designed to include both formative and summative elements. Currently, only formative evaluations have been conducted in this pre-pilot study, which helped to enhance the content and instructional methods for the forthcoming pilot study. They also assured that data gathering tools were harmoniously integrated into the course and were adequate for addressing the research questions of the project.

3.   Results and discussion

The first results from the pre-pilot study reveal that applying the ADDIE model for MOOC design can be challenging as it is addressed to anyone on the web. For instance, the collaborative environment created in the course and the tasks designed with such a purpose presented problems in terms of language barriers. Having an audience who is learning different languages limits the possibilities of peer to peer assessment. For this reason, some of the tasks needed redesign before the implementation in the pre-pilot and will need further adjustments for the pilot version of the course.

4.   Conclusions

The tests and improvements of this first version of the MOOC show that the principles and theory used for course and research design are adequate for fulfilling the project design objectives. Putting into practice the course design has demonstrated that it is possible to design user-friendly content which includes data gathering tools and use data gathering tools as part of the content in a connectivist MOOC. However, it is still in its embryonic stage after the pre-pilot course implementation so its effectiveness to achieve the learning and research goals was not fully evaluated. The upcoming piloting will allow final adjustments for its final release.

5.   Acknowledgements

The authors would like to thank David Alfter, Ph.D. student, University of Gothenburg, for bringing the team together and supporting the project in its initial phases.

References

Buckingham, D. (2007). Introducing identity. In D. Buckingham (Ed.), *Youth, identity, and digital media* (pp. 1-24). The MIT Press.

Davis, A. L. (2013). Using instructional design principles to develop effective information literacy instruction: the ADDIE model. *College & Research Libraries News, 74*(4), 205-207. https://doi.org/10.5860/crln.74.4.8934

Horwitz, E. K., Horwitz, M. B., & Cope, J. A. (1986). Foreign language classroom anxiety. *The Modern Language Journal, 70*(2), 125-132. https://doi.org/10.2307/327317

Oxford, R. (1990). Language learning strategies. In A. Burns & J. C. Richards (Eds), *The Cambridge guide to learning English as a second language* (pp. 81-90). Cambridge University Press.

Siemens, G. (2005). Connectivism: a learning theory for the digital age. *International Journal of Instructional Technology and Distance Learning, 2*(1), 3-10.

"My robot is an idiot!" – Students' perceptions of AI in the L2 classroom

Andrew Gallacher[1], Andrew Thompson[2], and Mark Howarth[3]

Abstract. Japanese university students (N=253) conversed with human and Artificially intelligent (AI) chatbot partners then recorded their perceptions of these interactions via open-ended written feedback. This data was qualitatively analyzed to gain a better understanding of the merits and demerits of using chatbots for English study from the students' perspective. Results suggest that, in its current state, students perceive the chatbot used in this study as a novelty rather than a legitimate language-learning tool and that it lacks the richness of interaction they could achieve with their peers. Ultimately, it is argued that educators should be more critical of incorporating AI technology in the second/foreign language (L2) classroom before it is ready for use.

Keywords: CALL, artificial intelligence, AI, chatbot, student perception.

1. Introduction

AI 'chatbots' provide an opportunity for independent conversational practice (Atwell, 1999) without the need for continual one-on-one support (Parker, 2007), making them an area of great interest within Computer-Assisted Language Learning (CALL) based research (Goda et al., 2014). Studies into the efficacy of chatbots as language learning tools have demonstrated a need for improvement before warranting greater adoption (Coniam, 2014; Fryer & Carpenter, 2006; Goda et al., 2014). However, the exponential rate of development of AI justifies routine and frequent 'checking in' with current iterations of these products, as ongoing

1. Kyushu Sangyo University, Fukuoka, Japan; gallacher@ip.kyusan-u.ac.jp
2. Kyushu Sangyo University, Fukuoka, Japan; thompson@ip.kyusan-u.ac.jp
3. Sojo University, Kumamoto, Japan; markwhowarth@gmail.com

How to cite this article: Gallacher, A., Thompson, A., & Howarth, M. (2018). "My robot is an idiot!" – Students' perceptions of AI in the L2 classroom. In P. Taalas, J. Jalkanen, L. Bradley & S. Thouësny (Eds), *Future-proof CALL: language learning as exploration and encounters – short papers from EUROCALL 2018* (pp. 70-76). Research-publishing.net. https://doi.org/10.14705/rpnet.2018.26.815

advancements make their feasibility of use for language practice simply a matter of time (Atwell, 1999; Fryer & Carpenter, 2006; Goda et al., 2014; Gulz, 2004; Morton & Jack, 2007; Parker, 2007).

With this in mind, the current study was designed to investigate the impact of using an artificially intelligent chatbot, known as *Cleverbot*, in a Japanese L2 classroom. As a part of this research, students' perceptions of AI versus human conversational partners were examined. The intervention utilized a task-based format with students performing spoken interviews with both AI and human partners in alternating sessions. Qualitative results obtained after each session were coded, and are presently discussed in relation to ongoing trends in CALL.

2. Methods

2.1. Participants

First and second year Japanese university students (N=253), studying English as a compulsory subject, took part in this study. Placement test results indicate a range of fluencies roughly equivalent to A1 to B2 on the Common European Framework of Reference for languages (CEFR).

2.2. Technology

Cleverbot (www.cleverbot.com) was created by Rollo Carpenter in 1988 (originally called *Jabberwacky*, Wikipedia contributors, 2018). It was designed to simulate human chat using AI algorithms that match input phrases and themes to those found within a continuously growing database of previously held conversations. It has had more than 279 million conversations to date, and passed the Turing Test in 2011 (Wikipedia contributors, 2018).

2.3. Instrument

Participants created questions asking for specific information using the prompts on their worksheets (see Figure 1). They then verbally asked these questions to either a human partner or *Cleverbot*. Partner responses were recorded on the worksheets in written form, as were students' perceived merits and demerits of having completed the activity with either an AI or human partner. The latter open-ended feedback was later translated then coded for analysis.

Figure 1. Conversation task worksheet

Student number: ☐☐☐☐☐☐☐	YEAR: 1 1ˢᵗ YEAR 2 2ⁿᵈ YEAR
	LEVEL: B BLUE R RED G GREEN
	TEACHER: T THOMPSON G GALLACHER H HOWARTH

PART 1
Work with a partner and write questions for the information below.

PART 2
Now ask your partner and write their answers below.

QUESTIONS

AI or HUMAN PARTNER *(circle one)*

1. Find out your partner's name:
Question ....

Answer 1. ....

2. Find out your partner's university major:
Question ....

Answer 2. ....

3. Find out how many classes your partner has per week:
Question ....

Answer 3. ....

4. Find out what classes your partner likes:
Question ....

Answer 4. ....

5. Find out what classes your partner dislikes:
Question ....

Answer 5. ....

6. Find out what your partner wants to do after university:
Question ....

Answer 6. ....

パートナーとの会話について、長所と短所を3つずつ挙げてください。

長所 ....
短所 ....

長所 ....
短所 ....

長所 ....
短所 ....

ENGLISH ACTIVITY
www.eltjapan.com

2.4.   Procedure

Four intervention sessions were conducted (two sessions each with AI and human partners) with participants alternating between partner types for each session. Previous to the initial intervention, participants were shown how to access and orally interact with *Cleverbot* (using the voice recognition function on their smartphones). After every session, participants were given five minutes to complete their conversation worksheets. Each session lasted approximately 15 minutes.

2.5.   Analysis

Completed worksheets were translated from Japanese into English where necessary. Students' reported merits and demerits of both AI and human partners were then coded in preparation for qualitative analysis. Codes for both partner types follow:

Human merits

- *Confirmable*: able to confirm understanding.
- *Contiguous*: can follow up conversation and ask for more detail.
- *Quick and reliable*: can complete quickly and rely on partner for response.

- *Natural*: facial expressions / emotions / voice easily understood.
- *Enjoyable/interesting*: interesting / fun / can make friends.
- *Discoverable*: can discover shared interests and learn about partner.
- *Forgiving*: more forgiving of mistakes (compared to voice capture on phone).
- *Appropriate*: stays on topic (appropriate responses to question asked).

Human demerits

- *Dependent on others*: cannot practice by yourself.
- *Limited responses*: receive one-word answers.
- *Misunderstanding*: hard to understand partner's pronunciation (ability).
- *Inability to check accuracy*: cannot check pronunciation / spelling / correctness (with phone's speech to text function).
- *Use of Japanese*: partner responds in Japanese.
- *Time consuming*: takes more time (because of follow up).
- *Lack of language ability*: lack of ability to use English (non-native partners).
- *Emotionally awkward*: feel shy or awkward / could lead to arguments.

AI merits

- *Independent*: can practice alone.
- *Quick response*: AI responds quickly and reliably to questions.
- *Ease of understanding*: replies in simple, easy English.
- *Smoothness of interaction*: one question, one answer no deviating.
- *Enjoyable/interesting*: enjoyable / fun / interesting.
- *Exposure to varied responses*: exposure to new vocabulary and phrases.
- *Speech capture useful*: speech-to-text was interesting and useful.
- *Accountability (error detection)*: valuable to English learning (checking pronunciation and spelling via the speech to text functions).

AI demerits

- *Non-contiguous*: cannot ask follow up questions.
- *Inappropriate response*: answers received often off topic.
- *Unnatural*: no facial, verbal, emotional cues.
- *Lack of audio response*: text only response / no listening practice.
- *Unintelligible response*: unable to understand the given response (ability?).
- *Audio capture unforgiving*: speech-to-text unforgiving for L2 pronunciation.

- *Uninteresting*: felt very industrial / like talking to a machine.
- *Unable to confirm understanding*: could not check meaning of responses.

3. Results and discussion

Table 1 depicts the overall number of responses for both human and AI partners. There were more reports of human partner merits than demerits overall, with the discrepancy between them being more than double. Conversely, AI partner demerits outnumbered merits, suggesting that students saw humans as better conversational partners than *Cleverbot*.

Table 1. Total number of responses

TOTAL RESPONSES		
	MERITS	**DEMERITS**
HUMAN Partner		
Session 1	176	75
Session 2	118	55
AI Partner		
Session 1	110	141
Session 2	92	107

Figure 2 and Figure 3 show the distribution of student responses for both human and AI partners between sessions. This illustrates the aspects of conversational interaction that participants found to be of benefit and/or detriment to their language practice.

Figure 2. Merits and demerits of human partner

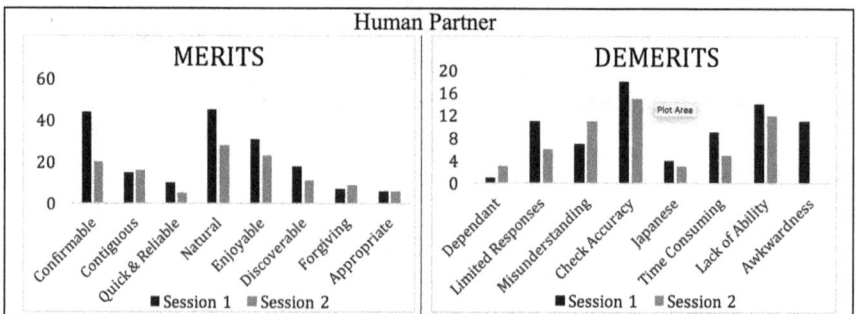

Naturalness of communication, the ability to confirm understanding/meaning, and the enjoyment of interaction were the most frequently reported merits of working with a human partner. The inverse of the first two were also reflected in the most commonly reported demerits of conversing with a human partner, namely: the inability to check accuracy (without the presence of an input/output field) and the misunderstanding of meaning. The third most reported demerit of human partners was a lack of English ability. Awkwardness disappeared as a category of response in the later session. Perhaps due to the students having become more comfortable with their classmates over time.

Figure 3.   Merits and demerits of AI partner

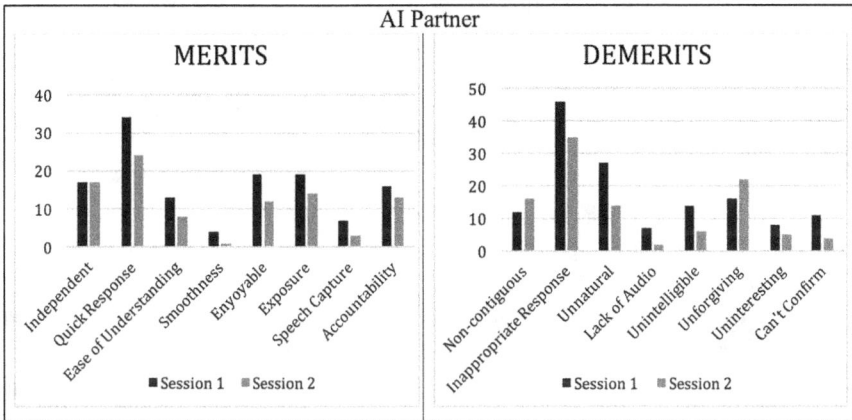

As for AI partners, the most cited merits were: the speed of response, independence of use, and the exposure to new forms of language. Top demerits included: the inappropriateness of responses, technical difficulties (speech to text function on smartphones), the unnaturalness of interaction, and a lack of being able to carry on the conversation. All aspects that are reminiscent of what separates man from machine, and that pose the most difficult hurdles to overcome in developing AI technology of this sort (Coniam, 2014; Fryer & Carpenter, 2006; Goda et al., 2014).

4.   Conclusions

In accordance with Atwell (1999) and Parker (2007), students saw the independence of conversing with *Cleverbot* as being beneficial for their English study. Other merits reported for AI partners had more to do with the speech-to-text function of the smartphone rather than the AI itself. Which suggests that the pre-existing functions on students' smartphones might provide the same benefits as some iterations of AI, without the added confusion of having to learn a new software platform.

In any case, it is clear that students do not see *Cleverbot* as a viable replacement for communication with another human being. Its lack of emotion, visible cues, and inability to confirm understanding were reported to be some of the major drawbacks to its form of interaction. Therefore, educators should be skeptical of incorporating current AI technology in the L2 classroom as frustration from interaction might outweigh any benefits to its inclusion within an English Curriculum. Future research would benefit from development of a quantifiable survey utilizing the categories presented herein that could provide a more consistent analysis across AI chatbot platforms.

References

Atwell, E. (1999). *The language machine: the impact of speech and language technologies on English language teaching*. British Council.

Coniam, D. (2014). The linguistic accuracy of chatbots: usability from an ESL perspective. *Text & Talk, 34*(5), 545-567. https://doi.org/10.1515/text-2014-0018

Fryer, L., & Carpenter, R. (2006). Emerging technologies. Language in action: from webquests to virtual realities. *Language Learning & Technology, 10*(3), 8-14.

Goda, Y., Yamada, M., Matsukawa, H., Hata, K., & Yasunami, S. (2014). Conversation with a chatbot before an online EFL group discussion and the effects on critical thinking. *Information and Systems in Education, 13*(1), 1-7. https://doi.org/10.12937/ejsise.13.1

Gulz, A. (2004). Benefits of virtual characters in computer based learning environments: claims and evidence. *International Journal of Artificial Intelligence in Education, 14*(3), 313-334.

Morton, H., & Jack, A. M. (2007). Scenario-based spoken interaction with virtual agents. *Computer Assisted Language Learning, 18*(3), 171-191. https://doi.org/10.1080/09588220500173344

Parker, L. (2007). Technology in support of young English learners in and out of school. In L. Parker (Ed.), *Technology-mediated learning environments for young English learners* (pp. 213-250). Routledge.

Wikipedia contributors. (2018, October 5). *Cleverbot*. In Wikipedia, The Free Encyclopedia. https://en.wikipedia.org/w/index.php?title=Cleverbot&oldid=862672526

From local to massive learning: unveiling the (re)design process of an English LMOOC based on InGenio materials

Ana Gimeno-Sanz[1], Ana Sevilla-Pavón[2], and Antonio Martínez-Sáez[3]

Abstract. This paper focusses on the (re)design and conversion process of small-scale English as a Foreign Language (EFL) online courseware into a Massive Open Online (Language) Course – or LMOOC, as it is commonly termed – for upper-intermediate learners of English offered on edX[4], one of the most popular MOOC platforms. It stems from the *InGenio First Certificate in English Online Course and Tester* (Gimeno-Sanz, Martínez-Sáez, & Sevilla-Pavón, 2011), which provides university students with autonomous study and self-evaluation materials for the preparation of B2-level[5] official English language exams. The authors discuss the differences between both platforms and the implications for language learning. They conclude that it is necessary to build language-learning-specific add-ons onto currently available MOOC platforms.

Keywords: online learning environments, open educational resources, massive open online language courses, InGenio FCE Online Course & Tester, upper-intermediate English language MOOC.

1.   Introduction

After designing and publishing a number of interactive multimedia courseware on CD-ROM, the CAMILLE Research Group at the Universitat Politècnica de

1. Universitat Politècnica de València, Valencia, Spain; agimeno@upvnet.upv.es
2. Universitat de València, Valencia, Spain; ana.m.sevilla@uv.es
3. Universidad Politécnica de Madrid, Madrid, Spain; antonio.martinezs@upm.es
4. https://www.edx.org
5. According to the Common European Framework of Reference for languages (Council of Europe, 2001)

How to cite this article: Gimeno-Sanz, A., Sevilla-Pavón, A., & Martínez-Sáez, A. (2018). From local to massive learning: unveiling the (re)design process of an English LMOOC based on InGenio materials. In P. Taalas, J. Jalkanen, L. Bradley & S. Thouësny (Eds), *Future-proof CALL: language learning as exploration and encounters – short papers from EUROCALL 2018* (pp. 77-82). Research-publishing.net. https://doi.org/10.14705/rpnet.2018.26.816

València (UPV) realised that the internet was rapidly becoming the future of Computer-Assisted Language Learning (CALL) so, at the turn of the century, a group of specialists started designing what was later to be known as the InGenio authoring tool and content manager. As described elsewhere,

> "InGenio, at the time (in 2000), was unique in a very important way; it was the first completely online CALL-dedicated authoring tool [– available worldwide –] based on the template approach to authoring (Kitts & Whittlestone, 1998, p. 4), that allowed language teachers to design their own materials, create a database with these materials – thus making it available to other users –, and automatically convert these materials into learner-ready courses, all on a cloud-computing basis" (Gimeno-Sanz, 2016, p. 1105).

Eighteen years later – a whole generation's worth of advancements in educational technologies – and despite the InGenio courseware still being used by EFL students at UPV, the CAMILLE Research Group decided to convert this Small Private Online Course (SPOC) into an internationally accessible LMOOC.

The resulting LMOOC, 'Upper-Intermediate English' (Gimeno-Sanz, Martínez-Sáez, & Sevilla-Pavón, 2018), is based on an English for specific purposes approach. As for the materials it is derived from, they have been piloted, validated and delivered through the InGenio Learning Management System over the past decade. Moreover, they are used by approximately 200 students from UPV every year. The move from a closed, restricted-access, low-scale course to an open, massive online course entails the redesign of the learning objects and resources in order to fit the new format.

The challenges faced during the (re)design process are discussed in the following section, particularly focussing on issues relating to (1) learner assessment and (2) sustainability (or as the conference theme suggests, 'Future-Proof CALL'). This EFL MOOC is the result of a collective effort through which both the developers and the institution are trying to find new ways of making learning more accessible, bearing in mind that education is a basic human right, as established in Article 26 of the United Nations' (1948) Universal Declaration of Human Rights (General Assembly Resolution 217 A, p. 76). Thanks to the use of internet-based tools, participants are granted access to high quality, free-of-charge study and self-assessment learning objects and materials that prepare them for official, high-stakes exams. In other words, this delivery mode makes learning more accessible for a larger number of learners, regardless of whether they come from academic or informal learning settings.

2.   Converting a SPOC into a MOOC: results

Owing to the fact that the InGenio authoring tool was designed specifically for self-access language learning purposes, it includes a number of features to support the acquisition of a foreign language through autonomous learning. As described in Gimeno-Sanz, Martínez-Sáez, Sevilla-Pavón, and de Siqueira Rocha (2011), some of the discipline-specific features include:

- (a) self-explanatory reference materials (grammar, use of language, etc.),

- (b) text-embedded hints to aid exercise completion,

- (c) immediate and delayed feedback (Pujolà, 2001),

- (d) self-assessment tools and exercises with limitation in number of attempts and time control,

- (e) performance and progress reports, as well as automatic scores,

- (f) help files describing how the online system works, and

- (g) audio enhancements of written text to simulate an immersion scenario.

Of these, only (a), (c), (d), and (e) were part of the edX platform, which meant that other alternatives for (b), (f), and (g) had to be sought. Provision of hints (b) was resolved by including 'reminders' and references to explanations in exercise headings. For platform functionality help (f), learners are redirected to the general edX learner Help Center, and audio enhancement (g) is provided by including audio files to enhance written text and by designing and embedding a voice-recording tool (Language Lab) in all of the exercises containing audio, allowing learners to compare their utterances to the models provided by native speakers (see Figure 1).

Furthermore, because InGenio courseware is designed to be used autonomously under the supervision of a tutor, with learners organised in closed groups – resembling face-to-face educational settings –, its online tutoring system allows tutors/teachers to access learner-generated audio and open text output, which can subsequently be corrected, marked, and scored. These scores are then automatically averaged with those calculated by the system itself (Sevilla-Pavón, Martínez-Sáez, & Macario de Siqueira, 2011). Consequently, due to the huge number of MOOC enrollees, this was one of the main features that had to be redesigned. In the MOOC version of the course, several solutions were found:

- Specially designed rubrics are provided to aid in self- and peer-assessment of learner-generated open text (writing practice exercises).

- Pronunciation and fluency practice is catered for by prompting learners to transcribe their oral production, requesting them to access external free text-to-speech software and, ultimately, have the software reproduce the written transcription of their oral text[6]. Correct oral reproduction of the written input is interpreted as an indication of success.

Another unique feature is InGenio's ability to create course-independent glossaries (which open up in pop-up windows upon clicking on a 'hot word') that authors can link to in any exercise. In the edX LMOOC, however, this deficiency was solved by incorporating automatically generated glossaries for each of the study units inserted into the Multidict dictionary interface[7], thus allowing learners to quickly seek definitions or translations into more than 100 languages – a true asset when considering that edX enrollees come from all five continents.

Lastly, whereas InGenio courseware users can upload recorded sound files for their tutors to correct and mark, given the enrolment numbers on edX – ranging in the tens of thousands –, upon designing the MOOC, the decision was made to compensate this absence, as described in Gimeno-Sanz (2017), by:

- organising scheduled instructor-led Google Hangouts[8] sessions to support synchronous oral interaction, and

- organising learner-driven speaking practice sessions using the Talkabout discussion planner, a tool that serves the purpose of organising speaking practice encounters so that students can interact live among themselves and practise the foreign language together through a Google Hangouts video conference.

---

6. https://www.naturalreaders.com/online
7. http://multidict.net
8. For more information, go to https://hangouts.google.com

Figure 1.   Sample reading comprehension exercise from the upper-intermediate EFL MOOC on the edX platform

3.   Conclusions

In order to gain in sustainability due to funding limitations at UPV to appropriately maintain and update the InGenio System, the CAMILLE Research Group decided to (re)design and transfer the *InGenio FCE Course & Tester* to the edX MOOC platform. This had major implications in terms of writing and speaking practice activities for which the MOOC platform was not prepared. This procedure has also proven that – as so many times warned in CALL systems and materials development – it is, in effect, not necessary to 'reinvent the wheel' by ensuring that the lessons learnt from the past are taken into account in present day CALL software development and implementation.

References

Council of Europe (2001). *Common European framework of reference for languages.* Cambridge University Press.

Gimeno-Sanz, A. (2016). Moving a step further from "integrative CALL". What's to come? *Computer Assisted Language Learning, 29*(6), 1102-1115. https://doi.org/10.1080/095882 21.2015.1103271

Gimeno-Sanz, A. (2017). Designing a MOOC for learners of Spanish: exploring learner usage and satisfaction. In K. Borthwick, L. Bradley & S. Thouësny (Eds), *CALL in a climate of change: adapting to turbulent global conditions – short papers from EUROCALL 2017* (pp. 122-127). Research-publishing.net. https://doi.org/10.14705/rpnet.2017.eurocall2017.700

Gimeno-Sanz, A., Martínez-Sáez, A., & Sevilla-Pavón, A. (2011). *InGenio FCE Online Course & Tester.* Universitat Politècnica de València.

Gimeno-Sanz, A., Martínez-Sáez, A., & Sevilla-Pavón, A. (2018). *Upper-intermediate English.* https://www.edx.org/es/professional-certificate/upvalenciax-upper-intermediate-english

Gimeno-Sanz, A., Martínez-Sáez, A., Sevilla-Pavón, A., & de Siqueira Rocha, J. M. (2011). Fostering autonomy in a pedagogically sound e-learning environment for learners of English for specific purposes. In S. Maruenda-Bataller & B. Clavel-Arroitia (Eds), *Multiple voices in academic and professional discourse: current issues in specialised language research, teaching and new technologies* (pp. 547-560). Cambridge Scholar Publishing.

Kitts, S. A., & Whittlestone, K. (1998). CALScribe: a multimedia template ideal for CALL development. *ReCALL, 10*(2), 4-11. https://doi.org/10.1017/S0958344000003682

Pujolà, J. T. (2001). Did CALL feedback feed back? *ReCALL, 13*(1), 79-98. https://doi.org/10.1017/S0958344001000817

Sevilla-Pavón, A., Martínez-Sáez, A., & Macario de Siqueira, J. (2011). Self-assessment and tutor assessment in online language learning materials: InGenio FCE Online Course and Tester. In S. Thouësny & L. Bradley (Eds), *Second language teaching and learning with technology: views of emergent researchers* (pp. 45-69). Research-publishing.net. https://doi.org/10.14705/rpnet.2011.000006

United Nations. (1948). *Universal declaration of human rights.* http://www.un.org/en/universal-declaration-human-rights

JYVÄSKYLÄN YLIOPISTO
UNIVERSITY OF JYVÄSKYLÄ

Who's got talent? Comparing TTS systems for comprehensibility, naturalness, and intelligibility

Jennica Grimshaw[1], Tiago Bione[2], and Walcir Cardoso[3]

Abstract. The current study compared five free Text-To-Speech (TTS) systems, selected based on characteristics such as availability and capabilities. Tasks were completed by 37 English learners to evaluate these systems in terms of their comprehensibility, naturalness, and intelligibility. Our findings indicate that IBM Watson and Google Translate are the best TTS systems, according to the evaluation criteria employed.

Keywords: text-to-speech synthesis, L2 pronunciation.

1. Introduction

Second language (L2) researchers have explored the pedagogical capabilities of TTS synthesizers for their potential to enhance the acquisition of writing (Kirstein, 2006), vocabulary, and reading (Proctor, Dalton, & Grisham, 2007), and pronunciation (e.g. Liakin, Cardoso, & Liakina, 2017). In addition, recent evaluations of TTS quality have attested that students perceive little difference between synthetic and human speech (Bione Alves, 2017; Cardoso, Smith, & Garcia Fuentes, 2015), suggesting that TTS technology is ready for pedagogical use not only because of its voice quality, but also because users may have become familiar with synthesized speech.

The availability of free web-based TTS applications is also promising (Karakaş, 2017), as L2 students can access these tools from any device. However, faced with

1. Concordia University, Montreal, Canada; jennica.grimshaw@concordia.ca
2. Concordia University, Montreal, Canada; tiagobione@gmail.com
3. Concordia University, Montreal, Canada; walcir.cardoso@concordia.ca

How to cite this article: Grimshaw, J., Bione, T., & Cardoso, W. (2018). Who's got talent? Comparing TTS systems for comprehensibility, naturalness, and intelligibility. In P. Taalas, J. Jalkanen, L. Bradley & S. Thouësny (Eds), *Future-proof CALL: language learning as exploration and encounters – short papers from EUROCALL 2018* (pp. 83-88). Research-publishing.net. https://doi.org/10.14705/rpnet.2018.26.817

a plethora of options, users may find it difficult to choose the most appropriate TTS system to use, particularly in terms of voice quality. As these technologies evolve, there is a need for regular evaluations to determine which systems will best suit L2 users' needs.

The current study compared a set of five TTS systems in terms of their comprehensibility, naturalness, and intelligibility, based on tasks completed by a group of English as a Second and Foreign Language (ESL/EFL) learners. It was guided by the following research question: which of the selected five TTS systems constitute the most pedagogically appropriate software in terms of their ability to produce speech that is comprehensible, natural, and intelligible?

2.   Method

While seven freely available TTS systems were originally considered for analysis, we decided to select a more manageable number of TTS systems for evaluation based on criteria that included: availability (web, iOS, Android), popularity (ratings on Google Play or the App Store), and other pedagogically-relevant capabilities (e.g. ability to control voice speed and pitch; see Barcroft & Sommers, 2005 for the rationale). Consequently, the number of TTS systems for evaluation was reduced to five: IBM Watson, Google Translate, LumenVox, NeoSpeech, and NaturalReader.

2.1.   Participants

Participants were 37 native speakers of Brazilian Portuguese (17 males, 20 females; all adults), living in Brazil (EFL; n=12) or abroad (ESL; n=25). The study targeted high-intermediate to advanced learners (self-prescribed) recruited over social media. For the purposes of the current analysis, results from both ESL and EFL groups were combined.

2.2.   Instruments

For each of the five TTS systems, one short story clip (20-30 seconds) and four short sentences were recorded using Audacity (or downloaded from the TTS application, if the option was available). Only default female voices were used in the recordings, as not all TTS systems offered male voices; all other default settings were also retained (speed, pitch, etc.) to replicate a user attempting to use the system without guidance. All recordings were placed into a quiz on a Moodle-based testing environment.

2.3.   Procedures

After participants gave their consent, they first practiced a set of ratings before completing a Moodle-based test, all of which was conducted remotely (online); the process lasted approximately 15 minutes. The participants were instructed to listen to each recording only once.

To evaluate the selected TTS systems in terms of comprehensibility and naturalness, participants listened to and rated recordings of short story clips from five different systems. They were also asked to transcribe four sentences produced by each TTS system (for a total of 20) as a measure of intelligibility.

2.4.   Data collection and analysis

Participants rated TTS voices based on a six-point Likert scale for comprehensibility (1=very difficult to understand, 6=very easy to understand) and naturalness (1=very unnatural, 6=very natural). For these items, descriptive statistics (means, standard deviations) were reported. For intelligibility, the data were measured according to transcription accuracy percentage, where participants could transcribe between 0% to 100% of each sentence correctly. It was assumed that more intelligible sentences would result in more accurately transcribed words.

3.   Results

3.1.   Comprehensibility

Participant comprehensibility ratings suggest that IBM's Watson TTS system is the most favorable (*M*=5.81, *SD*=0.46), followed by Google Translate (*M*=5.35, *SD*=0.82); see Table 1 for all ratings.

Table 1.   Comprehensibility ratings

TTS system	Mean	Standard deviation
IBM Watson	5.81	0.46
Google Translate	5.35	0.82
LumenVox	4.81	1.02
NeoSpeech	4.41	1.01
NaturalReader	3.78	1.46

3.2.   Naturalness

Participant ratings for naturalness follow a similar trend as comprehensibility, with Watson being ranked as most natural (M=4.87, SD=1.03), followed by Google Translate (M=3.73, SD=1.46); see Table 2.

Table 2.   Naturalness ratings

TTS system	Mean	Standard deviation
IBM Watson	4.87	1.03
Google Translate	3.73	1.46
NeoSpeech	3.14	1.25
LumenVox	3.08	1.19
NaturalReader	2.03	0.96

3.3.   Intelligibility

Accuracy percentages for the intelligibility task (Table 3) indicate that Watson's voice once again scored the highest (M=90%, SD=5%), followed by LumenVox (M=88%, SD=10%).

Table 3.   Intelligibility accuracy scores

TTS system	Mean	Standard deviation
IBM Watson	90%	5%
LumenVox	88%	10%
Google Translate	85%	7%
NaturalReader	85%	14%
NeoSpeech	79%	16%

4.   Discussion and concluding remarks

According to participant ratings, IBM Watson appears to be the most comprehensible and natural, followed by Google Translate. In terms of intelligibility, accuracy scores suggest that, once again, IBM Watson comes out on top, followed by LumenVox. One reason why IBM Watson outranks all others in these measures may be because it is a demo version of a new and highly advanced system which highlights the capabilities of state-of-the-art TTS (e.g. users can modify the voice's expression or pitch to make the voice sound apologetic or anxious; see demo: https://text-to-speech-demo.ng.bluemix.net). Google Translate may have also received high ratings because its synthesized voice is commonly used in many popular apps and websites. As a result, it is possible that participants may have already been familiar with the voice adopted in our study. Bione Alves (2017), for instance, noted that users' rating for comprehensibility and naturalness might increase as participants become more acquainted with synthetic voices.

There are several reasons that may explain the lower ratings for the other systems. As NaturalReader's default settings had the TTS voice play at a higher than normal speed, this may have influenced rater comprehensibility and naturalness. In the free version of NeoSpeech, soft music plays in the background as the voice speaks; this may have therefore interfered with user comprehensibility, while the creators of LumenVox may have focused on the quantity of voices they offer rather than quality. As we also only targeted one voice per system, ratings for the five systems may have varied if different voices had been used. Additionally, in reality, many TTS applications (including IBM Watson, Google Translate, NaturalReader, NeoSpeech) have user-controlled features that allow them to modify the speed of speech and/or repeat the speech as many times as necessary, a feature that may place some of these TTS systems at the same level, considering the three criteria adopted to evaluate them.

To conclude, the aim of this study was to evaluate and compare five TTS systems in terms of their comprehensibility, naturalness, and intelligibility, as assessed by a group of ESL/EFL learners. The results obtained in our analysis of participants' ratings and transcriptions suggest that, among the TTS systems considered, IBM Watson and Google Translate constitute, at present, the more pedagogically appropriate choices for L2 learners willing to enhance (in both quantity and quality) their access to the target language.

Assuming that the pedagogical use of TTS has the potential to extend the reach of the classroom (Bione Alves, 2017; Cardoso et al., 2015) and that it is beneficial for learning (Liakin et al., 2017), teachers can use one of these readily available systems to develop activities and tasks to provide additional listening and pronunciation practice. Although TTS systems are undergoing constant change, we hope that the criteria outlined here will help the language teacher to critically select the most pedagogically appropriate tool for their purposes.

5.   Acknowledgements

We would like to thank our participants and Paul John for his input. This project was partially funded by the *Social Sciences and Humanities Research Counsel of Canada.*

References

Barcroft, J., & Sommers, M. S. (2005). Effects of acoustic variability on second language vocabulary learning. *Studies in Second Language Acquisition, 27*(3), 387-414. https://doi.org/10.1017/S0272263105050175

Bione Alves, T. (2017). *Synthetic voices in the foreign language context*. Master's Thesis. Concordia University, Montreal, CA.

Cardoso, W., Smith, G., & Garcia Fuentes, C. (2015). Evaluating text-to-speech synthesizers. In F. Helm, L. Bradley, M. Guarda, & S. Thouësny (Eds), *Critical CALL – proceedings of the 2015 EUROCALL Conference, Padova, Italy* (pp.108-113). Research-publishing.net. https://doi.org/10.14705/rpnet.2015.000318

Karakaş, A. (2017). English voices in 'text-to-speech tools': representation of English users and their varieties from a World Englishes perspective. *Advances in Language and Literary Studies, 8*(5), 108-119. https://doi.org/10.7575/aiac.alls.v.8n.5p.108

Kirstein, M. (2006). *Universalizing universal design: applying text-to-speech technology to English language learners' process writing*. Doctoral dissertation. University of Massachusetts, Boston, MA.

Liakin, D., Cardoso, W., & Liakina, N. (2017). The pedagogical use of mobile speech synthesis (TTS): focus on French liaison. *Computer Assisted Language Learning, 30*(3-4), 348-365. https://doi.org/10.1080/09588221.2017.1312463

Proctor, C. P., Dalton, B., & Grisham, D. (2007). Scaffolding English language learners and struggling readers in a universal literacy environment with embedded strategy instruction and vocabulary support. *Journal of Literacy Research, 39*(1), 71-79.

Online English practice with Filipino teachers in university classrooms

Sandra Healy[1], Yasushi Tsubota[2], and Yumiko Kudo[3]

Abstract. Globalization has led to an increased need for Japanese students to improve their communicative abilities in order to compete on the world stage. As a result, the Japanese government has reformed the English education system in Japan to focus on more practical communication. Due to a lack of time and resources available to do this successfully, some institutions in Japan have introduced online components to their courses. This study examines both qualitative and quantitative data regarding students' engagement in online English education and some of the practical issues that can arise.

Keywords: computer-mediated communication, foreign language anxiety.

1.   Introduction

As a result of globalization, improvement of English language ability is extremely important for the future of Japan. The Japanese government is now reforming English education, but while various reforms have been introduced, they have not been enough to boost the level of English education. One of the biggest problems is the limited amount of time spent on practical English communication. To alleviate this, some institutions are introducing online English communication courses with teachers based in other countries. This study examines some of the issues that can arise in the use of online classes and reviews the results of both qualitative and quantitative research undertaken on the impact of online classes on the motivation, language anxiety, and level of English ability of the students.

1. Kyoto Institute of Technology, Kyoto, Japan; healy@kit.ac.jp
2. Kyoto Institute of Technology, Kyoto, Japan; tsubota-yasushi@kit.ac.jp
3. QQEnglish, Osaka, Japan; kudo_yumiko@qqeng.com

How to cite this article: Healy, S., Tsubota, Y., & Kudo, Y. (2018). Online English practice with Filipino teachers in university classrooms. In P. Taalas, J. Jalkanen, L. Bradley & S. Thouësny (Eds), *Future-proof CALL: language learning as exploration and encounters – short papers from EUROCALL 2018* (pp. 89-93). Research-publishing.net. https://doi.org/10.14705/rpnet.2018.26.818

2.   Method

Over three years, six groups of first year chemistry majors at a national university in Japan took part in synchronous, online sessions with teachers based in the Philippines. Before the sessions were held, the students were given a thorough orientation and assigned to groups which remained the same for all of the Skype sessions. The students used mini iPads and all of the sessions were recorded. The students were given a different topic for each session; self-introduction, Japanese life, Filipino life, and free choice, and were asked to research and prepare a five minute presentation individually. During the sessions, they gave their presentations, the Filipino teacher asked some questions and gave feedback, and then there was a short time for some whole group discussion.

Qualitative data was collected through the use of focused essays, a method recommended by MacIntyre, Burns, and Jessome (2011) which allowed us access to the thoughts and feelings of the students. The students had thirty minutes during class to write two essays, one on what they liked about the Skype sessions and the other about what they disliked. The answers were analysed using an open coding process adapted from Holton (2007). The quantitative data was collected using questionnaires using a Likert scale based on the *foreign language classroom anxiety scale* (Horwitz, Horwitz, & Cope, 1986) which was translated into Japanese and administered at the beginning and end of the sessions.

3.   Discussion

The data from the focused essays revealed five significant themes:

- perceived improvement in English language skills,

- increased motivation to study English,

- international posture,

- change in language user identity, and

- ambivalence about using English.

Firstly, many students remarked that they believed their English ability had improved, for example, "When I talked with them at last time I can speak fluently than for the first time". As the sessions were limited in number, the change in their language skills may not have been significant, however, the students' belief that there had been an improvement is important, as an emphasis on successful experiences should lead to an increase in motivation and self-confidence and in turn proficiency (MacIntyre & Gardner, 1991). Secondly, the students showed increased levels of motivation. Many compared the Skype sessions positively with their previous experiences learning English in school, for example, "Before English was just for tests now I can use English another way. I am fun". Working together in groups led to a positive atmosphere in the classroom which in turn helped build students' confidence and motivation (MacIntyre & Gardner, 1991).

The importance of international posture and identity was highlighted by the students. Yashima (2009) suggests that Japanese learners do not identify with native speakers of English, but view English as a medium through which communication with people from around the world is possible. Through the Skype sessions the learners were able to develop international, English-using versions of themselves,"I had never known interesting point about English before this class. But I can notice about talking with foreigner is very very interesting". The Japanese education system and the place of Japan in the outer circle of language users position Japanese learners in a passive role without a sense of ownership of the language. However, through speaking to the teachers in the Philippines, the students were able to develop an image of themselves as active users as we can see in the following comment, "I studied a lot for tests in high school, but I did not speak. I had to use my English to talk on Skype".

Notwithstanding the positive feedback regarding the Skype sessions, the students did express some ambivalence. The duality of their experience is captured in the following comment, "I liked it and I hated it. It was hard to do, my friends said too. But it was interesting". This comment highlights the mixed feelings and complicated processes the students are undergoing during L2 communication.

The results of the quantitative data revealed a complicated picture when the pre- and post-data were compared. The sessions clearly led to an increase in anxiety as can be seen in the answers to several questions. In Question 1 (*I feel nervous when I speak English*), there was a 12% increase in students who strongly agreed or agreed with the statement. Related to that, in Question 3 (*I feel nervous when I can't remember proper English phrases*), agreement increased significantly by 22%. Question 9 (*I feel embarrassed when I make mistakes*) showed a 10% increase, and finally Question 10 showed an 11% rise.

The data showing decreases in anxiety showed more complex changes. For example, in Question 11 (*I am afraid that other students think my English is poor*), there was a 10% decrease in the number of students who strongly agreed with this statement, but an 11% increase in students who agreed showing a slight reduction in anxiety levels. There was a 4% decrease in the number of students who agreed with Question 12 (*I am afraid the teacher will scold me when I cannot answer some questions*) and a 3% increase in students who disagreed also revealing a decrease in anxiety. Finally, Question 13 (*I feel upset when I hear other students' good pronunciation*) showed a similar pattern with an 8% decrease in students who disagreed and a 2% decrease in those who strongly disagreed.

We can see that there was an increase in anxiety concerning the learners' own performances, and a frustration with the disparity between the level of their thoughts and their linguistic ability. However, there was a decrease in anxiety related to external issues such as fear of negative evaluation from the other students or the teachers.

Several practical problems unique to studying online arose during the Skype sessions. One problem was some students hid their scripts out of view of the camera and just read their presentations, which was not allowed. It was also sometimes hard for the teachers to evaluate the students' body language and the volume of their speech due to the limitations of the computer or tablet. To solve this problem, we introduced wide conversion lenses and microphones for the Filipino teachers so they could see all the students easily, which has led to smoother group interaction and a reduction in the use of scripts.

Another problem was that the students presented in groups and sometimes those who had finished presenting lost interest and did not participate in the other students' presentations. In order to solve this problem we decided to give roles to each group member, such as Questioner, Time Keeper, and Recorder. We also introduced peer evaluation, which helped students to improve their reflective abilities and increase interaction. Finally, to improve the quality of the activities, all the students' presentations were video-recorded.

4.   Conclusions

In conclusion, the Skype sessions appeared to be beneficial to the students in a number of ways. Through practical experience communicating with the Filipino teachers, the students realized which areas of language learning they needed to focus on while building up their confidence and altering their self-perceptions to form images of themselves as successful language learners.

5.   Acknowledgements

This work was supported by JSPS KAKENHI Grant Numbers 16K02882.

References

Holton, J. A. (2007). The coding process and its challenges. In A. Bryant & K. Charmaz (Eds), *The Sage handbook of grounded theory* (pp. 265-289). Sage. https://doi.org/10.4135/9781848607941.n13

Horwitz, E. K., Horwitz, M. B., & Cope, J. (1986). Foreign language classroom anxiety. *The Modern Language Journal, 70*(2), 125-132. https://doi.org/10.1111/j.1540-4781.1986.tb05256.x

MacIntyre, P., Burns, C., & Jessome, A. (2011). Ambivalence about communicating in a second language: a qualitative study of French immersion students' willingness to communicate. *The Modern Language Journal, 95*(1), 81-96. https://doi.org/10.1111/j.1540-4781.2010.01141.x

MacIntyre, P. D., & Gardner, R. C. (1991). Investigating language class anxiety using the focused essay technique. *The Modern Language Journal, 75*(3), 296-304. https://doi.org/10.1111/j.1540-4781.1991.tb05358.x

Yashima, T. (2009). International posture and the ideal L2 self in the Japanese EFL context. In Z. Dörnyei & E. Ushioda (Eds), *Motivation, language identity and the L2 self.* Multilingual Matters. https://doi.org/10.21832/9781847691293-008

How much vocabulary is needed for comprehension of research publications in education?

Clinton Hendry[1] and Emily Sheepy[2]

Abstract. The American Education Research Association (AERA) is one of the largest education conferences in the world. Using the AERA Open Access Repository, we created a 5,000,000 word corpus of over 18,000 abstracts. We explored the coverages of the New General Service List (NGSL), the New Academic Word List (NAWL), and the Social Science Word List (SSWL). We found that the NGSL and NAWL provide approximately 90% coverage for abstracts from all 12 of the AERA's subject matter divisions. The SSWL showed little additional coverage. Our discussion highlights the research and pedagogical implications of our findings and the AERA abstract corpus.

Keywords: corpus-driven research, lexical frequency, reading comprehension.

1.   Introduction

AERA is currently one of the largest education conferences in the world, with more than 2,500 sessions and 15,000 people in attendance in 2017. At the time of this study, the AERA Open Access Repository contained all abstracts accepted from 2010-2017, separated into 12 divisions. It contains a wealth of contemporary education research in a variety of subdisciplines and offers a unique opportunity to develop a representative vocabulary corpus for education. This corpus allows us to estimate the vocabulary requirements required to participate in the education field in terms of reading and publishing academic works, and to test existing word lists for their coverage using authentic texts.

1. Concordia University, Montreal, Canada; clinton.hendry@concordia.ca
2. Concordia University, Montreal, Canada; emily.sheepy@concordia.ca

How to cite this article: Hendry, C., & Sheepy, E. (2018). How much vocabulary is needed for comprehension of research publications in education? In P. Taalas, J. Jalkanen, L. Bradley & S. Thouësny (Eds), *Future-proof CALL: language learning as exploration and encounters – short papers from EUROCALL 2018* (pp. 94-99). Research-publishing.net. https://doi.org/10.14705/rpnet.2018.26.819

Nation (2006) argues that corpus-driven word lists such as the General Service List (GSL) (West, 1953), and the Academic Word List (AWL) (Coxhead, 2000), can guide more efficient vocabulary learning.

The GSL, which consists of the 2,000 most frequent word families in English, could account for up to 80% of most written English works, while the AWL's 570 word families could account for up to an additional 10% of academic works (Nation, 2006). He also argues that although readers require knowledge of 98% of a text's vocabulary for comprehension, they can develop a strong foundation by learning just 2,570 word families for 90% coverage of most texts. However, the utility of these general purpose lists is debated in the field.

Hyland and Tse (2007) specifically call into question whether the AWL is actually representative of English academic writing because it ignores that different disciplines use different technical vocabulary. Many researchers have argued for the creation of more discipline-specific word lists that are more applicable to their respective areas (Nation & Kyongho, 1995). One recently developed technical word list is the SSWL (Chanasattru & Tangkiengsirisin, 2016).

For our study, we question whether the GSL, AWL, and the SSWL are sufficient for comprehension of research publications in education, specifically, the AERA annual conference. To answer this question, we will examine the coverage each list provides for all twelve AERA divisions. Our goal is to determine whether knowledge of the above lists would be sufficient to comprehend abstracts and presentations in the AERA conference, and likely education research as a whole.

2.   Methodology

2.1.   The AERA corpus

The AERA corpus is created from the titles and abstracts available in the AERA Open Access Repository and is divided into twelve divisions. In total, there are 18,669 abstracts, 4,361,577 tokens, and 46,772 unique words. We included only the titles and bodies of each abstract in the corpus. Additional information such as author names and keyword lists were removed as they were either irrelevant or might bias certain vocabulary over others. The breakdown of the corpus can be seen in Table 1.

Table 1.   AERA conference abstract corpus

Division	Abstracts	Tokens
Division A - Administration, Organization, and Leadership	1495	302459
Division B - Curriculum Studies	1303	330337
Division C - Learning and Instruction	3547	864120
Division D - Measurement and Research Methodology	1004	229040
Division E - Counseling and Human Development	419	99890
Division F - History and Historiography	326	67871
Division G - Social Context of Education	2326	647395
Division H - Research, Evaluation and Assessment in Schools	1188	266961
Division I - Education in the Professions	392	75733
Division J - Postsecondary Education	2035	333879
Division K - Teaching and Teacher Education	3400	765390
Division L - Educational Policy and Politics	1234	325688
All Divisions	18669	4361577

2.2.   NGSL, NAWL, and SSWL

We chose the NGSL and NAWL variants developed by Browne, Culligan, and Phillips (2013a, 2013b) as they were the most modern variants we were able to locate. Further details of their creation can be found at www.newgeneralservicelist.org.

The SSWL was created to be representative of vocabulary in the Social Sciences and to be used instead of the GSL or AWL (Chanasattru & Tangkiengsirisin, 2016). We decided to incorporate this list into our study because of its relevance to the subject matter.

After compiling the headword lists of the NGSL, NAWL, and SSWL, we used Lextutor's (lextutor.ca) 'Familizer' to create NGSL, NAWL, and SSWL word lists that include headwords and their derivatives. We opted to use word families to allow for better comparisons with earlier corpus-driven word list research (e.g. Coxhead, 2000; Nation, 2006).

Finally, to estimate the coverage of each list, we used Anthony's (2018) analysis toolkit AntConc using 'Stop Lists'. They allow us to determine what percentage of a given list of words (e.g. the AERA corpus) is comprised of another set of words (e.g. NGSL, NAWL, SSWL) by removing all instances of one list from another.

3.   Results

Each division was checked against the NGSL, the combined NGSL and NAWL (as the NAWL was made to work with the NGSL), the SSWL by itself, and the combined NGSL, NAWL, and SSWL.

The coverage was similar across all 12 divisions for all three word lists as seen in Table 2 with two notable exceptions. The combined NGSL + NAWL + SSWL saw much higher overall coverage in Division G ('Social Context of Education'). This implies that in Division G there was little overlap between the SSWL and the NGSL + NAWL word lists.

Table 2.   Coverages of the AERA divisions

Division	NGSL coverage	NGSL + AWL	SSWL	NGSL + AWL + SSWL
Division A	88.9%	91.3%	30.6%	91.6%
Division B	83.6%	87.2%	23.0%	87.4%
Division C	86.9%	90.7%	30.1%	91.0%
Division D	86.7%	90.3%	31.8%	90.5%
Division E	87.2%	90.3%	29.1%	90.5%
Division F	97.0%	86.7%	20.8%	87.0%
Division G	85.0%	88.2%	25.8%	98.2%
Division H	88.5%	91.4%	30.6%	91.7%
Division I	87.2%	91.3%	30.4%	91.5%
Division J	87.0%	90.3%	29.6%	90.6%
Division K	87.5%	90.9%	29.8%	91.1%
Division L	87.9%	90.4%	29.1%	90.7%
All Divisions	86.9%	90.2%	29.6%	90.4%

As seen above, the NGSL and NAWL consistently reach 90% coverage of the AERA divisions with only Divisions B, F, and G being slightly lower. The only division to see substantial gains from the SSWL was Division G, 'Social Context of Education'. This suggests that the SSWL does not contribute much coverage beyond the combination of the NGSL and NAWL.

4.   Discussion and conclusion

Our goal for this study was to explore the AERA corpus by checking the vocabulary requirements for comprehension by testing the coverages of the NGSL, NAWL, and SSWL. We were also interested in determining whether the specialized SSWL would see greater coverage when compared with the more general NGSL

+ NAWL, which in theory should be applicable to all academic discourse. Our data shows that the combined NGSL and NAWL saw approximately 90% coverage in all divisions which corresponds with the creators' expectations (Browne et al., 2013a, 2013b). The SSWL saw 20-30% coverage of any given division, but apart from Division G ('Social Context of Education'), it did not appreciably add to the coverage provided by the NGSL + NAWL. We argue that these results show that although the SSWL list is much smaller and more targeted, a learner would be just as successful studying the NGSL + NAWL. Although they might see further vocabulary gains with a more discipline-specific wordlist, the SSWL is not adequate. We believe this knowledge can help future academics in the field of education be more aware of the vocabulary requirements for participating in the field and will motivate future studies that use vocabulary word lists to help create more targeted pedagogical tools for English as a second language and English for academic purpose learning.

4.1. Limitations

This study's largest limitation is that our AERA abstract corpus is very specialized. It is debatable whether our results can be generalized to the field of education as a whole.

4.2. Future research

We hope to continue this research by incorporating other conferences' abstracts into our corpus. This will allow researchers to not only explore the AERA abstract corpus, but other education conferences too.

References

Anthony, L. (2018). AntConc (Version 3.5.7) [Computer Software]. Waseda University. http://www.laurenceanthony.net/software

Browne, C., Culligan, B., & Phillips, J. (2013a). *New Academic Word List*. http://www.newgeneralservicelist.org

Browne, C., Culligan, B., & Phillips, J. (2013b). *New General Service Word List*. http://www.newgeneralservicelist.org

Chanasattru, S., & Tangkiengsirisin, S. (2016). Developing of a high frequency word list in Social Sciences. *Journal of English Studies*, *11*, 41-87.

Coxhead, A. (2000). A new academic word list. *TESOL*, *32*(2), 213-238. https://doi.org/10.2307/3587951

Hyland, K., & Tse, P. (2007). Is there an "academic vocabulary"? *TESOL*, *41*(2), 235-253. https://doi.org/10.1002/j.1545-7249.2007.tb00058.x

Nation, I. (2006). How large a vocabulary is needed for reading and listening? *Canadian Modern Language Review*, *63*(1), 59-82. https://doi.org/10.3138/cmlr.63.1.59

Nation, I. S. P., & Kyongho, H. (1995). Where would general service vocabulary stop and special purposes vocabulary begin? *System*, *23*(1), 35-74. https://doi.org/10.1016/0346-251X(94)00050-G

West, M. (Ed.). (1953). *A general service list of English words, with semantic frequencies and a supplementary word list*. Longman.

JYVÄSKYLÄN YLIOPISTO
UNIVERSITY OF JYVÄSKYLÄ

Improve the chatbot performance for the DB-CALL system using a hybrid method and a domain corpus

Jin-Xia Huang[1], Oh-Woog Kwon[2],
Kyung-Soon Lee[3], and Young-Kil Kim[4]

Abstract. This paper presents a chatbot for a Dialogue-Based Computer Assisted Language Learning (DB-CALL) system. The chatbot helps users learn language via free conversations. To improve the chatbot performance, this paper adopts a Neural Machine Translation (NMT) engine to combine with an existing search-based engine, and also extracts a small domain corpus for the topics of the DB-CALL system so that the chabot's responses could be more related to the conversation topics. As a result of user evaluations, the performance of the chatbot was improved by using hybrid methods, achieving performance comparable to existing systems. The automatically extracted domain corpus has little help or even declines the chatbot performance as an auxiliary module of the DB-CALL system.

Keywords: DB-CALL, chatbot.

1.   Introduction

We have developed a DB-CALL system, GenieTutor, to help English language learners in Korea (Kwon, Kim, & Lee, 2016). Similar to other DB-CALL systems, GenieTutor asks questions on different topics according to given scenarios, and the learners answer questions to practise what they learned. In order to allow the user to communicate more freely with the system, we developed a search-based chatbot to assist GenieTutor. Chatbot normally indicates an open-domain dialogue system for chitchat, which deals with the out of topic conversations in GenieTutor. However,

1. Electronics and Telecommunications Research Institute, Daejeon, Korea; hgh@etri.re.kr
2. Electronics and Telecommunications Research Institute, Daejeon, Korea; ohwoog@etri.re.kr
3. Chonbuk National University, Jeonju, Korea; selfsolee@chonbuk.ac.kr
4. Electronics and Telecommunications Research Institute, Daejeon, Korea; kimyk@etri.re.kr

How to cite this article: Huang, J.-X., Kwon, O.-W., Lee, K.-S., & Kim, Y.-K. (2018). Improve the chatbot performance for the DB-CALL system using a hybrid method and a domain corpus. In P. Taalas, J. Jalkanen, L. Bradley & S. Thouësny (Eds), *Future-proof CALL: language learning as exploration and encounters – short papers from EUROCALL 2018* (pp. 100-105). Research-publishing.net. https://doi.org/10.14705/rpnet.2018.26.820

the student satisfaction on the free-talking was lower than our expectations (Huang, Lee, Kwon, & Kim, 2017).

This paper describes how we improved the chatbot performance. We first implemented the hybrid chatbot by introducing the NMT engine, combining it with the search-based engine, and then extracted the small domain corpus for the topics of the DB-CALL system to improve the chatbot's performance as an auxiliary system.

2.   Hybrid chatbot based on search and NMT engines

Last year, we developed a chatbot using the search engine Indri (Strohman, Metzler, Turtle, & Croft, 2005). It retrieves similar examples from dialogue corpuses which contain 410 thousand dialogue examples. A dialogue example consists of two utterances: one query utterance and one system response, which is also called one turn in a dialogue. If there is no similar example, the chatbot outputs random utterances to the user (Huang et al., 2017).

This year, we introduced an NMT engine OpenNMT (Klein et al., 2017) to generate responses if the search engine fails to get a similar example. The corpus for the NMT engine contains 1.4 million dialogue examples, which are from MovieDic (Banchs, 2012), BNC corpus[5], and our own dialogue corpus which has been built in the last decades.

A user evaluation involving 20 English learners was performed. The learners are the users of the DB-CALL system. They are asked to talk freely with the chatbot for 60 turns, and we got 1,211 user utterances in total. After chatting with the chatbot, the users assign 0 to 2 points to each response from the chatbot: 2 means the response is acceptable and satisfactory, 1 means it is acceptable but too general, 0 means the response is wrong. We evaluated the system with a percentage of responses that gained 1 and 2 points, and called it the acceptance rate.

Table 1 shows that comparing with the search engine (the first column), the NMT engine (the second column) gains a higher acceptance rate (72.15%>60.55) but lower satisfaction (2 points: 18.32%<34.74%). It means these two engines complement each other, and so a hybrid approach can help improve performance.

---

5. http://www.natcorp.ox.ac.uk/

As a result, the acceptance rate of the hybrid engine is 68.29% (the third column), which is much higher than 52.78% of the previous year (Huang et al., 2017).

Table 1.   Evaluation on the hybrid chatbot compared with Siri and Cleverbot

	Our chatbot			Siri	Cleverbot
Score	Search engine	NMT engine	Hybrid engine		
2	34.74%	18.32%	23.78%	22.96%	39.31%
1	25.81%	53.84%	44.51%	37.57%	17.01%
0	39.45%	27.85%	31.71%	39.47%	43.68%
Acceptance rate (>1)	60.55%	72.15%	68.29%	60.53%	56.32%

For comparative evaluation, the user utterances are also input to Siri and Cleverbot to get their responses. Siri is a task-oriented dialogue system which allows chitchat. Cleverbot is a chatbot which has been in online service for about 20 years and contains 150 million dialogue examples[6]. Table 1 shows that the accept rate of our hybrid chatbot is higher than both Siri and Cleverbot, which is quite encouraging considering the time and cost invested.

3.   Extracting the domain corpus for topic conversations

According to our experiments in the last year, the satisfaction on the chatbot as an auxiliary module of the DB-CALL system was much lower than that of the independent chatbot. We assumed that the performance could be raised if the chatbot responses could be more related to the given topics in DB-CALL systems (Huang et al., 2017). In this paper, we extracted a small domain corpus for the topics 'ordering food' and 'city tour' of the DB-CALL system to see if it helps.

To extract the domain corpus from the chatbot corpus, we firstly used the domain and topic labels of the examples. There are 156 thousand examples of domain labels like *study*, *business*, and *travel-meal*; and 39 thousand of them have more detailed topic labels like *reservation*, *cancel*, and *ordering*. Secondly, we extracted domain examples according to the domain weights they gain: the weight is directly proportional to the number of domain keywords in the example, and is

---

6. https://en.wikipedia.org/wiki/Cleverbot

inversely proportional to the example length. As the result, about 4.5 thousand and 2.8 thousand examples are extracted for 'ordering food' and 'city tour' topics, respectively.

The search engine corpus is separated into two parts. The search engine searches the small domain corpus before it searches the general corpus. The similarity threshold for in-domain search is lower than the one for general domain search, and the in-domain examples gain higher priorities when the similarities are the same with general domain examples.

The same 20 English learners were asked to have conversations with the DB-CALL system and finish the tasks like 'ordering food' or 'buying city tour tickets'. Free talking was allowed in the conversations. As results, we got 115 out of topic utterances which were replied to by the chatbot. The responses with and without the domain corpus were both produced for comparison.

Table 2 shows that the search engine gives responses to 59.13% of the user utterances without the domain corpus, and it is improved to 63.48% with the extracted domain corpus. The acceptance rate of the search engine is also improved from 30.43% to 32.17% with the domain corpus.

Table 2.   Evaluation on the chatbot as an auxiliary module in the DB-CALL system

	Coverage (search engine)	Acceptance rate (search engine)	Acceptance rate (hybrid engine)
Without domain corpus	59.13%	30.43%	41.74%
With domain corpus	63.48%	32.17%	40.00%

However, the acceptance rate with the hybrid engine is rather declined from 41.74% to 40.00%. One reason is according to the hybrid approach – most of the similar examples tend to be matched whether they are in-domain examples or not. The coverage is more improved by less similar examples, which improves the acceptance rate of the search engine, but the opportunity decreases for the NMT engine to generate more acceptable responses. It causes the overall acceptance rate to drop in the hybrid engine.

The other reason is that a DB-CALL system is supposed to play different roles in different topics. For example, the system should act as a waiter in the 'ordering food' domain. Following, the chatbot response is considered wrong although it is an in-domain response but more with a role of accompanying guests. Therefore, role information should be considered in addition to domain information in extracting a domain corpus.

> System (DB-CALL): What would you like to order?

> User: I'll have the sandwich the man is eating.

> System (chatbot): I'll have that too.

4. Conclusion

This paper presented a chatbot which combined an NMT engine with a search engine, and the evaluation showed that the hybrid approach improved the chatbot performance. We also extracted the domain corpus for the out of topic conversations in the DB-CALL system. The evaluation showed that, unlike the search-based engine, the performance declined in the hybrid engine. A brief discussion was held, and it seems more in-depth research is required in the future to improve the performance of the chatbot as an auxiliary module of the DB-CALL system.

5. Acknowledgements

This work was supported by the ICT R&D program of MSIP/IITP [2015-0-00187, Core technology development of the spontaneous speech dialogue processing for the language learning], and Electronics and Telecommunications Research Institute (ETRI) grant funded by the Korean government [18ZS1140 Conversational AI Core Technology Research].

References

Banchs, R. E. (2012). MovieDic: a movie dialogue corpus for research and development. *Proceedings of ACL*, 203-207

Huang, J.-X., Lee, K.-S., Kwon, O.-W., & Kim, Y.-K. (2017). A chatbot for a dialogue-based second language learning system. In K. Borthwick, L. Bradley & S. Thouësny (Eds), *CALL in a climate of change: adapting to turbulent global conditions – short papers from EUROCALL 2017* (pp. 151-156). Research-publishing.net. https://doi.org/10.14705/rpnet.2017.eurocall2017.705

Klein, G., Kim, Y., Deng, Y., Senellart, J., & Rush, A. M. (2017). OpenNMT: open-source toolkit for neural machine translation, *CoRR*, abs/1701.02810. http://arxiv.org/abs/1701.02810

Kwon, O.-W., Kim, Y.-K., & Lee, Y. (2016). Task-oriented spoken dialog system for second-language learning. In S. Papadima-Sophocleous, L. Bradley & S. Thouësny (Eds), *CALL communities and culture – short papers from EUROCALL 2016* (pp. 237-242). Research-publishing.net. https://doi.org/10.14705/rpnet.2016.eurocall2016.568

Strohman, T., Metzler, D., Turtle, H., & Croft, W. B., (2005). Indri: a language model-based search engine for complex queries. *Proceedings of the International Conference on Intelligence Analysis*.

Effects of web-based HVPT on EFL learners' recognition and production of L2 sounds

Atsushi Iino[1] and Ron I. Thomson[2]

Abstract. In English as a Foreign Language (EFL) situations, it is important for educators to improve learners' sound recognition skill due to the variation of English found in the world. Furthermore, perceptual skill is a foundation leading to intelligibility in production. This study examined the effects of using High Variability Phonetic Training (HVPT) in computer assisted pronunciation training on the recognition and production of English phonemes, which are challenging for Japanese learners of English. Between pre-, mid-, and post-tests, the learners completed training sessions three times a week in two sound environments. The results demonstrated improvement in recognition skill with larger effects immediately after training. For production skill, however, the effects were not large, with a mixed outcome against the improvement in perception. Further research is suggested under a condition in which articulation practice immediately follows identification of individual training items.

Keywords: pronunciation, HVPT (high variability phonetic training), computer assisted pronunciation training.

1.   Introduction

HVPT is a training method for learners to perceive L2 sounds produced by multiple talkers in multiple phonetic contexts, which has been applied to language programs for a variety of L1 due to its effectiveness and generalizability (Thomson, 2018). HVPT has been proven effective in helping learners to distinguish L2 sounds that are confusing due to their similarity to L1 sounds (Munro & Derwing, 2006). This perceptual training approach has also led to improvement in learner production by

1. Hosei University, Tokyo, Japan; iino@hosei.ac.jp
2. Brock University, St. Catharines, Ontario, Canada; rthomson@brocku.ca

How to cite this article: Iino, A., & Thomson, R. I. (2018). Effects of web-based HVPT on EFL learners' recognition and production of L2 sounds. In P. Taalas, J. Jalkanen, L. Bradley & S. Thouësny (Eds), *Future-proof CALL: language learning as exploration and encounters – short papers from EUROCALL 2018* (pp. 106-111). Research-publishing.net. https://doi.org/10.14705/rpnet.2018.26.821

way of better intelligibility scores (Bradlow, Akahane-Yamada, Pisoni, & Tohkura, 1999).

While numerous studies have examined the efficacy of HVPT for training Japanese listeners to perceive English /l/ and /r/ contrasts (Bradlow et al., 1999; Logan, Lively, & Pisoni, 1991, among many others), we are only aware of such studies being conducted in highly controlled phonetic laboratories. Further, with few exceptions, most studies have not examined whether this training transfers to production (Thomson, 2018). Finally, previous /l/-/r/ studies for Japanese learners focus on a binary distinction, which fails to recognize that English /r/-/w/ are also known to be confusable (Guion, Flege, Akahane-Yamada, & Pruitt, 2000).

In this study, Thomson's (2017) *English Accent Coach* is used because it comprises thirty distinct talkers for each sound in each phonetic context and has been gamified to make it more interesting to learners. The research questions are:

- What are the effects of HVPT on **perception of English /l/-/r/-w/ contrasts** over time in different phonetic environments?

- What are the effects of HVPT on **production** of the same sounds over time in different phonetic environments?

- What is the relationship between perception and production?

2.   Method

2.1.   Participants

The learners who agreed to participate in this research were freshman non-English majors in a university in Tokyo. They were enrolled in compulsory English courses consisting of two classes: Class A and Class B. By eliminating those who scored 100% on the pre-test and those who could not take all the tests, 30 students were eligible for data analysis: Class A (n=13; four males and nine females) and Class B (n=17; 11 males and six females). According to their TOEIC[3] listening scores (Class A, M=363.5, SD=48.5; Class B, M=277.2, SD=56.6), their English proficiency

---

3. Test of English for International Communication®

could be categorized as B1 in CEFR[4] levels based on the score bands provided by the test provider, the Institute for International Business Communication.

2.2.   Treatment

A pre-test and post-test design was adopted for a ten-week treatment period during the fall semester in 2017. During training, the target sounds were presented either in Consonant + Vowel (CV) environments or Consonant + Vowel + Consonant (CVC) environments, while the test stimuli utilized 100 CV items consisting of the three target consonants randomly followed by a vowel, such as /li/, /ru/ or /wa/. The sound combinations were also randomized as were the thirty talkers' stimuli. Mid-tests were conducted after five weeks only for perception. In the first and the tenth week, the participants' production was recorded by having them produce target items in the carrier phrase: "Now I say _____ ." (Thomson, 2012).

Training comprised three 200-item perceptual training sessions per week. Over the ten weeks, Class A learners were trained to perceive the English consonants in syllable-onset position in CV frames for the first five weeks, up to mid-test, followed by CVC frames for another five weeks and post-test. Class B was trained in the opposite order. In each of the classes they practiced first round of training in a week and assigned to do the rest during the week. They submitted three PDF feedback forms through Sakai, a course management system, every week. The researcher asked them to complete only one training session on a given day (i.e. they could not do multiple sessions back-to-back).

3.   Results and discussion

3.1.   RQ1: effects of HVPT on recognition over time

The means of the tests for the two classes exhibited medium and large effect sizes between pre- and post-tests (CV : Cohen's d=.78; CVC d=.58, Table 1). In both of the phonetic environments, HVPT training showed immediate positive effects and persistence (CV: pre- to mid-test in Class A, d=.46 ; mid- to post-test in Class B, d=.74). These results seem to be in accordance with the results of Logan et al. (1991) in that the linguistic environments for HVPT training makes a difference. In

---

4. Common European Framework of Reference for languages

addition, the CVC environment showed higher average scores than CV. The CVC stimuli, even non-words, may have sounded more word-like than the CVs.

Table 1. Mean of correct percentages (SD) in perception tests of CV and CVC environments

| | CV tests % | | | CVC tests % | |
	Pre	Mid	Post	Mid	Post
Class A	73.2 (17.5)	83.2(12.6)	83.7 (10.9)	87.3 (7.3)	96.9 (2.5)
Class B	68.6 (10.7)	73.4 (11.4)	84.5 (9.7)	94.6 (3.2)	94.1 (2.9)
Total	70.6 (14.1)	77.8 (12.7)	84.1 (10.1)	91.3 (6.1)	95.3 (3.2)

Among the three target phonemes, identification of /r/ was the lowest (50%), followed by /l/ (64%) and /w/ (90%) in the CV pre-test. However, the largest progress was made immediately after the training (30% in both environments). In comparison, /l/ made a maximum progress of 19% in CV and 12% in CVC. The sound of /w/ had high scores in the beginning (90%) and reached the ceiling (99%) over a short period.

3.2. RQ2: effects of HVPT on production over time

Approximately 13% increase was observed in CV and CVC production tests between pre- and post-tests (d=.44). Particularly, Class B showed larger progress both in CV and CVC environments with more than a 20% increase (Table 2). This positive transfer follows the findings of Bradlow et al. (1999) that perception-only training improves production. HVPT may have exerted more influence on learners at an intermediate level of L2 English rather than those at a higher level.

It was also found that the order of sound difficulty was the same as for perception. In addition, larger progress was observed in /l/ and /r/ in CVC than in CV. These similarities to perception may represent the distance between their L1 and L2 (Munro & Derwing, 2006).

Table 2. Mean of correct percentages (SD) in production tests of CV and CVC environments

| | CV test % | | CVC test % | |
	T1	T3	T1	T3
Class A	59.8 (15.4)	62.4 (22.3)	65.4 (13.1)	65.0 (22.6)
Class B	53.5 (35.6)	74.3 (23.2)	54.5 (22.1)	78.1 (17.5)
Total	56.3 (33.7)	69.0 (24.1)	59.4 (20.0)	72.2 (22.6)

3.3. RQ3: relationship between perception and production

Pearson's correlation coefficients between the recognition test gain and the production test gain were $r=-.20$ in CV, and $r=-.43$ in CVC. The results indicate the progress in production is not necessarily made by the participants who made progress in recognition. This gap may come from the EFL situation where the learners had limited opportunities of oral communication outside the classroom, yet perceptual foundation prepares learners for production.

4. Conclusion

This study found positive effects of HVPT in computer assisted pronunciation training on perception to a large degree, but a small degree on production. Despite the gap, it is significant for EFL learners to develop a robust acoustic image to be drawn on for production. In this sense, HVPT realized by *English Accent Coach* has a strong potential to change the paradigm of pronunciation learning and teaching in EFL environments.

5. Acknowledgements

We appreciate Dr. Brian Wistner (Hosei University) and Ms. Yukiko Yabuta (Seisen Jogakuin College) for their help in the rating of speech production.

References

Bradlow, A. R., Akahane-Yamada, R., Pisoni, D. B., & Tohkura, Y. (1999). Training Japanese listeners to identify English /r/and /l/: long-term retention of learning in perception and production. *Perception & Psychophysics, 61*(5), 977-985. https://doi.org/10.3758/BF03206911

Guion, S. G., Flege, J. E., Akahane-Yamada, R., & Pruitt, J. C. (2000). An investigation of current models of second language speech perception: the case of Japanese adults' perception of English consonants. *Journal of the Acoustical Society of America, 107*(5), 2711-2724. https://doi.org/10.1121/1.428657

Logan, J. S., Lively, S. E., & Pisoni, D. B. (1991). Training Japanese listeners to identify English /r/ and / l /: a first report. *Journal of the Acoustical Society of America, 89*(2), 874 -866. https://www.ncbi.nlm.nih.gov/pmc/articles/PMC3518834/

Munro, M., & Derwing, T. (2006). The functional load principle in ESL pronunciation instruction: an exploratory study. *System, 34*, 520-531. https://doi.org/10.1016/j.system.2006.09.004

Thomson, R. I. (2012). Improving L2 listeners' perception of English vowels: a computer-mediated approach. *Language Learning, 62*(4), 1231-1258. https://doi.org/10.1111/j.1467-9922.2012.00724.x

Thomson, R. I. (2017). English accent coach [Computer program]. Version 2.3. www.englishaccentcoach.com

Thomson, R. I. (2018). High variability [pronunciation] training (HVPT) --- A proven technique about which every language teacher and learner ought to know. *Journal of Second Language Pronunciation, 4*(2), 207-230. https://doi.org/10.1075/jslp.17038.tho

Successful telecollaboration exchanges in primary and secondary education: what are the challenges?

Kristi Jauregi[1] and Sabela Melchor-Couto[2]

Abstract. The TeCoLa project promotes telecollaboration to foster meaningful foreign language learning particularly in secondary schools throughout Europe. In 2018, a number of pilot experiences are being conducted. This paper focusses on one of these pilot experiences, where learners from a Dutch secondary school and a Spanish primary school telecollaborated in Spanish and English by carrying out four tasks (creation of vlogs) asynchronously and sharing them in their group's Padlet wall. Different sources of data were gathered (recordings, surveys, and interviews) in order to be able to disentangle the factors that might play a role in successful telecollaboration exchanges and language learning experiences. Overall learners seemed to enjoy the experience, but the Spanish participants found the exchanges much more meaningful than the Dutch ones. This might well be related to the autonomy given to the students, who might have needed further guidance to benefit fully from the exchange.

Keywords: telecollaboration, motivation, anxiety, primary/secondary/pre-university education, vlogs.

1. Introduction

The Erasmus+ project TeCoLa (2016-2019) promotes telecollaboration (Guth & Helm, 2010) to foster meaningful foreign language learning, particularly in secondary schools throughout Europe, while training and coaching teachers. Special attention is given to task development that facilitates authentic communication in the foreign language, intercultural experience, awareness raising, and competence

1. Utrecht University, Utrecht, the Netherlands; k.jauregi@uu.nl
2. University of Roehampton, London, United Kingdom; s.melchor-couto@roehampton.ac.uk

How to cite this article: Jauregi, K., & Melchor-Couto, S. (2018). Successful telecollaboration exchanges in primary and secondary education: what are the challenges? In P. Taalas, J. Jalkanen, L. Bradley & S. Thouësny (Eds), *Future-proof CALL: language learning as exploration and encounters – short papers from EUROCALL 2018* (pp. 112-117). Research-publishing.net. https://doi.org/10.14705/rpnet.2018.26.822

development in the Target Language (TL), taking into account the specific school contexts and tool affordances.

Several pilot experiences are being carried out in different TLs, making use of different technologies to engage young learners in telecollaboration practices. The TeCoLa team is interested in knowing which factors contribute to successful telecollaboration exchanges implemented at pre-university educational level. In this paper we focus on a pilot experience carried out among learners from secondary and primary schools who created cultural vlogs to inform their peers abroad about cultural issues in their country/region. These vlogs were shared via the online bulletin board Padlet.

Since very little is known about the factors that play a role in telecollaborative exchanges among young teen learners, our study focussed on the following: (1) the effects such exchanges have on these learners' motivations, and (2) the experiences they engender in learners and teachers who participate in them.

2. Method

2.1. Context

TeCoLa views diversity as a socially meaningful concept in education that should strategically lead towards understanding and valuing diversity as a prerequisite for an inclusive society. The present pilot consisted of a telecollaboration project between two schools at different educational levels (primary and secondary) in two different countries (Spain and the Netherlands).

Two TeCoLa coaches assisted the school teachers and monitored the experience. Together they analysed and compared the specific school contexts and curriculums. Because of technological limitations on the part of one school, it was decided that the telecollaborative exchange should be asynchronous. Using either their own smartphones or ones provided by their teachers, groups of learners from the two schools then created vlogs in their TL, which they shared with their partner groups abroad through a Padlet wall.

The participants of this exchange, which was carried out between April and June 2018, were 17 learners of Spanish from a Dutch bilingual secondary school (ages 13-14) and 22 learners of English from a Spanish primary school (ages 11-12).

The Dutch and the Spanish learners had an A2 proficiency level in their TL. A total of five groups were created in each school and subsequently paired with parallel groups in the other country. Separate Padlet environments were created for those international groups engaged in telecollaboration activities. The participants uploaded their group vlogs to their own shared Padlet and viewed and listened to the ones their partners abroad had recorded (see Figure 1).

Figure 1. Screenshot Padlet wall

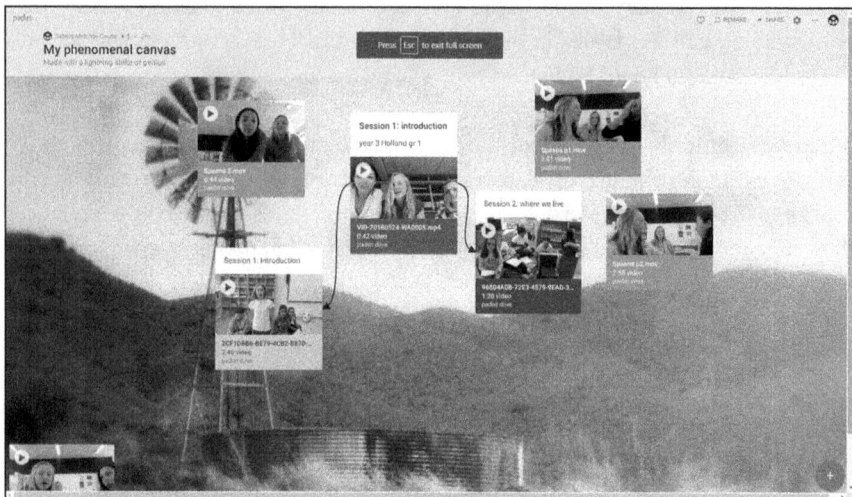

Four tasks (T1-T4) were created attending to the intercultural focus oriented educational programme that learners were following at both schools. In T1, learners introduced themselves and their school. In T2, they provided general information about their country/region. In T3, they informed their peers about what to see, where to go, and what to do when visiting their country/region. Finally, in T4, learners provided intercultural information about their region/country (how people live, what a regular day is like, how they celebrate their birthday, etc.).

Tasks 1, 2, and 4 were carried out in the TL (Spanish for the Dutch learners and English for the Spanish learners). The topic of T3 was more complex and it was decided that it would be carried out in Spanish for the Spanish learners and in English for the bilingual Dutch learners. This strategy enabled students to develop a range of language skills, namely oral expression and listening comprehension, both in their TL and mother tongue/proficient foreign language.

2.2. Instruments

The participants were required to complete a survey after every task consisting of ten five-point Likert scale items. All surveys were provided in the students' mother tongue and included closed items related to self-efficacy, anxiety, attitudes towards communication, technology, and the task (based on Jauregi, de Graaff, van den Bergh, & Kriz, 2012 and Jauregi & Melchor-Couto, 2017). The first survey included 15 additional open and closed items to gather background and learning preferences information. In the last one, students were also asked to rate the project.

The link to the Dutch surveys was distributed by email by the teacher after completion of each task. The surveys were printed out for the younger Spanish learners, who filled them in during their English classes. The results were then manually uploaded to the digital form. The Spanish learners' survey completion rate was considerably higher as compared to that of the Dutch learners, who responded to the survey only in certain sessions – the first survey was completed by all the participants (17), followed by ten, nine, and five respondents in subsequent sessions.

Four Spanish and three Dutch learners and their teachers were individually interviewed in their mother tongue at the end of the project in order to get a more in-depth view of how teachers and learners experienced the telecollaboration project.

3.   Results

3.1.   Motivational factors

The affective scores entered by Dutch and Spanish learners on the first and last sessions were compared (see Table 1). Learners' attitudes towards communicating in the TL were found to differ greatly among both groups, the Spanish learners valuing it with higher scores than the Dutch ones (Items 1 and 2). The comparison of T1 and T4 scores reveals a marked increase in the perceived usefulness of the exchange reported by the Spanish pupils, which is in contrast with the lower scores given in T4 by the Dutch learners. However, only five Dutch students responded to the survey circulated after T4 and therefore this value must be interpreted with caution. Self-efficacy values (Items 4 and 5) were similar for both groups, although a slight increase is observed amongst the Spanish learners on completion of the exchange regarding their perceived ability to express themselves in the TL (Item 5). Finally, both groups reported low levels of anxiety (Items 6 and 9), although the scores provided by the Dutch learners were slightly higher in both items.

Table 1.   Affective factors

Items		Dutch pupils				Spanish pupils			
		T1		T4		T1		T4	
		Mean	SD	Mean	SD	Mean	SD	Mean	SD
Attitudes	1. I learn a lot by using the TL to communicate with learners abroad	3.2	0.8	2.0	1.2	3.9	1.3	4.3	0.8
	2. I like to use the TL to communicate with learners abroad	3.4	1.0	3.4	1.1	4.0	1.1	4.0	1.0
Self-efficacy	4. I think that my TL competence is sufficient to communicate with learners abroad	3.1	1.1	3.2	0.8	3.0	0.8	3.2	1.2
	5. I express myself well in the TL	3.2	0.8	3.2	0.4	2.8	1.0	3.2	1.0
Anxiety	6. I'm afraid that my classmates will laugh at me when I use the TL	2.5	1.4	2.4	1.5	2.0	1.0	1.7	1.0
	9. I get nervous when I have to use technology to practise the TL	2.4	1.2	2.2	1.3	1.7	0.7	1.9	1.2

3.2.   Teachers' and learners' experience

Teachers' behaviour towards the project differed greatly. The Spanish teacher integrated the project in his classes and coached the learners during the whole process. For the Dutch teacher, the project was an add-on activity. The learners were supposed to work on the videos outside the classroom or during the last 10 minutes of the class. This teacher found the 'autonomy' with which learners had worked on the tasks as very relevant and meaningful. However, this 'autonomy' might have been experienced as 'lack of guidance' (learners received no feedback and not enough time to work on the tasks), as reported by the pupils interviewed. Most learners were positive about the project but especially the Spanish ones rated the telecollaborative experience with very high scores (Dutch learners' mean value: 3.8; Spanish: 4.6). The difference in age and educational school level did not seem to constitute a problem in the exchanges at all, as reported by six of the seven interviewed learners. In spite of the different approaches, both teachers were positive about the project as a whole and manifested their wish to repeat the experience next year by integrating it in the curriculum. Even the Dutch teacher seemed to realise that more guidance and monitoring was necessary to contribute to the meaningfulness of the activity for the learners.

4. Conclusions

This paper shows that telecollaboration projects across levels (secondary and primary education) can be valuable for learners, particularly if teachers are actively engaged in guiding them while respecting their autonomy. Further research will be required to analyse in more detail student attitudes regarding issues such as age difference, amongst others.

5. Acknowledgements

We would like to thank the teachers and students who participated in this exchange for their time and dedication in making this exchange a reality.

References

Guth, S., & Helm, F. (Eds). (2010). *Telecollaboration 2.0. Language, literacies and intercultural learning in the 21st century.* Peterlang Publishers. https://doi.org/10.3726/978-3-0351-0013-6

Jauregi, K., & Melchor-Couto, S. (2017). Motivational factors in telecollaborative exchanges among teenagers. In K. Borthwick, L. Bradley & S. Thouësny (Eds), *CALL in a climate of change: adapting to turbulent global conditions – short papers from EUROCALL 2017* (pp. 157-162). Research-publishing.net. https://doi.org/10.14705/rpnet.2017.eurocall2017.706

Jauregi, K., de Graaff, R., van den Bergh, H. & Kriz, M. (2012). Native non-native speaker interactions through video-web communication, a clue for enhancing motivation. *Computer Assisted Language Learning Journal*, 25(1), 1-19.

Using grammar checkers in the ESL classroom: the adequacy of automatic corrective feedback

Paul John[1] and Nina Woll[2]

Abstract. Our study assessed the performance of two Grammar Checkers (GCs), Grammarly and Virtual Writing Tutor, and the grammar checking function in Microsoft Word on a broad range of grammatical errors. The errors occurred in both authentic English as a Second Language (ESL) compositions and simple sentences we generated ourselves. We verified the performance in terms of (1) coverage (rates of error detection), (2) accuracy of proposed replacement forms, and (3) 'false alarms' (forms mistakenly flagged as incorrect). To the extent GCs provide accurate and comprehensive corrective feedback, they could relieve teachers of the time-consuming task of providing written feedback themselves. While inaccurate replacement forms and false alarms are relatively rare, we found GCs to have poor overall coverage (total error detection rates under 50%). Grammarly and Virtual Writing Tutor, however, outperform Microsoft Word. Coverage is also higher both for certain categories of error and for the sentences rather than the authentic compositions. Finally, although GCs do not provide comprehensive feedback, we suggest designing special activities that target select error types.

Keywords: grammar checkers, corrective feedback, focus-on-form, second language learning.

1. Introduction

Our study investigates the adequacy of automatic corrective feedback from GCs to determine their possible use in the ESL classroom. Written corrective feedback permits teachers to incorporate a focus on form into the communicative classroom, thereby promoting accuracy and preventing fossilization (Bitchener, 2008; Ferris,

1. Université du Québec à Trois-Rivières, Trois-Rivières, Canada; paul.john@uqtr.ca
2. Université du Québec à Trois-Rivières, Trois-Rivières, Canada; nina.woll@uqtr.ca

How to cite this article: John, P., & Woll, N. (2018). Using grammar checkers in the ESL classroom: the adequacy of automatic corrective feedback. In P. Taalas, J. Jalkanen, L. Bradley & S. Thouësny (Eds), *Future-proof CALL: language learning as exploration and encounters – short papers from EUROCALL 2018* (pp. 118-123). Research-publishing.net. https://doi.org/10.14705/rpnet.2018.26.823

Liu, Sinha, & Senna, 2013). Still, providing feedback is time-consuming, so the potential for GCs to relieve teachers' workloads is appealing. In essence, GCs look like an invaluable tool for the ESL context.

Important questions remain, however, concerning the quality of automatic corrective feedback. Previous studies have often adopted a narrow focus, evaluating GCs only on articles/determiners, prepositions, and collocations (De Felice & Pulman, 2008; Han, Chodorow, & Leacock, 2006). Research on the grammar checking function in automated writing evaluation systems has been more comprehensive (Dikli & Bleyle, 2014, on Criterion), but these systems are prohibitively expensive. In our view, an investigation of GCs available for little or no cost and on a wide range of grammatical issues is overdue. The current study thus addresses the following research questions:

- To what extent is automatic corrective feedback comprehensive and accurate?

- Do GCs perform better on certain grammar points than others?

2. Method

2.1. Data collection

We evaluated two leading online GCs (Grammarly and Virtual Writing Tutor) and the grammar checking function in Microsoft Word on errors from two sources: (1) authentic compositions (50 handwritten essays generated under exam conditions by 28 francophone TESL[3] students at a university in Quebec; 10M /18F; age 21-36); and (2) a set of 129 simple sentences containing errors we generated based on our knowledge of typical francophone errors.

Representative errors were selected from the compositions, and these errors and the simple sentences were run through the three GCs to verify coverage (error detection rates) and accuracy of proposed replacement forms. The 50 compositions and 129 sentences were then run through the GCs to establish rates of 'false alarms' (forms mistakenly flagged as incorrect).

---

3. Teaching English as a second language.

2.2.   Results

Table 1 shows how the GCs performed on the two sets of errors (compositions vs. simple sentences) in the different grammatical categories listed on the left. The results are presented as fractions, such that 2/4, for example, indicates that the GC identified two out of four errors (Gram=Grammarly; VWT=Virtual Writing Tutor). Though many of the error categories are self-evident, others may be elusive. By 'tense shift', we mean shifts primarily between past and present in contexts where either is acceptable. The category 'plural nouns' refers to failure to pluralize a noun or pluralization of a non-count noun. Possessive errors involve inappropriate use of either apostrophe + 's' or the periphrastic possessive with 'of'. Pronoun errors concern incorrect reference. The category 'relative clauses' refers to incorrect comma usage with restrictive and non-restrictive relative clauses.

Table 1.   Rates of error detection: compositions vs. simple sentences

	Grammatical categories	Compositions			Sentences		
		Word	Gram	VWT	Word	Gram	VWT
Verbs	Tense-aspect	2/4	1/4	2/4	1/9	4/9	0/9
	Verb form	1/3	3/3	2/3	2/13	8/13	8/13
	Subj-V agreement	0/3	3/3	0/3	0/6	6/6	6/6
	Tense shift	0/6	0/6	0/6	0/2	0/2	0/2
	Total	**3/16**	**7/16**	**4/16**	**3/30**	**18/30**	**14/30**
Nouns	Plural	1/3	3/3	3/3	4/20	11/20	11/20
	Possessive	0/5	3/5	2/5	0/4	0/4	0/4
	Pronoun	0/2	0/2	0/2	0/5	2/5	0/5
	Total	**1/10**	**6/10**	**5/10**	**4/29**	**13/29**	**11/29**
Preps	Wrong prep	0/3	1/3	1/3	0/10	8/10	8/10
	Missing prep	0/2	0/2	0/2	0/4	2/4	2/4
	Unnecessary prep	0/2	0/2	0/2	0/7	3/7	2/7
	Total	**0/7**	**1/7**	**1/7**	**0/21**	**13/21**	**12/21**
Words	Word order	0/3	0/3	0/3	3/18	7/18	3/18
	Word form	0/3	0/3	0/3	6/10	7/10	7/10
	Total	**0/6**	**0/6**	**0/6**	**9/28**	**14/28**	**10/28**
Misc.	Determiner	0/4	0/4	0/4	1/13	4/13	4/13
	Relative clause	0/3	0/3	0/3	2/8	1/8	0/8
	Total	**0/7**	**0/7**	**0/7**	**3/21**	**5/21**	**4/21**
	Grand totals	**4/46 (8.7%)**	**14/46 (30.4%)**	**10/46 (21.7%)**	**19 (14.7%)**	**63 (48.8%)**	**51 (39.5%)**

The grand totals in Table 1 indicate poor overall error detection (all below 50%). In addition, Microsoft Word achieves considerably lower coverage than the two online GCs, with Grammarly generally outperforming Virtual Writing Tutor: hence, Grammarly >> Virtual Writing Tutor >> Microsoft Word. Error detection is greater on simple sentences than on compositions. In addition, there are some grammatical categories in which Grammarly, and to a degree Virtual Writing Tutor, perform better: particularly verb forms, subject-verb agreement and plural nouns. They are also strong in the 'wrong preposition' and 'word form' categories, but only with simple sentences. Finally, we can report that incorrect replacement forms are rare: we found one inaccurate replacement for Grammarly, three for Virtual Writing Tutor and four for Microsoft Word.

While none of the GCs raised false alarms in the simple sentences, Grammarly shows a clear edge over both Virtual Writing Tutor and Microsoft Word for false alarms on the compositions (see Table 2). The absence of false alarms on the simple sentences is partly due to lack of opportunity (1,055 words in the sentences vs. 23,108 words in the compositions). Microsoft Word's relatively low number of false alarms is probably a function of its low rate of error detection.

Table 2.   Rates of false alarms

	Microsoft Word	Grammarly	Virtual Writing Tutor
Compositions	13	4	30
Simple sentences	0	0	0

3.   Discussion

We evaluated the performance of two online GCs, Grammarly and Virtual Writing Tutor, and the grammar checking function in Microsoft Word on a wide range of grammatical errors. The fact that Grammarly and Virtual Writing Tutor clearly outperform Microsoft Word in error detection suggests that learners should be wary of relying on this omnipresent word processor to check the accuracy of their writing. They might instead consider turning to an online GC for a fuller picture.

Nonetheless, Grammarly and Virtual Writing Tutor also show limited coverage – which parallels the findings in De Felice and Pulman (2008) and Han et al. (2006). An important implication is that ESL teachers cannot truly count on the technology to provide comprehensive written corrective feedback on student compositions. The fact that error detection rates were higher for the simple sentences than for the authentic compositions simply underscores this conclusion.

The low rates of inaccurate replacement forms and false alarms are encouraging for the ESL context. Inaccurate feedback could lead ESL learners seriously astray, particularly since they lack native speaker intuitions to override misleading feedback. It is encouraging that GCs perform strongly in some categories of error (verb forms, subject-verb agreement, plural nouns, wrong prepositions, and word forms). We suggest that teachers use GCs to target specific error types in student compositions and encourage students to scrutinize their own writing for errors that the GC might have overlooked. Furthermore, teachers can develop special activities containing errors that the GCs are capable of identifying. Students can first try to identify the errors themselves and then run the text through the GC to check their answers.

4.   Conclusions

While our findings show that GCs have poor overall coverage, Grammarly and Virtual Writing Tutor have higher coverage than Microsoft Word. GCs are also better at detecting errors in some categories than others and in specially composed simple sentences than in authentic compositions. Finally, both inaccurate replacement forms and false alarms are infrequent. Thus, though GCs cannot provide comprehensive corrective feedback on student compositions, they can be employed to target select error types in student writing and in specially developed activities alike. In this manner, GCs can be used effectively to incorporate a focus on form into the communicative ESL classroom.

5.   Acknowledgements

We appreciate the invaluable input of our colleagues, Mariane Gazaille and Walcir Cardoso, and research assistant, Michel Monier.

References

Bitchener, J. (2008). Evidence in support of written corrective feedback. *Journal of Second Language Writing*, *17*, 102-118. https://doi.org/10.1016/j.jslw.2007.11.004

De Felice, R., & Pulman, S. G. (2008). A classifier-based approach to preposition and determiner error correction in L2 English. In *Proceedings of the 22nd International Conference on Computational Linguistics* (COLING 2008), 169-176. https://doi.org/10.3115/1599081.1599103

Dikli, S., & Bleyle, S. (2014). Automated essay scoring feedback for second language writers: how does it compare to instructor feedback? *Assessing Writing, 22*, 1-17. https://doi.org/10.1016/j.asw.2014.03.006

Ferris, D., Liu, H., Sinha, A., & Senna, M. (2013). Written corrective feedback for individual L2 writers. *Journal of Second Language Writing, 22*, 307-329. https://doi.org/10.1016/j.jslw.2012.09.009

Han, N., Chodorow, M., & Leacock, C. (2006). Detecting errors in English articles usage by non-native speakers. *Natural Language Engineering, 12*(2), 115-129. https://doi.org/10.1017/S1351324906004190

JYVÄSKYLÄN YLIOPISTO
UNIVERSITY OF JYVÄSKYLÄ

Students' attitudes toward high-immersion virtual reality assisted language learning

Regina Kaplan-Rakowski[1] and Tomasz Wojdynski[2]

Abstract. This pilot study delivers a preliminary report on students' attitudes toward Virtual Reality Assisted Language Learning (VRALL). Learners ($N=22$) participated in a VRALL lesson and then completed a post-experience survey. Virtual Reality (VR) technology allows for learning experiences that increasingly remove geographic limitations to foreign language learners. Thanks to multisensory features of VR, including 360-degree, three-dimensional visualizations, students' experiences are highly immersive. Descriptive statistics provide preliminary evidence that VR technology is engaging and immersive for learners. Moreover, VR could play a role in Computer Assisted Language Learning (CALL), especially when pitfalls such as cybersickness are overcome.

Keywords: virtual reality, virtual reality assisted language learning, VRALL, students' attitudes, immersive learning environments.

1. Introduction

A common assumption is that the most effective way to learn a foreign language is through language immersion in the country where the language is spoken. High-immersion VR technology provides fairly realistic imitations of such settings. Learners can be welcomed in sensory-rich environments, allowing them to experience telepresence (i.e. the feeling of 'being there' in the target language country).

With the most recent release of advanced VR technology, interest in learning in VR environments is experiencing a rebirth. Unlike limited VR prototypes, the new

---

1. Valdosta State University, Valdosta, Georgia, United States; rkaplan@siu.edu
2. The School of Banking and Management, Cracow, Poland; tomwoj@wszib.edu.pl

How to cite this article: Kaplan-Rakowski, R., & Wojdynski, T. (2018). Students' attitudes toward high-immersion virtual reality assisted language learning. In P. Taalas, J. Jalkanen, L. Bradley & S. Thouësny (Eds), *Future-proof CALL: language learning as exploration and encounters – short papers from EUROCALL 2018* (pp. 124-129). Research-publishing.net. https://doi.org/10.14705/rpnet.2018.26.824

wave of VR headsets (especially Oculus and HTC Vive) is creating settings for immersive learning at an affordable cost. Researchers from multiple disciplines have explored learning in VR (Jensen & Konradsen, 2018). However, investigations in CALL are still limited.

VR-related areas that did gain interest from the CALL community were language learning with stereoscopic three-dimensional visualizations (Kaplan-Rakowski, 2016), in gaming (e.g. Cornillie, Thorne, & Desmet, 2012), and in virtual worlds (Kaplan-Rakowski, 2011; Sadler, 2017). While each of these areas was valuable to explore, they all involved low-immersion VR environments. Low-immersion VR can be experienced on a regular desktop Personal Computer (PC) with a two-dimensional monitor. High-immersion VR requires head-mounted displays, with sophisticated sensors that track users' head movements, allowing 360-degree visualizations which foster a sense of presence.

Given that positive attitudes toward a given technology are often associated with increased motivation for learning, how language learners perceive high-immersion VR is important to explore. Dolgunsöz, Yildirim, and Yildirim (2018) show that learners are motivated by VRALL. The intention of our project was to build on their study, testing a different sample and allowing for a more self-regulated experience using higher-immersion technology. The main goal of the study was to answer the research question: what are students' attitudes toward high-immersion VRALL?

2. Method

Our pilot study collected preliminary data regarding learners' (N=22) attitudes toward VRALL. Each participant filled out a demographic questionnaire and then completed a self-selected and self-conducted VRALL lesson. The final step was answering a series of survey questions. Microsoft Excel was employed to analyze data using descriptive statistics.

2.1. Participants

The urban Polish university students who volunteered to take part in the study were all adult males (median age=25). They had a minimum basic knowledge of English and were all information technology majors. They reported spending an average of eight hours per day using electronics. No students owned a VR device and only 9% had experience with using one. This raises the possibility of a novelty effect, which could be the focus of a follow-up study.

2.2. Instruments and procedure

Two instruments were used in the study: a demographics questionnaire and a survey completed after the VRALL lesson, which was conducted via the Mondly app (https://app.mondly.com/). The post-experience survey elicited responses regarding students' views on learning languages with VR. The participants were prompted to share their positive and negative views on VRALL. The format contained 'Yes/No', Likert-scale (range 1-5), and open-ended questions.

The experiment took place in a computer laboratory, and subjects were intentionally not told what to do in the lesson. In line with the Mondly app, learners used their own intuition, with little guidance given, to proceed with the lesson. The researcher assisted only in showing the participants how to wear the Oculus Go headset and how to calibrate and maneuver the VR mouse.

2.3. Lesson content

Mondly is a paid app featuring lessons with various themes designed for second language (L2) learning (e.g. "Greetings", "In a Restaurant", "Taxi Ride") in 28 different languages. Participants could select any theme but were restricted to choosing a new language for them.

Figure 1.   A screenshot of a Mondly lesson[3]: the learner, sitting in the backseat of the taxi, holds a conversation in a second language by selecting appropriate responses to the driver

3. Reproduced with kind permissions from © Mondly.

For example, a Mondly lesson creates a scenario of a student sitting in a virtual taxi and conversing with the driver in L2 (see Figure 1). The learner sees the surroundings in 360 degrees while the taxi is moving, which deepens the sense of presence. The taxi driver greets the student in L2, and the student must select the correct response from among a choice of phrases to proceed in the lesson. Voice recognition technology is used to detect the adequacy of the learner's response. The conversation lasts until the student fails to respond appropriately to the driver.

3.   Findings and discussion

Descriptive statistics provided preliminary results regarding the students' attitudes about the impact of VRALL. The majority (82%) of participants said that they wanted to study languages in VR, 9% reported that they did not, and the remaining 9% had no opinion. On a Likert scale (1=not engaging, 5=very engaging), the students reported their VR experience as engaging (median=4; mean=3.6). Figure 2 is a histogram of the distribution of the learners' engagement. The results show that the learners' attitudes toward VRALL are positive and their engagement is high. These findings are in line with the study by Dolgunsöz et al. (2018).

Figure 2.   Learners' engagement level in a VRALL lesson. The figure depicts study participants' response to the question: 'how engaging do you find the VRALL lesson?'

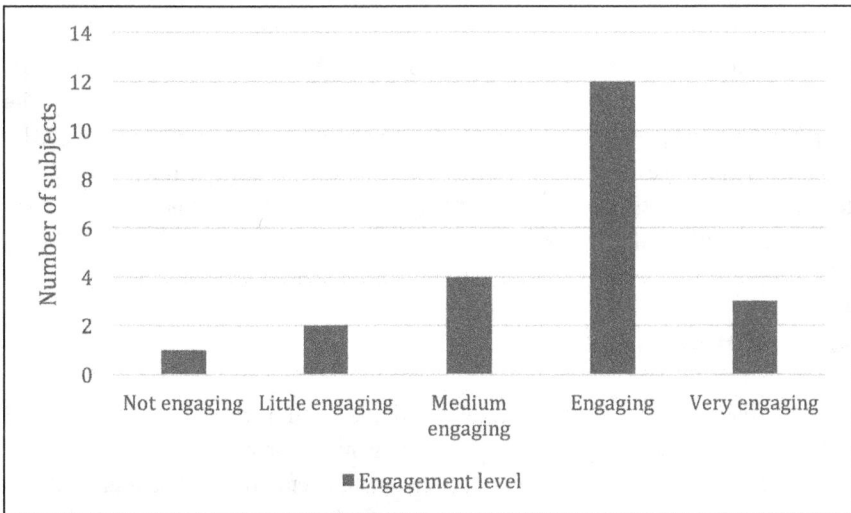

The majority of participants (91%) responded in the affirmative when asked: "Do you see any positive sides of learning languages in virtual reality?". Among their clarifying comments were: "learning in VR we can immerse ourselves better in what we are doing", "students can focus 100%", "there is a bigger use of imagination and emotional memory", and "very engaging activity; it minimizes the possibility of getting distracted". The remaining 9% of participants reported not seeing any positive sides.

Learners' insightful comments on the positive sides of VRALL reflect the reoccurring theme of increased immersion and extra focus. Wearing VR headsets could minimize distractions from external stimuli, which typically occurs while using a regular PC. Consequently, VR learning is more focused, another potential advantage that should be explored in more depth in future studies.

The survey also asked: "Do you see any negative sides of learning languages in virtual reality?". A substantial 41% acknowledged doing so. Some of these participants' comments were: "after a while you can get a headache", "VR is too absorbing", and "poor quality of the image, which causes eye tiredness and, consequently, discomfort".

Cybersickness, such as eye fatigue and dizziness, is often cited in the use of VR. However, the level of discomfort largely depends on the choice of VR experiences. More cybersickness is reported when the content is dynamic (e.g. cycling) than static (e.g. sitting). With time, the advancement of technology should correct this issue. Improvements have already been reported.

The final question was: "Some people claim that VR is the future of education. Do you agree with this statement? Justify your response with a comment". The majority (59%) of participants agreed; 14% disagreed. No opinion was expressed by 27%. Some justifications were: "new technology and its advancement encourages learning so it is necessary to take advantage of it" and "I think that no technology will be a substitute of an expert teacher".

4. Conclusions

Overall, the learners showed positive attitudes and high engagement toward VRALL. VR holds the promise of providing highly engaging experiences that allow learners to immerse themselves in foreign cultures and languages. The combination of high immersion with suppressed distraction open new possibilities for how VRALL could prove useful in language acquisition activities such as self-regulatory extramural language learning.

References

Cornillie, F., Thorne, S. L., & Desmet, P. (2012). Digital games for language learning: challenges and opportunities. *ReCALL, 24*(3), 243-256. https://doi.org/10.1017/S0958344012000134

Dolgunsöz, E., Yildirim, G., & Yildirim, S. (2018). The effect of virtual reality on EFL writing performance. *Journal of Language and Linguistic Studies, 14*(1), 278-292.

Jensen, L., & Konradsen, F. (2018). A review of the use of virtual reality head-mounted displays in education and training. *Education and Information Technologies, 23*(4), 1515-1529. https://doi.org/10.1007/s10639-017-9676-0

Kaplan-Rakowski, R. (2011). Teaching foreign languages in a virtual world: lesson plans. In G. Vincenti & J. Braman (Eds), *Multi-user virtual environments for the classroom: practical approaches to teaching in virtual worlds* (pp. 438-453). IGI Global. https://doi.org/10.4018/978-1-60960-545-2.ch026

Kaplan-Rakowski, R. (2016). *The effect of stereoscopic three-dimensional images on recall of second language vocabulary.* Unpublished doctoral dissertation. Southern Illinois University, Carbondale, IL.

Sadler, R. W. (2017). The continuing evolution of virtual worlds for language learning. In C. A. Chapelle & S. Sauro (Eds), *The handbook of technology and second language teaching and learning* (pp. 184-201). Wiley-Blackwell. https://doi.org/10.1002/9781118914069.ch13

Advantages and disadvantages of digital storytelling assignments in EFL education in terms of learning motivation

Naoko Kasami[1]

Abstract. Digital storytelling is an educational practice which has attracted the attention of many experts. However, there has been little research on the disadvantages of digital storytelling assignments from the students' perspectives in English as a Foreign Language (EFL) education. Addressing difficulties or problems which are likely to occur in integrating digital storytelling in language learning would provide better insights for education in the future. Thus, this study aims to examine not only the advantages but also the disadvantages of introducing digital storytelling assignments in EFL education by focusing on learners' motivation. To achieve the aim of this study, data was obtained from questionnaire surveys in six courses entitled 'Information English' for students in Japan. Though most students were motivated for learning with digital storytelling assignments, there were also some students who were less motivated. The findings from students' comments revealed that it would be effective to provide specific instruction based on (1) proper guidance of effective narration, (2) the condition of having sufficient time to accomplish the assignment, (3) technical support, and (4) information ethics.

Keywords: digital storytelling, advantage, disadvantage, motivation.

1. Introduction

The main aim of this study is to reveal the advantages and disadvantages faced by Japanese university students in conducting digital storytelling assignments in

1. J. F. Oberlin University, Tokyo, Japan; naoko.kasami@gmail.com

How to cite this article: Kasami, N. (2018). Advantages and disadvantages of digital storytelling assignments in EFL education in terms of learning motivation. In P. Taalas, J. Jalkanen, L. Bradley & S. Thouësny (Eds), *Future-proof CALL: language learning as exploration and encounters – short papers from EUROCALL 2018* (pp. 130-136). Research-publishing.net. https://doi.org/10.14705/rpnet.2018.26.825

EFL classrooms. Information and Communication Technologies (ICT) constitute an integral part of the teaching and learning environment and become more important in language education (Penner & Grodek, 2014). Digital storytelling is an educational practice which has received attention in the literature. For instance, Robin (2006) states that "Digital Storytelling has become a powerful instructional tool for both students and educators" (p. 709) and the StoryCenter website[2] indicates that "digital storytelling can be an incredibly powerful way to foster creativity, engage [the] community, transform perspectives, and encourage reflect[ion] upon learning and life processes" (para 1). Language learning can also be promoted with digital storytelling, as Ohler (2013) pointed out that digital storytelling has great potential to help students learn language because of the interplay between writing, speaking, and listening.

Despite the considerable amount of research that has been conducted on digital storytelling, the focus has often been on their advantages. It was stated that while some disadvantages were noted, overall, the advantages of digital storytelling outweighed the disadvantages (De Jager et al., 2017). However, it is this researcher's belief that focusing on the disadvantages or difficulties of digital storytelling would be effective for overcoming the shortcomings and utilizing the advantages. Hence, the following specific research questions were addressed:

- What are the advantages of digital storytelling assignments in EFL courses in terms of student motivation for learning?

- What are the disadvantages of digital storytelling assignments in EFL courses in terms of student motivation for learning?

- What factors are necessary to overcome difficulties?

2. Background and method

2.1. Background

The author has focused on the effectiveness and advantages of digital storytelling in a previous study (Kasami, 2017), where results show that most students

---

2. https://www.storycenter.org/public-workshops/edu-intro-to-ds

(77.77%) were motivated for learning with digital storytelling assignments more than with the traditional storytelling assignments. However, there were still some students (7.94%) who were less motivated (Kasami, 2017). Consequently, it was necessary to find out and overcome these difficulties in order to improve teaching and learning.

2.2.   Method

The courses and data collection in this paper were conducted as outlined in this researcher's previous study (Kasami, 2017), with new data from the courses held in the following academic terms. This study focuses on the practices of six courses entitled 'Information English' for students at the Faculty of Information and Communications in Japan. The courses, with 153 students in total, were held during the fall term of 2015 and spring term of 2016. This study comprised 96 students who had answered all (pre, midterm, and post) questionnaires and had taken three tests under the same conditions as those in the previous research. The open-ended questions were presented to ask 'good' and 'bad' points about the digital storytelling assignment in the post questionnaire. Sixty-six out of 96 students commented. Out of these responses, two comments were not related to motivation and 64 comments were chosen which related to motivation for learning. From the comments, advantages and disadvantages were analyzed and factors for overcoming difficulties were explored.

3.   Results and discussion

3.1.   Advantages

Students were asked "Please write down good points of the digital storytelling assignment if there are any". Positive comments were given by 48 students. From all of the comments, the author and another collaborator collected keywords. Keywords which had a frequency of more than two are shown in Figure 1. Some students' comments had multiple keywords. From the many students who responded very positively towards the digital storytelling, the principal keywords included 'English', 'Movie / PC', 'Create' and 'Interesting / Fun'.

When asked about the advantages of introducing digital storytelling in EFL courses, most students referred to their attractive features. The following responses are some examples of positive comments (Figure 2).

Figure 1. Keywords of advantages

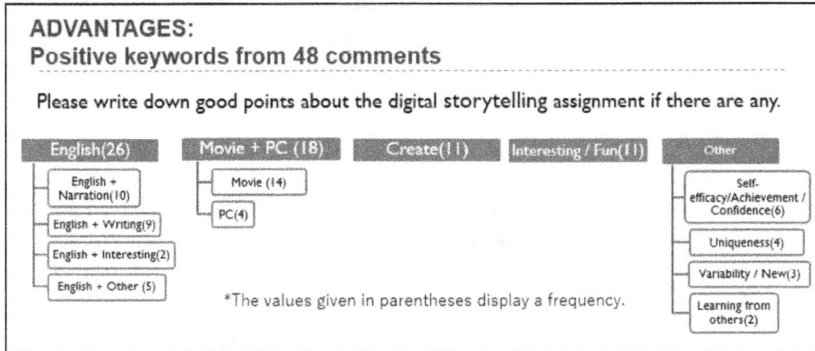

ADVANTAGES:
Positive keywords from 48 comments

Please write down good points about the digital storytelling assignment if there are any.

English(26)

English + Narration(10)

English + Writing(9)

English + Interesting(2)

English + Other (5)

Movie + PC (18)

Movie (14)

PC(4)

Create(11)

Interesting / Fun(11)

Other

Self-efficacy/Achievement / Confidence(6)

Uniqueness(4)

Variability / New(3)

Learning from others(2)

*The values given in parentheses display a frequency.

Figure 2. Examples of positive comments

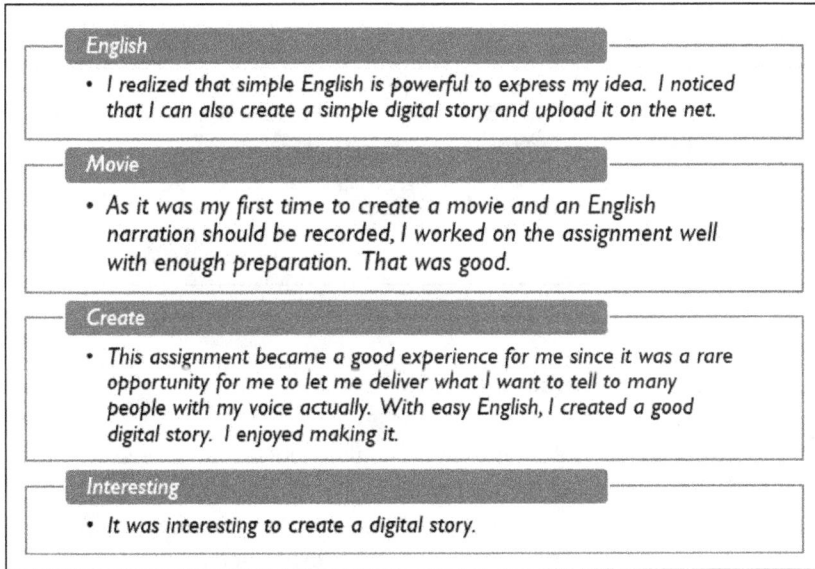

English

• I realized that simple English is powerful to express my idea. I noticed that I can also create a simple digital story and upload it on the net.

Movie

• As it was my first time to create a movie and an English narration should be recorded, I worked on the assignment well with enough preparation. That was good.

Create

• This assignment became a good experience for me since it was a rare opportunity for me to let me deliver what I want to tell to many people with my voice actually. With easy English, I created a good digital story. I enjoyed making it.

Interesting

• It was interesting to create a digital story.

3.2. Disadvantages

Students were asked "Please write down the bad points of the digital storytelling assignment which should be improved if there are any". Negative comments were given by 16 students. All of the comments were classified into the four categories; (1) Narration Difficulties (n=6), (2) Shortage of Time (n=5), (3) PC Problems (n=3), and (4) Copyright (n=2).

When asked about the disadvantages of introducing digital storytelling in EFL courses, 16 negative comments were received from the students, including some from those who were satisfied with the digital storytelling assignment. The following responses are some examples of negative comments (Figure 3).

Figure 3.   Examples of negative comments

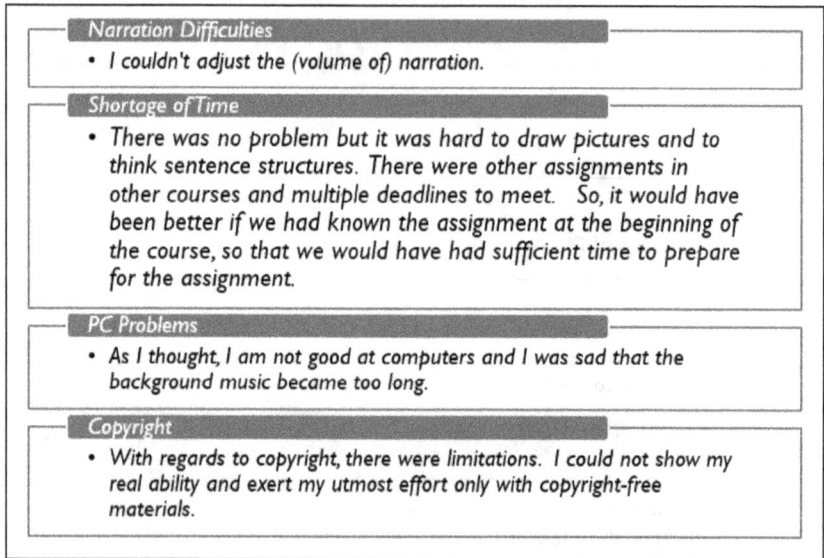

> **Narration Difficulties**
> * I couldn't adjust the (volume of) narration.
>
> **Shortage of Time**
> * There was no problem but it was hard to draw pictures and to think sentence structures. There were other assignments in other courses and multiple deadlines to meet. So, it would have been better if we had known the assignment at the beginning of the course, so that we would have had sufficient time to prepare for the assignment.
>
> **PC Problems**
> * As I thought, I am not good at computers and I was sad that the background music became too long.
>
> **Copyright**
> * With regards to copyright, there were limitations. I could not show my real ability and exert my utmost effort only with copyright-free materials.

3.3.   Factors for overcoming difficulties

The following are some potential solutions to the problems encountered.

First, the most frequently occurring problems related to recording narration with a microphone. These problems were solved by allowing students to use additional headphones or setting the device options. Another problem was the volume of narration being set too low and some narrations were not clearly audible. To solve this problem, it was necessary to recommend that students rehearsed and checked the volume of their recorded narration at the beginning of each step. It was also effective for considering the balance of narration and selecting appropriate background music.

Second, five students indicated that there was not sufficient time to create their digital stories. It was inferred that the students who experienced difficulties with writing scenarios in English and who spent longer periods writing fell behind schedule. Consequently, the time period for creating the digital story became limited. In order to improve this problem, it was necessary to emphasize time management skills to meet their deadlines. It was also recommended that the schedule should be less tight. If there was sufficient time, effective peer-feedback could be provided as well as teacher support.

Third, three students commented that they were demotivated because of their lower computer literacy skills and experienced difficulty with using computers. The most technically challenging parts should be explained adequately, especially adding music to the movie file, adjusting the timing of the music, and rerecording narrations.

Fourth, the copyright issues are very important in this kind of assignment. Since this format is digital, it is very important to consider how to deal with digital information, so basic information ethics become very significant. Many students would like to include their favourite music, anime, and characters, however, in many cases, this is not allowed as it infringes various copyrights and portrait rights. Therefore, it was necessary for students to use copyright free pictures and music. These issues should be explained in the early stages of the project repeatedly.

4.   Conclusions

The purpose of this study was to clarify the advantages and disadvantages faced by digital storytelling assignments in EFL. The results show that most students expressed positive views on digital storytelling assignments and considered movies and ICT both interesting and useful for English learning.

Regarding disadvantages, this research identified four problems. The findings suggested that teachers should provide specific instruction based on (1) proper guidance of effective narration, (2) the condition of having sufficient time to accomplish the assignment along with suitable advice, (3) technical support with troubleshooting tips, and (4) copyright and portrait rights which are related to information ethics.

More comprehensive views and in-depth analyses should be conducted in future research. Future studies should discuss how these improvements in instruction affect student learning motivation for better education.

5.   Acknowledgements

I would like to thank Dr Julian Lewis for his advice on my paper.

References

De Jager, A., Fogarty, A., Tewson, A., Lenette, C., & Boydell, K. M. (2017). Digital storytelling in research: a systematic review. *The Qualitative Report, 22*(10), 2548-2582.

Kasami, N. (2017). The comparison of the impact of storytelling and digital storytelling assignments on students' motivations for learning. In K. Borthwick, L. Bradley & S. Thouësny (Eds), *CALL in a climate of change: adapting to turbulent global conditions – short papers from EUROCALL 2017* (pp. 177-183). Research-publishing.net. https://doi.org/10.14705/rpnet.2017.eurocall2017.709

Ohler, J. B. (2013). *Digital storytelling in the classroom: new media pathways to literacy, learning, and creativity* (2nd ed.). https://doi.org/10.4135/9781452277479

Penner, N., & Grodek, E. (2014). Integrating multimedia ICT software in language curriculum: students' perception, use, and effectiveness. *The EUROCALL Review, 22*(1), 20-39. https://doi.org/10.4995/eurocall.2014.3637

Robin, B. (2006). The educational uses of digital storytelling. In C. Crawford, R. Carlsen, K. McFerrin, J. Price, R. Weber & D. Willis (Eds), *Proceedings of SITE 2006--Society for Information Technology & Teacher Education International Conference* (pp. 709-716).

Examining student perceptions about smartphones to understand lack of acceptance of mobile-assisted language learning

Olivia Kennedy[1]

Abstract. Problematic smartphone usage has been widely recognized (e.g. Al-Barashidi, Bouazza, & Jabur, 2015; Chóliz, 2012). However, few researchers have investigated the relationship between students' feelings towards their smartphones and their acceptance of Mobile-Assisted Language Learning (MALL). This exploratory study of thirty-six Japanese high-school students sought to understand their overwhelming reluctance to use the popular language-learning application, Duolingo. Fewer than half of the students used the application, with several failing to even install it on their device. Small group interview discussions were conducted to clarify and gain insight into the participants' feelings and motivations about the use of their smartphones.

Keywords: technology acceptance, MALL, mobile-assisted language learning, smartphones.

1.   Introduction

Smartphones present enormous difficulties for the teachers of the 36 Japanese high school students at the center of this study. All participants have had a smartphone for between one and seven years (M=3.39 years), as do some 81.4% of Japanese teenagers (Ministry of Internal Affairs and Communications, 2017). Rather than fight against the students' desire to keep their phones turned on and within easy reach during lessons, it was decided instead to integrate smartphone usage into classes. Duolingo, a popular free language-learning application, was carefully

1. Ritsumeikan University, Osaka, Japan; okennedy@fc.ritsumei.ac.jp

How to cite this article: Kennedy, O. (2018). Examining student perceptions about smartphones to understand lack of acceptance of mobile-assisted language learning. In P. Taalas, J. Jalkanen, L. Bradley & S. Thouësny (Eds), *Future-proof CALL: language learning as exploration and encounters – short papers from EUROCALL 2018* (pp. 137-141). Research-publishing.net. https://doi.org/10.14705/rpnet.2018.26.826

introduced to the students. Often successfully adopted due to its accessibility via smartphone, gamified interface, and variety of activities available (Munday, 2016), it seemed ideal for these students. Duolingo has been criticized due to its lack of pragmatic content, but has been shown to be effective if used in addition to classroom learning for beginners (Ahmed, 2016). In the present study, however, engagement was minimal with some participants simply pretending to install Duolingo in the two class periods that were set aside for the purpose, and more than half not using it at all in the following eight weeks. This article describes the qualitative study that was undertaken to explore whether students' relationship with their phones could account for this failure.

2.   Methods

Six randomly assigned group interviews were held, audio-recorded, and later transcribed. Gender balance was maintained between groups of six members. All participants (36 Japanese high school students) were given the option to not take part in this study, and privacy was carefully maintained. Discussions were in the participants' native Japanese, and every effort was made not to influence their responses. It should be noted that Duolingo was intentionally not mentioned by the researcher so as to be able to judge whether it emerged as an important theme. Similarly, discussions were not guided by the researcher unless the participants were off-topic. Only the following very general prompts were used to start the discussion and to get participants back on-topic, or when conversation stalled:

- When did you get your smartphone?

- What do you like about your smartphone?

- What don't you like about your smartphone?

3.   Results

Four major themes emerged: convenience, information, contact, and overuse.

3.1.   Convenience

The most common theme mentioned by participants was how convenient life with a smartphone has become. 'Convenient' occurred 30 times in interviews with

23 individual speakers. Approximately a third of the total discussion time was dedicated to this topic. Four of the six groups (A, C, D, E) talked about how easy it is to listen to music using the website YouTube (http://www.youtube.com) when they are able to connect to wifi. Another conversation thread in Groups A, D, and E was the convenience of being able to listen to music on their smartphones, rather than a dedicated player.

Another example raised in five of the six groups (A, B, D, E, F) that many students agreed with was about how having a smartphone has made commuting easier because they can check up-to-date train schedules. This allows them more flexibility in planning.

3.2.   Information

This theme is also connected with the smartphone's ability to provide information and was raised by nine individuals, representing all groups. These participants described using their smartphones to understand the content of lessons or what people around them are discussing, to (1) check what was said on a television program the previous evening so as to be able to join a conversation, (2) explore song lyrics so as not to appear foolish when discussing the meaning of a song, or (3) verify the closing time of a particular store. Only one participant raised the idea that the smartphone is a useful tool when finding information to complete homework. The other members of his group teased him about this, perhaps showing their own disregard for academic study and the importance of doing homework.

3.3.   Contact

All groups discussed how their smartphones meant that they could readily contact parents, siblings, friends, coaches, teammates, and after-school employers. One male participant in Group C raised how he could comfortably send text messages to his father. Another member of the group said that his father lived apart from the family, too. The first speaker said that this was not the case, but that it was somehow easier to talk to his father by text than face-to-face. His comments were acknowledged by the group with comments of affirmation. A female participant further added that it is always a good plan to prepare her mother for truly difficult topics by sending a text before she wants to talk to her about something important. In line with Christensen's (2009) research, these three examples illustrate the role that the mobile phone plays as an interface between the participants and their parents in allowing for easier communication.

Four participants (in Groups A, C, F) mentioned that they had finally managed to persuade their parent/s to purchase them a smartphone as it would allow for easier communication. In Groups C and F, the discussion then turned to how some parents had purchased devices for the participants without being requested to for this very reason.

3.4.   Overuse

The final theme that emerged in the group discussions was about smartphone overuse and the impact that such overuse could have. One male participant described lying in bed using various applications and websites until he drifts into sleep. When his smartphone buzzes with a new notification, he wakes to read it and uses his device until he drifts off to sleep again. The other five students in his group listened carefully, nodding in agreement. It should be noted that this participant did not identify himself as having an issue with overuse.

A full 25% talked about problems controlling their own smartphone use:

> "I use it more than I need to, and I don't really like that".
> "Once I touch it, I can't stop, and that's a problem for me".
> "I have to study, but I use my phone. At that time, having a phone is a problem for me".

In three separate groups a participant used the word "addicted" or "addictive", and other members of those groups nodded. Whether this was in agreement or sympathy, is unclear.

> "I'm afraid that I'm getting addicted".
> "It's highly addictive and I can't resist".
> "I'm so addicted that it's like one of my organs".

4.   Discussion

Despite a total of 32 ten-minute sessions of lesson time having been allocated to Duolingo, neither the application or its usage in class was mentioned by a single participant in the group interviews. Very few students used the application throughout the semester, and several did not even install it. There are numerous possible interpretations, but perhaps most pertinent here is not that the students did not value Duolingo, or that they did not recognize the importance of the time given in each class to work on it. Rather, for these students, smartphones are not a tool to be used for formal education, but a personal helpmeet that they control and administer themselves, as shown by three of the four themes – convenience, information, and contact – that emerged in their interviews. The fourth theme, about overuse of smartphones, was a problem expressed by 25% of the class. All but one of the students who did not install Duolingo fall into this group. Perhaps it can be seen that because they already feel that their phones are too addictive, they do not want to increase their smartphone usage. Future research will explore this hypothesis, with a survey and further group discussion interviews planned for early in the next school semester that will probe the specific issues of overuse and addiction.

5.   Conclusions

By examining the participants' largely unprompted small group discussions about their smartphones, the present study offers a glimpse into how Japanese teenagers feel about their ever-present devices. The picture that has emerged – that participants view their phones as personal helpmeets – allows for a much more targeted selection of an application for language learning in the future. It is therefore recommended that rather than choose applications based on popularity or availability, educators select materials that answer not only the academic goals of the institution, but also the learning needs of the students who will use them.

References

Ahmed, H. (2016). Duolingo as a bilingual learning app: a case study. *Arab World English Journal, 7*(2), 255-267. https://doi.org/10.24093/awej/vol7no2.17

Al-Barashidi, H. S., Bouazza, A., & Jabur, N. H. (2015). Smartphone addiction among university undergraduates: a literature review. *Journal of Scientific Research and Reports, 4*(3), 210-225.

Chóliz, M. (2012). Mobile-phone addiction in adolescence: the test of mobile phone dependence (TMD). *Progress in Health Sciences, 2*(1), 33-44.

Christensen, T. H. (2009). 'Connected Presence' in distributed family life. *New Media & Society, 11*(3), 433-51. https://doi.org/10.1177/1461444808101620

Ministry of Internal Affairs and Communications. (2017). *White Paper on Information and Communications 2017*. http://www.soumu.go.jp/johotsusintokei/whitepaper/eng/WP2017/2017-index.html

Munday, P. (2016). The case for using Duolingo as part of the classroom experience. *RIED, 19*(1), 83-101.

JYVÄSKYLÄN YLIOPISTO
UNIVERSITY OF JYVÄSKYLÄ

Using the digital storytelling app and software Moxtra to extend student presentations beyond the classroom

Tim Knight[1]

Abstract. This paper explains how the mobile app and computer software Moxtra[2] has augmented presentation and oral communication classes at the university level. Even the free version of Moxtra allows students to compile a digital portfolio of presentation and storytelling work, involving voice and visuals, to which both the teacher and fellow students have access. In a Mobile Assisted Language Learning (MALL) set up in particular, the app provides a workspace of language exploration where students can encounter each other beyond the classroom, and actively participate in the benefits of multimedia learning (Mayer, 2009). Feedback can be given after a presentation, and also beforehand during vital preparation time. The app encourages students to practice their presentations and helps the teacher when it comes to the assessment of students' work.

Keywords: MALL, presentations, digital portfolio, blended learning.

1. Introduction

Presentation assignments are a common task for students at the tertiary level and they fit well into increasing demands from education ministries for 'active learning' by students (Jones & Palmer, 2017), as the "core elements of active learning are student activity and engagement in the learning process" (Prince, 2004, p. 1). Researching a topic and preparing a presentation on it involves students in an active process, and being able to present to an audience is an important skill. And yet public speaking is often cited in surveys as one of the scariest prospects for most people (e.g. Burgess, 2013).

1. Shirayuri University, Tokyo, Japan; tknight@shirayuri.ac.jp
2. http://moxtra.com/

How to cite this article: Knight, T. (2018). Using the digital storytelling app and software Moxtra to extend student presentations beyond the classroom. In P. Taalas, J. Jalkanen, L. Bradley & S. Thouësny (Eds), *Future-proof CALL: language learning as exploration and encounters – short papers from EUROCALL 2018* (pp. 142-146). Research-publishing.net. https://doi.org/10.14705/rpnet.2018.26.827

Thus, language teachers need to think about various things before requiring students to make presentations. Apart from the matter of stress, which many students feel when having to present (King, 2002), "whole class talks [...] take time and limit individuals' speaking opportunities" (Knight, 2018, p.113). Having students present in a round-robin fashion allows more speaking time. This is achieved because each student presents to three or four students only, and being an active audience member when the others in the group do their presentation. Then new groups are made and everyone presents again. Everyone presents three or four times. The round-robin format also creates a more informal, intimate and more relaxed atmosphere in which to present, which is useful when the students are lacking in confidence.

The biggest problem with the presenting-to-small-groups format, however, is that the chance for each presentation to be seen by everyone (including the teacher) is restricted. In a class of about 20 students, it is likely that only about half will see each presentation. This is where the free mobile app and computer software Moxtra comes in: it allows and encourages student interactions and appreciation of each other's work beyond the classroom. The aim of this paper is to explain how Moxtra has benefited the author's presentation classes at the university level.

2. Tools and procedures

After researching an agreed topic, students prepare slides of pictures, text, and graphs on their phones using one of the slideware apps – Keynote, PowerPoint, or Google Slides. The research and preparation is done partly in class and partly as homework. In class, the students download the Moxtra app and accept an invitation from the teacher to join 'a conversation'. One of the main attractions for this author to use Moxtra was the software's 'mobile-first architecture'[3]. It should be noted, however, that the first time administrators invite people to join, they have to type in the email addresses of the invitees. This is the one slightly time-consuming task, for which a computer is useful. Once the students have joined Moxtra (with an email address and password of their choosing), it is quick and easy to make a conversation with the same group, or other members, again.

Once students have joined the group conversation (it is best to make a new one for each presentation project), they should make a folder under their own name. If

3. http://moxtra.com/

they do not, the conversation will get disorganized, as files or pictures are uploaded and get mixed up. When each member keeps their own work inside their folder, everything is clear and tidy. Conversation members can upload various kinds of files from anywhere, including linked apps on their phone or from cloud storage.

Any other group member can immediately access everyone else's work, so even at this stage, feedback can be given on the proposed slides for the presentation. Spelling errors or information lacking from a presentation can be noticed and feedback swiftly given, and acted on.

The teacher can give feedback on students' slides, and suggest where more research is needed. Students can therefore develop the presentation more, making changes and corrections on their slides just as on a draft of an essay.

At this point in the course, in class students present 'live', in the small group format, as described in the introduction.

Once their visual aids are in order, students can record over them. Presenters simply swipe left as they speak to move to the next slide. While recording, presenters or storytellers can also make annotations on slides, and draw freely on the app's whiteboard. The free version of Moxtra allows a time limit of ten minutes for one recording. It is possible both to pause while recording, and to discard a finished recording if the speaker wants to try again. A saved presentation results in an mp4 file, which can be viewed on any group member's device or even downloaded and shared in other ways.

The final activity in the project is to require students to comment, within Moxtra, on class members' presentations. It gives them a chance to see and hear those presentations they were not able to experience live. Comments can be written or recorded, and responded to, at any time. Teachers can keep these digital presentations as a record, and use them when grading at the end of the course.

3.   Discussion

The reason for introducing Moxtra into the course was as follows. In the first class of the course for second year, two classes of female Japanese university students, each with just under 20 students, have been asked about their attitudes to presenting. The survey was made and the data collected in a Google Form, with the link distributed through the class learning management system.

Students answered the questions on their phones. For three years (2016-2018), the results have been consistent. A little more than half have agreed that it is useful to have good presentation skills. However, about half declare that they do not like presenting. Thus, this author sees one of his tasks as creating a supportive atmosphere in which the students can start to enjoy the process of making presentations and building their confidence. The combination of using the round-robin presenting format, with shared digital presentations and written and spoken feedback given in Moxtra outside and beyond class meetings, seems to be working to this end. In the first year of using this framework, in 2016, the clear 'dislikes' for presenting had fallen from 43.3% at the start of the course to 11.8% three months later. The figures were similar among the most recent cohort. Furthermore, in a new follow-up survey about using Moxtra, answered by the 2018 cohort, after the students had completed two presentation projects, over 92% said they found the app very useful or somewhat useful "as a way of getting further language practice". At least from the perception point of view, these responses vindicated the author's decision to use Moxtra.

Moreover, by sharing their presentations in Moxtra, students could actively participate in the benefits of multimedia learning (Mayer, 2009). However, to benefit properly from the use of Moxtra in presentation projects, the students and teacher need to be comfortable with using mobile devices in class. Even a few years ago, Hockley (2013) referred to this form of "mobile literacy" as "an increasingly important skill" (p. 4). Most students seem to have acquired it. They are able to use presentation apps with dexterity, and quickly find their way round Moxtra after a brief demonstration on the big screen. However, it should be acknowledged that the occasional student says they find it 'difficult' to use at first. A future step will be to examine the digital portfolios closely to see how instrumental Moxtra was in the actual development of the students' speaking and presentation skills.

4.   Conclusions

This paper has explained how using the free app and software Moxtra can augment the process of student presentations. This is especially true when the round-robin presentation format is used, a format particularly suited for students who lack confidence or do not like presenting. Moxtra is a convenient medium for providing feedback both before and after presentations, for providing language practice for presenters and listeners, and as a means for students in a class to view all their classmates' presentations. It may also be helpful for teachers when grading students.

References

Burgess, K. (2013, October 30). Speaking in public is worse than death for most. *The Times*. https://www.thetimes.co.uk/article/speaking-in-public-is-worse-than-death-for-most-5l2bvqlmbnt

Hockley, N. (2013). Mobile learning. *ELT Journal, 67*(1), 80-84. https://doi.org/10.1093/elt/ccs064

Jones, B. A., & Palmer, R. (2017). Active learning in Japanese university EFL classes: clarifying the construct. *Hirao School of Management Review, 7,* 107-125.

King, J. (2002, March). Preparing EFL learners for oral presentations. *The Internet TESL Journal, VIII*(3).

Knight, T. (2018). Extending class presentations beyond the classroom with Moxtra. In A. B. Gallagher (Ed.), *The 2017 PanSIG journal: expand your interests* (pp. 113-118). http://pansig.org/publications/2017/2017_PanSIG_Journal.pdf?

Mayer, R. (2009). *Multi-media learning*. Cambridge University Press. https://doi.org/10.1017/CBO9780511811678

Prince, M. (2004). Does active learning work? A review of the research. *Journal of Engineering Education, 93*(3), 223-231. https://doi.org/10.1002/j.2168-9830.2004.tb00809.x

Mobile assisted language learning in the workplace – developing the context-aware learning application Appla

Johanna Komppa[1] and Lari Kotilainen[2]

Abstract. This paper discusses the possibilities for Mobile-Assisted Language Learning (MALL) in the workplace. We present an on-going project on developing a language learning application Appla and report on a pilot study of its use. The Appla application is based on speech recognition: it records and transcribes the ongoing interaction the language learner/employee is involved in and provides information about it (e.g. transcriptions of conversations, word lists). Thus, the application is context-aware (cf. Stockwell, 2016), i.e. the learning material is gathered from real interaction around the learner. The target group of the application consists of adult L2 learners, who have basic knowledge of Finnish and who want to improve (professional) Finnish language skills. In the pilot study reported, the Appla application was tested in simulated work-like tasks by second language speakers.

Keywords: context-aware, learning applications, less taught languages, MALL, second language learning, speech recognition.

1. Introduction

In Finland, as in many other European countries, the public sector language training, so-called integration training, for adult second language learners aims to achieve the level B1 in the Common European Framework of Reference for languages (CEFR, 2001). After achieving this level, the availability of language

1. University of Helsinki, Helsinki, Finland; johanna.komppa@helsinki.fi
2. University of Helsinki, Helsinki, Finland; lari.kotilainen@helsinki.fi

How to cite this article: Komppa, J., & Kotilainen, L. (2018). Mobile assisted language learning in the workplace – developing the context-aware learning application Appla. In P. Taalas, J. Jalkanen, L. Bradley & S. Thouësny (Eds), *Future-proof CALL: language learning as exploration and encounters – short papers from EUROCALL 2018* (pp. 147-152). Research-publishing.net. https://doi.org/10.14705/rpnet.2018.26.828

training decreases dramatically. However, many learners would benefit from more advanced Finnish courses, since level B1 does not suffice for professions which require high education and in which the work is mostly done via language, e.g. white-collar work. The need for further education also applies to many learners who already have a workplace. In this paper, we present a mobile application, which is developed for those more advanced language learners (and their teachers), and report a pilot study that shows how the application may be utilised.

Our ideological background is in language learning in interaction and situated learning (Lave & Wenger, 1991). The critical catalyst has been the idea that the classroom is not the most efficient place to learn professional language. At the same time, it is known that working itself does not guarantee language learning (e.g. Strömmer, 2016). Interaction in the workplace does offer possibilities for learning, but these affordances could be exploited more effectively.

For the better exploitation of the affordances workplaces provide, we have developed a language learning application Appla. Our target group is adult L2 learners who have basic knowledge of Finnish and who want to improve Finnish language skills at work. From a technical point of view, the application is based on speech recognition: it turns the ongoing conversations around the users into language learning materials. As such, the application is learner-centred and context-aware (cf. Stockwell, 2016), which means that the learning materials are collected around the user. In this regard, there is a considerable difference between Appla and the traditional language learning applications in which the learning materials are usually ready-made. The benefits from a context-aware approach are evident since the learning materials reflect the linguistic reality of the user. The Appla application may benefit not only L2 learners in workplaces but also L2 teachers by helping them to design material for teaching particular vocabulary, expressions, and grammar in different workplaces.

In this paper, we present a pilot study of the use of the Appla application. The research questions are (1) how the test users address language issues while using the Appla application, and (2) whether the test users find the application useful.

From the broader point of view of MALL-studies, we investigate if the existing speech recognition technologies (in this case Google API) are sufficient for supporting independent language learning, especially in less resourced languages such as Finnish. With Appla, we want to contribute to the discussion on the future of MALL, which Burston (2015) has encouraged.

2. Methods

2.1. Task and participants

We arranged four test sessions in the universities in the Helsinki region. Each session lasted 45-90 minutes and included two different tasks and a reflective interview after the test. Seventeen voluntary testers were university students with Finnish skills B1 or higher. Testers used mobile phones provided by the researchers.

The first research question is answered through a task in which test users wrote an invitation according to the instruction given orally by the researcher and transcribed by the Appla application. The way in which the test users accomplished the writing task – with the help of the Appla transcript – was video-recorded and analysed. After the task, the students were interviewed in order to answer the second research question.

2.2. Technical overview of the Appla application used in the study

Appla is a mobile application which records interaction around the user, transcribes the interaction into text, and displays it on the mobile device and on the desktop in real time. On the desktop, the system creates word clouds based on the transcribed material. Also, the user may create their own list of essential words by clicking on the words in the word cloud (see Figure 1).

Figure 1. Desktop view

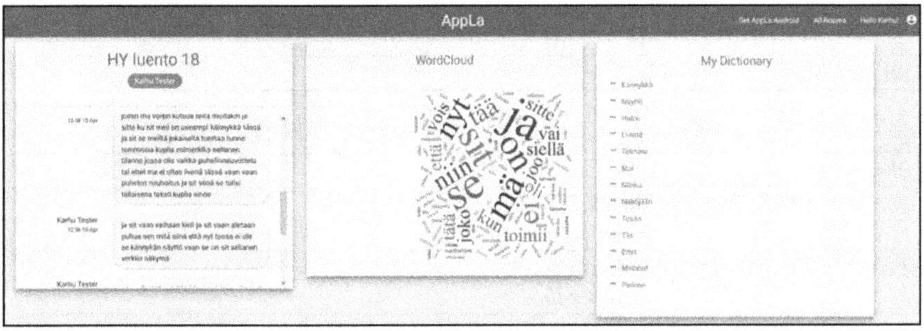

Appla is an Android application, and the speech recognition feature is powered by Google Cloud Speech API (for details, see Nguyen, 2017). The application is designed to work both as a real-time guide and as a material bank for individualised language studies. Used simultaneously with an ongoing conversation (e.g. a meeting), the Appla gives information about the ongoing interaction. After the recording, the user may utilise the transcription and the word cloud by building their own contextually relevant vocabulary. The transcription is also well-suited to function as a material for the language teacher – or a colleague supporting the learner.

3.   Results

The pilot study shows that the test users employed the transcriptions as an affordance for language learning. That is seen in the actions of the test users in following ways: they check lexical details from the transcript, they copy and modify the formulations from the transcript, and they start language-related discussions based on the transcript. Table 1 (see Sidnell & Stivers, 2013 for transcription details) illustrates the first mentioned. The test users are writing an invitation according to the instruction given orally and transcribed by Appla (more detailed analysis, see Komppa & Kotilainen, forthcoming).

Table 1.   Checking a lexeme

Line	Test user	Transcription
01	T1:	alumnit; *alumni*
02		(.)
03	T1:	antavat työvinkkejä; *give work tips*
04		(2.8)
05	T2:	<°antavat°> *give*
06		(2.0)
07	T2:	°työ° *work*
08		(1.5)
09	T1:	työnhaku (.) vinkkejä. vai? *job application tips or*
11	T2:	oliko. joo. tuo; *was it yes that*

In Lines 1-2, test user T1 is dictating the text to T2 who is writing the invitation on the paper. The dictation includes the word *työvinkkejä* ('work tips'). When T2, who reads aloud while writing, reaches the word (Line 7), he immediately leans towards the phone where the Appla transcription is on display and points to the phone with his pen. In Line 9, T1 leans towards the phone and suggests an alternative word, *työnhakuvinkkejä* ('job application tips'), which is confirmed by T2 (Line 11). After the extract, T2 continues writing the invitation. He now uses the word *työnhakuvinkkejä*, found in the Appla transcript.

According to the interviews, test users found the application useful, for instance, for internships and other situations outside the language class. The idea that the application provides the user with an archive of workplace language to be studied later was anticipated. The shortcomings in the quality of transcription were addressed but were not seen as severe. Some test users emphasised that it was difficult to understand spoken language in written format.

4.   Discussion

According to the pilot study, the Appla transcription seems to open up various possibilities for situated language learning (as discussed in Wagner, 2015). For example, the testers orient to the transcription as a source of words and linguistic formulations (e.g. in Table 1). Besides, the transcript serves as a starting point for language-related discussions. The test users found the application useful even though the imperfect quality of the transcriptions was addressed in the interviews.

5.   Conclusions

With Appla we investigate how to support MALL in workplaces. Our approach is learner-based and its core is on speech recognition; the application makes a transcript of the interaction around the user and affords them possibilities to use the interactions as study material. In this way, the application supports a non-native employee and her work community to turn the workplace into an effective language learning environment. The pilot study is promising, and though more research is needed, this kind of approach could have practical implications for both L2 learners and L2 teachers.

6.   Acknowledgements

We would like to thank our project team, Harri Airaksinen, Olli Alm, Bao Nguyen, Tien Pham, Johanna Olkku, and Hanna Rajalahti, and the University of Helsinki and Kone Foundation for supporting this project.

References

Burston, J. (2015). Twenty years of MALL project implementation: a meta-analysis of learning outcomes. *ReCALL,* 27(1), 4-20. https://doi.org/10.1017/S0958344014000159

CEFR. (2001). *Common European framework of reference for languages: learning, teaching, assessment.* Council of Europe. Cambridge University Press.

Komppa, J., & Kotilainen, L. (forthcoming). Mobiiliteknologia kielenoppijan apuna. Esimerkkinä puheentunnistus ja Appla-sovellus. In L. Kotilainen, S. Kurhila & J. Kalliokoski (Eds), *Ulos opetustilanteesta. Kielenoppimisen laajenevat kontekstit.* SKS.

Lave, J., & Wenger, E. (1991). *Situated learning. Legitimate peripheral participation.* Cambridge University Press. https://doi.org/10.1017/CBO9780511815355

Nguyen, B. (2017). *Assisting language learning with Appla application.* Bachelor thesis. Metropolia UAS. http://urn.fi/URN:NBN:fi:amk-201705239648

Sidnell, J., & Stivers, T. (2013). *The handbook of conversation analysis.* Wiley-Blackwell.

Stockwell, G. (2016). Mobile language learning. In F. Farr & L. Murray (Eds), *The Routledge handbook of language learning and technology.* Routledge.

Strömmer, M. (2016). Affordances and constraints: second language learning in cleaning work. *Multilingua,* 35(6), 697-721. https://doi.org/10.1515/multi-2014-0113

Wagner, J. (2015). Designing for language learning in the wild: creating social infrastructures for second language learning. In T. Cadierno & S. W. Eskildsen (Eds), *Usage-based perspectives on second language learning.* Mouton de Gruyter.

Task graph based task-oriented dialogue system using dialogue map for second language learning

Oh-Woog Kwon[1], Young-Kil Kim[2], and Yunkeun Lee[3]

Abstract. This paper presents a rule-based task-oriented dialogue system for second language learning and a knowledge extraction method which automatically extracts the training data for Natural Language Understanding (NLU) and dialogue rules for dialogue management from a Dialogue Map (DM). The DM consists of turn-by-turn utterances between the system and the learner. Therefore, the proposed method can automatically extend a new dialogue domain by constructing a dialogue map with a simple format. We constructed two dialogue maps for English and Korean, respectively, and implemented English and Korean task-oriented dialogue systems using the DMs. In the experiments, although the turn success rates are relatively low (78.1% in English and 78.76% in Korean), the task success rates are 90.83% in English and 99.17% in Korean. The systems constructed by the proposed method should enable learners to communicate successfully in the topic despite some mistakes in the system responses.

Keywords: knowledge extraction method, task-oriented dialogue system, second language learning, dialogue map.

1.   Introduction

Speech dialogue system technology is a promising tool to use in Computer-Assisted second Language Learning (CALL). Through dialogue with the system, we expect to improve learners' second language skills. Generally, the dialogue system suitable for CALL can be viewed as a Task-oriented Dialogue System (TDS) rather than a chatbot system, as it is necessary to be able to converse with the subject in a

1. Electronics and Telecommunications Research Institute, Daejeon, Korea; ohwoog@etri.re.kr
2. Electronics and Telecommunications Research Institute, Daejeon, Korea; kimyk@etri.re.kr
3. Electronics and Telecommunications Research Institute, Daejeon, Korea; yklee@etri.re.kr

How to cite this article: Kwon, O.-W., Kim, Y.-K., & Lee, Y. (2018). Task graph based task-oriented dialogue system using dialogue map for second language learning. In P. Taalas, J. Jalkanen, L. Bradley & S. Thouësny (Eds), *Future-proof CALL: language learning as exploration and encounters – short papers from EUROCALL 2018* (pp. 153-159). Research-publishing.net. https://doi.org/10.14705/rpnet.2018.26.829

specific situation (Johnson & Valente, 2009). Most TDSs are implemented as a slot-filling dialogue model which is not suitable for language learning because a slot-filling dialogue consists of only simple request and response pairs.

We already proposed a Task Graph Dialogue Model (TGDM) that enables topic conversation in various situations (Choi, Kwon, Kim, & Lee, 2016). The model can divide a complex topic task into smaller subtasks and define the order between them. In TGDM, subtasks are defined as nodes and the order as edges. We also suggested a DM based on TGDM, which can be constructed by educators who do not know the dialogue systems (Choi et al., 2016).

In this paper, we introduce a knowledge extraction method platform that automatically convert a DM into the knowledge of a TGDM-based TDS to create a dialogue system for a new topic.

2. Automatic knowledge extraction for TGDM-based TDS

2.1. TGDM

TDS needs a dialogue model that enables dialogue between learners and the system to perform a specific task. The dialogue model defines the dialogue strategy and response of the system to a learner's utterance on the dialogue context. In the model, the utterances and the dialogue context are represented by dialogue acts and slots. A dialogue act is a function of utterance and a slot is a semantic concept in the conversation. For example, in 'ordering food task', the utterance *I want to have a coffee* is represented by *want_a_food(beverage='coff ee')*, which consists of the dialogue act *want_a_food*, as well as the beverage slot and its value *coffee*.

The proposed TGDM divides a complex task into small subtasks and places order constraints amongst the subtasks. TGDM is similar to finite-state transition models. Dialogue models of individual subtasks are implemented as a hybrid dialogue model of a slot-filling and information state. Therefore, TGDM is hybridised with different models, where expression ability of TGDM is more powerful than other models. Also, TGDM can (1) have the advantage that subtasks can be used for other tasks and (2) analyse learner's utterance and generate its system response according to subtasks.

2.2. DM for TGDM

DM is a method of expressing TGDM in a dialogue script manner. Figure 1 shows the ordering food task in the snack bar as DM. The ordering food task is divided into six subtasks that consist of turn-by-turn dialogue. The diversity of the conversation flow is made by the learner's various responses to a system utterance. In DM, each terminal turn of the subtask contains the next subtask information (for further details of DM, see Choi et al., 2016).

Figure 1.   An example of DM for 'ordering food task'

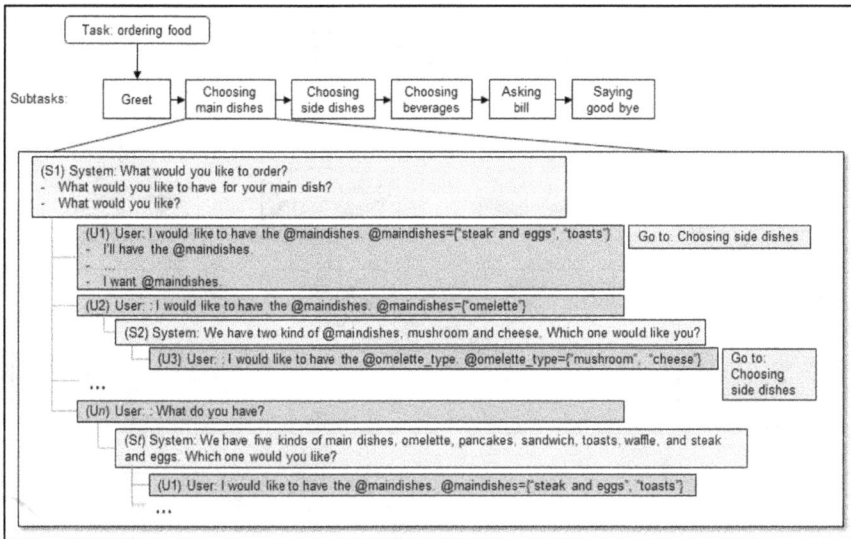

2.3.   Automatic knowledge extraction using DMs

In this section, we introduce a method that can build a dialogue system for a new task by writing a machine readable DM. Figure 2 shows an overview of our TDS and also the procedures of automatic knowledge extraction method which automatically extracts the knowledge needed by our TDS from the DM.

Our TDS consists of a Structured Support Vector Machine (SSVM) based NLU (Kwon, Lee, Kim, & Lee, 2015), task graph-based dialogue management, and a generation template based Natural Language Generation (NLG). First, SSVM-based NLU analyses the learner utterance and determines the intention using

SSVM training data. Then, task graph-based dialogue management locates the appropriate system response for the learner intention on the context using dialogue rules and updates the context. Finally, NLG generates the system utterance from a template of the selected system response.

Figure 2.   Automatic knowledge extraction for TGDM-based TDS using DM

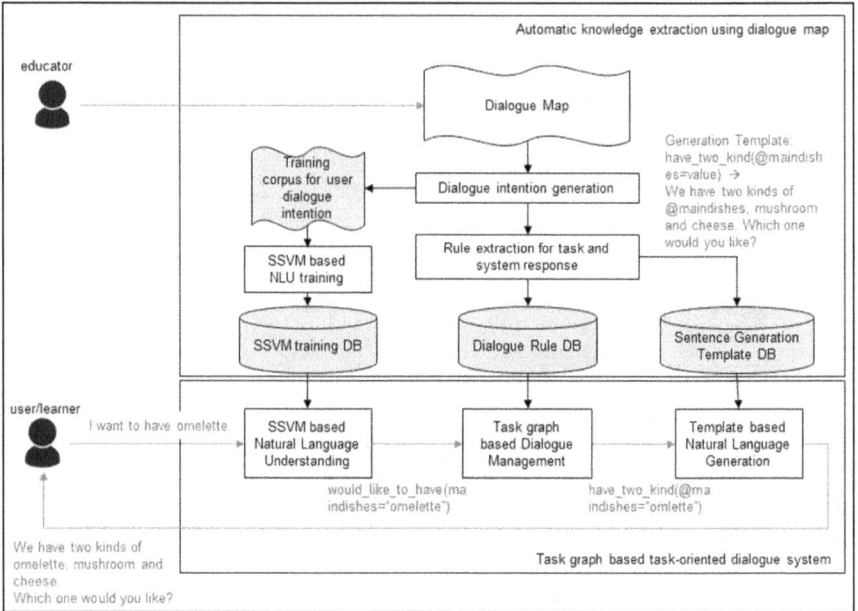

Automatic knowledge extraction methods using DMs consist of dialogue intention generation, SSVM based NLU training, and rule extraction. Dialogue intention generation automatically makes the intention for each utterance in DMs using its predicate and object, which are analysed by shallow parser. If the utterance has no object or the object is a slot, it sets the dialogue act with the predicate, otherwise, with a combination of the predicate and object. For example, Utterances U1, U2, and U3 of Figure 1 have the same predicate *would like to have*, but have different objects. So, the intention generation makes the intention *would_like_to_have(@maindishes='value')* for U1 and U2, and the intention *would_like_to_have(@omelette_type='value')* for U3.

SSVM training data consists of triples of user sentences of DMs, slot-annotated sentences, and its intentions automatically generated by dialogue intention generation. The SSVM-based NLU training module trains slot classification using sentences and their slot-annotated sentences, as well as intention classification using sentences and their intentions.

Dialogue rules are generated after dialogue intention generation. The rules are divided into subtask movement rules and turn-by-turn rules. Subtask movement rules consist of a movement condition and a subtask information for the current subtask and the next subtask. The movement condition is defined as the terminal utterance's intention and/or all slots and their values as appear in the path from the initial utterance to the terminal utterance.

Turn-by-turn rules consist of activating the condition and the action to be performed when the condition is satisfied. The rules are extracted from each turn-by-turn utterance. Its condition is constructed by the subtask information, previous intention, and its talker (system or user/learner), and its action is current intention and its talker. From the rules, we may determine a proper system response intention to the user/learner's input on the context, and also proper utterances of the next user/learner's turn to current system response.

Sentence generation templates are easily generated from the utterance pattern of the DM. The templates are classified by the intention and the subtask.

3.   Preliminary experiments and discussion

We implemented English and Korean TDSs. The language educators constructed two DMs and implemented two TDSs using the DMs through the proposed knowledge extraction method for each language. To evaluate the performance, we recruited 20 second language learners for each language. The learners freely talked on the given task and conducted four conversations with each other topic on each task.

Table 1 shows the experiment results. The turn success rates to evaluate whether the system responded correctly to learners' utterances are 78.1% in English and 78.76% in Korean, and the task success rates to evaluate whether learners completed the conversation with the system in the topics are 90.83% in English and 99.17% in Korean. There were little differences in the performance depending on the number of learners' conversation attempts. According to these preliminary results, we believe the systems constructed by writing DMs may have the performance to communicate successfully with learners in the topic despite a rather low success rate; this will be further explored.

Table 1. The experiment results

Language	Task	Task success rate %	Turn success rate %
English	ordering food	88.33	78.74
	city tour ticketing	93.33	77.45
	both	90.83	78.10
Korean	ordering Korean food	100	81.41
	clothes shopping	98.33	75.65
	both	99.17	78.76

Task success rate (%) = (number of task completed dialogue) / (total number of dialogue) x 100
Turn success rate (%) = (number of correct system's responses to learners' utterances) / (total number of learners' utterances) x 100

4. Conclusions

This paper describes an automatic knowledge extraction method developing TDS using the DM. Through the experiments, the performance of the TDS constructed by writing a DM showed that second language learners could successfully practice conversations on a given topic. With the proposed automatic knowledge extraction method, we expect that anyone could construct dialogue systems for language learning. In future research, we will investigate whether educators can build DMs quickly and easily and collect more data to further improve the system's success rate.

5. Acknowledgements

This work was supported by the ICT R&D programme of MSIT/IITP. [2015-0-00187, Core technology development of the spontaneous speech dialogue processing for the language learning].

References

Johnson, W. L., & Valente, A. (2009). Tactical language and culture training systems: using AI to teach foreign languages and cultures. *AI Magazine, 30*(2), 72-83. https://doi.org/10.1609/aimag.v30i2.2240

Choi, S. K., Kwon, O. W., Kim, Y. K., & Lee, Y. K. (2016). Using a dialogue system based on dialogue maps for computer assisted second language learning. In S. Papadima-Sophocleous, L. Bradley & S. Thouësny (Eds), *CALL communities and culture – short papers from EUROCALL 2016* (pp. 106-112). Research-publishing.net. https://doi.org/10.14705/rpnet.2016.eurocall2016.546

Kwon, O.-W., Lee, K., Kim, Y.-K., & Lee, Y. (2015). GenieTutor: a computer assisted second language learning system based on semantic and grammar correctness evaluations. In F. Helm, L. Bradley, M. Guarda & S. Thouësny (Eds), *Critical CALL – proceedings of the 2015 EUROCALL conference, Padova, Italy* (pp. 330-335). Research-publishing. net. https://doi. org/10.14705/rpnet.2015.000354

Antipodal communication between students of German in Finland and in New Zealand via Facebook

Vera Leier[1] and Kirsi Korkealehto[2]

Abstract. This reflective practice paper presents an excerpt of the outcome of a telecollaboration project between two tertiary institutions in New Zealand and Finland. Twenty-six intermediate students of German in the two countries used a Facebook-group to write about given topics which were part of their final assessment. The posts were a combination of video uploads, audio recordings, and writing which is in line with the multimodal meaning-making theory (Kress & van Leeuwen, 2001). The task design was guided by O'Dowd and Ware's (2009) three-layer approach design. The study investigates how students perceive the collaboration using the Facebook group and how the multimodal approach helps the students to develop their digital literacies. The data collected for the study included a mixed-methods approach with pre- and post-questionnaires, semi-structured interviews and Facebook logs. Results show that students learned more about each others' culture and improved their German at the same time.

Keywords: telecollaboration, Facebook, German.

1.   Introduction

Widely accessible and user friendly social networking sites have allowed students to connect with friends world-wide and develop an international network. Social Networking Sites (SNSs) are perceived as authentic communication platforms by language learners. Bringing SNSs into the language classroom to connect learners of German from two different parts of the world to create a collaborative learning environment within the principles of constructivism (Ellis, 2003) seems a natural continuation of the students' online life they are already leading (Boyd, 2014).

1. University of Canterbury, Christchurch, New Zealand; vera.leier@canterbury.ac.nz
2. Kajaani University, Kajaani, Finland; kirsi.korkealehto@kamk.fi

How to cite this article: Leier, V., & Korkealehto, K. (2018). Antipodal communication between students of German in Finland and in New Zealand via Facebook. In P. Taalas, J. Jalkanen, L. Bradley & S. Thouësny (Eds), *Future-proof CALL: language learning as exploration and encounters – short papers from EUROCALL 2018* (pp. 160-164). Research-publishing.net. https://doi.org/10.14705/rpnet.2018.26.830

This study is based on a telecollaboration task that was set up on a Facebook group between two sets of learners of German. Tertiary students from New Zealand and Finland communicated over a period of six weeks for an enhanced collaborative learning experience. In this study, we wanted to find out how the students perceived the work on the Facebook platform and how the multi-modal approach helped them to develop into a community of learners. For this research, we posed the following questions:

- How do students perceive class collaboration using a Facebook group?

- How does the multimodal approach help students to develop into a community of learners?

2. Method

2.1. The project and the participants

The study took place in German language courses in Finland and New Zealand. Both classes were B1 level. The telecollaboration task took part over a period of six weeks and was part of the overall assessment of the two classes. The 26 students, 14 from New Zealand and 12 from Finland, were given five tasks based on the three-layer design (O'Dowd & Ware, 2009). The tasks were organised in three main categories (Table 1). The first task type comprised of information exchange tasks. Task type two involved comparison and analysis; the students had to comment on other students' Facebook posts and draw comparisons between the two different cultures. This information exchange type triggered reflection about their own culture and enhanced intercultural understanding. The final task type was a collaborative task, a joint product of the two groups. The students were assigned to groups of four students, two students of each class. The task design was supported by multimodal meaning-making theory (Kress & van Leeuwen, 2001).

Table 1. Tasks and topics of the exchange

Tasks	Topics
Task type one: information exchange Video: individual introductions Photos, weblinks: local culture and people	Make a video not longer than 3 minutes, introduce yourself and your hobbies. Presenting your hometown and family. The distant partners are required to comment on at least two of the posts.

Task type two: comparison and analysis Photos: comparing Photos, weblinks: comparing	Writing about food in your country supported by photos. Presenting your favourite clothes shop using external web links and photos. The distant partners are required to compare the information with their country.
Task type three: collaboration PowerPoint: presentation about a given topic in pairs of 3-4 students from both classes.	Comparing Christmas, summer holidays or national holidays in the two countries.

The groups doing the PowerPoint presentation were made up of three or four students from both classes, the groups were assigned by the teachers. The students had free choice of the software to use for the presentation.

2.2.　Data collection and data analysis

A post-questionnaire was created using google software; it included 11 multiple choice questions and nine open-ended questions asking about their perception of the project and consisted of multiple choice questions applying a five point Likert scale ranging from strongly agree to strongly disagree. The data also consisted of semi-structured interviews conducted after the project had finished.

Coding was derived from students' online answers and interview responses. The researchers read and identified common phrases, key themes, and patterns concerning student perception of the use of Facebook and their views on the multimodal design.

3.　Results and discussion

The study has given some insight into how students perceive Facebook as a platform to communicate with peers they have not met before. The results showed that the majority of the students (80%) perceived the tasks and the experience on the Facebook site as favourably. One student commented in an interview "I have learned more about both of our cultures while improving my German".

Several students commented that they gained confidence and found the course content very interesting. They enjoyed the choice of topics; they believed that the topics were interesting for both developing cultural knowledge and building up their vocabulary:

"the artefacts are good, all people eat, all people wear clothes, etc.".

"I learned many new words to do with food".

Some students found it challenging to communicate with strangers, they commented that

"it is sometimes hard to communicate with different people in different places or it is hard to start making contact with people you've never seen and probably will never see again".

The tasks were set up that so that they had to communicate in different modes: video, audio, photos, and texts. The students answered in the post-questionnaire in favour of written text as a communication media. Photos might have been too personal, one student commented in an interview, that while he was posting a photo of his family on a public platform, he felt uneasy about this. The introductory video was also perceived by students as intimidating: "It was intimidating, I did not like to show my face to strangers". This statement is in line with Ware and Kramsch (2005), who recommend that in-depth intercultural understanding needs to be carefully set up in a dialogical setting.

Overall, Facebook as a platform was perceived as an easy place to communicate, "Facebook is a good platform, everyone who takes the class uses it anyway". Especially the New Zealand students benefited from developing the unique virtual community of German learners; it eased their feeling of linguistic isolation. They commented "there were many different people from all over learning German".

4. Conclusions

The study described how students from two very different parts of the world can connect with each other using technology and the common medium of the German language. The main aim was to provide the students in both classes with an additional dimension of authentic course content. It was interesting for the teachers to see that writing was still the preferred medium.

Although the project was of a small scale with only 26 participants and over a short period of time, it was a rewarding activity for the students to gain cultural insight into a new culture. Most of the students expressed the wish to continue with the exchange. Unfortunately, setting up an exchange with students on the opposite hemisphere brings problems with respect to term schedules and time differences. We were very fortunate that we found a six-week slot in our teaching schedule that worked for both countries. Problems with the time difference were minimised because we set up the telecollaboration based on asynchronous communication.

The short opportunity the students had was very enriching and added Finland and New Zealand onto the travelling map for the students involved. In the future, we will try to set up online exchange possibilities over an extended period and preferably with more chances for the students to talk to each other. The students should also have the opportunity to get to know each other in individual dialogues before moving to the more public class overarching SNSs.

5.   Acknowledgements

We would like to thank all the students and the student teacher who took part in this study.

References

Boyd, D. (2014). *It's complicated: the social lives of networked teens.* Yale University Press.

Ellis, R. (2003). *Task-based language learning and teaching.* Oxford University Press.

Kress, G., & van Leeuwen, T. (2001). Multimodal discourse: the modes and media of non-temporary communication. Arnold.

O'Dowd, R., & Ware, P. (2009). Critical issues in telecollaborative task design. *Computer Assisted Language Learning, 22*(2), 173-188. https://doi.org/10.1080/09588220902778369

Ware, P., & Kramsch, C. (2005). Towards an intercultural stance: teaching German and English through telecollaboration. *Modern Language Journal, 89*(2), 190-205. https://doi.org/10.1111/j.1540-4781.2005.00274.x

JYVÄSKYLÄN YLIOPISTO
UNIVERSITY OF JYVÄSKYLÄ

Aucune anomalie détectéé ! Practice your French while piloting a spaceship

Denis Liakin[1], Walcir Cardoso[2],
David Waddington[3], and Natallia Liakina[4]

Abstract. This study explores the pedagogical use of *Astronautes Français Langue Seconde (Astronautes FLS)*, a cooperative digital game, in second/foreign language (L2) French teaching. It has two goals: (1) to introduce *Astronautes FLS* and its conceptualization, and (2) to report the results of a feasibility study in which we examined the pedagogical viability of the game as well as learners' perceptions of the game, across two proficiency groups. The results of the feasibility study suggest that the game is positively perceived by the participants in many factors known to contribute to language learning (e.g. it increased their motivation to learn).

Keywords: digital gaming, French as a second language, L2 speaking, L2 listening.

1. Introduction

The pedagogical use of digital gaming has been expanding in popularity and is gradually being applied to L2 contexts (Godwin-Jones, 2014), with results supporting the hypothesis that its use can enhance learners' L2 acquisition (e.g. Sykes & Reinhardt, 2013). When these games are presented in a mobile format, they have the potential to offer the same benefits of digital gaming while also maintaining the portability and accessibility attributes of mobile devices (Stockwell, 2010). Some of these benefits (or four *themes* – see below) include students' increased *motivation* (Ducate & Lomicka, 2009), *enjoyment* (Allen, Crossley, Snow, &

1. Concordia University, Montreal, Canada; denis.liakin@concordia.ca
2. Concordia University, Montreal, Canada; walcir.cardoso@concordia.ca
3. Concordia University, Montreal, Canada; david.waddington@concordia.ca
4. McGill University, Montreal, Canada; natallia.liakina@mcgill.ca

How to cite this article: Liakin, D., Cardoso, W., Waddington, D., & Liakina, N. (2018). Aucune anomalie détectéé ! Practice your French while piloting a spaceship. In P. Taalas, J. Jalkanen, L. Bradley & S. Thouësny (Eds), *Future-proof CALL: language learning as exploration and encounters – short papers from EUROCALL 2018* (pp. 165-170). Research-publishing.net. https://doi.org/10.14705/rpnet.2018.26.831

McNamara, 2014), and *comfort* (Liakin, Cardoso, & Liakina, 2017), which may potentially lead to a positive impact on *learning* (Kukulska-Hulme, 2016).

The first goal of this paper is to introduce a mobile digital game, *Astronautes FLS*, created to motivate L2 learners to practice French. *Astronautes FLS* (http://astronautesfls.ca) is a non-serious cooperative game inspired by *Spaceteam ESL* (http://spaceteamesl.ca). To play the game, groups of two or more players engage in speaking, reading, and listening to time-sensitive instructions to pilot a spaceship. To survive, players must read and orally communicate instructions with their peers and, at the same time, press buttons on a control panel on their mobile devices (iOS, Android) to keep the spaceship afloat, as illustrated in Figure 1.

Figure 1.   The interface of *Astronautes FLS*

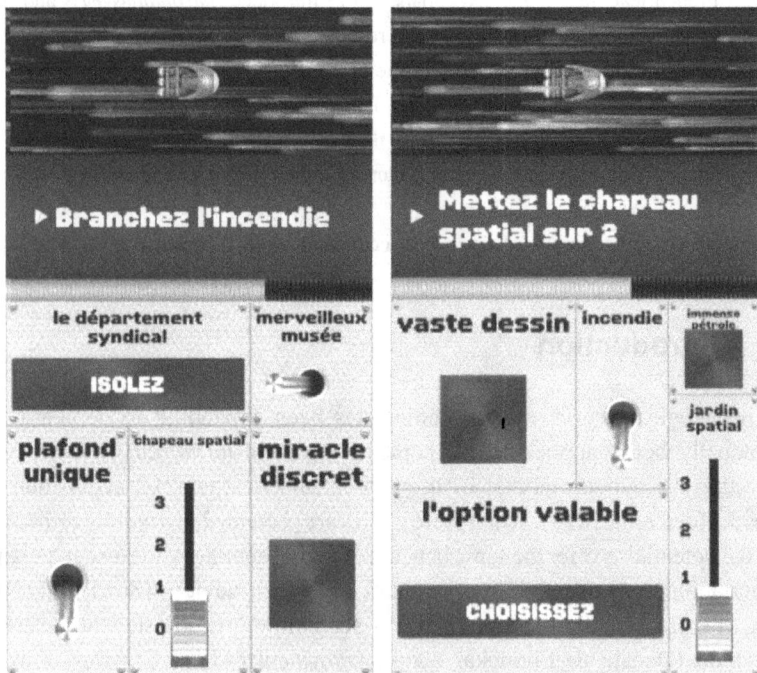

Our second goal is to report the results of a feasibility study in which we examined the pedagogical viability of *Astronautes FLS* (i.e. its ability to promote the four themes discussed above) across two proficiency groups (i.e. to determine the level appropriateness of the game), as well as learners' perceptions of the game's pedagogical potential.

2. Method

2.1. The conceptualization of *Astronautes FLS*

The conceptualization of *Astronautes FLS* included the selection of a lexicon from the 5,000 most frequently used words in French (i.e. with each 1,000 frequency band constituting a 'proficiency level'), thus allowing learners to practice what they already know in an automatized manner (Nation & Newton, 2009). As game levels increase, so does the complexity of the vocabulary and related pronunciation (Cardoso, Grimshaw, & Waddington, 2015, p. 103). *Astronautes FLS* also offers a practice feature that can be used as a technology-enhanced 'listen-and-repeat' activity. This feature allows players to select vocabulary lists based on the level of difficulty and listen to a recording of the selected words. Players also have the option to record themselves saying the words, allowing them to compare their own recordings with those provided by the game. For details, visit http://astronautesfls.ca.

2.2. Feasibility/perception study

Based on Grimshaw and Cardoso (2018), we adopted a mixed-methods approach for data collection and analysis, using data from surveys and focus group discussions.

2.2.1. Participants

Seventeen participants from two Anglophone universities in Montreal were recruited and stratified among two proficiency groups in French: seven low-intermediate and ten upper-intermediate participants (A2 and B1+ levels respectively, according to the Common European Framework of Reference for languages). The rationale for excluding beginners is that *Astronautes FLS* presupposes basic knowledge of French, as players are required to read, hear, and orally react to time-sensitive commands.

2.2.2. Instruments, data collection, and procedure

During a four-week period, participants played the game individually at home or at their university and used the practice pronunciation feature for at least one hour per week. After this period, they were invited to play in group sessions so that the researchers could observe their interactions during gameplay. At the end of these sessions, a 15-statement survey (using a five item Likert scale, where 1=negative and 5=positive) was distributed to participants to obtain their perceptions of the game. It asked students questions about the impact *Astronautes FLS* had on their learning experience, according to the four themes established earlier: the game's ability to increase students' *motivation, enjoyment, comfort,* and *learning.* We also conducted focus group discussions in which participants were encouraged to expand on their perceptions of the game.

3.   Results

Table 1 shows that the participants perceived *Astronautes FLS* highly positively across the four composite themes, with mean values at or above the 'agree with' level.

Table 1.   Survey results of two proficiency groups

Survey questions	Mann-Whitney U Test	Proficiency			
		B1 + (n=10)		A2 (n=7)	
		Mean	SD	Mean	SD
1. Increased motivation	.417	4.2	0.79	3.77	1.11
2. Increased level of comfort	.193	4.4	0.8	3.9	1.18
3. Sense of enjoyment	.133	4.77	0.43	4.29	0.9
4. Impact on learning, improvement	.475	4.14	0.78	4.29	1.08

The results of the nonparametric tests using an Independent Samples Mann-Whitney U Test indicate that there were no significant differences between the two groups for the four composite variables, as shown in Table 1. This indicates that participants perceived the pedagogical affordances of *Astronautes FLS* similarly, regardless of their level of proficiency in French.

These results were corroborated by statements during focus group discussions, in which the participants stated that *Astronautes FLS* (1) increased their motivation to practice/learn (e.g. "It forced me to speak in French, and read, and my friends were correcting my pronunciation"), (2) created a comfortable environment in which to use the language (e.g. "It was so engaging, because you just kind of immerse yourself, in that I just don't think about how accurate I am"), (3) provided an overall sense of enjoyment (e.g. "that way people can get more familiar and we could have more fun in class"), and (4) positively impacted their learning (e.g. "It made me correct my pronunciation, because you have the chance to repeat some words, pronounce it better next time").

4.   Discussion and concluding remarks

The main goals of this study were to introduce *Astronautes FLS*, a non-serious cooperative digital game created to motivate L2 learners to learn and practice French, and to examine the game's pedagogical potential via an investigation of learners' perceptions across two proficiency groups.

Our results show that *Astronautes FLS* was perceived positively across the four major composite themes included in the study and that, regardless of their level of French proficiency, the participants of both groups perceived the pedagogical affordances of the game similarly. As such, these findings corroborate our hypotheses that the pedagogical use of *Astronautes FLS* could lead to students' increased *motivation* (Ducate & Lomicka, 2009), *enjoyment* (Allen et al., 2014), *comfort* (Liakin et al., 2017), and consequently have a positive impact on *learning* (Kukulska-Hulme, 2016).

Some of the methodological limitations of this study include the small number of participants and the short duration of the study. In future research, we would like to verify whether the participants' positive perceptions about the game's positive impact on learning are reflected in actual learning gains in terms of vocabulary and pronunciation (including holistic measures such as intelligibility and comprehensibility, and more specific measures such as fluency in speaking, listening and reading).

Our results suggest that *Astronautes FLS* is a fun and engaging game for the L2 classroom with great potential to motivate students and contribute to creating a comfortable and joyful learning environment. It encourages fluency through input (reading, listening) and output (speaking intelligibly) practice, and creates a non-threatening environment to experiment with language which could be 'anytime anywhere' – one of the pedagogical affordances of *Astronautes FLS*.

5.   Acknowledgements

Thanks to the participants and the following individuals for their contribution to this study: Jennica Grimshaw, Henry Smith, Katia Primeau, Sonia Corbeil, Anne-Marie Sénécal, Rhonda Chung, June Ruivivar, and Jeremy Lane.

This project was partially funded by the *Social Sciences and Humanities Research Council* (Canada).

References

Allen, L., Crossley, S., Snow, E., & McNamara, D. (2014). L2 writing practice: game enjoyment as a key to engagement. *Language Learning & Technology, 18*(2), 124-150.

Cardoso, W., Grimshaw, J., & Waddington, D. (2015). Set super-chicken to 3! Student and teacher perceptions of Spaceteam ESL. In F. Helm, L. Bradley, M. Guarda & S. Thouësny, Sylvie (Eds), *Critical CALL – Proceedings of the 2015 EUROCALL Conference, Padova, Italy* (pp. 102-107). Research-publishing.net. https://doi.org/10.14705/rpnet.2015.000317

Ducate, L., & Lomicka, L. (2009). Podcasting: an effective tool for honing language students' pronunciation? *Language Learning & Technology, 13*(3), 66-86.

Godwin-Jones, R. (2014). Games in language learning: opportunities and challenges. *Language Learning & Technology, 18*(2), 9-19.

Grimshaw, J., & Cardoso, W. (2018). Activate space rats! Fluency development in a mobile game-assisted environment. *Language Learning & Technology, 22*(3), 159-175.

Kukulska-Hulme, A. (2016). *Personalization of language learning through mobile technologies: part of the Cambridge papers in ELT series*. Cambridge University Press.

Liakin, D., Cardoso, W., & Liakina, N. (2017). Mobilizing instruction in a second-language context: learners' perceptions of two speech technologies. *Languages, 2*(3), 11, 1-21. https://doi.org/10.3390/languages2030011

Nation, I. S. P., & Newton, J. (2009). *Teaching ESL/EFL listening and speaking*. Routledge.

Stockwell, G. (2010). Using mobile phones for vocabulary activities: examining the effect of the platform. *Language Learning & Technology, 14*(2), 95-110.

Sykes, J., & Reinhardt, J. (2013). *Language at play: digital games in second and foreign language teaching and learning*. Pearson.

From computer-assisted language learning to digitally mediated intercultural communication

Paul A. Lyddon[1]

Abstract. Digital technologies have proliferated communications between speakers of different languages, but the widespread use of online machine translation has now become a disruptive force for foreign language education, as it permits intelligible exchanges between persons with little or no knowledge of a foreign tongue. As machine translation technology only continues to improve, the entire purpose of foreign language learning, computer-assisted or otherwise, may one day soon likely be called into question. While nothing is ever truly future-proof, the sustainability of foreign language education may require a shift in focus, away from traditional language acquisition and toward social semiotic awareness and multimodal intercultural communication. This paper describes a reconceptualization of language education from this proposed perspective. It then suggests possible roles for digital technologies in sustainable language teaching.

Keywords: symbolic competence, intercultural communicative competence, sustainable foreign language teaching.

1.   Introduction

Technological development has facilitated globalization, which in turn has brought formerly distant peoples from diverse cultures into much more frequent contact with one another and, thus, unquestionably increased the need for communication between them. However, the degree to which the normalization of such intercultural interactions has correspondingly increased the need for additional language proficiency (aside from English) is debatable, as globalization has also led to significant cultural homogenization and language extinction. Moreover,

1. University of Shizuoka, Shizuoka, Japan; palyddon@u-shizuoka-ken.ac.jp

How to cite this article: Lyddon, P. A. (2018). From computer-assisted language learning to digitally mediated intercultural communication. In P. Taalas, J. Jalkanen, L. Bradley & S. Thouësny (Eds), *Future-proof CALL: language learning as exploration and encounters – short papers from EUROCALL 2018* (pp. 171-175). Research-publishing.net. https://doi.org/10.14705/rpnet.2018.26.832

public pages on internationally popular social media platforms reveal countless examples of 'good enough' communication between interlocutors with sometimes very limited knowledge of each other's linguistic code. Whether these types of exchanges are the product of machine translation, emergent pidgins, or some combination thereof, to deny their existence or acceptability would be unrealistic. In short, digital technologies have fundamentally altered the nature of modern communication, and foreign language educators would be wise to take these developments into consideration in envisioning their professional future.

2.   Background

Most introductory-level foreign language study being compulsory, its justification has long been an important concern. Fortunately, with the advancement of digital technologies and the advent of the Internet, computer-assisted language learning has progressed from the largely drill-based applications of its earliest years to the custom-made collections of atomized didactic resources of today (Gimeno-Sanz, 2016), now often including tools for bringing learners together online to provide them with real opportunities for actual communication.

However, a critical distinction needs to be made here between language acquisition and mere use. While computer-mediated communication activities and social media interactions may arguably be more interesting and enjoyable than traditional classroom-based lessons, these types of exchanges often exhibit liberal code mixing, which, though undeniably permissible if not absolutely obligatory in these situations, does not readily promote the pushed output that might motivate mastery of linguistic forms with potentially greater currency.

A parallel phenomenon even more threatening to foreign language education than code mixing, however, is the indiscriminate use of machine translation. As freely available online tools have now made possible the instant translation of dozens of languages into countless others with a mere click of a button, naïve language users may be reinforced in the common misconception of communication as a more or less mathematical process, whereby messages are formulaically encoded into their equivalent linguistic symbols in the head of one person and then methodically transmitted for systematic decoding by another. Such a view may be fine if one simply wants to know the gist of what is being said, but it renders the issue of language acquisition in this case virtually irrelevant. In some ways, this predicament might be considered an unfortunate extension of undisciplined communicative language learning, whereby 'good' communication has been universally supplanted by the 'good enough', only now it is no longer even human learners producing the target language.

Given the increasingly integrated and interdependent economies in our globalized society, international communication is indeed more necessary than ever, but the implications for foreign language education are anything but clear. Of course, for the foreseeable future, there will still be a demand for highly proficient foreign language users who master the traditional body of relevant linguistic knowledge and skills. However, these individuals have always comprised but a fraction of total enrollments. Thus, in light of these recent and rapid technological developments and the trending responses to them, some key questions for the profession are these: What do most L2 learners really need to know in order to be able to effectively communicate for their own purposes? And how might that impact on our pedagogy?

3.   Discussion

Even if learners could manage translations of low-context transactional language without machine assistance, we would do well not to insist, as there is little workplace demand for humans to perform routine, repetitive, and predictable tasks that machines can accomplish faster and more economically (Ford, 2015). Instead, we should emphasize skills that machines neither currently possess nor are soon likely to, such as creativity and critical thinking. In this vein, we should first try to dispel the misconception of communication as mainly denotative, transactional language by highlighting the connotative and interactional aspects. For example, learners should be made to reflect on what they are actually trying to achieve with language and how. Borrowing a core tenet from mainstream translation theory, we must go beyond lexico-grammatical issues and carefully examine the textual and pragmatic (Baker, 1992).

Next, we need to foster symbolic competence, that is, understanding of the complexity, ambiguity, and formal meanings of communication (Kramsch, 2006). Learners need to be able to recognize the meaning potentials of various semiotic resources, each with its own conventional sociocultural and historical uses and significations. They need to be cognizant of probable interpretations, all the while maintaining awareness of the ever-present possibility of divergence. Furthermore, they must acknowledge form (including not only linguistic but also non-linguistic modes of expression) as having sociocultural implications even when seemingly lacking semantic significance. To this end, teachers need to adopt a "multilingual mindset", which Kramsch (2014) characterizes as embracing "diversity of meaning, as expressed through the different codes, modes, modalities, and styles that have currency in a global world that is now constantly and ubiquitously interconnected" (p. 253).

In addition to symbolic competence, we should also foster intercultural communicative competence, starting with raising learners' sociolinguistic and cultural self-awareness. Although national identity and presumed culture play pivotal roles in interlingual encounters (Byram, 1997), learners should realize that every individual, regardless of national origin, represents a unique constellation of differing gender, ethnicity, age, and social class group memberships and that all communication is, thus, essentially intercultural. In this way, they can come to appreciate their foreign language learning experience even if they never again have opportunity to use the language itself. To this end, we should help learners recognize conventional uses and interpretations of various semiotic resources within the competing discourse communities to which these individuals already belong. One way this goal might be advanced is through explicit treatment of often unconscious and implicit factors that shape all our communications, whether or not they occur in discernibly different linguistic varieties. Following the discourse approach of Scollon and Scollon (2001), we can then assist learners in improving their ability both to reduce ambiguity through greater shared knowledge about participant identities and to deal with any miscommunication that still inevitably arises.

Finally, as to the specific role of digital technologies in these efforts, a non-exhaustive list of a few of the possibilities includes the following:

- cross-cultural comparisons of authentic multimedia texts modeling pragmatic language use between interlocutors with different social roles and relationships;

- instruction on effective online dictionary and translator use, especially in conjunction with corpus analyses to highlight collocational associations and contextual constraints;

- discourse analyses of recorded online intercultural exchanges; and

- online games, including not only drills but also role plays.

The point here is not to imply anything novel in the individual or collective pedagogical use of authentic multimedia texts, online linguistic reference and research tools, online exchanges, or online games themselves. Rather it is to suggest a shift in their focus, away from the acquisition of primarily linguistic elements and toward an informed understanding and the skillful use of multimodal semiotic resources.

4. Conclusion

While digital technologies have brought the world's peoples into closer contact, they have also disrupted conventional interlingual communications such that the end goal of foreign language education is now ironically in question. In response, we must shift our pedagogical focus from transactional to interactional language use and expand the traditional notion of language arts to include not only linguistic modes of meaning-making but non-linguistic ones as well. Moreover, we should teach the use of digital media for integrating these various semiotic resources into rich, multimodal expressions of thought and feeling in order to foster greater symbolic and intercultural competence. In this way, we can hope to make our profession the truly humanistic endeavor it should be.

References

Baker, M. (1992). *In other words: a coursebook on translation*. Routledge.

Byram, M. (1997). *Teaching and assessing intercultural communicative competence*. Multilingual Matters.

Ford, M. (2015). *Rise of the robots: technology and the threat of a jobless future*. Basic Books.

Gimeno-Sanz, A. (2016). Moving a step further from "integrative CALL": what's to come? *Computer Assisted Language Learning, 29*(6), 1102-1115. https://doi.org/10.1080/095882 21.2015.1103271

Kramsch, C. (2006). From communicative competence to symbolic competence. *Modern Language Journal, 90*(2), 249-252. https://doi.org/10.1111/j.1540-4781.2006.00395_3.x

Kramsch, C. (2014). The challenge of globalization for the teaching of foreign languages and cultures. *Electronic Journal of Foreign Language Teaching, 11*(2), 249-254.

Scollon, R., & Scollon, S. W. (2001). *Intercultural communication: a discourse approach*. Blackwell.

Introducing the European NETwork
for COmbining Language LEarning
and Crowdsourcing Techniques (enetCollect)

Verena Lyding[1], Lionel Nicolas[2], Branislav Bédi[3], and Karën Fort[4]

Abstract. We present enetCollect, a large European network project funded as a COST Action that sets ground for combining crowdsourcing with IT technologies used in areas such as language learning and Natural Language Processing (NLP). This project tackles a major challenge of bringing together interdisciplinary researchers to foster language learning of all European citizens from diverse socio-demographic, cultural, educational, and linguistic backgrounds. It aims at unlocking a crowdsourcing potential available for all languages, including less widely spoken languages, in order to create language resources and achieve a coverage of material for teaching the languages. It will meet its research and capacity-building goals by creating an international community of researchers that will work on producing a comprehensive theoretical framework and running prototypical experiments to benefit a wide range of users and languages, while considering ethical, legal, and business issues. This article informs about its objectives, expected impact and strategic organisation that contribute to reaching its flexible and sustainable success goals.

Keywords: crowdsourcing, computer assisted language learning, language resources, COST Action.

1. Eurac Research, Bolzano, Italy; verena.lyding@eurac.edu
2. Eurac Research, Bolzano, Italy; lionel.nicolas@eurac.edu
3. University of Iceland, Reykjavík, Iceland; brb19@hi.is
4. Sorbonne Université, Paris, France; karen.fort@sorbonne-universite.fr

How to cite this article: Lyding, V., Nicolas, L., Bédi, B., & Fort, K. (2018). Introducing the European NETwork for COmbining Language LEarning and Crowdsourcing Techniques (enetCollect). In P. Taalas, J. Jalkanen, L. Bradley & S. Thouësny (Eds), *Future-proof CALL: language learning as exploration and encounters – short papers from EUROCALL 2018* (pp. 176-181). Research-publishing.net. https://doi.org/10.14705/rpnet.2018.26.833

1.   Introduction

EnetCollect was founded as a large European network project through COST Association for four years starting from March 2017. The project tackles the major European challenge to foster the language learning of all citizens with diversified cultural, educational, linguistic, and socio-demographic backgrounds by combining the well-established domain of language learning (Godwin-Jones, 2011) with recent crowdsourcing approaches (Brabham, 2008).

The demand for language learning is continuously increasing due to ongoing globalisation and political happenings, i.e. migration. Also, learner profiles are getting more diversified in terms of the learners' language backgrounds, daily realities, and communicative needs. This calls for more adapted learning content to optimally serve the individual learner, and to increase the ecology of learning (Blewitt, 2006). At the same time, the Internet has opened new possibilities for a collaborative development; sharing and reusing content for language learning has never been easier.

2.   Objectives and approach

EnetCollect aims to research and promote the possibilities that crowdsourcing offers for language learning. It can provide a long-term solution to the complex and ever-changing demands on language learning by involving the 'crowd' in creating and improving language learning materials.

In Computer Assisted Language Learning (CALL), Duolingo (von Ahn, 2013) is an example of a language-learning platform which follows a similar logic as enetCollect in offering free learning services for numerous languages while crowdsourcing lessons and translations through exercises.

EnetCollect distinguishes two forms of crowdsourcing approaches, as follows. *Explicit* crowdsourcing involves a crowd that intentionally participates in data creation, i.e. by providing language content for teaching and curricula design for specific languages. It is based on the 'wisdom-of-the-crowd' approach that enables stakeholders to collaboratively create resources of common interest, as implemented for example in the language learning platform Memrise, the online dictionaries Dict.cc, Wiktionary, Lingobee (Procter-Legg, Cacchione, & Petersen, 2012), and the well-known Wikipedia. *Implicit* crowdsourcing involves a crowd that is not necessarily aware of its participation. It includes generating exercises and content based on learner's achievements, e.g. Games-With-A-Purpose (GWAPs) (Chamberlain et al., 2013; Lafourcade, Brun, & Joubert, 2015). The learners' activities are monitored in terms of difficulties and errors, the efficiency in completing different exercises, and learning analytics. This involves features from intelligent CALL (iCALL) (Gamper & Knapp, 2002). Based on this, enetCollect will explore new opportunities for autonomous and life-long learning, and concentrate on the practical implementation of theories with regard to learning materials that respond not only to the learner's individual pace but also to the content and, as opposed to Duolingo, to the overall curricula design for each language individually.

3.   Structure of the network and implementation strategies

The network is structured into five specialised Working Groups (WGs) and three coordination groups (Outreach, Exploitation, and Dissemination). It is steered by the Core Group and the Management Committee (MC) (see Figure 1). About 200 researchers from more than 40 countries representing different domains, e.g. CALL, crowdsourcing, NLP, e-lexicography, computer science, ethics, law, and business have joined forces. WG1 deals with approaches for the collaborative creation of teaching content (*explicit* crowdsourcing). WG2 is concerned with the integration of *implicit* crowdsourcing techniques into interactive learning content (e.g. gap filling exercises), which allows for the harvesting of information and data about learners. WG3 researches the usability and user experience of learning platforms in order to assure to attract and retain enough learners and tutors. WG4 addresses technical challenges related to an online learning environment for numerous distributed clients, such as scalability and robustness. Finally, WG5 deals with ethical, legal, and commercial perspectives. The coordination groups, i.e. Outreach, Exploitation, and Dissemination, support the WGs with transversal tasks enabling optimal communication and knowledge exchange within and outside of enetCollect.

The objective is to carry out the groundwork for setting into motion a new research and innovation trend for the creation of online language learning solutions. The WGs will explore innovative approaches for the production and enhancement of online teaching materials, the opportunities posing the integration of crowdsourcing techniques into learning environments, and the blending of learning content with gamification and data harvesting. This effort can particularly be beneficial for less widely taught languages with smaller speaker communities that have limited language resources (Mariani, 2015) because it will enable them to gather data for teaching and provide these to learners, who would otherwise have a very limited access to such materials. While for lesser spoken languages it can be particularly challenging to involve a sufficient number of participants, the extent of the network, together with the gamification layer, comprehensiveness, and online nature of its approach, foster participation and support to a maximum. Depending on the type of language resources dealt with, the completion of material gathering can be achieved with semi-automatic methods (Sagot, 2010) related to *explicit* and *implicit* crowdsourcing, which will collaboratively devise lesson content (*explicit* crowdsourcing) and generate exercise content for individual learners based on their progress and feedback (*implicit* crowdsourcing).

Figure 1.   Organisational structure of enetCollect

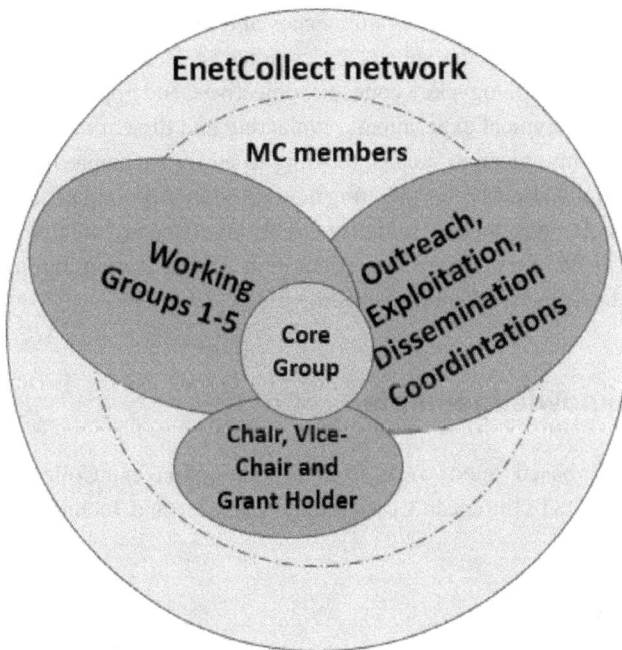

Having a manpower producing language resource materials can result in high costs (Böhmová, Hajic, Hajicova, & Hladka, 2001), but crowdsourcing offers a cost-effective solution. For instance, both Wikipedia, which redefined the domain of encyclopedias, and reCAPTCHA, have made the highly laborious task of manual writing and annotation possible by obtaining a workforce from the crowd. The content providers will upload and share content via telecollaboration across the boundaries of local territories, thus making it available as free, partially free, or paid, all depending on the business scheme, maintenance, and overall support of official authorities. The assurance of quality can also be part of a crowd feedback. Different types of users will evaluate the usefulness and trustworthiness of content via different reward and feedback mechanisms. The problem of ethics is also a very important in this context and will be addressed in connection with data collection and usage, and personal data protection using an ethics by design approach (Spiekermann, 2015).

4.   Conclusion and future work

EnetCollect aims both at reviewing the state-of-the-art in order to gather and compile an overview of relevant approaches and techniques, and at achieving a shared understanding of the subject by creating an interdisciplinary framework for defining its terminology, key concepts, objectives, and opportunities. It aims at carrying out prototypical experiments, evaluating and disseminating their results. It possesses communication means allowing to easily exchange information and reach relevant stakeholders for targeting new research stays, organised workshops, training schools, and funded initiatives. The involvement of new and current members will be pursued through promotion of the Action through relevant channels of the research domains concerned.

5.   Acknowledgements

This article is based upon work from COST Action enetCollect (CA16105) supported by COST (European Cooperation in Science and Technology).

References

Blewitt, J. (2006). *The ecology of learning. Sustainability, lifelong learning and everyday life.* (1st ed.). Earthscan.

Böhmová, A., Hajic, J., Hajicova, E., & Hladka, B. (2001). The Prague dependency treebank: three level annotation scenario. In A. Abeillé (Ed.), *Treebanks: building and using syntactically annotated corpora.* Kluwer Academic Publishers.

Brabham, D. C. (2008). Crowdsourcing as a model for problem solving. An introduction and cases. *Convergence: The International Journal of Research into New Media Technologies, 14*(1), 75-90. https://doi.org/10.1177/1354856507084420

Chamberlain, J., Fort, K., Kruschwitz, U., Lafourcade, M., & Poesio, M. (2013). Using games to create language resources: successes and limitations of the approach. In I. Gurevych et al. (Eds), *The people's web meets NLP. Theory and applications of natural language processing* (pp. 3-44). Springer. https://doi.org/10.1007/978-3-642-35085-6_1

Gamper, J., & Knapp, J. (2002). A review of intelligent CALL systems. *Computer Assisted Language Learning, 15*(4), 329-342. https://doi.org/10.1076/call.15.4.329.8270

Godwin-Jones, R. (2011). Emerging technologies : mobile apps for language learning. *Language Learning & Technology, 15*(2), 2-11. http://llt.msu.edu/issues/june2011/emerging.pdf

Lafourcade, M., Brun, N. L., & Joubert, A. (2015). *Games with a purpose (GWAPs)*. Wiley. https://doi.org/10.1002/9781119136309

Mariani, J. (2015). Technologies de la langue : état des lieux. In *Proceedings of the workshop on the Technologies pour les Langues Régionales de France, Meudon, France*.

Procter-Legg, E., Cacchione, A., & Petersen, S. A. (2012). Lingobee and social media: mobile language learners as social networkers. *Paper presented at the International Association for Development of the Information Society (IADIS) International Conference on Cognition and Exploratory Learning in Digital Age (CELDA), Madrid, Spain, Oct 19-21, 2012*. https://eric.ed.gov/?id=ED542698

Sagot, B. (2010). The Lefff, a freely available and large-coverage morphological and syntactic lexicon for French. In *Proceedings of the 7th international conference on Language Resources and Evaluation (LREC 2010), Valletta, Malta. May 2010*.

Spiekermann, S. (2015). *Ethical IT innovation: a value-based system design approach*. CRC Press. https://doi.org/10.1201/b19060

Von Ahn, L. (2013). Duolingo: learn a language for free while helping to translate the web. In *Proceedings of the 2013 international conference on Intelligent user interfaces* (pp. 1-2). ACM. https://doi.org/10.1145/2449396.2449398

Tracking and analysing the learner behaviour of non- and low-literate adults in an online literacy training environment

Eva Malessa[1]

Abstract. This study investigated what log files can reveal about learner behaviour of low- and non-literate adults learning to read for the first time in Finnish as a second language. The participants' reading development was supported by practising in an online training environment. Log files, automatically created user-computer interaction records, were chosen as empirical evidence as their analysis enables in-depth post-activity exploration of student behaviour. The quantitative analysis resulted in user profiles containing information on learner engagement, performance and productivity. Overall, the results demonstrate that individual learning performance, process, and progress can be studied and reflected on holistically by investigating the individual's digital learning footprints, their log files. Log files are an accurate and precise, yet currently underemployed research tool. More easy-to-use tools for non-experts are in demand, as current Data Mining (DM) tools are designed for computer scientists and need to be developed further to become accessible and applicable by practitioners and educational researchers.

Keywords: log files, learner behaviour, late literacy, computer-assisted language learning.

1.   Introduction

A growing number of low- and non-literate adults are immigrating to highly literate countries. According to Cucchiarini, van de Craats, Deutekom, and Strik (2013, p. 96), 10-15% of the European immigrant population is estimated to be non- or

1. University of Jyväskylä, Jyväskylä, Finland; eva.i.malessa@jyu.fi

How to cite this article: Malessa, E. (2018). Tracking and analysing the learner behaviour of non- and low-literate adults in an online literacy training environment. In P. Taalas, J. Jalkanen, L. Bradley & S. Thouësny (Eds), *Future-proof CALL: language learning as exploration and encounters – short papers from EUROCALL 2018* (pp. 182-187). Research-publishing.net. https://doi.org/10.14705/rpnet.2018.26.834

low-literate. In Finland, the world's most literate country (Miller & McKenna, 2016), adult non-literacy is highly unusual and consequently, there is a paucity of academic research on how non-literate adults acquire skills in Finnish as their second language (for a review see Malessa, 2018). In practice, basic language courses are often insufficient to achieve functional literacy, even in the very transparent Finnish orthography (see Tammelin-Laine & Martin, 2015).

The 'Digital Literacy Instructor' (DigLin) was pioneered to provide Computer-Assisted Language Learning (CALL) support to low- or non-literate migrants learning to read in English, Finnish, German, or Dutch. The project (2013-2015), funded by the European Commission, enabled the development of the DigLin software which provided systematic instruction in sound-letter connections, basic decoding, and word recognition. The DigLin training environment included 300 words with seven different exercise types, including 'Listen and drag the letters' (DL) and 'Listen and drag the words' (DW), see Figure 1 below.

Figure 1. Screenshot of a DL (left) and DW (right) task

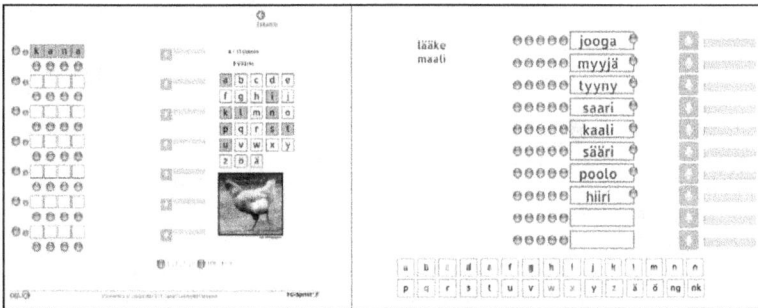

The aim of the current mixed-method study was to analyse the learners' log files automatically generated during the use of the software and to explore what log files can reveal about learner behaviour.

2. Method

2.1. Tracking computer-user interaction with log files

This study's seven participants tested the DigLin software for a period of four to six months (for details see Malessa & Filimban, 2017). The learners' software use, including mouse/keyboard movements and microphone recordings, was automatically tracked by log files. Time-stamped log files provide detailed and objective tracking data that can be employed to make inferences about learner knowledge, processes, and strategies (Chapelle, 2007, pp. 98-99). They are currently underemployed mainly due to the extensiveness of their collected interaction records (Bruckman, 2006, p. 1449), illustrated by Figure 2.

Figure 2.   Extract of a DigLin log file

```
7632;"[""04FIN""314""]";"FIN";"2014-10-30 09:21:20";"2014-10-30 09:23:58";"Drag the letters
4a";"[{""type"":""play_word_sound""  data"":""sauna""      timestamp"":""2014-10-30
09:21:20""    data_extra"":""""}     {""type"":""hide_word_picture""       data"":""""
    timestamp"":""2014-10-30 09:21:21""  data_extra"":""""}
    {""type"":""show_word_picture""     data"":""sauna""      timestamp"":""2014-10-30
09:21:21""    data_extra"":""""}    {""type"":""letter_drag""     data"":""s""
    timestamp"":""2014-10-30 09:21:26""  data_extra"":""""}
    {""type"":""letter_drag_right""  data"":""""     timestamp"":""2014-10-30 09:21:28""
data_extra"":""""}      {""type"":""letter_drag""     data"":""a""
    timestamp"":""2014-10-30 09:21:32""  data_extra"":""""}
    {""type"":""letter_drag_right""  data"":""""     timestamp"":""2014-10-30 09:21:34""
data_extra"":""""}      {""type"":""letter_drag""     data"":""u""
    timestamp"":""2014-10-30 09:21:34""  data_extra"":""""}
    {""type"":""letter_drag_right""  data"":""""     timestamp"":""2014-10-30 09:21:42""
data_extra"":""""}      {""type"":""letter_drag""     data"":""n""
    timestamp"":""2014-10-30 09:21:44""  data_extra"":""""}
    {""type"":""letter_drag_right""  data"":""""     timestamp"":""2014-10-30 09:21:45""
data_extra"":""""}      {""type"":""letter_drag""     data"":""a""
    timestamp"":""2014-10-30 09:21:49""  data_extra"":""""}
    {""type"":""letter_drag_right""  data"":""""     timestamp"":""2014-10-30 09:21:49""
```

Figure 2 presents the user interaction in a DL exercise. The documentation (workload) of dragging the letters for the word *sauna* (09:21:21-09:21:49 =29 seconds) emphasises the comprehensiveness of log file raw data. The workload contains details regarding the exact start/end date of the event, exercise type, type of actions taken, data involved, and provided feedback (right/false).

2.2.   Raw data preparation and DM procedures

DigLin's log file dataset provided the empirical data for this study. Log files were accessed via phpMyAdmin and extracted for pre-processing, followed by DM, in which data is stored electronically in existing databases and the search is automated or augmented by computers (Witten, Frank, & Hall, 2011, p. 3). An initial analysis of the raw dataset supplied 3,141 log files. The data was then prepared for DM.

An event log dataset of 2,497 log files was created for the qualitative analysis, excluding no event data. For DM of this extensive database, computerised, Educational Data Mining (EDM) tools were investigated. However, faced with a limited timescale, non-expert computing skills, and the lack of an easy-to-use tool, EDM was conducted manually with the computer software Excel. Furthermore, the scope of this study's qualitative analysis was limited to 133 log files. The data were restricted to the exercise types DL and DW (see Figure 1) as both focus on the initial stages of reading development, training visual/aural grapheme-phoneme correspondences.

3.   Results and discussion

This study's motivation was to investigate "what learners actually do, not what the researcher assumes instructions and task demands will lead learners to do" (Swain, 1998, p. 80). The results indicate that even though the testing sessions were relatively long (averaging 60 minutes), users were actively engaged, spending their time almost exclusively on-task. Log files' workloads record user actions and system feedback, thus providing information on how successful users perform in specific exercises. The overall success rate for letter drags in DL was unexpectedly high (78.81%), however, the users' performance was only studied for the specific skills trained in the exercises and therefore universal statements about learner proficiency are impossible to make. Further, the log files revealed that learner productivity did not equal learner performance, as the most industrious decoder was not the most successful, nor the most successful the most productive.

Qualitative log-file analysis showed that learners employed various ways to solve tasks and all strategies were not equally well-suited for all users. In many instances, the lack of successful strategies indicated an inability to learn independently, while increased autonomy and decoding proficiency were seen to stem from an increased use of efficient strategies. As log files track every single event, they show whether and how often learners make use of the provided help tools. In DL users could press buttons to listen to letter and word sounds for the words they were decoding, in DW they could listen to the words' letter sounds and were provided with an additional helptool, a soundbar (see Figure 1). The results indicate a correlation between learner proactivity, using the tools independently, and decoding success.

"Sometimes the absence of activity can be as revealing as its presence" (Bruckman, 2006, p. 1451), and log files prove that learners do not always do what they are expected to, e.g. independently exploring and employing all provided resources (word sets, exercises, help tools). These revelations should be taken into account to enhance the CALL application's design and effectiveness. Additionally, the results also emphasise weaker students' need for more instruction and help regarding successful strategies.

4.   Conclusions

This study has been a challenging, yet rewarding exploration of a new realm, log files. In sum, even though manual DM is very time-consuming and cumbersome, the results also show that it is not impossible. Nevertheless, this study acknowledges that the manual mining procedure applied to the overwhelming abundance of log files made the analysis highly prone to human error and possibly weakened the scientific rigor of the current study to some degree. Log files provide unique and innovative research data, but easy-to-use tools for non-experts are urgently needed to benefit from the valuable knowledge hidden away in the computer mines. As EDM is a relatively young research field, it remains to be seen *when* not whether EDM can make a contribution to research "in terms of providing tools and techniques that educational technology researchers can easily grasp and apply to their own research" (Angeli et al., 2017, p. 227).

References

Angeli, C., Howard, S. K., Ma, J., Yang, J., & Kirschner, P. A. (2017). Data mining in educational technology classroom research: can it make a contribution? *Computers & Education, 113*, 226-242. https://doi.org/10.1016/j.compedu.2017.05.021

Bruckman, A. (2006). Analysis of log file data to understand behavior and learning in an online community. In J. Weiss, J. Nolan, J. Hunsinger & P. Trifonas (Eds), *International handbook of virtual learning environments* (pp. 1449-1465). Springer. https://doi.org/10.1007/978-1-4020-3803-7_58

Chapelle, C. A. (2007). Technology and second language acquisition. *Annual Review of Applied Linguistics, 27*, 98-114. https://doi.org/10.1017/S0267190508070050

Cucchiarini, C., van de Craats, I., Deutekom, J., & Strik, H. (2013). The digital instructor for literacy learning. In B. Badlin, T. Hueber, G. Bailly, D. Demolin & F. Raby (Eds), *Proceedings of SLaTE 2013* (pp. 96-101). Grenoble.

Malessa, E. (2018). Learning to read for the first time as adult immigrants in Finland: reviewing pertinent research of low-literate or non-literate learners' literacy acquisition and computer-assisted literacy training. *Journal of Applied Language Studies, 12*(1), 25-54. https://doi.org/10.17011/apples/urn.201804051932

Malessa, E., & Filimban, E. (2017). Exploring what log files can reveal about LESLLA learners' behaviour in an online CALL environment. In M. Sosiński (Ed.), *Language and literacy. Teaching LESLLA students. Proceedings of the 12th annual LESLLA symposium* (pp. 149-159). University of Granada.

Miller, J. W., & McKenna, M. C. (2016). *World literacy: how countries rank and why it matters.* Routledge. https://doi.org/10.4324/9781315693934

Swain, M. (1998). Focus on form through conscious reflection. In C. Doughty & J. Williams (Eds), *Focus on form in classroom second language acquisition* (pp. 64-81). Cambridge University Press.

Tammelin-Laine, T., & Martin, M. (2015). The simultaneous development of receptive skills in an orthographically transparent second language. *Writing Systems Research, 7*, 39-57. https://doi.org/10.1080/17586801.2014.943148

Witten, I. H., Frank, E., & Hall, M. A. (2011). *Data mining: practical machine learning tools and techniques* (3rd ed.). Morgan Kaufmann.

JYVÄSKYLÄN YLIOPISTO
UNIVERSITY OF JYVÄSKYLÄ

Exploring virtual collaborative writing in the EFL classroom

Antonio Martínez-Sáez[1], Avelino Corral-Esteban[2],
and Margarita Vinagre-Laranjeira[3]

Abstract. With the integration of new technologies in the foreign language classroom, the practice of collaborative writing has gained renewed attention, although some questions still remain unanswered regarding the extent to which these tools help learners in their writing when compared to more traditional learning contexts (Elola & Oskoz, 2010). In order to explore these issues, we analysed the written production of 84 undergraduate students of English as a Foreign Language (EFL) using the LIWC2015[4] software. The analysis revealed significant differences in categories such as word count, clout, emotional tone, or analytical thinking when comparing the texts written by an experimental and a control group. Moreover, regarding discourse, some differences were observed in terms of the way information was presented and structured.

Keywords: language learning, collaborative writing, virtual collaboration, discourse analysis.

1. Introduction

The effects of collaborative writing – "the co-authoring of a text by two or more writers" (Storch, 2013, p. 2) – has become the focus of much research in recent years. Some studies suggest "that collaborative writing promotes reflective thinking,

---

1. Universidad Politécnica de Madrid, Madrid, Spain; antonio.martinezs@upm.es
2. Universidad Autónoma de Madrid, Madrid, Spain; avelino.corral@uam.es
3. Universidad Autónoma de Madrid, Madrid, Spain; margarita.vinagre@uam.es
4. Linguistic Inquiry and Word Count. Software published by Pennebaker Conglomerates, Inc, Austin, TX, USA. For more information go to http://liwc.wpengine.com/how-it-works/

How to cite this article: Martínez-Sáez, A., Corral-Esteban, A., & Vinagre-Laranjeira, M. (2018). Exploring virtual collaborative writing in the EFL classroom. In P. Taalas, J. Jalkanen, L. Bradley & S. Thouësny (Eds), *Future-proof CALL: language learning as exploration and encounters – short papers from EUROCALL 2018* (pp. 188-192). Research-publishing.net. https://doi.org/10.14705/rpnet.2018.26.835

---

focusses attention on grammatical accuracy, lexis, and discourse, and encourages a pooling of knowledge about language" (Donato, 1994; Storch, 2013, cited in Oskoz & Elola, 2011, p. 209). In order for collaborative writing to be successful, some authors have mentioned that students have to become truly involved and engaged in the activity (e.g. Oskoz & Elola, 2011).

However, there are still some unanswered questions regarding the differences between the process of collaborative writing in more traditional contexts and in those in which technology has been integrated in the classroom. We are referring more specifically to telecollaborative environments, which are gaining renewed attention and becoming more relevant among researchers who study their effects on collaborative writing (Elola & Oskoz, 2010). In this study, we have used the term *telecollaboration* to refer to an activity in which students, who are in face-to-face environments, use technologies to collaborate (Vinagre, 2016). In its more strict sense, this activity refers to students who are located in different countries and use technologies to carry out tasks or project work together.

Given its potential, in this study we analyse the collaboratively written production of a group of students who worked in this environment (experimental group) and that of another group who wrote collaboratively in class (control group).

2. Complexity, accuracy, fluency, and discourse analysis

Complexity, accuracy, and fluency "represent three dimensions of L2 production" and are "of value to L2 language teachers as they can use the research findings to improve their practice and their students' language performance" (Craven, 2017, p. 25). In general terms and in line with Craven's (2017) definitions, complexity is seen as "the use of more challenging and difficult language"; accuracy as "the degree of conformity to certain language usage norms", primarily in lexicon and grammar; and fluency as "a person's general language proficiency in relation to ease and smoothness of speech or writing" (p. 25).

In order to compare the written production of both groups, we decided to use LIWC2015 software since some of the variables it measures (see below) are based on the complexity and fluency factors mentioned above. Besides, the software also analyses other relevant features for this study – including cohesive devices such as reference, repetition, substitution, ellipsis, conjunction, and connectors (Schiffrin, 2001).

3.   Method

Eighty-four first year students of English at Autónoma University of Madrid participated in this study. Their levels of proficiency in the foreign language ranged from a B1 to a C1 (all according to the Common European Framework of Reference for Languages).

Students were divided randomly into two groups. Students in the experimental group used Google Docs as a technological tool to write a joint collaborative essay based on a list of suggested topics working in small groups. Similarly, students in the control group used pen and paper to carry out the same task also working in small groups. Eleven texts in total were produced by the experimental and the control group respectively.

The texts were then introduced in LIWC2015. This tool processes text files and displays categories such as word count, analytical thinking, clout, authentic, emotional tone, words per sentence, words including more than six letters, the total number of function words, etc. Furthermore, as explained on this software's website, "the text analysis module [...] compares each word in the text against a user-defined dictionary"[5]. Most of its output variables are expressed as percentage of total words, with the exception of Word Count (WC; raw word count), mean Words Per Sentence (WPS), and four summary variables: *analytic*, *clout*, *authentic*, and *tone*. These summary variables are "standardised composites which have been converted to percentiles based on large corpora of texts described in the *LIWC2015 Language Manual*" (Pennebaker, Booth, Boyd, & Francis, 2015, pp. 6-7).

4.   Results and discussion

The results show that there were some significant differences between the texts produced by both groups in some of the categories analysed by LIWC2015. For instance, the total number of words written by the students in the experimental group was 2,452, whereas the control group wrote only 1,451. The group working in the virtual environment also obtained higher results in the following categories (definitions available from Pennebaker et al., 2015, p. 22): *clout*, which reflects "a higher level of expertise and confidence" (experimental group: 93.21 / control group: 80.73); *tone*, which is "associated with a more positive and upbeat style" (experimental: 77.55 / control: 12.87); and *function words* (experimental: 52.98 / control: 50.03).

---

5. http://liwc.wpengine.com/how-it-works/

In contrast, as illustrated in Table 1, the control group achieved higher results in other categories such as *analytical thinking*, i.e. "more formal, logical, and hierarchical thinking", and *authentic*, associated with "a more honest, personal, and disclosing text" (Pennebaker et al., 2015, p. 22).

Table 1.   Results of the analysis of the rest of variables

	Analytic	Authentic	Words/sentence	Words > 6 letters
Control group	83.33	13.33	17.91	21.23
Experimental group	45.89	5.99	13.78	18.11

These results suggest that students in the experimental group tended to be more productive, showed a higher level of expertise, and felt more confident and positive. However, students in the control group preferred to adopt a more formal and personal approach to the task. Besides, they wrote longer and more complex words. A plausible explanation for these findings could be that students in the control group tended to focus more on the task itself, on what and how they wrote it, and at the same time they reflected more on the format and wording of their final joint essay. The experimental group, on the other hand, seemed to focus more on the collaborative interaction than on the task, as can be deduced from their levels of confidence and positivity (Vinagre & Corral, 2017).

As regards discourse analysis tokens, some differences were observed in terms of the way information was presented and structured. As already mentioned, students in the control group tended to focus mostly on formal aspects, such as a more frequent and accurate use of cohesive devices and adequate paragraph separation, whereas those in the experimental group focussed more on content and included a higher number of new relevant ideas related to the topic of their essays. In this respect, it is possible that by giving priority to the collaborative interaction over the task, the students in the experimental group feel freer to explore and discuss other relevant ideas that can enrich their task.

5.   Conclusions

The findings suggest that the students in the control group were more focussed on the variables based on complexity, which highlights the idea that they might adopt a more reflective and even cautious attitude in face-to-face interaction when having to reach agreements on the words and structure of their essays. Other factors explaining these results could be related to the importance of reinforcing and constructing a more positive and desirable personal identity. In contrast, students using the technological tool to write their joint essay achieved better results in the variables based on fluency. Moreover, these findings suggest that in a telecollaborative environment, students feel freer to explore, discuss, and add more ideas and thus write longer texts since they might also tend to adopt a less inhibited attitude.

6. Acknowledgements

This research was funded by the Spanish Ministry of Economy and Competitiveness (EDU2014-54673R).

References

Craven, L. (2017). Measuring language performance: complexity, accuracy and fluency measures. *The 2017 WEI International Academic Conference Proceedings.* https://www.westeastinstitute.com/wp-content/uploads/2017/02/Laurence-Craven.pdf

Donato, R. (1994). Collective scaffolding in second language learning. In J. Lantolf & G. Appel (Eds), *Vygotskian approaches to second language research* (pp. 33-56). Ablex.

Elola, I., & Oskoz, A. (2010). Collaborative writing: fostering foreign language and writing conventions development. *Language Learning & Technology, 14*(3), 30-49.

Oskoz, A., & Elola, I. (2011). Meeting at the Wiki: the new arena for collaborative writing in foreign language courses. In M. J. Lee & C. McLoughlin (Eds), *Web 2.0-based e-learning: applying social informatics for tertiary teaching.* Information Science Reference. https://doi.org/10.4018/978-1-60566-294-7.ch011

Pennebaker, J. W., Booth, R. J., Boyd, R. L., & Francis, M. E. (2015). *Linguistic inquiry and word count: LIWC2015 Operator's Manual.* Pennebaker Conglomerates.

Schiffrin, D. (2001). Discourse markers: language, meaning, and context. In D. Schiffrin, D. Tannen & H. E. Hamilton (Eds), *The handbook of discourse analysis.* Blackwell Publishers.

Storch, N. (2013). *Collaborative writing in L2 classrooms.* Multilingual Matters. https://doi.org/10.21832/9781847699954

Vinagre, M. (2016). Developing key competences for life-long learning through virtual collaboration: teaching ICT in English as a medium of instruction. In C. Wang & L. Winstead (Eds), *Handbook of research on foreign language education in the digital age* (pp. 170-187). IGI Global. https://doi.org/10.4018/978-1-5225-0177-0.ch008

Vinagre, M., & Corral, A. (2017). Evaluative language for rapport building in virtual collaboration: an analysis of appraisal in computer-mediated interaction. *Language and Intercultural Communication, 18*(3), 335-350. https://doi.org/10.1080/14708477.2017.1378227

Analysing students' perceptions of two learning and evaluation modalities in the InGenio FCE Online Course and Tester

Antonio Martínez-Sáez[1], Ana Sevilla-Pavón[2], and Ana Gimeno-Sanz[3]

Abstract. Instructors have to make important decisions regarding the type of assessment that will finally be implemented when producing online learning materials, since this has a noticeable effect in terms of the methodology, the approach, and the attitude of all the actors involved (Goertler, 2011). This study investigates students' perception of tutor assessment and self-assessment in an online upper-intermediate level English course (described in Martínez-Sáez, 2015) and testing tool (described in Sevilla Pavón, 2013). After the implementation of these learning resources through the online authoring tool and content manager InGenio[4], 95 students participated in the study conducted for the validation stages. The statistical analysis of the data gathered by means of questionnaires showed that the students highly appreciated the freedom to learn at their own pace offered by these two modalities which can contribute to autonomous progress and learning.

Keywords: attitudes, assessment, online resources, validation.

1.   Introduction

Students' attitudes and motivation are two components which play a central role in language learning (Grzib-Schlosky, 2002; Martínez-Sáez, 2015). These features, along with learners' specific goals, interests, needs, or expectations, were deemed key to strategic objectives during the production of the InGenio learning resources,

1. Universidad Politécnica de Madrid, Madrid, Spain; antonio.martinezs@upm.es
2. Universitat de València, València, Spain; ana.m.sevilla@uv.es
3. Universitat Politècnica de València, València, Spain; agimeno@upvnet.upv.es
4. InGenio was designed and developed at Universitat Politècnica de València

How to cite this article: Martínez-Sáez, A., Sevilla-Pavón, A., & Gimeno-Sanz, A. (2018). Analysing students' perceptions of two learning and evaluation modalities in the InGenio FCE Online Course and Tester. In P. Taalas, J. Jalkanen, L. Bradley & S. Thouësny (Eds), *Future-proof CALL: language learning as exploration and encounters – short papers from EUROCALL 2018* (pp. 193-199). Research-publishing.net. https://doi.org/10.14705/rpnet.2018.26.836

and have been the basis for the research described in this paper. The resulting courseware comprises an online course and a tester aimed at helping students track their own progress before facing any official upper-intermediate English exam – B2-level according to the Common European Framework of Reference for Languages (CEFRL).

Upon designing and developing the courseware, research was conducted on the importance of assessment within the learning process and the theoretical distinction between several pedagogical strategies in an attempt to improve the learning and evaluation method offered to the final users. The authors explored how online authoring tools and content managers, and in particular, InGenio, contribute to effectiveness and efficiency when two modalities such as self-assessment and tutor assessment are integrated into the resulting resources in order to allow students to monitor their process. One of the main advantages reported was the flexibility and adaptability provided to the students by this type of system (Sevilla-Pavón, Martínez-Sáez, & Macario de Siqueira, 2011).

In the design and development stages, special attention was paid to the variants known as tutor assessment, i.e. an autonomous online learning process monitored by a lecturer, and self-assessment, i.e. an autonomous online learning process in which students receive previously designed automatic feedback, hints, as well as model answers (both in the written and oral sections). The first modality "leads to the development of the students' autonomy and sense of responsibility over the learning process, while enabling students to get as much help and support as they need from a human tutor in order to both complete the different tasks and attain the target level of language" (Sevilla-Pavón et al., 2011, p. 47). The second modality "enables students to conduct their own learning process and to assess their own learning achievements in an independent and autonomous way" (Sevilla-Pavón et al., 2011, p. 47). These were the two learning and evaluation methods which were finally integrated into the courseware in order to respond to the highly demanding requirements and standards of an effective self-access online course (Gimeno-Sanz, 2009; Levy & Stockwell, 2006).

2.   Method

This paper addresses a specific part of the InGenio Course and Tester validation study conducted throughout two consecutive academic years (2011-12 and 2012-13). A total number of 95 undergraduate students took part in it. They had previously enrolled on the course 'Computer-Assisted English' (4.5 ECTS), an online subject offered at Universitat Politècnica de València. All students were granted access to the *InGenio FCE Online Course & Tester* (Module 1)[5] and were asked to complete all their contents in one semester. Therefore, all the students engaged in both tutoring assessment and self-assessment, i.e. the two learning and evaluation variants finally incorporated into the resulting courseware.

Two different questionnaires (available from Martínez-Sáez, 2015) were designed so as to monitor students' progress and perceptions of a wide variety of components before (pre-course survey) and after (post-course survey) completing the first module of the Course and Tester. Among the components measured by these surveys administered through Google Forms, the following stand out: (1) length, usefulness, and effectiveness of the theoretical and practical contents; (2) the templates provided by the online authoring tool; (3) feedback; (4) interaction between the user and the platform; and (5) the range of assessment options.

Thus, in this part of the study, the participants rated and evaluated the above-mentioned learning and assessment modalities. They also compared them with other learning scenarios in order to determine which alternative would best suit their needs and interests. In so doing, the fourth part of the pre-course survey was entitled 'Learning styles' and included two multiple-choice and two open-ended questions. As for the post-course survey, it was based on a 7-point Likert scale and included several enquiry items relating to learning and assessment modalities. These items were queried in two different sections: 'General features' and 'Student self-assessment and personal comments', comprised of four and seven questions, respectively.

Due to the significant amount of data retrieved through the two questionnaires, only the most outstanding findings relating to the aims of this paper will be included.

3. Results and analysis

3.1. Pre-course survey

In the initial questionnaire, the 95 students had to decide on the best way to learn a language; their preference went for a Face-to-Face (F2F) course in the classroom with a teacher (see Figure 1). These preferences can be compared with the results displayed in Figure 3.

---

5. The first module of the Course and Tester was implemented in 2011.

Figure 1.   The best way to learn a language is… (pre-course survey)

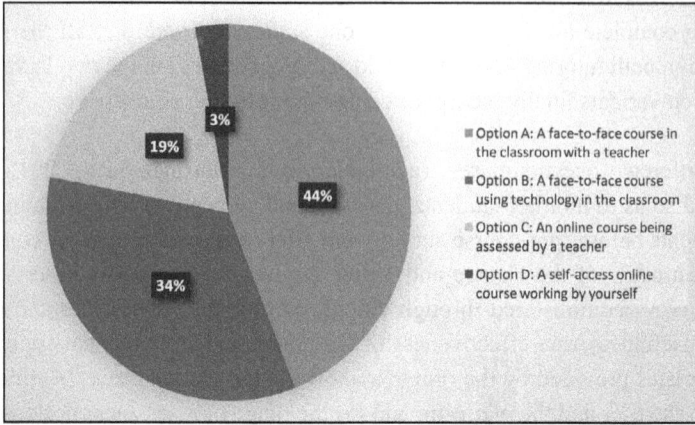

Figure 2 illustrates the participants' perceptions when asked about the most appropriate assessment modality in that particular online learning context. In the open-ended questions, a high number of students reported that flexibility is seen as an essential component when learning a language and that they highly valued feedback provision.

Figure 2.   Which learning modality would you prefer?

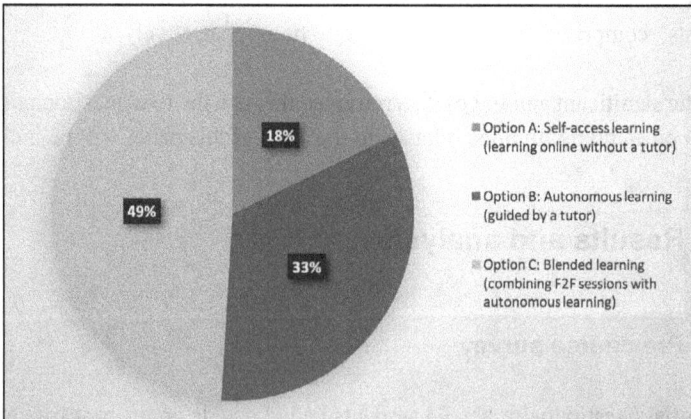

3.2.   Post-course survey

A total number of 49 students completed all the Course and Tester contents and tasks and participated in this survey. In Section A, they rated four factors relating to the learning and assessment modalities. As shown in Table 1, the participants reported that "the Course and Tester encouraged autonomous / independent learning" (Item 17). A high number also emphasised how "they enjoyed having freedom to organise their time their own way" (Item 19) and "being able to self-assess their progress by accessing the assessment reports" (Item 21). Furthermore, the feedback they received was seen as very useful and relevant by most of the students.

Table 1.   Section A (Likert scale)

	1	2	3	4	5	6	7
Item 17			6%	12%	33%	39%	10%
Item 19		2.5%	2.5%	16%	12%	20%	47%
Item 21			2%	14%	31%	29%	24%

Section C, the third part of the post-course questionnaire, provided evidence of students' very positive attitude towards the use of technology and, in particular, to online environments after completing the Course and Tester. They also found it very easy to work autonomously.

Figure 3 illustrates that the students' general perception of the best modality to join a language course had experienced some changes when compared with the same question in the first questionnaire. The percentages of Options C and D were still very low in the final survey. However, there was an increase of 11% in the number of students who opted for Option B, which had a clear negative impact on Option A.

Figure 3.   The best way to learn a language is… (post-course survey)

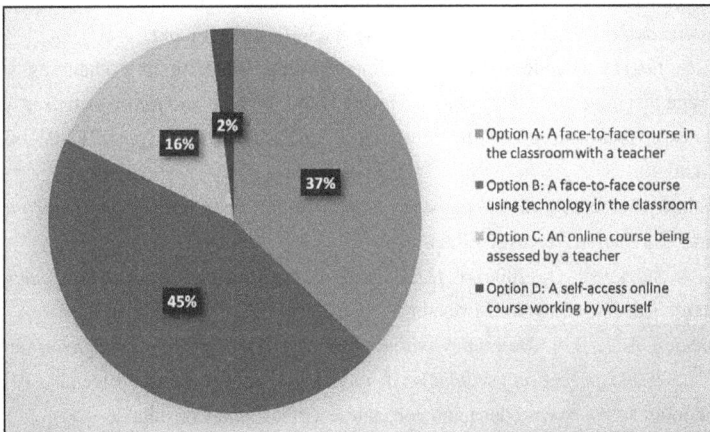

4.   Conclusions

As seen in the previous section, students' perceptions of the courseware and most of the components were very positive. An outstanding number welcomed features such as being able to self-assess their own progress and felt comfortable working in an online environment. However, when asked about their general perception of the best modality to take a language course, a significant number of learners still reported a preference for a hypothetical blended-learning alternative combining the F2F classroom component being assisted by a lecturer or tutor with an appropriate use of the online resources provided. Even though technology, flexibility, and adaptability were seen as fundamental and motivating features, the support given by the human component was highly appreciated.

5.   Acknowledgements

We would like to thank the Valencian Regional Government (Generalitat Valenciana).

Antonio Martínez-Sáez and Ana Sevilla-Pavón were still holders of a four-year research grant (FPI) when the data began to be collected.

References

Gimeno-Sanz, A. (2009). Online courseware design and delivery: the InGenio authoring system. In I. González-Pueyo, C. Foz Gil, M. Jaime Siso & M. J. Luzón Marco (Eds), *Teaching academic and professional English online* (pp. 83-105). Peter Lang.

Goertler, S. (2011). Blended and open/online learning: adapting to a changing world of language teaching. In N. Arnold & L. Ducate (Eds), *Present and future promises of CALL: from theory and research to new directions in language learning* (pp. 471-502). CALICO Publications.

Grzib-Schlosky, G. (2002). *Bases cognitivas y conductuales de la motivación y emoción*. Centro de Estudios Ramón Areces (CERA).

Levy, M., & Stockwell, G. (2006). *CALL dimensions: options and issues in computer-assisted language learning*. Lawrence Erlbaum.

Martínez-Sáez, A. (2015). *Materiales online para el aprendizaje y la evaluación del inglés: análisis, diseño, propuesta y validación de recursos*. Doctoral Thesis. Universitat Politècnica de València. https://www.educacion.gob.es/teseo/irGestionarConsulta.do

Sevilla-Pavón, A., Martínez-Sáez, A., & Macario de Siqueira, J. (2011). Self-assessment and tutor assessment in online language learning materials: InGenio FCE Online Course and Tester. In S. Thouësny & L. Bradley (Eds), *Second language teaching and learning with technology: views of emergent researchers* (pp. 45-69). Research-publishing.net. https://doi.org/10.14705/rpnet.2011.000006

Sevilla Pavón, A. (2013). *Desarrollo, implementación y validación de recursos multimedia para la enseñanza y la evaluación del nivel B2 de inglés en contextos de educación superior a través del sistema InGenio*. Doctoral Thesis. Universitat Politècnica de València.

JYVÄSKYLÄN YLIOPISTO
UNIVERSITY OF JYVÄSKYLÄ

Automatic scaffolding for L2 listeners by leveraging natural language processing

Maryam Sadat Mirzaei[1], Kourosh Meshgi[2], and Toyoaki Nishida[3]

Abstract. This paper introduces a new captioning tool, Partial and Synchronized Caption with Hints (PSCH), as a means to facilitate second language (L2) listening by providing cues for ambiguous and difficult words/phrases in the caption while filtering out the easy words. Each word in the caption is synchronized to the corresponding audio to enable text-to-speech mapping. The words to be shown in the caption are carefully selected by defining the features that lead to listening difficulty. The hints are generated in the form of short explanations/definitions of the words to allow for meaning construction and resolving difficulties on-the-fly. With the use of Natural Language Processing (NLP) tools and word sense disambiguation, we tried to generate appropriate hints for the selected words to provide instantaneous and minimally intrusive assistance. Experimental results revealed that learners' scores significantly increased when they used PSCH compared to having no hints. Furthermore, PSCH received positive learner feedback in providing appropriate and useful hints for improving listening comprehension.

Keywords: partial and synchronized caption, L2 listening difficulty, word ambiguity, instantaneous hints.

1. Introduction

L2 listening entails constant effort as the listeners need to process each part of the input quickly, without having the option to return to the earlier points. Learners must go through perception, recognition, comprehension, meaning construction, ambiguity resolution, and inferencing, etc. in a short time (Rost, 2005), which

1. Kyoto University, Kyoto, Japan; mirzaei@ii.ist.i.kyoto-u.ac.jp
2. Kyoto University, Kyoto, Japan; meshgi-k@sys.i.kyoto-u.ac.jp
3. Kyoto University, Kyoto, Japan; nishida@i.kyoto-u.ac.jp

How to cite this article: Mirzaei, M. S., Meshgi, K., & Nishida, T. (2018). Automatic scaffolding for L2 listeners by leveraging natural language processing. In P. Taalas, J. Jalkanen, L. Bradley & S. Thouësny (Eds), *Future-proof CALL: language learning as exploration and encounters – short papers from EUROCALL 2018* (pp. 200-206). Research-publishing.net. https://doi.org/10.14705/rpnet.2018.26.837

imposes large working memory loads (Chang, 2009). To foster L2 listening, captioning is used as a popular tool that facilitates the comprehension of the input by allowing for reading the text along with listening to the audio. The use of captions, however, is subjected to some limitations as it promotes more reading than listening, thus inhibiting listening skill development (Pujolà, 2002).

To alleviate these problems, we introduced a Partial and Synchronized Captioning (PSC) system which selects limited numbers of words/phrases and presents them in the caption by synchronizing each word to its relevant speech segment (word-level text-to-speech alignment). The selection of words in PSC is based on the factors that cause difficulty for L2 listeners, such as word frequency, specificity, and speech rate. Additionally, more acoustic features were added by extracting the Automatic Speech Recognition (ASR) system's errors as a source that indicates perception difficulties in the given audio (Mirzaei, Meshgi, & Kawahara, 2018).

Through the experiments, Mirzaei et al. (2018) found that PSC can assist L2 listeners by successfully detecting and presenting difficult segments. However, further observations suggested that merely showing the words in the captions may not provide the optimal assistance, especially for words out of the learner's vocabulary reservoir. In such cases, learners' attention is confined to the ambiguous segment, which inhibits them from moving on to process the next input. This happens particularly for those who overemphasize on using bottom-up strategies and word-by-word decoding (Osada, 2004).

Figure 1. Screenshot of a TED talk with PSCH, which includes instantaneous hints

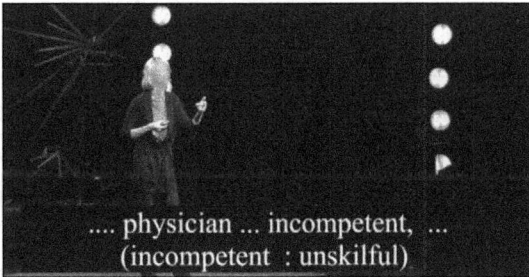

To address this issue, we augmented PSC with Hints (PSCH) to provide minimal assistance on the spot, when learners encounter difficult/ambiguous segments. This assistance is provided in the form of context-matching synonyms, short definitions, named entity tags, or co-references for such segments (Figure 1). Only 30% of the words are shown in PSC and one-third of these words are accompanied with hints, to promote more listening than reading and using top-down strategies for comprehension.

2. Instant scaffolding for L2 listeners

The process of generating PSCH involves: (1) determining the words/phrases that need supplementary description or clarification, and (2) providing useful description for them to assist learners.

First, we focus on the problematic categories that were specified by L2 listeners including: low-frequency, technical, ambiguous, and polysemous words, proper nouns, named entities, ambiguous references, and uncommon/multi-purpose abbreviations. Low frequency words were detected in PSC by referring to the corpora (BNC and COCA). For detecting other categories, however, we use NLP techniques for parsing, analyzing, extracting information (e.g. named entities and part-of-speech), and resolving ambiguities (e.g. co-references and word sense) of the transcript. We leverage the state-of-the-art open-source NLP libraries such as CoreNLP (Manning et al., 2014), NLTK, and spaCy.

We used the Term Frequency/Inverse Document Frequency (TF/IDF) index and/ or domain-specific encyclopedias to find technical/specific jargon, WordNet synset size to detect polysemous/homonym words, named-entity recognizers and part-of-speech taggers to identify proper nouns, and Wikipedia and the Urban Dictionary to determine symbolic names and abbreviations (Figure 2).

Figure 2. PSCH system architecture

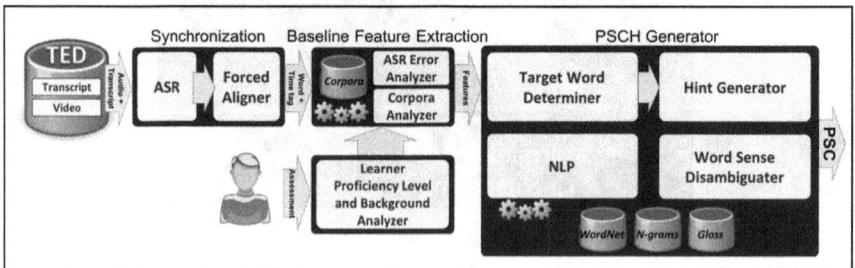

Next, the proper hints for each category are retrieved from in-house and online resources. A synonym is selected as the hint for low-frequency words (e.g.

cobble→put together). Wikipedia and glosses are consulted for word definitions and abbreviation expansions (e.g. neocortex→part of mammalian brain). Short descriptions are retrieved for proper nouns, named-entities, and symbolic names from Wikipedia and the Google search engine (e.g. Basel→city in Switzerland, big apple→New York City). The referent of references is displayed as a reminder hint if their co-reference was distant. For words with different meanings (e.g. polysemous words), we employed word sense disambiguation to find the most probable meanings from available synonyms/descriptions.

The hints provided to the learners should be short, helpful, and relevant. To this end, we seek the shortest description for the word or generate one by searching for the keywords in the retrieved description. Along with this, a filtering process assures that the final hint includes high-frequency words that are familiar for the learner. We carefully controlled the display of hints. Hints appeared in sync with the utterances and remained for a pre-defined duration, providing enough time for reading and processing the input.

3.   Experimental evaluation

3.1.   Participants

Our participants were 30 graduate and undergraduate students of intermediate English levels with TOEIC[4] scores ranging from 810-920.

3.2.   Procedure

The participants were asked to watch a series of short segments (two to three minutes) from eight TED talks using Baseline PSC (no hint) and PSCH (with hints). We selected 40 words from the videos that appeared in PSC, among which only 15 words were supplemented by hints and were used as the target words of our experiment. The rest were used as distractors.

First, the participants watched all the videos with the baseline PSC followed by a listening test on 40 words. The listening test was made by extracting short audio clips (10~15 seconds) from the experimental videos. The participants were asked to write the meaning of each word in the given context.

---

4. Test of English for International Communication®

Next, participants watched the videos with PSCH in shuffled order. On average, each video segment included six hints. Learners were then asked to take the same listening test only on the 15 target words with hints. We aimed to see the participants' performance on the target words before and after receiving the hints. A questionnaire was designed to elicit learner feedback on the usefulness of PSCH.

4.   Results and discussion

Figure 3(a) shows the result of participants' scores on defining the target words before and after receiving hints, which indicates a significant increase by the use of PSCH as compared to PSC. Figure 3(b) shows how the participants' answers changed before and after receiving hints. Results revealed that in most cases the answers were corrected after receiving hints (55%) but there were cases where participants could answer the questions correctly without having the hints (29%). Participants noted that in these cases hints were mostly used as a confirmation rather than assistance.

Figure 3.   (a) Participants scores using PSC (with no hints) and PSCH (with hints);
(b) Distribution of participants' answers before and after receiving hints

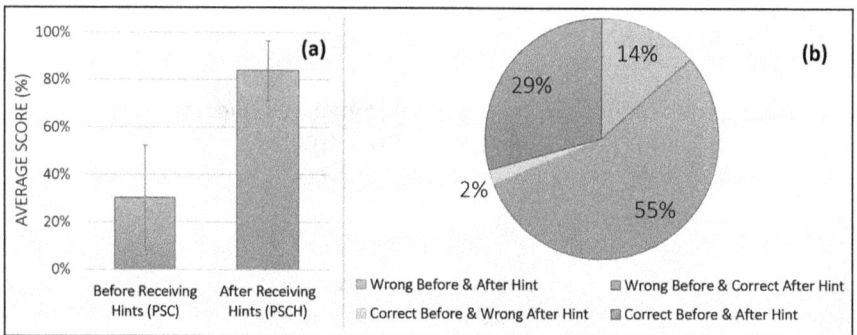

Figure 4 demonstrated learner feedback on PSCH and the type of hints provided during the experiment. The figure suggests that the majority of the participants found the hints easy to understand, useful to resolve difficulty, and helpful to comprehend the content on-the-fly, which highlights the benefit of instantaneous assistance and concurrent lexical support to facilitate L2 listening (Rost, 2005). It was noted, however, that at some points hints were not necessary as the words were easy or common, whereas, for some other words, participants preferred to receive hints. This emphasizes the importance of adjusting the type and frequency of the hints with the learner's level and needs to provide more effective assistance (Durlach & Lesgold, 2012).

Figure 4. 5-point Likert-scale questionnaire on PSCH

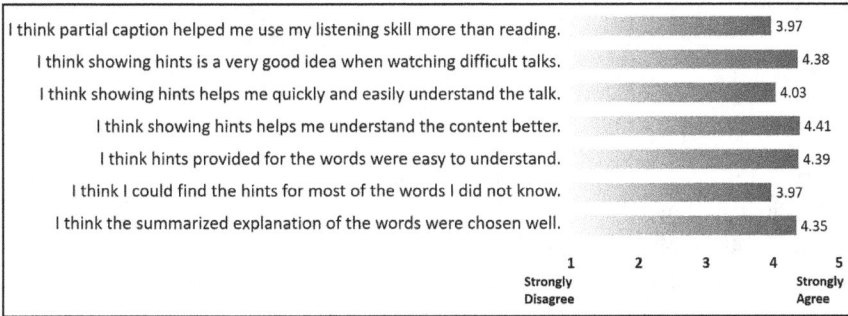

I think partial caption helped me use my listening skill more than reading.	3.97
I think showing hints is a very good idea when watching difficult talks.	4.38
I think showing hints helps me quickly and easily understand the talk.	4.03
I think showing hints helps me understand the content better.	4.41
I think hints provided for the words were easy to understand.	4.39
I think I could find the hints for most of the words I did not know.	3.97
I think the summarized explanation of the words were chosen well.	4.35

1 Strongly Disagree   2   3   4   5 Strongly Agree

5. Conclusions

This paper investigated the use of PSCH as a captioning system that detects difficult words in the listening material and presents them in the caption while supplementing some of them with hints in the form of short definitions when necessary. PSCH aims to provide necessary but minimal assistance to foster L2 listening by delivering instantaneous hints. Experimental results suggested that using PSCH has significantly assisted L2 listeners to disambiguate the content when listening on-the-fly and facilitated listening to the authentic materials. Findings also suggested that further improvement is needed by considering each individual's requirement to provide more learner-specific assistance.

6. Acknowledgements

This study was supported by Japan's MEXT Kakenhi grant No.17K02925. Baseline PSC was developed under supervision of Professor Tatsuya Kawahara, to whom we are always grateful.

References

Chang, A. C. S. (2009). Gains to L2 listeners from reading while listening vs. listening only in comprehending short stories. *System, 37*(4), 652-663.

Durlach, P. J., & Lesgold, A. M. (2012). *Adaptive technologies for training and education.* Cambridge University Press. https://doi.org/10.1017/CBO9781139049580

Manning, C. D., Surdeanu, M., Bauer, J., Finkel, J., Bethard, S. J., & McClosky, D. (2014). The Stanford CoreNLP Natural Language Processing Toolkit. In *Proceedings of ACL* (pp. 55-60).

Mirzaei, M. S., Meshgi, K., & Kawahara, T. (2018). Exploiting automatic speech recognition errors to enhance partial and synchronized caption for facilitating second language listening. *Computer Speech & Language, 49*, 17-36. https://doi.org/10.1016/j.csl.2017.11.001

Osada, N. (2004). Listening comprehension research: a brief review of the past thirty years. *Dialogue, 3*, 53-66.

Pujolà, J. T. (2002). CALLing for help: researching language learning strategies using help facilities in a web-based multimedia program. *ReCALL, 14*(2), 235-262. https://doi.org/10.1017/S0958344002000423

Rost, M. (2005). L2 listening. In E. Hinkel (Ed.), *Handbook of research in second language teaching and learning* (pp. 503-527). Erlbaum.

JYVÄSKYLÄN YLIOPISTO
UNIVERSITY OF JYVÄSKYLÄ

Language learning through conversation envisioning in virtual reality: a sociocultural approach

Maryam Sadat Mirzaei[1], Qiang Zhang[2],
Stef van der Struijk[3], and Toyoaki Nishida[4]

Abstract. This study proposes a virtual reality platform for language learners to practice a Target Language (TL) and develop cross-cultural competencies through interaction with peers or an AI-agent (limited scope), followed by a scheme for engaging learners to envision their conversations by disclosing their thoughts, reasoning, feelings, and expectations. This platform, Virtual Reality Conversation Envisioning (VRCE), enables the learners to fully share a contextual, immersive environment, simulated in Virtual Reality (VR), to have free conversations by performing role-plays on proposed topics. VRCE is designed to provide first person views during conversation and third person views during envisioning so that learners can take the role of participants and meta-participants at each phase. Learners envision the conversation individually at certain points during the role-play review. Their envisioning is then shared with their conversational partner to detect the misunderstandings, observe the situation from each other's perspective, and to learn about sociocultural cues that led to the different viewpoints. Participants' envisioning revealed interesting differences in their understanding of a shared situation. Findings showed that VRCE is an effective medium to raise learner collaboration and develop cross-cultural competencies.

Keywords: conversation envisioning, cross-cultural competencies, virtual reality, collaborative learning.

1. RIKEN AIP, Kyoto, Japan; maryam.mirzaei@riken.jp
2. Kyoto University, Kyoto, Japan; qiang.zhang@ii.ist.i.kyoto-u.ac.jp
3. Kyoto University, Kyoto, Japan; stef@ii.ist.i.kyoto-u.ac.jp
4. Kyoto University, Kyoto, Japan; nishida@ii.ist.i.kyoto-u.ac.jp

How to cite this article: Mirzaei, M. S., Zhang, Q., Van der Struijk, S., & Nishida, T. (2018). Language learning through conversation envisioning in virtual reality: a sociocultural approach. In P. Taalas, J. Jalkanen, L. Bradley & S. Thouësny (Eds), *Future-proof CALL: language learning as exploration and encounters – short papers from EUROCALL 2018* (pp. 207-213). Research-publishing.net. https://doi.org/10.14705/rpnet.2018.26.838

1.   Introduction

There has been increasing interest in the use of virtual worlds and simulated games for promoting language learning, raising cultural awareness, and developing communicative competencies (Deutschmann & Panichi, 2013; Peterson, 2011). Such platforms often focus on teaching discrete cultural points to the learners (Cheng, Yang, & Andersen, 2017), promote grammar and vocabulary acquisition (Johnson & Valente, 2009), and support real-time communication to fulfill a quest (Thorne, 2008). However, there is a paucity of research on making a platform that focuses on free-form conversation, the meta-analysis of the interactions, and knowledge transfer to develop a set of culture general skills. In today's culturally diverse world, the use of a foreign language has become the main means of communication among people of various backgrounds. However, when using a foreign language to interact with peers from different cultural backgrounds, building common ground on-the-fly becomes a challenge. It is known that learners bring their background culture to the conversation even when using a foreign language (Lado, 1964). This transfer effect can lead to interesting cross-cultural communications as well as peculiar misunderstandings that can be investigated to develop sociocultural competencies.

This paper proposes a platform to support real-time conversation between learners or with an AI agent (with limited scope) in VR and to envision the conversation by including learners and teachers as meta-participants for making a detailed contrastive analysis of the interactions. We conducted an experiment to see if the framework is effective in developing learners' cross-cultural competencies and smoothening conversations. We analyzed the learners' interactions and envisioning during the experiment from a sociocultural perspective.

2.   VRCE

VRCE has two modes, role-play and envisioning. It offers access to engage in social interaction with peers, native speakers of English, and an AI-agent (role-play), and endows learners with deft tools to reflect on their interactions and further perform a contrastive analysis of their reflections (envisioning). A series of negotiation scenarios such as bargaining, job offer, etc. were designed as a basis for learners' interaction. An AI agent is built to interact with learners by showing appropriate verbal and non-verbal reactions to the learner input on the given scenarios. The agent's reaction is taken from real-world scenarios and is augmented by the sociocultural notes, cues on the reasoning behind the agents' behavior, and hints for expected reactions, provided by meta-participants' analysis. During the interaction with the agent, learners could benefit from the envisioning notes that clarified why the conversation led to a particular direction. This part demonstrates how envisioning can help understanding the conversation better and what it takes to envision a conversation as a meta-participant.

Voice chat was used to support real-time communication and a motion capture system was used to track the participants' gestures and project them into their avatars to allow for natural communication. The platform is designed to support recording, rewinding and replaying learner collaborations and enables the learners to review, revise, or analyze their interactions. Learners can move back and forth through the branches of the conversation to revise their decisions or interaction (first person view) or later review their conversation as meta-analyzers to interpret their actions, provide notes on instances of cultural implications, and envision the conversation (third person view). In envisioning mode, VRCE allows the teachers, conversation analysts, or other learners (observers) to add indicators on different points of the conversation to prompt for participants' envisioning. The system requests explanation using the rubric shown in Figure 1.

Figure 1. VRCE for role-play and envisioning: (a,b) role-play in first person view, (c) role-play review in third person view and envisioning rubric, (d) envisioning provided by the participant

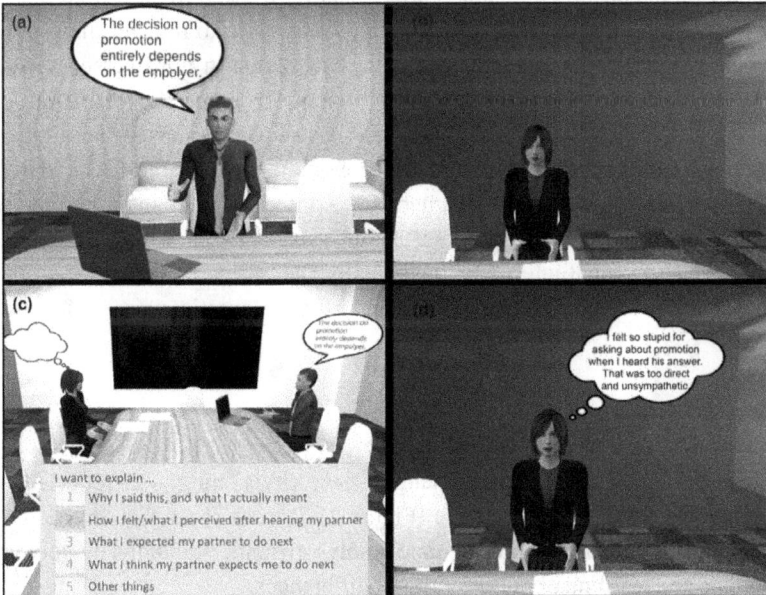

During envisioning, teachers can join the shared space to elicit learner's explanation and to provide them with necessary scaffold. After envisioning, the system allows for replaying the conversation augmented by the envisioning notes. This would serve as an example scenario with sociocultural cues to the other learners so that they can replay this scenario while benefiting from the cultural points provided by their peers earlier.

3. Experimental analysis

3.1. Participants

The participants in this study were 34 upper-intermediate learners of English from different cultural backgrounds. Participants were carefully grouped into pairs with different cultural backgrounds (e.g. Japanese versus French).

3.2. Procedure

The participants were placed in different rooms and did not meet each other before the experiment. They received a role-play scenario with secret conditions specified for each role. The conditions were set to encourage each participant to negotiate for achieving the desired outcome. Participants were asked to perform a role-play in first person view using VR. Motion capture was used to transfer their gestures into their avatars. The teacher observed the interaction in third person view and assigned indicators at various intervals to prompt for learners' explanation in the envisioning phase. After the role-play, each participant reviewed the interaction individually (third person view) and envisioned the conversation particularly for teacher-specified points. Next, learners were informed that their partner went through the same envisioning process, and their explanations will be exchanged to see if they had different interpretations. Finally, the two participants were asked to meet each other, have a short discussion and fill out a questionnaire.

4. Results

Learners' feedback after they exchanged their envisioning was reflected on a five point Likert scale questionnaire (Figure 2). Results show that envisioning in VRCE helped the learners to detect and resolve misunderstandings by comparing viewpoints and learning about the cultural differences.

Figure 2.   Participants' feedback on a five point Likert scale questionnaire for exchanged envisioning

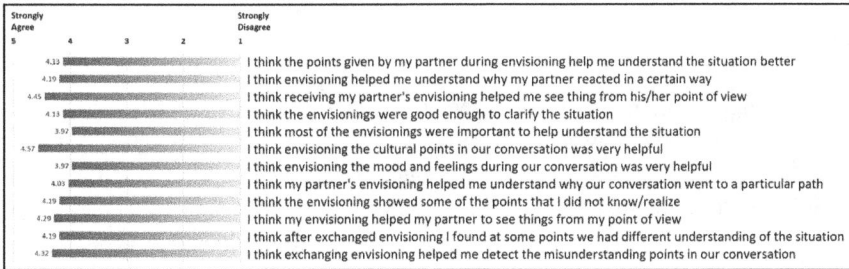

This result is supported by the collected data from the interactions and envisioning. Figure 3 shows an excerpt of the learners' interaction and their individual envisionings. As can be seen, what counted as an annoying direct question in one's culture and an instance of galling one's pride, was no more than a simple question out of curiosity that can be asked directly in another culture. By comparing the envisioning, both participants realized that they had different understandings of the same situation. Another interesting point in this excerpt is the negotiation of meaning when one participant misuses the word "disposable", which is noted by the peer.

Figure 3.   A sample excerpt of role-play and envisioning

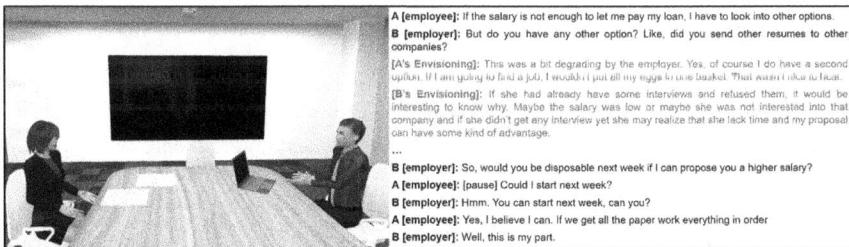

5.   Discussion and conclusion

Results suggest that the majority of participants highlighted the effectiveness of VRCE in facilitating cross-cultural interactions. Participants noted that contrastive analysis of their envisioning significantly assisted them in interpreting their interaction accurately, which in turn may lead to smoother future communication with their partner. Learners also pointed that reviewing the interaction in the third person view facilitated meta-analysis of the conversation and raised meta-linguistic awareness. One main complaint about this system was the lack of facial expressions in VR, which can be addressed by using a web-based 3D version in future.

Further analysis of participants' interactions in VRCE showed rich use of the TL both during role-play and envisioning. VRCE can be an effective medium to improve learner competencies by inducing activities that elicit TL dialogues. These activities involve collaboration, assistance, and co-construction such as negotiation of meaning, asking for clarification, resolving misunderstandings, and receiving support from more proficient peers, that are conducive to the operation of zones of proximal development (Vygotsky, 1978). It can be inferred from the observations that with frequent instances of collaborative learning (e.g. explaining specific cultural points) using the TL during role-play, envisioning and discussion, this framework can promote TL learning. Data showed that learners' interactions involved a high degree of learner input, as they actively engaged in the interpretations of the TL use and sociocultural points which promoted critical thinking. Finally, the game-like nature of the scenario raised learner motivation and the use of our fully immersive environment allowed the participants to get into their roles and benefit from situated and experiential learning (Kolb, 2014). In this view, VRCE is anticipated to promote fluency and smoother cross-cultural interaction in the long-term.

References

Cheng, A., Yang, L., & Andersen, E. (2017). Teaching language and culture with a virtual reality game. *2017 CHI Conference on Human Factors in Computing Systems* (pp. 541-549). ACM. https://doi.org/10.1145/3025453.3025857

Deutschmann, M., & Panichi, L. (2013). Towards models for designing language learning in virtual worlds. *International Journal of Virtual and Personal Learning Environments, 4*(2), 65-84. https://doi.org/10.4018/jvple.2013040104

Johnson, W. L., & A. Valente. (2009). Tactical language and culture training systems: using AI to teach foreign languages and cultures. *AI Magazine, 30*(2), 72-83. https://doi.org/10.1609/aimag.v30i2.2240

Kolb, D. A. (2014) *Experiential learning: experience as the source of learning and development.* FT press.

Lado, R. (1964). *Language teaching.* McGraw-Hill.

Peterson, M. (2011). Toward a research agenda for the use of three-dimensional virtual worlds in language learning. *CALICO Journal, 29*(1), 67-80. https://doi.org/10.11139/cj.29.1.67-80

Thorne, S. L. (2008). Transcultural communication in open internet environments and massively multiplayer online games. In S. Magnan (Ed.), *Mediating discourse online* (pp. 305-327). John Benjamins. https://doi.org/10.1075/aals.3.17tho

Vygotsky, L. (1978). *Mind in society*. MIT Press.

Vlogging in Toronto: learning Finnish through collaborative encounters

Anu Muhonen[1] and Riikka Kujanen[2]

Abstract. This case study is excerpted from a larger study where we explore collaborative encounters, i.e. practices and discourses, within a blended learning project where vlogging, i.e. video blogging, is used in Finnish language learning. The data has been collected in 2017-2018 during an intermediate Finnish course at the University of Toronto. In this paper, we investigate one student assignment and analyse what kind of collaborative encounters the use of vlogging creates outside the classroom. We analyse the discourse within the vlog with the support from ethnographically collected data (semi-structured interviews and written reflections). This study shows that vlogging implements the adoption of different collaborative encounters; a free time activity with friends creates a space for authentic and collaborative language learning.

Keywords: vlogging, collaboration, discourse, language learning, ethnography.

1. Introduction

Education is experiencing a shift from accessing and sharing information to designing communities where participants are actively engaging in deep and meaningful learning (Vaughan, Cleveland-Innes, & Garrison, 2013). In the *Finnish Studies Program* at the University of Toronto, vlogging is used as a language learning practice in an attempt to create meaningful and authentic opportunities for language use and to create spaces to learn collaboratively. Because of the long distance to Finland and only a few opportunities to meet Finnish speakers in Toronto, students have a limited exposure to Finnish outside the classroom. Encountering authentic language environments is, however, crucial for learning.

---

1. University of Toronto, Toronto, Canada; anu.muhonen@utoronto.ca
2. University of Toronto, Toronto, Canada; riikka.kujanen@gmail.com

How to cite this article: Muhonen, A., & Kujanen, R. (2018). Vlogging in Toronto: learning Finnish through collaborative encounters. In P. Taalas, J. Jalkanen, L. Bradley & S. Thouësny (Eds), *Future-proof CALL: language learning as exploration and encounters – short papers from EUROCALL 2018* (pp. 214-219). Research-publishing.net. https://doi.org/10.14705/rpnet.2018.26.839

Earlier studies have explored blogging as a tool for building communities between students (Ducate & Lomicka, 2008; Petersen, Divitini, & Chabert, 2008). Vlogging is reported to increase student talk time (Huang, 2015; Watkins, 2012). In this paper, we take a close look at one vlog produced by a student, Lisa, for a course task, where she talks about "Finnish things in Toronto". This paper analyses what kind of collaborative encounters the creation of this vlog creates outside the classroom. This is excerpted from a study where we explore altogether 31 vlogs within an intermediate Finnish language course in 2017-2018.

2. Aims, method, and data

In addition to the broadcasted and transcribed discourse in Lisa's vlog, the data consists of two sets of written reflections by Lisa based on the assignment. Further, we also conducted two semi-structured interviews based on the reflections. By analysis of the discourse (Blommaert, 2005) and the ethnographic data, we explore the following:

- What kind of collaborative encounters took place while Lisa was creating the vlog?

- How do they connect to Lisa's language learning?

3. Results: layers of collaborative encounters in vlogging in Finnish

When Lisa was given the assignment, she chose to vlog about her visit to a Finnish sauna in her friend's house. She says that selecting the topic "was very spontaneous", and continues: "they had a sauna in their basement, I just thought oh that's Finnish". A casual free-time activity created a setting to vlog, practise, and learn.

3.1. Layers of discourse in the sauna

Lisa engages her friends Anna and Jeff in her learning practice, and they are featured in the sauna vlog (see Table 1). The discourse begins, when Lisa describes the setting in Finnish ("olemme saunassa") and says that she loves the sauna. By referring to the participants as "we", she demonstrates that vlogging is a collaborative practice. She further says that she is in her friend Anna's sauna. Anna records the video and moves the camera to feature her face, when her name is mentioned (line 4). When Lisa suddenly (line 4) forgets what she was planning to utter, Anna (line 6) helps her by whispering "ystävien kanssa" (with friends). Lisa repeats the sentence "minä ystävien kanssa saunassa" and the vlog ends when Jeff throws water on the hot stones and utters "heitän löylyä".

Table 1.   Sauna vlog

1	Lisa	olemme saunassa <we are in the sauna>
2		minä rakastan sauna <I love sauna>
3		koska se on hauskaa <because it is fun>
4		ja tämä on Annan sauna <and this is Anna's sauna>
5		((the camera turns to Anna and back to Lisa))
6	Anna	((whispering)) ystävien kanssa <with friends>
7	Lisa	mina ystävien kanssa saunassa <I with friends in the sauna>
8	Jeff	heitän löylyä <I am throwing water on the hot stones>
9		((sound of water touching the hot stones))

3.2.   Layers of collaboration in language learning

Lisa engages her friends in her learning throughout the task. She reflects: "I wrote the script myself first and then Anna checked it over to make sure it made sense, then we rehearsed it a lot". Lisa revised and practised the content with Anna, who speaks Finnish. She practised the pronunciation of the discourse and repeated it to memorise it. Earlier research has shown that vlogging is beneficial for practising vocabulary and oral communication skills (Huang, 2015; Watkins, 2012; Yeh, 2018), the same can be witnessed here.

Lisa's learning practice involves collaboration in different layers. She reflects: "I think I learned, well, it was fun because we had three levels going on", and continues, "Anna was helping me and then I was helping Jeff so there is like this chain happening". While Lisa teaches Finnish to non-Finnish-speaking Jeff and engages him in the discourse, Anna mentors Lisa, even by assisting her to remember the lines in the sauna (line 5). Lisa continues: "Having Jeff there was interesting because I would translate what it was to Jeff so for me it was very educational having him there". In her reflections, she also writes positively about the support she received from Anna's family:

> "I learned a lot from Anna and her parents, and they taught me new words. For example, 'heitän löylyä' is what you say in the sauna, but I had no idea until Anna and her family taught me that".

The casual free time interaction with Anna and her family, and their genuine interest towards Lisa's vlogging assignment, enabled this collaborative learning practice to happen.

3.3.   Layers of community support and feedback

Activating friends in the process created a positive learning experience. Lisa says that having Anna in the vlogs "was always very fun for me", and continues, it was "fun for her too so she kinda wanted to help or be featured". Collaborating with a friend who is "really interested" created a supportive learning space and made Lisa even more inspired to learn and practise Finnish. Lisa considers the feedback positive and describes that Anna is "not judgmental so I can do whatever and she just laughs".

Lisa reflects: "The most fun was seeing the final product, as well as filming with friends". When creating the vlog at her friend's house, an authentic audience was created, as Lisa says "Anna's parents loved [it so much] that they showed the whole family, they thought that was great". Anna's family considered vlogging an innovative learning activity and expressed a genuine interest both in the process and in the final outcome.

Collaboration involves a purposeful partnering of students to solve and accomplish relevant and meaningful tasks. It provides a space to test and validate personally constructed knowledge. (Vaughan et al., 2013, pp. 119-120). By creating the vlog outside of the classroom and including her friends in the process, Lisa expanded her learning community, which also offered her supportive feedback. This made the assignment meaningful and authentic.

Earlier studies report that blogging has a positive impact on student interaction, self-expression, and self-evaluation (Trajtemberg & Yiakoumetti, 2011), and most importantly, speaking, reading, and writing skills (Armstrong & Retterer, 2008). As Lisa reflects, "speaking Finnish outside of the classroom was very beneficial to me and the most educational part"; vlogging implements the adoption of different layers of collaborative encounters outside the classroom.

4.   Conclusions

Social media applications' greatest asset in pedagogy is to bring students together in communities where they can interact and collaborate. The use of social media

– in our case vlogging – shifts learning from accessing and sharing information to designing communities of inquiry where participants can actively engage in meaningful collaborative learning (see Vaughan et al., 2013).

In this paper, we have analysed the different layers of how Lisa engages her friends in her vlogging, and how her friends participate in these by supporting and giving feedback. We have shown that a casual free-time activity with friends actually enables the creation of an encounter where authentic discourse in Finnish helps Lisa to learn Finnish in a genuine collaboration. Through vlogging, communities are created (Vaughan et al., 2013, pp. 119-120). Collaborative encounters outside the classroom take place in many layers: Lisa learns together with her friends; she also teaches her friend Jeff.

The vlog was, as part of the course assignment, published for peers to explore, and was further used as material by the teacher in the classroom. We explore these encounters elsewhere. This paper demonstrates, however, that Lisa's vlogging practice involved more layers than interacting and sharing information with peers and the teacher.

Vlogging has not been used in our field, and our project is on the frontier of a new Finnish as a foreign language pedagogy.

References

Armstrong, K., & Retterer, O. (2008). Blogging as L2 writing: a case study. *AACE Journal, 16*(3), 233-251.

Blommaert, J. (2005). *Discourse.* Cambridge University Press. https://doi.org/10.1017/CBO9780511610295

Ducate, L., & Lomicka, L. (2008). Adventures in the blogosphere: from blog readers to blog writers. *Computer Assisted Language Learning, 21*(1), 9-28. https://doi.org/10.1080/09588220701865474

Huang, H.-C. (2015). From web-based readers to voice bloggers: EFL learners' perspectives. *Computer Assisted Language Learning, 28*(2), 145-170. https://doi.org/10.1080/09588221.2013.803983

Petersen, S. A., Divitini, M., & Chabert, G. (2008). Identity, sense of community and connectedness in a community of mobile language learners. *ReCALL, 20*(3), 361-379. https://doi.org/10.1017/S0958344008000839

Trajtemberg, C., & Yiakoumetti, A. (2011). Weblogs: a tool for EFL interaction, expression, and self-evaluation. *ELT Journal, 65*(4), 437-445. https://doi.org/10.1093/elt/ccr015

Vaughan, N. D., Cleveland-Innes, M., & Garrison, D. R. (2013). *Teaching in blended learning environments: creating and sustaining communities of inquiry.* Au Press.

Watkins, J. (2012). Increasing student talk time through vlogging. *Language Education in Asia, 3*(2), 196-203. https://doi.org/10.5746/LEiA/12/V3/I2/A08/Watkins

Yeh, H.-C. (2018). Exploring the perceived benefits of the process of multimodal video making in developing multiliteracies. *Language Learning & Technology, 22*(2), 28-37.

Testing the reliability of the New General Service List Test (NGSLT) in order to better evaluate Japanese university students' written receptive vocabulary levels

Paul Nadasdy[1], Kazumi Aizawa[2], and Tatsuo Iso[3]

Abstract. The New General Service List Test (NGSLT) (Stoeckel & Bennett, 2015) was designed as a diagnostic test to measure students' written receptive vocabulary knowledge. This test battery was developed based upon the New General Service List (NGSL) (Browne, 2013), which makes it appealing to teachers in Japan, and especially those who see vocabulary as key to English as a foreign or second language learning. The research focused on finding out whether and to what degree the test accurately and reliably measures students' vocabulary knowledge, and to find if there are any incongruences with the scores on this test and those on extraneous standards. Three versions of the NGSLT were distributed and a triangulation method was used to analyze the data, with the findings suggesting that the NGSLT may be less a measure of students' knowledge of the target words than a measure of how well they can understand the answer choices.

Keywords: new general service list test, reliability, vocabulary testing.

1.   Introduction

The NGSL (Browne, 2013), an upgrade on West's (1953) General Service List (GSL), is a list of high-frequency English words that has been compiled as an educational resource. As it has been well established through corpora studies, only a small number of words from the large amounts of vocabulary available cover the running words in a wide range of texts – 4,000 word families provide around 95%

1. Tokyo Denki University, Tokyo, Japan; nadasdy@cck.dendai.ac.jp
2. Tokyo Denki University, Tokyo, Japan; aizawa@cck.dendai.ac.jp
3. Tokyo Denki University, Tokyo, Japan; tiso@mail.dendai.ac.jp

How to cite this article: Nadasdy, P., Aizawa. K., & Iso, T. (2018). Testing the reliability of the New General Service List Test (NGSLT) in order to better evaluate Japanese university students' written receptive vocabulary levels. In P. Taalas, J. Jalkanen, L. Bradley & S. Thouësny (Eds), *Future-proof CALL: language learning as exploration and encounters – short papers from EUROCALL 2018* (pp. 220-224). Research-publishing.net. https://doi.org/10.14705/rpnet.2018.26.840

coverage (Nation, 2006) – and the NGSL has contributed to the available tools by adding more contemporaneous language.

Researchers have been encouraged to use the list as a resource to devise pedagogical tools. One such instrument includes Stoeckel and Bennett's (2015) NGSLT, designed to measure L2 learners' written receptive knowledge of the NGSL. Though a bilingual form has now been published (Stoeckel, Ishii, & Bennett, 2018), at the time of this study, the original monolingual NGSLT was being used as a measure. At this time, the authors were considering whether the original NGSLT could be used to influence design of a placement test at a technical university in northeast Tokyo. What follows is a test of the reliability of the original NGSLT (Stoeckel & Bennett, 2015) using a triangulation method to answer the following questions:

- Does the NGSLT accurately and reliably measure students' vocabulary knowledge?

- Are there discrepancies between the scores of the NGSLT and those on extraneous standards?

2. Method

2.1. Participants

A total of 98 Japanese first-year university students completed all the necessary processes in their regular classes. The students' English level was around A2, making use of the NGSLT a suitable means of testing of their vocabulary knowledge.

2.2. Procedure

Three versions of the test were distributed: The original NGSLT (a multiple-choice, monolingual version, EE), a version where students had to translate target words (TR), and a multiple-choice version with Japanese translations added for target words (EJ). The participants also took the TOEIC[4] as an English proficiency measure (scores range from 195 to 595). Online versions of the test were administered via Google Docs to five intact classes during seven lessons

---

4. Test of English for International Communication®

over a period of two months to avoid practice effects. At first, the EE, comprised of 100 items in English, was distributed during week one. Over the subsequent five weeks, the test was split into five sections, reflecting the five, 20-item bands of the NGSLT and students translated the English target words into Japanese (TR). A list of possible answers was created to identify correct and incorrect answers and the actual rating was done by a computer to eliminate any rater variables. Lastly, in week seven, the EJ version was distributed. Due to occasional absences and lack of TOEIC scores, some data had to be eliminated from the final set. The population of participants who qualified for the final count reduced to 98 from 105 at completion. For the analysis, scores from EE and EJ versions, as well as students' current TOEIC scores, were compared to see if a gap exists in the comparative data.

3.   Results

As a measure of test performance, a Cronbach alpha showed a reliability for the three tests at .90 (EE), .83 (EJ), and .89 (TR). Results in Table 1 show there was a discrepancy between levels one and two in the EJ version of the test and a considerable drop between levels four and five on the EE. Results also showed that mean scores of the EJ were statistically significantly higher than the EE. Furthermore, the differences in average scores between EE and EJ across five frequency bands were also significant, with the participants performing better on the EJ. It was also discovered that correlations between TOEIC scores and the EE or EJ version of the NGSLT were rather weak (r=.31 and .37, respectively).

Table 1.   Descriptive statistics of tests

	Overall	1	2	3	4	5
EE	72.06 (12.02)	16.26 (3.18)	15.61 (3.02)	15.4 (2.21)	13.69 (3.02)	11.1 (3.17)
EJ	90.8 (6.28)	18.54 (1.87)	18.8 (1.29)	18.55 (1.2)	18.22 (1.47)	16.68 (2.31)
TR	50.57 (12.14)	12.15 (4.35)	10.76 (2.72)	10.01 (2.84)	9.74 (3.23)	7.91 (3.27)

As can be seen in Figure 1, there is a gap between the two lines between levels four and five, and there is a considerable drop on the EE side at this level. However, with some help in the Japanese version via translations, there is a distinct difference at levels four and five. As expected, the participants did not perform on the TR as well as on the EE or EJ, confirming that it is more difficult to translate the examples than choose the right answers. There was no interaction observed among the three versions of the test, indicating no NGSL levels acted irregularly in any of the versions of the test.

Figure 1.   Comparison of EE, EJ, and TR

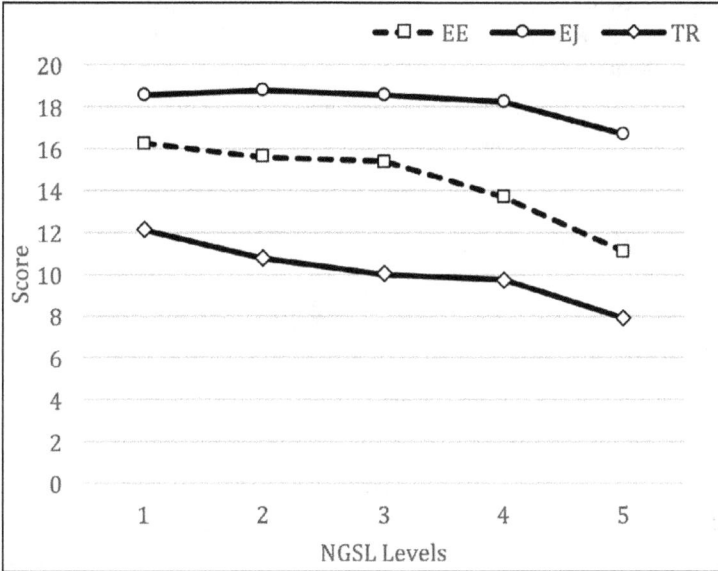

4.   Discussion

It appeared that students did not understand the answer choices in the EE version, suggesting that this may have interfered with how well the test was determining vocabulary level. Results showed that students all did well on the Japanese version of the test, but that did not reflect the range of TOEIC scores. Taken together, these results suggested that participants had difficulty figuring out the meanings of the language used in the possible answers in the EE. Given the fact that the participants were given the translation of the target words, it was apparent that they did not understand in what sense the target words were described in the sample sentences.

The lack of stronger correlation between both versions of the NGSLT and the TOEIC test implied a threat to the validity of the NGSLT, at least when the test takers are similar to the participants in the current study. There also appears to be a ceiling effect in the Japanese version as average scores were high across the board, which may also apply to issues in the English version. As the original validation tests of the NGSLT mainly checked to see whether the test accurately reflected knowledge of the NGSL, there may have been a discrepancy in how it reflected students' actual levels of English, as the triangulation of results in our study proved that there was a discrepancy between what the NGSLT measured and the students' TOEIC scores. Some help given via the translations in the Japanese version resulted in there being a distinct difference at levels 4 and 5. That gap suggests test takers did not completely understand the answer choices. Therefore, we conclude that the original NGSLT appears to be less a test of vocabulary knowledge of target words and more a test of understanding the possible answer choices.

5.   Conclusions

Analyzing the reliability and validity of vocabulary tests is vital if we want to be more informed of the potential gaps in our students' knowledge. From this, we can make better pedagogical choices based on their needs. This study set out to use a triangulation method to see if the original NGSLT withstood scrutiny. The NGSLT is no doubt a good measure of the knowledge of the NGSL, and the more recent bilingual version has gone some way to rectifying potential issues with the test. We showed, however, that there may be a slight weakness in the levels of the original test. Results suggest the effectiveness of our triangulation method in identifying potential weaknesses in tests of written receptive knowledge. Therefore, we will continue to analyze the accuracy of tests like these in order to use them to help us better understand our students' levels of vocabulary knowledge.

References

Browne, C. (2013). The new general service list: celebrating 60 years of vocabulary learning. *The Language Teacher*, *37*(4), 13-16. https://jalt-publications.org/files/pdf-article/37.4tlt_featureds.pdf

Nation, P. (2006). How large a vocabulary is needed for reading and listening? *Canadian Modern Language Review*, *63*(1), 59-82. https://doi.org/10.3138/cmlr.63.1.59

Stoeckel, T., & Bennett, P. (2015). A test of the new general service list. *Vocabulary Learning and Instruction*, *4*(1), 1-8.

Stoeckel, T., Ishii, T., & Bennett, P. (2018). A Japanese-English bilingual version of the new general service list test. *JALT Journal*, *40(*1), 5-21. https://www.jalt-publications.org/node/2/articles/24281-japanese-english-bilingual-version-new-general-service-list-test

West, M. (1953). *A general service list of English words*. London: Longman, Green & Co.

Integrating #FLIrish101 in an LMOOC – learner engagement and pedagogical approach

Mairéad Nic Giolla Mhichíl[1],
Conchúr Mac Lochlainn[2], and Elaine Beirne[3]

Abstract. Course specific hashtags are a feature of Massive Open Online Courses (MOOCs) delivered through many of the major MOOC platforms. Their pedagogic objective is usually considered as a means to facilitate social learning and collaboration between learners. Research into the use of hashtags by learners illustrates limited engagement and integration within their learning experience (Veletsianos, 2017) and that MOOC providers use course hashtags mainly as a means of promotion and marketing. This paper presents the findings of an analysis of the use of the #FLIrish101 by a cohort of learners undertaking a Language MOOC (LMOOC) designed for ab initio learners of Irish. The LMOOC is delivered through the FutureLearn platform. The paper outlines the main findings from an analysis of the Twitter dataset to interpret the LMOOC's learner use of the hashtag. The paper critiques the implicit research design, pedagogical principles and engagement strategies employed by the LMOOCs academic designers to integrate the hashtag as a purposeful means to support collaborative language learning outside the confines of the MOOC platform

Keywords: hashtag, learning design, language learning MOOC, LMOOC.

1.   Introduction

Dublin City University launched the *Irish101: Introduction to Irish Language and Culture* on the FutureLearn platform in 2018 as part of the *Fáilte ar Líne*

1. Dublin City University, Dublin, Ireland; mairead.nicgiollamhichil@dcu.ie
2. Dublin City University, Dublin, Ireland; conchur.maclochlainn@dcu.ie
3. Dublin City University, Dublin, Ireland; elaine.beirne4@mail.dcu.ie

How to cite this article: Nic Giolla Mhichíl, M., Mac Lochlainn, C., & Beirne, E. (2018). Integrating #FLIrish101 in an LMOOC – learner engagement and pedagogical approach. In P. Taalas, J. Jalkanen, L. Bradley & S. Thouësny (Eds), *Future-proof CALL: language learning as exploration and encounters – short papers from EUROCALL 2018* (pp. 225-229). Research-publishing.net. https://doi.org/10.14705/rpnet.2018.26.841

('Welcome Online') project co-funded by the Irish Government. The LMOOC is designed for A1 learners of the Irish language and is part of a suite of courses being developed for the global audience.

This paper reports mainly on learner engagement with the #FLIrish101 and critiques the use of the hashtag within the LMOOC. Research on the pedagogical integration of Twitter into MOOCs reveals limited engagement with hashtags (Veletsianos, 2017). However, Twitter is noted to support participatory culture amongst users where they can share and interact on specific themes, interests, or events (Page, 2012). From a learning perspective, the provision of informal learning and engagement opportunities are reported to enhance learning performance (Jones, 2011; Kassens-Noor, 2012). The underlying pedagogical objective adopted within the Irish101 LMOOC was to integrate #FLIrish101 as a means by which learners could actively produce language outside of the confines of the platform, thus underpinning a constructivist approach to learning along with the social aspects of learning (Conole & Alevizou, 2010). This objective was aligned with Borau, Ullrich, Feng, and Shen's (2009) findings which found that learners within their study found it easier to communicate in the target language on Twitter.

2. Method

2.1. Assessing learner engagement

Within the LMOOC, learners were encouraged to complete simple language production activities outside of the platform using the #FLIrish101. The findings presented are based on an analysis of those tweets which used the #FLIrish101 during the first iteration of the LMOOC and the comments placed in the comments forum of the LMOOC.

Tweets were downloaded from Twitter using a simple screen scraping approach. The data set was cleaned to remove promotional and other non-relevant tweets to provide a final dataset of 145 tweets from learners over a four-week period in early 2018. All LMOOC comments were downloaded and mined using keywords (such as 'social media', 'twitter', and 'facebook') to develop a corpus of approximately 67 comments (out of over 24,000 course-wide) specifically relating to Twitter and tweeting. A thematic analysis of the comments was conducted and cross-validated by the researchers.

2.2. Findings from tweets and platform comments

The tweets themselves spanned a broad range of perspectives and functions, with some specifically engaging with learning activity:

"Maidin mhaith! Tá sé fliuch inniu. #FLIrish101 #Gaelige" [*Translation*: Good morning. It's wet today] (Learner A, 2018).

Other tweets were not linked to learning activities:

"#FLIrish101 My view of a recent sunset here in the USA. Have a great weekend everyone. I love this Irish class through FutureLearn" (Learner B, 2018).

The total number of learners who utilised Twitter was low, with a small number who tweeted more often and did not support continuous interactions with most threads limited to one response. The main themes to emerge from learner comments within the platform included a reluctance to using Twitter as a channel to produce language outside of the platform due to (1) an absence of knowledge regarding Twitter and (2) a preference to remain in-platform. Furthermore, the lack of a Twitter account was viewed with concern by some learners:

"What happens if you do not tweet or twitter or whatever it is called? The wording is encouraged but it looks like I will miss a whole portion of the course" (Learner C, 2018).

Others recognised the value of using Twitter and social media as a means by which they could engage with other learners outside of the platform to produce language, whilst some learners indicated their preference to use alternative social media tools:

"An interesting mix of language and historical material, especially around Ogham and trees. I need more practice at talking - have set up a Twitter account @X and have met a couple of learners there" (Learner D, 2018).

"I use Facebook but not Twitter" (Learner E, 2018).

An important contextual theme to emerge from the data was that some voluntarily referred to their age to contextualise their comments with both positive and negative perspectives for Twitter and social media:

"I have no idea about Twitter and/or Facebook but think I could cope with this comments page. Hope I can keep up" (Learner F, 2018).

"BTW Im 68 and have been computing since 1987. I use Facebook but not Twitter" (Learner G, 2018).

3.   Discussion

In general, engagement with Twitter by Irish101 learners was low, particularly when contrasted with the vibrant forum use by learners within the LMOOC. This finding is aligned with Veletsianos's (2017) contention regarding the limited interaction of many MOOC learners with in-course hashtags. The implication may well be that learners view the platform as a safe learning environment, with learners reluctant to move outside it. Concern for privacy was thought by the researchers to be linked to this, though further qualitative research would be needed to support this contention. The conceptual distinction, between 'private' or 'personal' in-course activity, and 'public' space, is both interesting and important to explore, as several learners explicitly mentioned their negative attitudes towards social media participation. It also suggests that despite prompts, the function of social media activity was invariably secondary and thus 'invisible' in grading/completion and may need to align more closely with these to encourage meaningful engagement. The potential value of learner interaction via social media as relates to language learning is large, however, and suggests there are good reasons to consider doing so. Finally, an interesting factor relates to course demographics; learners referenced their age to frame opinions regarding social media. The majority of learners were over 55. This age group was usually categorised as either 'Hobbyists' i.e. those who learned for specific hobbies, or 'Vitalisers' i.e. those who enjoy a wide range of experiences and learning for its own sake as a means of development (FutureLearn, 2017). Such categorisation is important particularly for reflection during the iterative redesign of the LMOOC to recognise the cohorts' social media experience, which are likely dependent on their wider experiences and beliefs.

4.   Conclusions

Although the integration of Twitter as a means to informally support learners to produce language outside of the platform was attempted, it was in the main not embraced by most learners. Although a reluctance to use Twitter was expressed by some, a group of learners did take it upon themselves to make use of Facebook, specifically a group established by one Irish101 learner linked to the project's Facebook page. That group has 43 learners, with substantial discussion and evident engagement. This bottom-up activity demonstrates that social media can be useful for learners as part of an informal learning setting. The difficulty of integrating Twitter into the design of an LMOOC was realised in Irish101. The conception that focussing on learning design alone may increase engagement with Twitter as per Veletsianos's (2017) conclusions is problematic as the findings of this study suggest. Learner concerns relating to their uses and knowledge of the social media tool and their conceptions of privacy should also be factored into facilitating a supportive digital language learning experience.

5.   Acknowledgements

The research was co-funded by the Irish Government's Department of Culture, Heritage and the Gaeltacht under the 20-Year Strategy for the Irish language with support from the National Lottery.

References

Borau, K., Ullrich, C., Feng, J., & Shen, R. (2009). *Microblogging for language learning: using Twitter to train communicative and cultural competence.* Springer-Verlag. https://doi.org/10.1007/978-3-642-03426-8_10

Conole, G., & Alevizou, P. (2010). *A literature review of the use of Web 2.0 tools in Higher Education.* HEA.

FutureLearn. (2017). *Who are our Learners? Part 4: The 'Leisure' archetypes.* https://about.futurelearn.com/research-insights/learners-part-4-leisure-archetypes

Jones, A. (2011). How Twitter saved my literature class: a case study with discussion. In C.Wankel (Ed.), *Teaching arts and science with the new social media : cutting-edge technologies in higher education* (pp. 91-105). Emerald.

Kassens-Noor, E. (2012). Twitter as a teaching practice to enhance active and informal learning in higher education: the case of sustainable tweets. *Active Learning in Higher Education, 13,* 9-21. https://doi.org/10.1177/1469787411429190

Page, R. (2012). The linguistics of self-branding and micro-celebrity in Twitter: the role of hashtags. *Discourse & Communication, 6,* 181-201. https://doi.org/10.1177/1750481312437441

Veletsianos, G. (2017). Toward a generalizable understanding of Twitter and social media use across MOOCs: who participates on MOOC hashtags and in what ways? *Journal of Computing in Higher Education, 29*(1), 65-80. https://doi.org/10.1007/s12528-017-9131-7

An Scéalaí: synthetic voices for autonomous learning

Neasa Ní Chiaráin[1] and Ailbhe Ní Chasaide[2]

Abstract. This paper details the motivation for and the main characteristics of *An Scéalaí* ('*The Storyteller*'), an intelligent Computer Assisted Language Learning (iCALL) platform for autonomous learning that integrates the four skills; writing, listening, speaking, and reading. A key feature is the incorporation of speech technology. Speech synthesis provides aural feedback which draws the learners' attention to errors in the text. Natural language prompts focus on common spelling and grammatical errors, further guiding the learners' ability to revise and self-correct written materials. While *An Scéalaí* is still in early stages of development, results of a feasibility study are positive and point towards directions for further development.

Keywords: autonomous learning, speech technology, iCALL platform.

1.   Introduction

An Scéalaí ('*The Storyteller*') is an iCALL platform that incorporates speech synthesis and deploys it for autonomous learning, in the sense of directed learning initially leading to self-supported learning (description of current version in Ní Chiaráin & Ní Chasaide, 2018). It entails training in all four language skills, with a particular emphasis on written accuracy, both in terms of the spelling rules of the language and the frequently linked grammatical rules, developing awareness of the morphophonemics of Irish.

The platform (Figure 1) invites the user to contribute regular diary-style entries. The written text is then spoken aloud by the synthesis engine to allow learners to *hear* where there are errors in the text. Subsequently, specific spelling/grammatical errors are highlighted in colour, and the user is encouraged to review and correct

1. Trinity College, Dublin, Ireland; neasa.nichiarain@tcd.ie
2. Trinity College, Dublin, Ireland; anichsid@tcd.ie

How to cite this article: Ní Chiaráin, N., & Ní Chasaide, A. (2018). An Scéalaí: synthetic voices for autonomous learning. In P. Taalas, J. Jalkanen, L. Bradley & S. Thouësny (Eds), *Future-proof CALL: language learning as exploration and encounters – short papers from EUROCALL 2018* (pp. 230-235). Research-publishing.net. https://doi.org/10.14705/rpnet.2018.26.842

their input again. The specific errors targeted for correction will be adapted to the learner and introduced in a stepwise fashion (no more than three errors highlighted at a time in an attempt to avoid cognitive overload). When the diary entry is complete, the user records their own reading of the passage and listens back to compare it to the native models (synthesised).

Figure 1.   Screenshot illustrating *An Scéalaí* main features

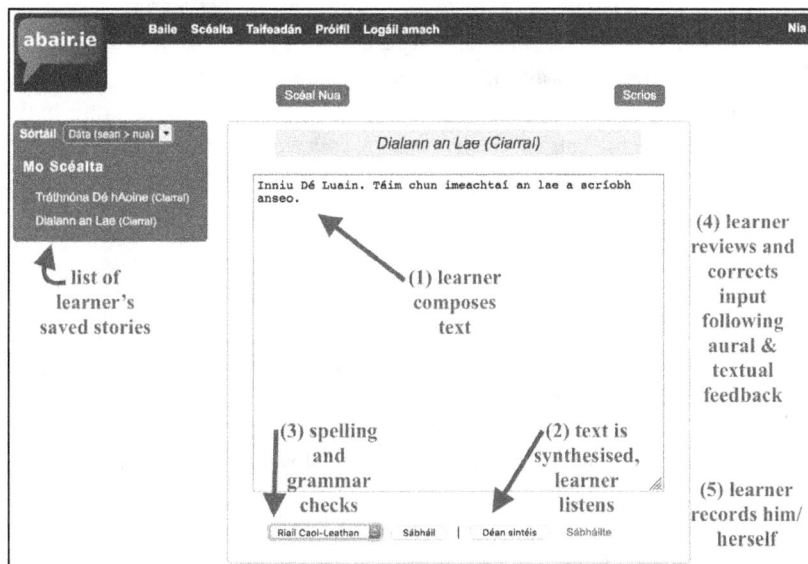

The users' written and spoken input are retained and provide learner corpora, essential for the further development of the system. It is currently undergoing development and is freely available online. It aims not only to provide tools for teachers' own lifelong professional development, but also a tool which they can adapt for use in their classrooms.

This paper aims to discuss the theoretical background of *An Scéalaí* along with findings from a feasibility study of the developing system.

2.   Theoretical background

The current theoretical framework is based on 'experiential' or 'hands-on' learning, where the task is meaningful and students engage in reflective activity, (Dewey, 1997), combined with the sociocultural approach to language teaching and learning frequently referred to as a communicative approach. A common criticism of the latter approach is that it sometimes fails to bring along those writing skills that create the "all-important interface between explicit processes of language learning and implicit processes of spontaneous language use" (Little, Dam, & Legenhausen, 2017, p. 210). *An Scéalaí* places an initial emphasis on those writing skills and integrates them with the other three language skills.

The *use* of the target language is key to the learning process as learning happens by doing (and by making errors and learning from these). With a view to facilitating autonomy (intentional learning), the present application entails a personalised diary-style writing task (Rosenblatt, 1978). Learners' reflective contributions instantiate meaningful language use, serving as a vehicle for making/correcting written errors in a way that links the written to oral/aural skills.

3.   Language learning goals

Key goals of the platform are that:

- hearing the text spoken (synthetic speech) will increase learners' error detection rate, as errors will simply 'sound wrong';

- the built-in specific error prompts will improve learners' revision of the written text;

- the specific correction prompts linked to the auditory (synthesis) feedback will increase learners' understanding of the connection between pronunciation and Irish spelling rules; and

- the platform will motivate students to spend time on language learning tasks (self-correction).

4.   Feasibility study

A feasibility study was conducted in parallel with the system's development. Five student teachers in the first year of a two-year Master's programme participated. It formed part of an elective taught module on teaching (any subject) through the medium of Irish. The students had all successfully passed the Irish language proficiency test at B2 level (see www.teg.ie). Student intrinsic motivation was high.

Six weeks of diary entries were included as part of the study. Students were awarded 10% of their module marks for contributing diary entries – they were simply asked to contribute *something* each week. One limiting factor was that the participating students were involved in a busy Master's programme with considerable workloads.

5. Study outcomes

Some objective and some subjective results emerged as presented below.

5.1. Objective results

Learners produced a considerable amount of written material, clearly warming to the reflective writing task. On average they contributed 567 words weekly, well in excess of what was expected.

The content of the learners' diary entries showed they were engaged and actively reflecting on their language learning journey.

The learners didn't listen and correct as much as would be expected given the volume of written work. This usefully points to the need for a built-in requirement that learners listen back to their written work and correct errors (where they can) before progressing with further writing.

Spelling corrections, which were expected to be easily corrected through listening, were missed by some students who clearly did not 'hear' their mistakes. This highlights a fundamental issue in the teaching of Irish pronunciation. Phonological awareness of the sound contrasts of Irish (very different from English) is often poor, even among teachers, and thus the important underpinning of fundamental spelling rules is missing. This does not, as such, reflect on the present application but rather points to the need for specific resources geared to training the sound contrasts of the language as a precursor to spelling and literacy. A parallel project is currently underway which is geared to this particular problem in Irish language learning (Ó Broin, Barnes, Ní Chiaráin, & Ní Chasaide, forthcoming).

5.2. Subjective results

Learners reported the experience of using *An Scéalaí* as enjoyable and spent considerable time writing despite a very heavy schedule. Their enthusiasm and level of usage resulted in system glitches being identified and fixed.

The use of synthesis for self-correction was well understood and positively received (*aha moment!*). For some, the linkage between pronunciation and spelling rules was a revelation, glimpsed for the first time. As mentioned, however, this was not true of all students.

Learners enjoyed the autonomous nature of the platform. Frequently commented on was the relative anonymity of an automatic system where learners did not feel judged by their 'teacher'.

Learners agreed they did not spend as much time evaluating, revising, editing their written work as would have been desirable. This may to some extent reflect the time constraints under which students were operating. However, it undoubtedly also reflects a general tendency for students to shy away from revisions and self-correction, something which underlines the need for this type of application.

The unconstrained personal aspect of the writing was positively received compared to the more 'boring' written exercises they are accustomed to.

Student teachers were enthusiastic that the platform would be adaptable to their own classrooms. Specifically mentioned was the fact that the system provides the repetitive corrective feedback that reinforces the teachers' efforts. The fact that this platform helps younger students towards becoming autonomous learners was also positively commented on.

Further comments suggested that the availability of the platform on mobile devices would be desirable leading to increased levels of use (less setup time wastage). An extension of the error correction facilities, preferably with an interactive dimension, was also highlighted.

6. Conclusions

Current indications are that the platform is going in the right direction to meet its learning objectives, particularly the benefits of using synthetic speech as a mechanism that facilitates integration of oral/aural and writing skills. The study has provided insight into how the next iteration may be adapted, e.g. to ensure that students engage to a greater degree with the correction of their written work.

The spoken and written corpus collected to date is currently being analysed to provide pointers for the steps of corrective feedback to introduce next.

The auditory dimension is undoubtedly helpful for the development of learners' pronunciation, even though it is clear that for some (most learners in all likelihood) specific training in the phonological contrasts of the language will be required – something that is beyond the scope of *An Scéalaí*.

Fuller trials involving student teachers as well as classroom learners will be carried out. Tasks will be adapted as appropriate. Although *An Scéalaí* was specifically developed for Irish language learners, the principles and implementation should be usable for other languages for which high quality speech synthesis is available.

References

Dewey, J. (1997). *Democracy and education: an introduction to the philosophy of education.* Free Press [First published 1916].

Little, D., Dam, L., & Legenhausen, L. (2017). *Language learner autonomy: theory, practice and research.* Multilingual Matters. https://doi.org/10.21832/LITTLE8590

Ní Chiaráin, N., & Ní Chasaide, A. (2018). Recycling learner data for acquisition of targeted linguistic features: a custom-built iCALL platform. In J. Colpaert, A. Aerts & F. Cornillie (Eds), *Proceedings of CALL your DATA* (pp. 292-295). Brugge, KULeuven & imec.

Ó Broin, D., Barnes, E., Ní Chiaráin, N., & Ní Chasaide, A. (forthcoming). A story based game for teaching phonetics for the Irish language. In *Proceedings of European Conference for Game Based Learning 2018.*

Rosenblatt, L. (1978). *The reader, the text, the poem: the transactional theory of the literary work.* Southern Illinois University Press.

Self-directed learning and the teacher's role: insights from two different teaching contexts

Louise Ohashi[1]

Abstract. There has been interest in learner autonomy in the field of language education for many years but the role of the teacher remains uncertain. In Japan, where this research was conducted, it is not commonplace for comprehensive programs that foster autonomous learning to be integrated into formal English education, but some institutions and educators have taken steps in this direction. This study gives an overview of two different contexts in which teacher support for autonomous learning was woven into English education at Japanese universities; firstly, in a course that was dedicated to self-directed learning and secondly, in a speaking course that included a self-directed learning strand. Survey data that were collected from 50 students in these two contexts suggest that the support given in both course types was largely beneficial to learners, with similar outcomes in many areas but a noteworthy difference in the amount of time spent studying outside of class.

Keywords: learner autonomy, self-directed learning, language learning, digital technology.

1. Introduction

To become fully proficient in a language, students generally need to look beyond their course-based studies and seek opportunities for autonomous, out-of-class learning. The path to efficient and sustained self-directed learning is not without its challenges, but educators can play an integral role in enhancing students' opportunities to gain the skills and motivation required (Blidi, 2017; Lai, 2017). In Japan, there is not a comprehensive system in place for fostering autonomous

1. Meiji University, Tokyo, Japan; ohashi@meiji.ac.jp

How to cite this article: Ohashi, L. (2018). Self-directed learning and the teacher's role: insights from two different teaching contexts. In P. Taalas, J. Jalkanen, L. Bradley & S. Thouësny (Eds), *Future-proof CALL: language learning as exploration and encounters – short papers from EUROCALL 2018* (pp. 236-242). Research-publishing.net. https://doi.org/10.14705/rpnet.2018.26.843

learning at the tertiary level. However, there is support available, with some universities offering credit-bearing self-directed learning courses (Curry, Mynard, Noguchi, & Watkins, 2017) and others providing self-access learning centers (Mynard, 2016). This study contributes to the existing body of work in this field by examining different ways in which English learners were offered support for self-directed learning at two private universities in Tokyo, Japan. While the two contexts are compared, the main aim of this study was not to assess which was more beneficial to learners, but rather to draw on the researcher's own teaching settings to provide examples of ways that educators can successfully support out-of-class learning in different contexts.

2.   Method

This study presents ways self-directed learning was integrated into two first-year university subjects that students were required to take for two 14-week semesters. Students in one university took a self-directed learning course (hereafter SDL course/students) for 90 minutes once per week and students in the other university took an English speaking skills course (hereafter Regular Course or RC students) for 100 minutes twice per week. In the latter course, approximately 20 minutes of class time each week was spent on self-directed learning tasks, with longer sessions held several times throughout the course.

Both groups followed the same basic pattern with different degrees of detail and extension work. Support commenced by guiding students to reflect on their language learning history and share it with their teacher and classmates. After that, both groups learnt about tools and methods for English study, with the teacher and students introducing a range of education-driven CALL/MALL[2] tools and other digital tools that could be exploited for language learning purposes as well as some paper-based tools such as graded readers and proficiency test textbooks. Another key component of each course was planning-action-reflection cycles, which had the following components:

- outline long-term and short-term goals,

- identify tasks that will build towards goals,

- list the tasks in a SMART[3] way,

---

2. Computer Assisted Language Learning/Mobile Assisted Language Learning
3. SMART: Specific, Measurable, Achievable, Relevant and Time-related; alternate versions of this acronym exist.

- discuss the plans in class,

- take action outside of class,

- discuss the action (or inaction) in class,

- reflect on the experience,

- modify plans if necessary, and

- continue the cycle.

The first step was done as a writing task for homework then discussed in class. Students were told about the teacher's long-term goals and Figure 1 was used to show how one of the major goals could be broken down into smaller goals, with facilitative tasks identified. For steps two and three, students made a similar chart for their own goals then learned about SMART plans and applied this principle to create learning plans. Steps four to nine became a cycle during term-time and all steps except the discussions were encouraged during university breaks.

Figure 1.   Model for connecting tasks with goals

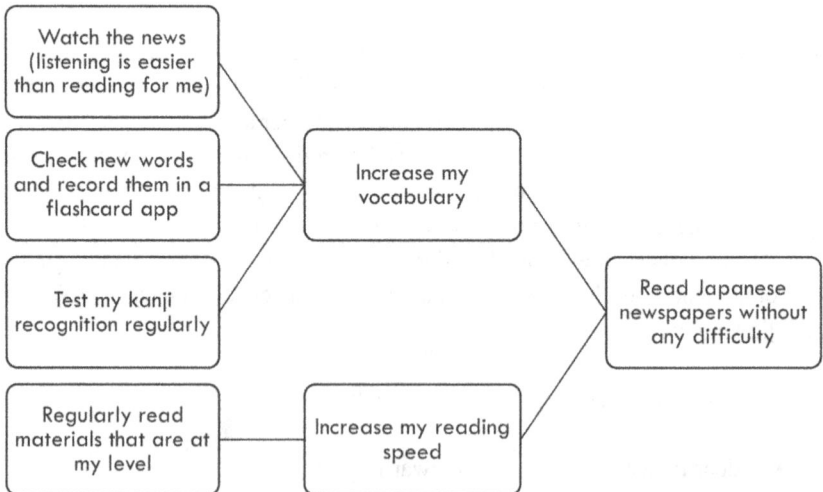

The major difference between the two courses related to the amount of support that was provided for each step. For example, SDL students did extra preparation for their learner histories by watching and reading models online and significantly more time was spent on learning about useful tools and study methods, with a lot of support through Moodle, which was used for course management. Moreover, while RC students made short learning plans in note form, SDL students wrote detailed plans based on models from the teacher. Furthermore, student interaction about planning, action, and reflection was limited to brief, in-class discussions for RC students, but SDL students had time for lengthier group discussions and also did three presentations about their planning-action-reflection cycles, including face-to-face and pre-recorded ones that they shared online.

At the end of the academic year, anonymous survey data were collected from 50 students, with 38[4] SDL participants and 12 RC participants. Key findings are discussed below.

3.   Results and discussion

To gain insight into the value of steps taken to support self-directed learning, students were asked to rate the usefulness of various aspects of their course on a four-point Likert scale. Figure 2 shows that the vast majority in both contexts found it *useful* (combined figures for *very useful* and *somewhat useful*) to make and review plans, share plans and actions with their teacher and classmates and learn about their classmates' out-of-class study/use of English.

In terms of learning about resources, Figure 3 indicates that a marginally higher proportion of students found it useful to learn about ways to improve their English outside of class with digital technology than with non-digital tools, and more students found it beneficial learning about tools from the teacher than other students. However, in all cases, most students found value in these aspects, which suggests building these features into the courses was worthwhile.

The greatest discrepancy between the groups was found in the amount of time spent studying outside of class. Students were asked to estimate the average amount of time they spent on self-study each week, choosing from categories that rose in 30-minute increments (e.g. about 30 minutes, about 60 minutes). In Japan, the typical length of a university lesson is 90 minutes so responses have been amalgamated in Figure 4 to show those who did at least one extra lesson's worth of study and those who did less. The results show that SDL students were more likely

---

4. This figure is an amalgamation of two separate classes.

to study for approximately 90 minutes or longer, with an 18 percentage point gap during the term and a 24 percentage point gap during university breaks. Without further investigation, it cannot be claimed that the additional support students received in the SDL course is responsible for these gaps, but the discrepancy warrants further research.

Figure 2.   Perceptions of the usefulness of making, reviewing, and sharing learning plans/actions

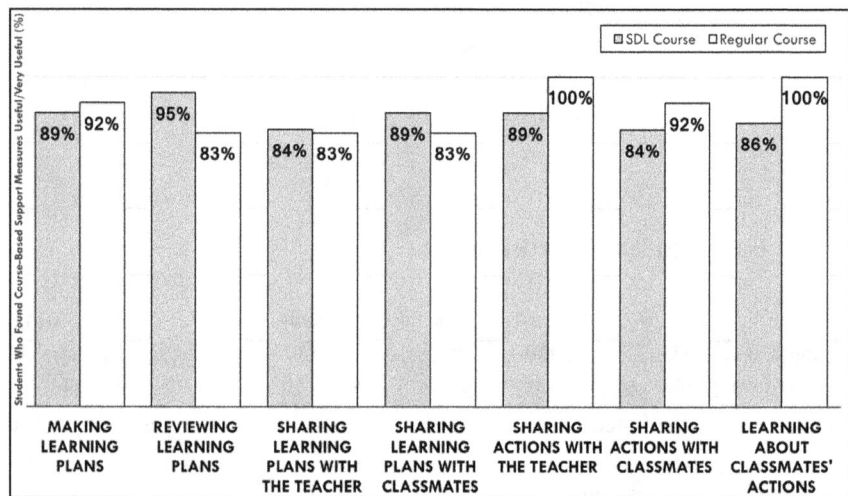

Figure 3.   Perceptions of the usefulness of learning about study tools from others

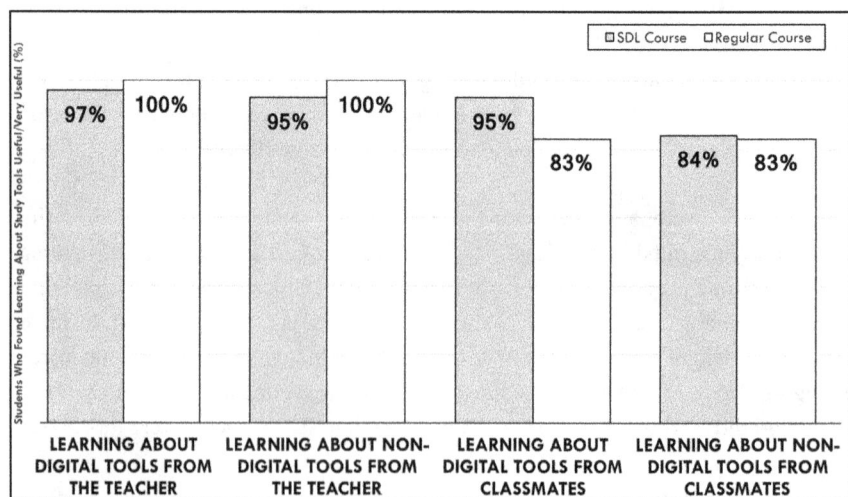

Figure 4. A comparison of out-of-class study time by course

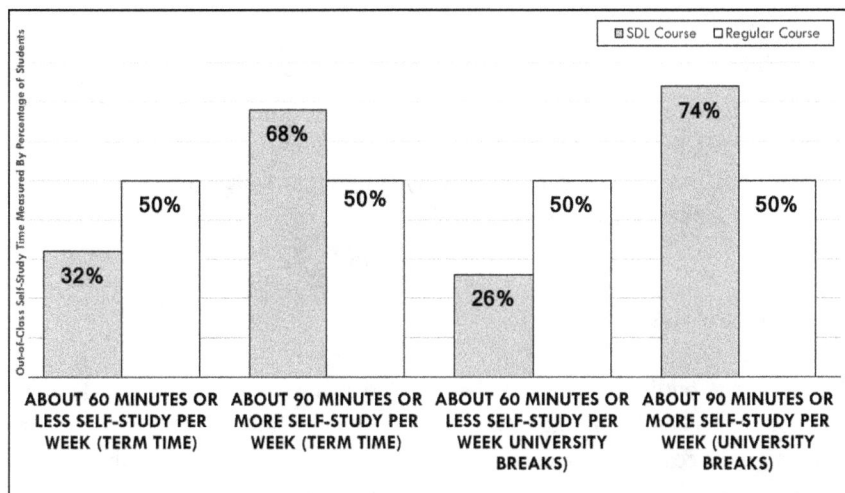

Open responses from students also highlighted numerous benefits to students, including the following:

- **Identifying future goals**: "[The course] helped me think about my future plans, and what I want to do in the future became a bit more clear".

- **Developing planning skills**: "I learned the importance of setting a short and REACHABLE goal because I had almost never achieved big and long-term goals".

- **Learning new study skills**: "Thanks to [the] 5-week feedback presentations, I learned and found [a] variety of ways of learning English. I could find new studying methods so I will do it from now and am motivated now".

- **Planning as a motivator**: "By making a study plan, it motivated me to actually study English and reach goals".

- **Gaining motivation from others**: "I was so motivated to study English. Especially, when my friend told me how much he studied English and its outcome, I was so encouraged to study English".

However, some students did not like certain activities, with one noting, "I was not really motivated because when I do something I planned, I feel that I have the duty to do that". Furthermore, a student from the SDL course wrote, "I was a little not motivate[d] because sharing the information can be done in [a] short time and also we did similar things through the first semester which made me less motivated". For this learner, the repetition of the cycle had become unproductive and the time allocated was excessive. Further investigation into how widespread this sentiment is in similar settings would be worthwhile.

4.   Conclusions

This study has outlined ways in which teachers can support autonomous learning and shows the potential they have to influence students' out-of-class actions through in-class guidance. It was beyond the scope of the study to thoroughly evaluate whether the support given to SDL or RC students was more beneficial to learners, but the results suggest the SDL students were generally willing to spend more time developing their language skills outside of class. In future research, it would be valuable to extend this work by collecting qualitative data to investigate further how and why the types of teacher support outlined in this study can influence learners.

References

Blidi, S. (2017). *Collaborative learner autonomy*. Springer. https://doi.org/10.1007/978-981-10-2048-3

Curry, N., Mynard, J., Noguchi, J., & Watkins, S. (2017). Evaluating a self-directed language learning course in a Japanese university. *International journal of self-directed learning, 14*(1), 17-36.

Lai, C. (2017). *Autonomous language learning with technology: beyond the classroom.* Bloomsbury.

Mynard, J. (2016). Self-access in Japan: introduction. *Studies in self-access learning journal, 7*(4), 331-340.

Can 360 virtual reality tasks impact
L2 willingness to communicate?

Kevin Papin[1]

Abstract. This paper presents a research proposal that aims at examining the impact of communicative tasks mediated by Virtual Reality (VR) on second language (L2) Willingness To Communicate (WTC) outside of the classroom. The study will take place in Montreal, a Canadian city known for its regional variety of French and the bilingualism of its population, which is challenging for international students trying to practice the target language outside of the classroom. A mixed-methods approach will be used to follow the evolution of WTC levels while exploring in more depth students' perceptions of the virtual activities and their WTC.

Keywords: virtual reality, L2 willingness to communicate, task-based language teaching.

1.   Introduction

Since the communicative approach and task-based language teaching have placed communication at the center of L2 teaching, the use of authentic learning material and simulation have been identified as two efficient strategies to improve learner's communicative competence (Ellis, 2003). Researchers have pointed out, however, that while some L2 learners with high linguistic skills are reluctant to initiate communication in L2, other learners, with less developed language skills, are eager to engage in conversations using the L2. This paradox can be understood through the concept of L2 WTC, defined as "a readiness to enter into discourse at a particular time with a specific person" (MacIntyre, Dörnyei, Clément, & Noels, 1998, p. 547). Although it is a complex model, literature has clearly identified that L2 anxiety and L2 Self-Perceived Communication Competence (SPCC) are the two main antecedents of L2 WTC. Since researchers have suggested that

1. McGill University, Montreal, Canada; kevin.papin@mcgill.ca

How to cite this article: Papin, K. (2018). Can 360 virtual reality tasks impact L2 willingness to communicate? In P. Taalas, J. Jalkanen, L. Bradley & S. Thouësny (Eds), *Future-proof CALL: language learning as exploration and encounters – short papers from EUROCALL 2018* (pp. 243-248). Research-publishing.net. https://doi.org/10.14705/rpnet.2018.26.844

the development of L2 WTC be made the ultimate goal of L2 teaching, teachers interested in doing so should try to create learning material that help to reduce L2 anxiety while increasing L2 SPCC.

Empirical research indicates that computer-mediated communication has a positive effect on increasing L2 learners' WTC by lowering language anxiety (Rankin, Gold, & Gooch, 2006) and increasing SPCC (González-Lloret, 2017). One avenue for research that has not received careful attention is the pedagogical use of 360 VR, which relies on 360 photos and videos that can be displayed either on a computer (or phone) screen, or on a VR headset. In both cases, due to its immersive and real-life nature, and based on previous research showing that virtual environments can help lower anxiety (Grant, Huang, & Pasfield-Neofitou, 2013) while improving communicative and cultural skills (Johnson & Valente, 2009), we propose that the introduction of communicative tasks based on quasi-authentic VR simulations in the L2 classroom will positively impact L2 French WTC by preparing students for real life encounters in the L2, and thus reducing anxiety and increasing SPCC (Figure 1). As such, our research questions are the following: (1) how can quasi-authentic VR simulation contribute to L2 WTC and its two main antecedents, SPCC and L2 anxiety?, and (2) how do students perceive class communicative tasks using VR in preparing them for actual L2 use outside of the classroom?

Figure 1. The hypothesized impact of the introduction of quasi-authentic VR simulations on L2 WTC (dotted lines)

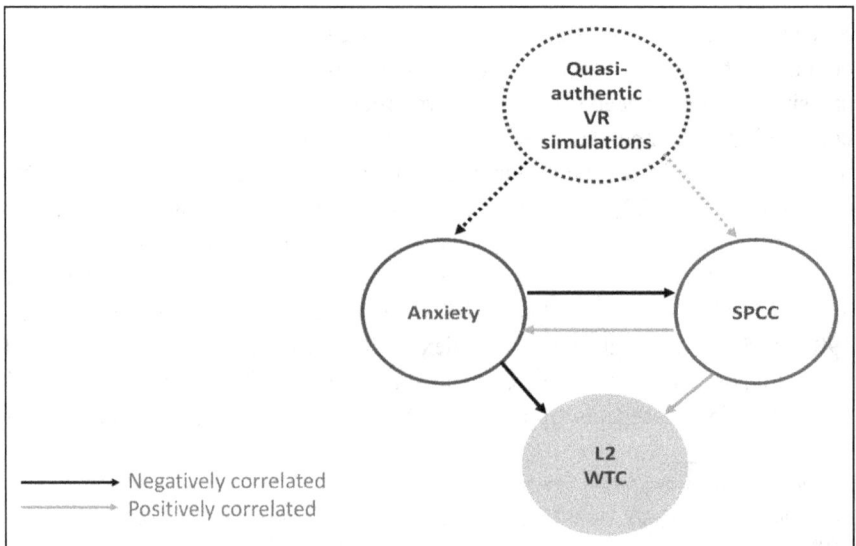

2. Method

2.1. Participants

The study will take place in a Montreal university setting, at a beginner level L2 French course over a period of ten weeks. To examine the impact of the communicative VR tasks on learners' L2 WTC, we will recruit 28 students (A2 level, according to the Common European Framework of Reference for languages). They are international students with low to moderate L2 WTC facing challenges to communicate in French outside the classroom. Many speak English as a first or second language.

2.2. Procedures

During the ten-week period, students will complete three VR communicative tasks reproducing scenarios that can be encountered in everyday life, such as ordering a hot drink in a café. The tasks will be anchored in the reality of the Montreal context: participants will be exposed to a variety of accents and local vocabulary during the VR tasks.

2.3. Material development

A Samsung Gear video camera will be used to shoot the 360 videos (to be used in the VR scenarios) in three different Montreal locations: a café, a bar and a grocery store. Volunteers (local French speakers) will be recorded while asking questions and giving instructions in French based on a pre-written scenario. The recordings will serve as prompts for the VR communicative tasks. The videos will be uploaded to YouTube and then embedded in an online learning platform that students will use to perform the tasks. The online platform will feature a speech-recognition tool that will be able to identify students' oral responses to the 360 video prompts and automatically play the next corresponding prompts (branching).

2.4. Instruments

Given the fact that 360 VR is still a technology in its infancy in L2 teaching, this research can be defined as an exploratory study, relying on survey questionnaires and qualitative data from student logbooks and focus groups. Mixed methodology allows for the observation of the psycho-affective variables underlying L2 WTC

(L2 anxiety and SPCC) while examining students' perceptions and reactions following the introduction of the VR material from a sociocultural perspective.

2.4.1. Surveys

At the beginning and end of the ten-week period, the participants will fill out pre-test/post-test surveys in which they will be asked to rate their levels of L2 WTC, anxiety, and SPCC. These surveys will rely on validated quantitative questionnaires using Likert scales (e.g. the 20-item L2 WTC questionnaire from MacIntyre, Baker, Clément, & Conrod, 2001) followed by open-ended questions that will give participants the opportunity to elaborate on their self-reported levels of L2 WTC, anxiety, and SPCC. Descriptive and inferential (correlative) statistics will be run on *SPSS 25.0* to analyse the results for questions using Likert scales.

2.4.2. Journals

Participants will also be asked to keep a journal during the ten-week period in order to reflect on their learning experience in Montreal and their willingness to communicate outside the classroom. To guide them in this reflection, they will be presented with different types of questions related to the use of VR in the classroom, their willingness to use the L2, and their actual use of L2 outside the classroom.

2.4.3. Focus groups

Finally, towards the end of the ten-week period, during focus group discussions, students will be invited to expand on the reflection initiated in their journal. These discussions, in groups of five to six students, will take place outside of class time and will be filmed. Transcriptions of the focus groups will be analysed using *QDA Miner 5.0*.

3. Discussion

Since research on the pedagogical implications of L2 WTC has not received appropriate attention (Gregersen & MacIntyre, 2013), this study will make a valuable contribution to the field of L2 learning. Even if no study has yet looked at VR tasks using 360 videos, results showing the positive impact of gamified virtual environments on L2 WTC (Reinders & Wattana, 2014) lead us to believe that the introduction of 360 VR tasks could increase students' L2 WTC. This research could also pave the way to the creation of a framework for the design of 360 VR tasks for the L2 classroom, therefore helping task designers to avoid pitfalls such as *edutainment* (O'Brien & Levy, 2008).

One of the limitations of this study might be the bias of some participants due to the introduction of VR, a relatively new technology in the L2 classroom. However, this potential limitation could be mitigated due to the fact that by the beginning of the study, participants will already have performed one non-interactive task using VR as part of the regular course activities.

4.   Conclusion

This study will focus on the pedagogical implications of L2 WTC. It will examine students' perceptions of 360 VR communicative tasks and seek to determine how their introduction in the L2 classroom impacted the students' L2 WTC outside of the classroom.

5.   Acknowledgements

We would like to thank the following individuals for their contribution to the shaping of this study: Patricia Lamarre, Walcir Cardoso, and Ahlem Ammar.

References

Ellis, R. (2003). *Task-based language learning and teaching*. Oxford University Press.

González-Lloret, M. (2017). Technology and task-based language teaching. In C. A. Chapelle & S. Sauro (Eds), *The handbook of technology and second language teaching and learning* (pp. 234-247). Wiley Blackwell.

Grant, S. J., Huang, H., & Pasfield-Neofitou, S. E. (2013). Language learning in virtual worlds: the role of foreign language and technical anxiety. *Journal for virtual worlds research, 6*(1), 1-9.

Gregersen, T., & MacIntyre, P. D. (2013). *Capitalizing on language learners' individuality: from premise to practice* (Vol. 72): Multilingual Matters.

Johnson, W. L., & Valente, A. (2009). Tactical language and culture training systems: using AI to teach foreign languages and cultures. *AI magazine, 30*(2), 72-83. https://doi.org/10.1609/aimag.v30i2.2240

MacIntyre, P. D., Baker, S. C., Clément, R., & Conrod, S. (2001). Willingness to communicate, social support, and language-learning orientations of immersion students. *Studies in second language acquisition, 23*(3), 369-388. https://doi.org/10.1017/S0272263101003035

MacIntyre, P. D., Dörnyei, Z., Clément, R., & Noels, K. A. (1998). Conceptualizing willingness to communicate in a L2: a situational model of L2 confidence and affiliation. *The Modern Language Journal, 82*(4), 545-562. https://doi.org/10.1111/j.1540-4781.1998.tb05543.x

O'Brien, M. G., & Levy, R. M. (2008). Exploration through virtual reality: encounters with the target culture. *Canadian modern language review, 64*(4), 663-691. https://doi.org/10.3138/cmlr.64.4.663

Rankin, Y. A., Gold, R., & Gooch, B. (2006). 3D role-playing games as language learning tools. In *Eurographics (Education Papers)*.

Reinders, H., & Wattana, S. (2014). Can I say something? The effects of digital game play on willingness to communicate. *Language learning & technology, 18*(2), 101-123.

Creative Muscle: the serious learning game

Giouli Pappa[1] and Salomi Papadima-Sophocleous[2]

Abstract. "Serious Games [SGs] are applications combining educational content with gameplay by integrating learning objectives into a game-like environment" (Thillainathan & Leimeister, 2014, p. 1). However, they have not been used much in language teacher education and training (Ulicsak, 2010). This paper describes the design of *Creative Muscle*, a SG and its use to train second language practitioners/ Master of Arts (MA) in Computer Assisted Language Learning (CALL) student-teachers in the use of Singularity Viewer Virtual World (VW) for online micro teaching. This game-based training was delivered in three one-hour sessions. *Creative Muscle* was based on creative writing as a metaphor. Data included the researchers' personal observations, screen recordings of students' participation, and the participants' reflective journal entries. The findings gave insights into the effectiveness of the use of the 3D SG as a VWs' training mechanism. Students' feedback further provided ideas for game improvement which indicated a good understanding of the game, and of VWs.

Keywords: serious games, virtual worlds, online second language teacher education.

1.　Introduction

"Entertainment games that educate players are widely referred to as Serious Games (SGs)" (Stege, Van Lankveld, & Spronck, 2011, p. 1). SGs represent an acknowledged potential for instruction where users can practice knowledge and skills, because they are able to strongly motivate learners of all ages and backgrounds with their immersive game-like environments. While SGs' potential for teacher education has been noted (De Gloria, Bellotti, & Berta, 2014), SG user studies in language teacher education and training have been underreported

1. Cyprus University of Technology, Limassol, Cyprus; giouli.pappa@cut.ac.cy
2. Cyprus University of Technology, Limassol, Cyprus; salomi.papadima@cut.ac.cy

How to cite this article: Pappa, G., & Papadima-Sophocleous, S. (2018). Creative Muscle: the serious learning game. In P. Taalas, J. Jalkanen, L. Bradley & S. Thouësny (Eds), *Future-proof CALL: language learning as exploration and encounters – short papers from EUROCALL 2018* (pp. 249-254). Research-publishing.net. https://doi.org/10.14705/rpnet.2018.26.845

(Ulicsak, 2010). This paper describes how *Creative Muscle,* a story driven SG designed to train language teachers in the use of VWs, was used in an online teacher education programme.

Second/Foreign Language (L2/FL) teacher education programmes have only recently applied teacher training in the simulation field of VWs (Pappa & Papadima-Sophocleous, 2016). Although VWs have attracted a lot of attention, communication and disorientation issues within the VWs and the steep learning curve were addressed as influencing participants' performance in the use of this technology (Guichon & Hauck, 2011). For this reason, *Creative Muscle* was designed to train six language practitioners/MA in CALL student-teachers how to use a VW. It particularly aims to make them familiar with and develop skills in using the Singularity Viewer VW for their online microteaching. This intervention lies within the realms of possibility that SGs and VWs may offer a stress-free and safe environment for experimentation in a real life-like environment (Ulicsak, 2010).

SGs need to have a strong connection with the learning process so as to give the sense of an expanded reality. In an attempt to create instructionally sound and relevant learning experiences for language practitioners, the metaphor of creative writing was used in the game as a learning mechanism.

Creative Muscle was designed and developed by Researcher 1 (see Figure 1). Each level was designed by combining classical platform and role-play game elements with quizzes, puzzles, and riddles as learning mechanics. All elements are materialised through the metaphor of creative writing as the main learning mechanism. Creative writing was specifically chosen as it derives from practitioners' language learning and teaching context.

The game starts with a brief introduction in which the player is shown that the playable character is trapped in a dark isolated room. In the first level, the player is introduced to the communication and orientation techniques. The character has to move around the room to discover the tools that will help him to improve his memory and escape his reality, and in that way progress in the game. To achieve this, the player has to solve issues related to his present location, with the help of a non-player character. He must follow instructions and solve quizzes while exploring the room. In the second level, the player learns how to move faster in the environment and how to store and retrieve objects from his inventory. A riddle guides the level and upon its completion, the player teleports to the third and final level of the game. In the third level, the player is required to make decisions within limited time. To do this, he has to resort to everything he has learned during Levels 1 and 2.

Figure 1. *Creative Muscle*: the serious learning game

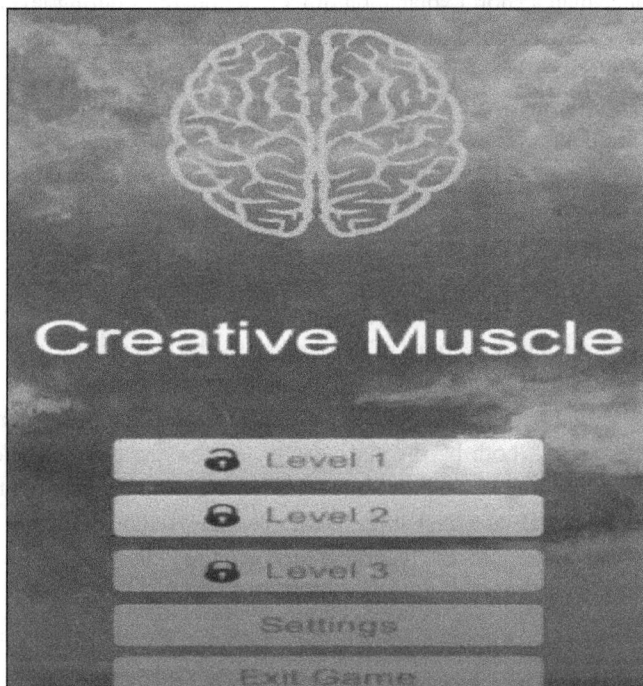

2. Method

2.1. Participants

The participants of this study were six female L2 practitioners from Cyprus, also full-time and part-time students of an online Master's programme in CALL. Serious gaming and VWs were completely new to all the participants.

2.2. Procedure

The intervention took place online, as part of the participants' studies. It was designed and delivered in the form of three one-hour online sessions, similar to the number of levels of the game. During these webinars, Researcher 1 introduced the concept of SGs and its related use to the participants. This occurred during the sixth week of the academic semester 2016-2017.

The game was made available to the participants to use autonomously with no other guidance than a short explanation of its functionalities during level one. The participants screen-recorded their gameplay. Upon completion of each level, the issues encountered were explained within the game and over the pre-arranged one-to-one tutorials between Researcher 1 and the participants. Users thus had the opportunity to express their emotions and understanding to the researcher, reflect on their experiences, and record them later in their reflective journal entries.

2.3.   Data collection

This study used a mixed-method data collection approach. Data included the researcher's personal observations of Researcher 1, who was also the webinar tutor, screen recordings of students' participation, and the participants' reflective journal entries. The virtual performance of the participants was screen-recorded with the use of Atube catcher, both by the participants and the researcher. Students were instructed to record the whole procedure in order to evaluate their performance in their reflection journals at a later stage. Data were analysed qualitatively through a transcribing and coding process regarding their acquired knowledge of what a VW is and what tools can be used.

3.   Findings and discussion

This study investigated the use of the *Creative Muscle* SG as a teacher training for VWs to six language practitioners, new to the 3D environment concept. The most common theme emerging from all collected data was participants' anxiety for this new kind of training. As extensively reported in SGs literature, there are frequent feelings of initial anxiety or discomfort in the use of a new technology, especially when SGs do not create relevant learning experiences for language practitioners: "But I don't like or play games. How can a game help me in my classroom?" (Student 2).

Despite these negative feelings, all six immediately started playing the game and they all managed to complete all three levels at their given time, according to the researcher's observations: "It was a hands-on experience – while frightening in the beginning" (Student 4). The completion of the game and therefore, the participants' training relied heavily on the sense of presence. The feeling that "they were there" (Student 5) was the second highly rated aspect of their training: "Good games are immersive and challenge and support players to approach, explore, and overcome problems" (Bellotti, Berta, & De Gloria, 2010). As all participants mentioned during their following-up tutorials, they were curious to see what a VW is like. They raised questions regarding how they could use VW in their practices and how VWs differ from SGs. The latter signified their progress in the 3D environment understanding. Their familiarisation with the VWs' provided tools was indicated by their point of interest: "Can we **store objects** from the game in our **inventory** and retrieve them in virtual world micro-teaching?" (Student 1). The skill of storing/retrieving objects was based on the immediate feedback they received within the game. The feedback enabled them to "remember what they had used" (Student 1). The progressive appearance of the key buttons for navigation and communication in the environment from the very first level appeared catalytic for the learning process of how to use a VW. This was proved with the completion of the final level of the game. The participants resorted to everything they had learned in Levels 1 and 2 in order to navigate properly and not get disoriented. One important finding was the participants' suggestions for improvement of the *Creative Muscle* on their own initiative. This could also be considered as proof of good understanding of a 3D environment through a SG.

4. Conclusion

It is hoped that we provided a good understanding of what *Creative Muscle* SG is and can be used for. Changes are planned to improve the game and to further test it with more participants.

5. Acknowledgements

We would like to thank the students who participated in this study.

References

Bellotti, F., Berta, R., & De Gloria, A. (2010). Designing effective serious games: opportunities and challenges for research. *International Journal of Emerging Technologies in Learning (iJET)*, *5*(3), 22-35. https://doi.org/10.3991/ijet.v5s3.1500

De Gloria, A., Bellotti, F., & Berta, R. (2014). Serious games for education and training. *International Journal of Serious Games*, *1*(1), 1-11. https://doi.org/10.17083/ijsg.v1i1.11

Guichon, N., & Hauck, M. (2011). Teacher education research in CALL and CMC: more in demand than ever. *ReCALL*, *23*(3), 187-199. https://doi.org/10.1017/S0958344011000139

Pappa, G., & Papadima-Sophocleous, S. (2016). A CALL for evolving teacher education through 3D microteaching. In S. Papadima-Sophocleous, L. Bradley, & S. Thouësny (Eds), *CALL communities and culture – short papers from EUROCALL 2016* (pp. 369-374). Research-publishing.net. https://doi.org/10.14705/rpnet.2016.eurocall2016.590

Stege, L., Van Lankveld, G., & Spronck, P. (2011). Serious games in education. *International Journal of Computer Science in Sport*, *10*(1), 1-9.

Thillainathan, N., & Leimeister, J. M. (2014). Serious game development for educators – a serious game logic and structure modeling language. *In 6th International Conference on Education and New Learning Technologies Barcelona, Spain*. https://www.alexandria.unisg.ch/233433/1/JML_484.pdf

Ulicsak, M. (2010). *Games in education: serious games – a Futurelab literature review*. FutureLab. https://www.nfer.ac.uk/publications/FUTL60/FUTL60.pdf

JYVÄSKYLÄN YLIOPISTO
UNIVERSITY OF JYVÄSKYLÄ

How MISSION BERLIN gamified
my FL/L2-German class – a six-week journey

Bart Pardoel[1], Salomi Papadima-Sophocleous[2],
and Androulla Athanasiou[3]

Abstract. This paper contributes to a better understanding of the affordances of gamification in Foreign or Second Language (FL/L2) education, specifically in the context of a secondary school. An Exploratory Research (ER) was conducted, aiming to examine how gamification affects secondary school learners' experience in the FL/L2 classroom. A six-week technology-assisted gamified mobile language course for German as a Foreign Language (GFL), called MISSION BERLIN, was developed, implemented, and evaluated. Data collection methods include semi-structured focus group interviews with all students, an online survey and Moodle logs. Results indicate that there are certain game elements that are more useful in a mobile Moodle environment than others, and that structure and duration of the course, as well as technical issues, influence the students' learning experience. The paper concludes with suggested improvements and final considerations for the implementation of a gamified mobile course for FL/L2 learning.

Keywords: foreign language learning, gamification, Moodle, MALL.

1.   Introduction

Current generation students are different in the way they learn and in the way they process information. They are used to interactive, dynamic content and information on demand. This is a world in which action is triggered by rewards, fun, and competition (Zarzycka-Piskorz, 2016). Such characteristic game elements

1. Cyprus University of Technology, Limassol, Cyprus; b.pardoel@gmail.com
2. Cyprus University of Technology, Limassol, Cyprus; salomi.papadima@cut.ac.cy
3. Cyprus University of Technology, Limassol, Cyprus; androulla.athanasiou@cut.ac.cy

How to cite this article: Pardoel, B., Papadima-Sophocleous, S., & Athanasiou, A. (2018). How MISSION BERLIN gamified my FL/L2-German class – a six-week journey. In P. Taalas, J. Jalkanen, L. Bradley & S. Thouësny (Eds), *Future-proof CALL: language learning as exploration and encounters – short papers from EUROCALL 2018* (pp. 255-260). Research-publishing.net. https://doi.org/10.14705/rpnet.2018.26.846

can be adapted for the needs arising during language classes (Danowska-Florczyk & Mostowski, 2014).

Using game elements outside a game context and applying them to, in this case, a GFL classroom, is a process called 'gamification'. This concept draws on the *self-determination theory* (Ryan & Deci, 2000) and the *theory of flow* (Csikszentmihályi, 1975). A person might experience *flow*, the "holistic sensation that people feel when they act with total involvement" (Csikszentmihályi, 1975, p. 36), when they feel their skills are good enough to overcome challenges.

Although the application of gamification in the area of education has a high prospective (Kapp, 2012; Simões, Redondo, & Vilas, 2013), remarkably few papers about gamification for FL/L2 learning in a secondary school context have been published (e.g. Dicheva, Dichev, Agre, & Angelova, 2015; Garland, 2015; Hamari, Koivisto, & Sarsa, 2014). This study examines the students' experience with MISSION BERLIN, a six-week gamified mobile online language course at A1 level for Dutch secondary school students.

In the following sections, we describe the methodology employed, followed by the main results and conclusions drawn from this research.

2. Method

2.1. The setting

The study took place in a small pre-vocational public school in the Netherlands. As a part of the mandatory programme, GFL at A1 level is offered to all students. In this study, two groups with a total of 39 (m=16/f=23) students between 13 and 14 years old participated as an 'intact class' (Mackey & Gass, 2005, p. 142). Nearly all of them stated that they play games, ranging from digital or mobile games to board or card games. When playing MISSION BERLIN, the students used the school's Wi-Fi connection and their own mobile devices.

2.2. Research design and data collection

An exploratory research approach was adopted to examine how gamification affects secondary school learners' experience in the FL/L2 classroom. The data were collected in a mixed methods procedure: quantitative data from the Moodle logs, consisting of 45,003 students' interactions with the website, and qualitative data from the focus group interviews, held at the end of the six-week course. A concurrent embedded design model (Creswell, 2009) was then used to collect and analyse the data, using triangulation to compare the statements in the focus group interviews with the Moodle logs.

2.3. Gamified course design

As shown in Figure 1, the participants used the Moodle platform, where they 'travelled through Germany by train', and 'visited several important German cities'.

After six weeks, the students 'arrived' at their final destination: Berlin. Each city contained some compulsory and optional challenges that, when finished, gave rewards to students. By completing optional challenges, the students could collect rare items.

During the course, the students were encouraged to complete individual and collaborative challenges, take quizzes, collect and construct artefacts, and gain coins and tickets in order to proceed through the game (see Figure 2).

Figure 1. Students use their mobile devices to access the Moodle platform

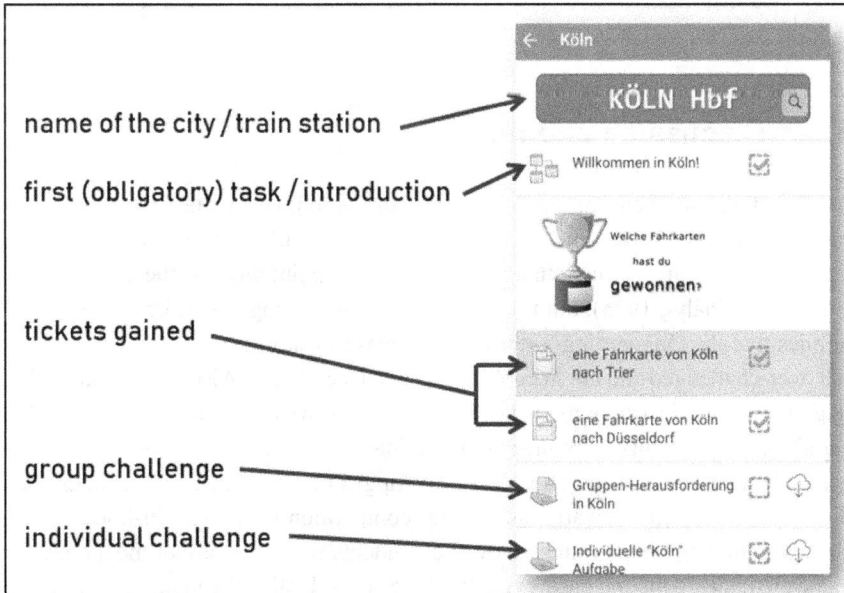

Figure 2.   Basic structure of the learning path per city

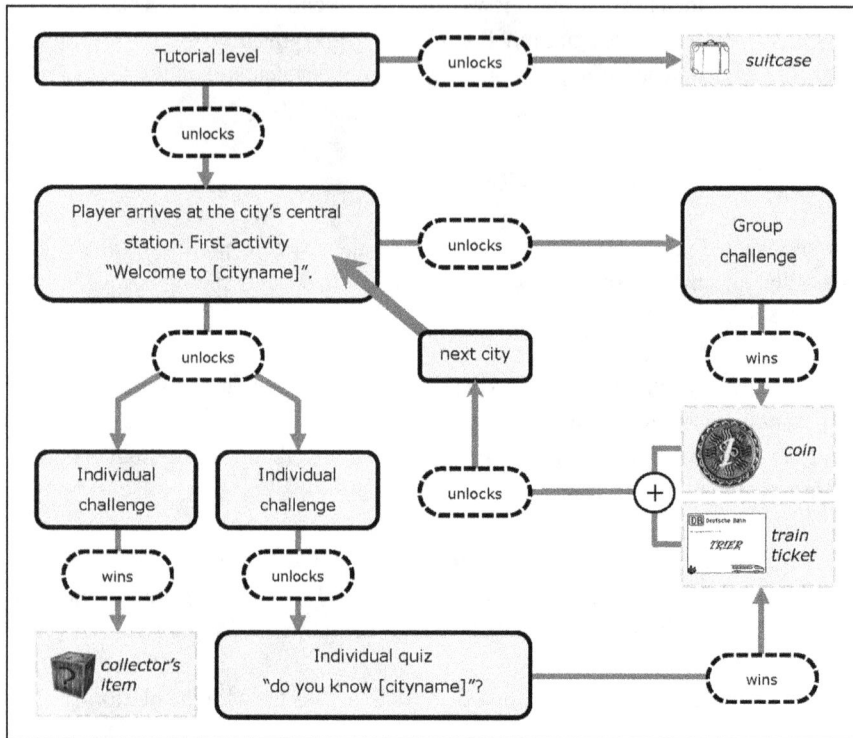

3.   Discussion and findings

As stated in the focus group interviews, the activities in the first cities were perceived as too hard, whereas activities in later cities proved to be of little challenge. This means that students only at some point were in the state of flow (Csikszentmihályi, 1975), but this was not the case during the entire game. It also implies that the Onboarding/Tutorial phase was too short, as the students initially felt over-challenged and not in control (Ryan & Deci, 2000). Also, more scaffolding (e.g. tutorial, L1 instructions) is needed. Moreover, what becomes apparent is that certain game elements were more popular than others. The most popular abstract game elements were cooperation and unlocking content. These elements addressed the players' need for rewards and group competition (Zarzycka-Piskorz, 2016). However, findings in this study show that students were unaware of most concrete game elements, with one clear exception: the coins. Unlike the items, which where only noticed by three students, two-third of the students knew exactly how many coins they collected after finishing MISSION BERLIN. Initially, the coins were implemented to unlock cities, as shown in Figure 1, but gradually they replaced other game elements' functions. For example, some students thought of them as rewards, which reduced the need for a badge, or used them to compare their progress in the game with other students, thereby ignoring any team leaderboards or progress bars. Coins are countable, gradable items, which makes them comparable to other students.

Other findings in this study suggest that the duration of the gamified course is a decisive factor for a positive learning experience. When the students (n=17) mentioned the duration of the course, most students (n=11) specifically stated that a shorter four-week course would keep MISSION BERLIN more challenging; only one student preferred a longer playtime. Any technical issues may also affect the student's learning experience negatively, as ten out of 35 suggestions for improvement were grouped around technical malfunctioning of the gamified system. Finally, log results indicate that the more active students are in class, the more likely it is they continue to play when they are at home.

4.   Conclusions

The results of this study imply that there is a positive impact on learners' experience in a secondary school context, provided there are not too many technical issues. More importantly, the data analysis has revealed specific conditions under which a gamified language course can be more or less effective. From the results of this study, we may conclude that gamification in a mobile context seems to work best in short sprints of four weeks. A longer duration of the course would have a negative effect on student's experience. However, a different setup (e.g. more cities, more coins) could extend the optimal duration.

Results also indicate that more scaffolding is needed, especially in the beginning. Furthermore, results strongly suggest that specific game elements (coins, levels, unlocking content, retrying, feedback) have more impact on students' experience than others.

Finally, high-active students are more likely to play in their leisure time. Low-active students will play only during school. Overall, in order to improve the students' experiences, MISSION BERLIN 2.0 could be re-designed based on the comments of the majority of the study's participants.

References

Creswell, J. W. (2009). *Research design: qualitative, quantitative and mixed approaches*. Sage Publications. https://doi.org/10.2307/1523157

Csikszentmihályi, M. (1975). Beyond boredom and anxiety: experiencing flow in work and play. *The Jossey-Bass Behavioral Science Series*.

Danowska-Florczyk, E., & Mostowski, P. (2014). Gamification as a new direction in teaching Polish as a foreign language. *ICT for Language Learning*, 0-3.

Dicheva, D., Dichev, C., Agre, G., & Angelova, G. (2015). Gamification in education: a systematic mapping study. *Journal of Educational Technology & Society*, *18*(3), 75-88. https://doi.org/10.1109/EDUCON.2014.6826129

Garland, C. M. (2015). *Gamification and implications for second language education: a meta analysis*. Culminating Projects in English.

Hamari, J., Koivisto, J., & Sarsa, H. (2014). Does gamification work? - A literature review of empirical studies on gamification. In *Proceedings of the Annual Hawaii International Conference on System Sciences* (pp. 3025-3034). https://doi.org/10.1109/HICSS.2014.377

Kapp, K. (2012). *The gamification of learning and instruction: game-based methods and strategies for training and education*. John Wiley & Sons.

Mackey, A., & Gass, S. M. (2005). *Second language research: methodology and design* (2nd ed.). Lawrence Erlbaum Associates, Inc.

Ryan, R. M., & Deci, E. L. (2000). Self-determination theory and the facilitation of intrinsic motivation, social development, and well-being. *American Psychologist*, *55*(1), 68-78. https://doi.org/10.1037/0003-066X.55.1.68

Simões, J., Redondo, R. D., & Vilas, A. F. (2013). A social gamification framework for a K-6 learning platform. *Computers in Human Behavior*, *29*(2), 345-353. https://doi.org/10.1016/j.chb.2012.06.007

Zarzycka-Piskorz, E. (2016). Kahoot it or not? Can games be motivating in learning grammar? *Teaching English with Technology*, *16*(3), 17-36.

Language education culture and practice under change at *JAMK Language Centre*

Pirkko Pollari[1] and Tuula Kotikoski[2]

Abstract. Universities of applied sciences in Finland are higher education institutions with emphasis on practical working life skills and strong links with working life. Students typically study in field-specific groups where they receive language and communication instruction alongside their professional courses. The development of language and communication studies is the chief responsibility of *JAMK Language Centre* at *JAMK University of Applied Sciences*. To create flexibility in language and communication teaching and to improve language and communication teachers' working practices, a two-year project was started at *JAMK Language Centre* in autumn 2017. In the experiment, JAMK´s students in Finnish degree programs began studying languages and communication in multidisciplinary groups instead of field-specific groups. There were administrative reasons as well as a pedagogical development aims behind the change. Two Strengths, Weaknesses, Opportunities, Threats (SWOT) analyses have been performed to find out about the experiences of the *JAMK Language Centre* staff members regarding the change. So far the experiment has been both challenging and rewarding and it continues until 2019 when the final results can be seen. The aim of this article is to present the first phase of the experimental project highlighting the experiences of the *JAMK Language Centre* staff.

Keywords: digitalization, language teaching, multidisciplinary student groups, paradigm change.

1. JAMK University of Applied Sciences, Jyväskylä, Finland; pirkko.pollari@jamk.fi
2. JAMK University of Applied Sciences, Jyväskylä, Finland; tuula.kotikoski@jamk.fi

How to cite this article: Pollari, P., & Kotikoski, T. (2018). Language education culture and practice under change at JAMK Language Centre. In P. Taalas, J. Jalkanen, L. Bradley & S. Thouësny (Eds), *Future-proof CALL: language learning as exploration and encounters – short papers from EUROCALL 2018* (pp. 261-265). Research-publishing.net. https://doi.org/10.14705/rpnet.2018.26.847

1.   Introduction

The literature on the future needs for working life emphasizes working in networks and complex problem solving (see e.g. Davies, Fidler, & Gorbis, 2011; Fidler, 2016). According to Davies et al. (2011), most real-life problems require a multidisciplinary approach to solve them. For example, Metsäportti and Saarinen (2017) have experimented with multidisciplinary nursing and engineering student groups when teaching English to them. We wanted to experiment this multidisciplinary approach with JAMK students from all Finnish degree programs, and started in autumn 2017.

In the past, different degree programs of *JAMK University of Applied Sciences* ordered their mandatory language and communication courses (English for Working Life, Swedish for Working Life, and Communication Skills for Working Life) from *JAMK Language Centre* once per year. This model was not flexible enough to meet the changing and increasing needs of degree programs and their students, especially the growing demand of online courses. Since *JAMK Language Centre* was now in charge of the entire language and communication course offering, it meant that the teachers had more freedom to choose the course modes they preferred. This change contributed to teachers' pedagogical development, e.g. how to implement online teaching flexibly and interactively in a student friendly way. The research focuses on the teachers' experiences of how they perceive the new situation and what implications it has on their teaching practices.

2.   Method

2.1.   SWOT analyses

In her doctoral thesis begun in 2017, Tuula Kotikoski studies the paradigm change at *JAMK Language Centre*. The first steps of the research consisted of two SWOT analyses which were performed in August 2017 and May 2018. Both the administrative staff (N=3) and language teachers (N=19) wrote about their concerns and expectations regarding the new system and teaching multidisciplinary groups.

3.   Discussion

In autumn 2017, with the experiment starting, expectations were very high and almost the entire staff was full of optimism: 20 out of 22 SWOT respondents felt the new multidisciplinary approach offered a way to help the *JAMK Language Centre* administration with the planning and implementation of courses. In addition, studying in this new system would empower the students in many ways: they could choose when (wide selection of courses), where (four campuses), and how (face-to-face, online, or blended learning) they would like to complete their mandatory language and communication studies. Teachers would be able to connect and communicate with students from different study fields.

In the 2017 SWOT questionnaire, the expectation of the lecturers was that they would now gain further control over their own annual teaching schedule timetables with a more even distribution of courses and a better balance of implementation modes. In the old implementation model, the autumn and spring terms could potentially be very unbalanced for many lecturers. In addition, the new approach would lessen the lectures' need for special knowledge of their students' particular fields of study, since the groups could be very heterogeneous and a stronger emphasis could be placed on making the course content generic. Prior to 2017, some lecturers had specialized their teaching within certain fields of study. The 2017 SWOT analysis revealed that a few lecturers, understandably, were disappointed and felt their motivation sinking since they felt that their long specialized teaching expertise was no longer needed.

Nevertheless, the overall view of the staff was generally very positive and the lecturers were looking forward to more collaboration in the form of creating materials together and implementing new ways to deliver the contents of their courses. During the 2017-2018 academic year, *JAMK Language Centre* allocated some resources to lecturers willing to create materials, which consisted mostly of generic themes and some specific materials for JAMK's various fields of study (e.g. nursing, engineering, and business) for the new multidisciplinary groups. Several respondents were very excited since they felt they were creating something new in collaboration with their colleagues. The younger lecturers, in particular, perceived an opportunity to gather new material for their multidisciplinary groups. Material repositories were created on the learning platform at JAMK for language and communication studies to be used in online courses. Many new digital tools were experimented with and information on their uses was shared and discussed in staff workshops. For example, Kahoot!, Padlet, Screencast-O-Matic, and some other tools were taken into use.

In the 2018 SWOT questionnaire (N=22 respondents), the reported atmosphere was still optimistic overall, and there seemed to be a consensus that multidisciplinary groups are easier to teach. The group dynamics in the new multidisciplinary classes were now highlighted by many respondents. The learning situations were more authentic and resembled real working life situations. The administrative staff has found ways to successfully direct all students to language study groups. According to lecturers, some students have really enjoyed the multidisciplinary groups. One respondent stated that the silent students were more active as members of multidisciplinary groups. However, at the beginning of a new course, students needed more time to get acquainted with one another.

4.   Conclusions

For the *JAMK Language Centre* lecturers, the academic year 2017-2018 was a time of learning and adapting. They felt that it was more interesting to work with their students and that there was an aspect of unpredictability as well, since the composition of the groups could be quite random. The year was also replete with professional development activities, collaboration with colleagues creating new materials, and the challenge of working with students from unfamiliar fields of study. According to two SWOT analyses, some lecturers were stressed and anguished as they felt they were drifting away from their own comfort zones because of the experiment.

For the administration of *JAMK Language Centre*, the biggest challenge was to determine the right amount and the right mix of courses to offer to meet the demand. Since certain courses received too few enrollments, not all of the courses could be implemented. Likewise, there was added stress and anguish for teachers who wondered what would happen if their annual quota of working hours could not be realized.

Online learning has gained great popularity among JAMK students since it is sometimes difficult for them to find suitable or convenient times for classes. Online language and communication courses are now more popular than ever. During the experiment the group sizes varied; sometimes the groups were very small, and sometimes too large. It seems that within certain degree programs there is not yet a sufficient understanding of how the new system works. It also appears that there is a general lack of awareness with regard of the vast selection of language and communication courses on offer. Finally, one *JAMK Language Centre* staff member expressed a weakness in the new system: "If perceived quality slips as a result of the recent changes, there may eventually be an even stronger push to get things back to the way they were before the changes were made". There is still one year left of the experiment in which languages are taught in multidisciplinary groups using different study modes (face-to-face, online, or blended). During the academic year 2018-2019, a decision will be made whether to continue the experiment or return to the former model.

5.   Acknowledgements

We would like to thank Jason Stevens for his valuable feedback on this article.

References

Davies, A., Fidler, D., & Gorbis, M. (2011). *Future work skills 2020*. Institute for the Future for the University of Phoenix Research Institute. http://www.iftf.org/uploads/media/SR-1382A_ UPRI_future_work_skills_sm.pdf

Fidler, D. (2016). *Future skills*. Update and literature review. Prepared for ACT Foundation and The Joyce Foundation. Institute for the Future. http://www.iftf.org/fileadmin/user_upload/ downloads/wfi/ACTF_IFTF_FutureSkills-report.pdf

Metsäportti, M., & Saarinen, K. (2017). A fast track to professional English – engineering and health care students collaborating in an online course. *Language Teaching Tomorrow*. http:// urn.fi/urn:nbn:fi:jamk-issn-2343-0281-27

Discourses in place: technology and language experts negotiating solutions for a language learning application

Maritta Riekki[1] and Leena Kuure[2]

Abstract. This study explores the nature of collaboration between language students and technology developers while designing an application for language teaching. This project was part of a university course on language learning and teaching in technology-rich environments. An important aspect of the course was to help the university students to explore and extend their understandings of language teaching and being language teachers. One of the student teams on the course had the opportunity of acting as language (pedagogy) experts while working with technology experts, negotiating directions for the application under development. Such a collaborative relationship together with the support of the course was expected to provide the participants with new perspectives, helping them to detach themselves from narrow conceptions of language pedagogy. Video materials were stored from different phases of the project. The design concepts and reflection papers produced by the students were also used in the analysis. The research drew on nexus analysis. The findings suggest that multidisciplinary collaboration can be fruitfully integrated into language teacher education to provide the students with experiences and perspectives for assuming an active role in technology development for language learning, and, additionally for seeing this type of cooperation as an essential element of their language teacher professionalism.

Keywords: professional development, multidisciplinarity, sense making, nexus analysis.

1. University of Oulu, Oulu, Finland; maritta.riekki@oulu.fi
2. University of Oulu, Oulu, Finland; leena.kuure@oulu.fi

How to cite this article: Riekki, M., & Kuure, L. (2018). Discourses in place: technology and language experts negotiating solutions for a language learning application. In P. Taalas, J. Jalkanen, L. Bradley & S. Thouësny (Eds), *Future-proof CALL: language learning as exploration and encounters – short papers from EUROCALL 2018* (pp. 266-271). Research-publishing.net. https://doi.org/10.14705/rpnet.2018.26.848

1.   Introduction

As our technology-rich environments of everyday life and education are changing, language teachers also need to rethink their pedagogic roles, designs, and practices in a new light (Blin & Jalkanen, 2014). One site for appropriating new kinds of language teacher professionalism is the development of applications for language learning/teaching together with technology specialists. Language teachers and researchers have been involved in numerous projects where new environments have been under construction and applied in practice (see ReCALL[3]). However, research in the field rather focuses on aspects of language learning and pedagogic approaches than on the development of technologies. Language teachers and students have been participating in technology development often as usability testers and focus group informants. It seems that language teachers could have a stronger role in developing technology-mediated learning environments for language pedagogy in the modern world. This, however, requires new kinds of expertise and agency in multidisciplinary collaboration, which the current language teacher education seldom supports concretely (Riekki, 2016).

This study focuses on collaboration between two teams, one with expertise in language pedagogy and the other in technology. The context for the study was a Master's level course on language learning and teaching in technology-rich environments where two technology developers were invited to work together with one of the project teams on the course, designing an application for use in language teaching. One of the developers was a doctoral student (ubiquitous computing) and the other a Master's student (information networks). The study draws on a nexus analysis (Scollon & Scollon, 2004) and a multimodal (inter)action analysis (Norris, 2011) using multiple types of data. This allows exploring collaboration in situ as an aggregate of discourses echoing the past and emanating new discourses.

2.   Research materials and approach

2.1.   Research materials

The aim of this study was to shed light on the nature of collaboration between language students and technology developers. The language team joined the technology team not only to test the application but also to act as language teaching

---

3. https://www.cambridge.org/core/journals/recall

specialists in the course of the design process. Different types of research materials were gathered, e.g. video materials from the planning, testing and evaluation sessions, which took place beyond the course meetings. In addition to the video data, reflection papers and design concepts written by the students were consulted.

2.2.   Research approach

The research proceeded by examining the video data through the lens of nexus analysis, which sees social action and interaction as an intersection of interaction order, historical body, and discourses in place (Scollon & Scollon, 2004). Discourses in place refers to the social semiotic meaning making that emerges in a social arrangement by which people come together. Interaction order implies the mutual relationships and power configurations between the participants. Historical body is used to describe the life experiences of the social actors involved in the action. Nexus analysis is characteristically ethnographic, yet historical, in its approach (Scollon & Scollon, 2004). Some aspects of multimodal (inter)action analysis were also used in the examination of the research materials, so as to trace identity work arising in the collaborative situations (Norris, 2011).

3.   Discussion

Riekki (2016) has pointed out in earlier research with the same materials the diversity of discourses circulating in the design sessions: aspects of application design, teamwork, teacher education, technology use in language teaching, language teachers' professional practice, and the nature of language learning. The present study explores the collaborative dynamics of action and interaction as well as the competing discourses circulating in the discursive space of the design meetings.

Figure 1 illustrates the arrangement in a typical design session: the technology developers (Alex and Riina) are positioned closer to the data projector screen and the language students (Samuel, Tuomas, Ilkka, Aaro, and Jouni) at the other end of the table as a group.

In the sessions, the interaction order between the participants was quite balanced as the language students were positioned both by the technology developers and by themselves as collaborative partners instead of mere test users. This was done by giving others opportunities for expressing their views and negotiating for meanings, which led to extended discussions in comparison to minimal question-answer exchanges. In the language team, Aaro and Samuel were more active in taking turns but they did this by voicing the outcomes of the whole team. The other team members were giving their consent through multimodal means such as nods, gazes, affirmative expressions, and quick consultations in the team. The technology experts' questions prompted longer discussions and sense making in relation to the application, its technical solutions, its use in the field of language pedagogy, and possibilities for further development. The developers' questions were at times what can be expected in usability testing or application development, inviting direct answers. However, more general questions were also asked to prompt discussion around the language teachers' work-life practices. The developers also gave lots of space for the language students to share their views on the working process related to application design. The students wished, for example, more detailed advance information on technical aspects to be able to anticipate some of the constraints of programming in the ideation phase.

Figure 1.   The setting in a meeting between the language and technology teams

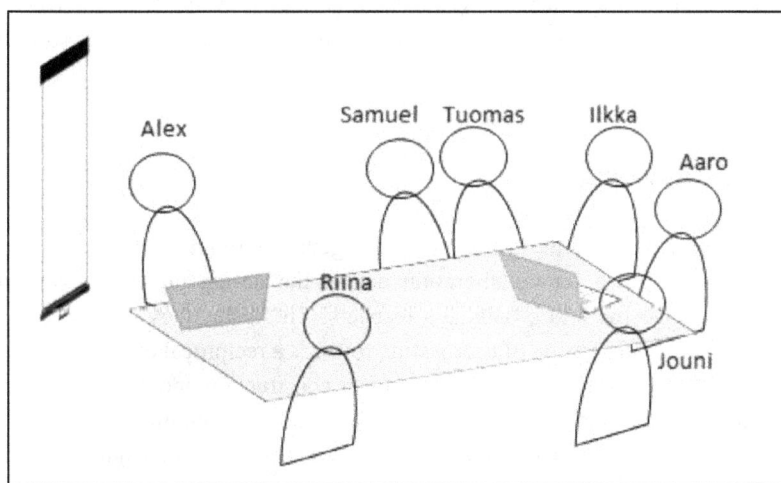

There was also negotiation for meanings in the sessions concerning the focus of evaluation in commenting the use of the application. The technology experts seemed to expect that the evaluation would focus on the application itself, while the students were broadening the discussion to the field of language pedagogy more generally. The technology experts seized this opportunity and joined such exchanges. All in all, the interactions throughout the working process seemed to provide space for genuine collaboration instead of the simple developer vs. test user setting.

Further, the discussions in the meeting involved tensions related to the experiences of the participants and accustomed practices (historical bodies) in language learning and teaching. Discourses of the tradition were intertwining with discourses of change: classroom-based, textbook-driven teaching of the four skills of language competence in contrast with supporting learning as a situated, sociocultural enterprise more broadly. Moreover, the students were anticipating challenges in trying to surpass traditional language pedagogy as digitally literate professionals, showing agency as future language teachers.

No particularly novel pedagogic solutions for technology development were presented, however. Nevertheless, there were several indications of the language students seeing the broader uses of the application than just completing a game task through a device. Thus, their discourses circulating the design sessions reflected modern views of language learning, also reflected in the curricula. The technology experts were open to these discussions, but their primary aim was to produce a functioning language learning application. The students were in their discussions bringing forth identity elements (Norris, 2011) not only of language teachers, language students, and teacher students, but also of design team members and language experts.

4.   Conclusion

The study showed how the teams created together, through multimodal means, a fruitful atmosphere for collaboration during the design project as part of a university course for future language teachers. The technology experts stepped aside from the configuration of user testing towards a reciprocal exchange of ideas about the language learning application under construction and, hence, about the nature of language learning, language teaching, and programming, as well as the role of technology in language pedagogy. The discourses around language learning echoed past and current practices anticipating future directions. There seems to be a need for renewal in language teacher education to support students in broadening their view of the profession, taking also an active role in technology design for language pedagogy.

5.   Acknowledgements

We would like to thank the language students and the technology researchers/ developers for participating in this study.

References

Blin, F., & Jalkanen, J. (2014). Designing for language learning: agency and languaging in hybrid environments. *APPLES – Journal of applied language studies, 8*(1), 147-170. http://apples. jyu.fi/ArticleFile/download/433

Norris, S. (2011). *Identity in (inter)action: introducing multimodal (inter)action analysis.* De Gruyter Mouton. https://doi.org/10.1515/9781934078280

Riekki, M. (2016). Navigating change: nexus-analytic explorations in the field of foreign language education. *Acta Universitatis Ouluensis B. Humaniora, 146.*

Scollon, R., & Scollon, S. W. (2004). *Nexus analysis. Discourse and the emerging Internet.* Routledge. https://doi.org/10.4324/9780203694343

The acquisition of French vocabulary
in an interactive digital gaming context

Avery Rueb[1], Walcir Cardoso[2], and Jennica Grimshaw[3]

Abstract. *Prêt à Négocier* (PàN) is an interactive digital information gap game designed to help French students improve their interaction skills. In this study, we examined the effects of its use on improving French learners' vocabulary. Following a pretest/posttest design, we compared the development of 20 French words between an experimental and a control group. Although both groups followed a similar trajectory in vocabulary learning, some participants benefited from the proposed game-based pedagogy more than others due to individual differences. Our findings highlight how interactive and meaningful games such as PàN can complement and enhance the learning of second/foreign language (L2) vocabulary.

Keywords: gaming, L2 learning, oral interaction.

1. Introduction

Oral interaction is an L2 competency that is required for the completion of everyday tasks such as talking on the phone or engaging in face-to-face conversations with peers or teachers. Because it requires the learner to exchange information with a partner by speaking and understanding what is being said efficiently in real time (i.e. fluently), oral interaction is not easy for L2 learners to master. An important aspect of developing interaction skills is the mastery of L2 vocabulary, particularly the words that are required for fluent communication (Nation, 2009). Traditionally, teachers have used paper-based information gap activities (Larsen-Freeman & Long, 1991) to promote interaction for the learning of a variety of L2 skills (e.g.

1. Vanier College, Montreal, Canada; rueba@vaniercollege.qc.ca
2. Concordia University, Montreal, Canada; walcir.cardoso@concordia.ca
3. Concordia University, Montreal, Canada; jennica.grimshaw@concordia.ca

How to cite this article: Rueb, A., Cardoso, W., & Grimshaw, J. (2018). The acquisition of French vocabulary in an interactive digital gaming context. In P. Taalas, J. Jalkanen, L. Bradley & S. Thouësny (Eds), *Future-proof CALL: language learning as exploration and encounters – short papers from EUROCALL 2018* (pp. 272-277). Research-publishing.net. https://doi.org/10.14705/rpnet.2018.26.849

de la Fuente, 2006). However, with the rise of 'anytime, anywhere learning', L2 students and instructors are willing and ready to invest in mobile-assisted learning (Stockwell, 2010), especially in an autonomous manner to enhance their experience (Lai, Yeung, & Hu, 2016). This study contributes to this area of research by examining the effects of a mobile digital game, PàN, as a tool to assist in the acquisition of vocabulary in L2 French.

PàN is a digital information gap game designed to help French students improve their oral interaction skills. The game can be played on computers, tablets, and smartphones in both the classroom as a face-to-face conversation and/or out of the classroom with a built-in audio chat feature. To play the game, students have three minutes to both exchange information about the product they are buying/selling as well as to agree on the item's final price (see Rueb, Cardoso, & Grimshaw, 2016 for an introduction to the game). Figure 1 illustrates a seller's user interface for the English version of the game, showing a car for sale and related negotiable features (e.g. air conditioning, automatic transmission).

Figure 1.   PàN: interface

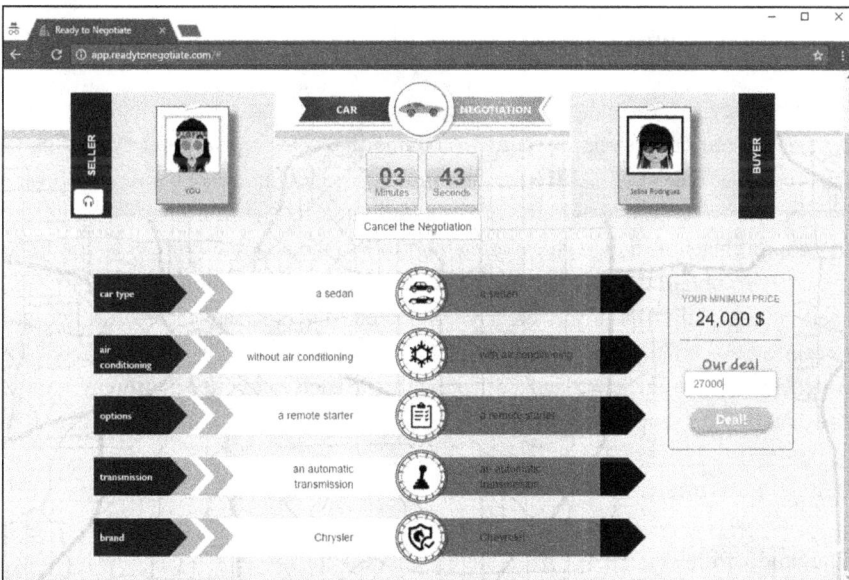

The goal of this study is to examine the effects of the pedagogical use of PàN on improving French learners' vocabulary. We hypothesized that the game would positively impact French vocabulary acquisition in the context of L2 learning based on de la Fuente (2006). As such, our research question was the following: Can PàN help French learners improve their French vocabulary more than paper-based, gamified information gap activities?

2. Method

2.1. Participants and experimental groups

To investigate the effects of PàN on vocabulary acquisition, we examined two groups of intermediate-level French as second language learners (total N=29) in a classroom setting over a period of four weeks. The participants were post-secondary (CEGEP, or General and Vocational College) students at an Anglophone college in Montreal, Quebec. They were stratified into two experimental (intact) groups: while the experimental group (n=17) played PàN, the control group (n=12) played paper-based, gamified information gap activities, which attempted to emulate the same types of oral interactions found in the digital game.

2.2. Procedures

In game-playing, the participants negotiated orally and synchronously with a partner for the purchasing or renting of items like cars, houses, and even trips to the moon (see Rueb et al., 2016 for details). As it is a competitive game, pairs of L2 learners were required to use their oral interaction skills and appropriate vocabulary in a comprehensible and persuasive manner to win the negotiation (e.g. to convince the other to obtain the best final price on a product). In addition, vocabulary was used meaningfully (i.e. it was clearly connected to personal experiences), helping to reinforce acquisition (Meara, 1996). Game playing sessions were held twice a week, 25 minutes each, and had a different theme each week (i.e. apartment rentals, cars, apartments, and pirate ships).

2.3. Instruments

The study followed a pre/post/delayed posttest design that measured learners' vocabulary development using Meara and Buxton's (1987) 60-item yes/no test.

The 60 items were broken into three word groups: (1) 20 game words selected randomly from the four negotiation themes in the aforementioned Procedure section (the target words used in our study); (2) 20 non-game words (used as distractors); and (3) 20 imaginary, pseudo English words (used as a means to control for guesses and 'slips of the mind'). On the test sheet, participants indicated if they knew a word (e.g. by underlining or circling the corresponding option) and were attributed a point for every game word identified correctly. Students who identified more than 4 imaginary words from the list were eliminated from the study. The pretests were administered immediately before the first treatment, the posttest immediate after the final one, and the delayed posttests two weeks after the treatment.

3. Results

A preliminary independent-samples t-test was conducted to compare the two groups at the pretest, which revealed that the experimental (M=6.47, SD=2.70) and control groups (M=4.08, SD=1.50) were not comparable at the outset; $t(28)$=2.87, p=.008. However, the nonsignificant p value observed on the Box's Test of Equality of Covariance Matrices (p=.28) reassured us that multivariate tests could be performed.

Consequently, we conducted follow-up Within-Subjects ANOVAs, which showed a significant effect for time (Wilks' Lambda=0.18, $F(2,27)$, 59.19, p=.000), but no time versus group interaction (Wilks' Lambda=0.82, $F(2,27)$, 2.95, p=.069). This means that while both groups significantly improved over time, the difference observed cannot be attributed to the treatment received by the participants, as both groups behaved in a relatively similar manner. Table 1 provides the means and standard deviations of the vocabulary gains involving the target words for each group at each test.

Table 1.   Vocabulary gains for game words (N=20)

Group	Pretest		Posttest		Delayed posttest	
	M /20	SD	M /20	SD	M /20	SD
Experiment	6.47	2.70	14.24	4.42	13.35	5.82
Control	4.08	1.50	9.23	2.98	9.77	4.25

Although noticeable gains were observed on the posttest (PàN: M=14.24 vs. Control: M=9.23), this difference was not deemed significant, possibly due to the high standard deviations found in the experimental group (see forthcoming discussion). Figure 2 illustrates the development paths observed among the two groups over time.

Figure 2.   Vocabulary learning: groups over time

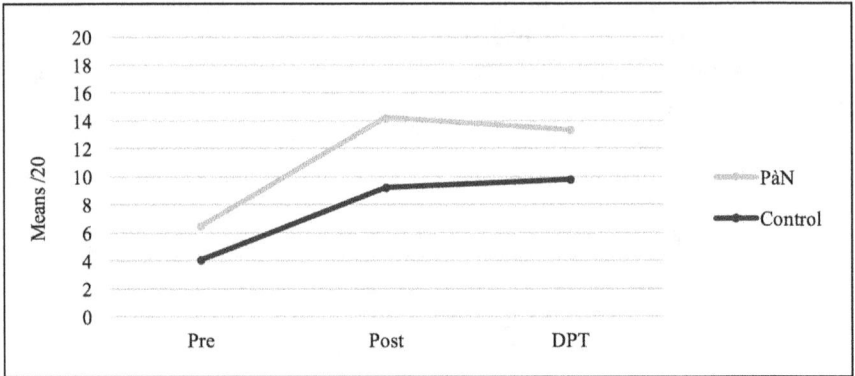

4.   Discussion

Can PàN help French learners improve their French vocabulary? Based on an exclusively statistical analysis of our results, digital game-playing had limited pedagogical value for vocabulary acquisition in comparison with traditional (but gamified), paper-based information gap activities. We highlight the term *limited pedagogical value* because we found evidence that PàN-based learning was beneficial for *some* users. For example, while one game-playing participant went from two known items on the pretest to 17 on the two posttests (an 850% increase), another improved by a mere 100%, going from four on the pretest to eight and seven on the respective posttests. These discrepancies might explain the higher standard deviations observed within the experimental group and no time versus group interaction among the groups.

5.   Conclusion

Our findings highlight how interactive games such as PàN can enhance the learning of L2 vocabulary for *some* participants, possibly due to: (1) individual differences observed in L2 vocabulary development (e.g. Dóczi & Kormos, 2016) and, as we hypothesize, (2) some of the game's affordances – e.g. its ability to promote autonomous learning (Lai et al., 2016), in a fun and competitive (and consequently motivating) environment (Rueb et al., 2016). Because interactive games such as PàN can also help increase student interest and engagement in the learning process, we believe they are another viable option for teachers' pedagogical toolboxes.

6.   Acknowledgements

We would like to thank participants. This study was partially funded by the *Social Sciences and Humanities Research Council of Canada* (SSHRC).

References

De la Fuente, M. J. (2006). Classroom L2 vocabulary acquisition: investigating the role of pedagogical tasks and form-focused instruction. *Language Teaching Research, 10*(3), 263-295. https://doi.org/10.1191/1362168806lr196oa

Dóczi, B., & Kormos, J. (2016). *Longitudinal developments in vocabulary knowledge and lexical organization.* Oxford University Press. https://doi.org/10.1093/acprof:oso/9780190210274.001.0001

Lai, C., Yeung, Y., & Hu, J. (2016). University student and teacher perceptions of teacher roles in promoting autonomous language learning with technology outside the classroom. *Computer Assisted Language Learning, 29*(4), 703-723. https://doi.org/10.1080/09588221.2015.1016441

Larsen-Freeman, D., & Long, M. (1991). *An introduction to second language acquisition research.* Longman

Meara, P. (1996). The classical research in L2 vocabulary acquisition. In G. Anderman & M. Rogers (Eds), *Words words words; the translator and the language learner* (pp. 27-40). WBC Book Manufacturers Ltd.

Meara, P., & Buxton, B. (1987). An alternative to multiple choice vocabulary tests. *Language Testing, 4*(2), 142-154.

Nation, I. S. P. (2009). *Teaching ESL/EFL reading and writing.* Routledge.

Rueb, A., Cardoso, W., & Grimshaw, J. (2016). Developing oral interaction skills with a digital information gap activity game. In S. Papadima-Sophocleous, L. Bradley & S. Thouësny (Eds), *CALL communities and culture – short papers from EUROCALL 2016* (pp. 397-402). https://doi.org/10.14705/rpnet.2016.eurocall2016.595

Stockwell, G. (2010). Using mobile phones for vocabulary activities: examining the effect of the platform. *Language Learning & Technology, 14*(2), 95-110.

Learning outcomes and learners' impressions of parallel and monolingual concordancers

June Ruivivar[1] and Cynthia Lapierre[2]

Abstract. Monolingual and parallel concordancers have both been found to benefit second-language (L2) grammatical development. However, the relative benefits of these two concordancer types remains unclear. The present study compares learning outcomes and learners' perceptions of a monolingual English (Corpus of Contemporary American English, COCA) and a French-English parallel concordancer (Tradooit), using verb-preposition collocations as a target feature. Students in an advanced English as a second language (ESL) course completed three concordancing activities where they used either Tradooit (for French L1 speakers) or COCA (for other L1s) to formulate rules for challenging verb-preposition collocations (e.g. *arrive in/at*). Pre- and post-tests showed significant learning gains for both groups, which were maintained in delayed post-tests; however, perception questionnaires showed that Tradooit was perceived as easier and more useful for language learning. We suggest that these differences may be due to the type of cognitive work involved in L1-L2 comparison versus L2 pattern-finding, but that these two processes may both lead to noticing and learning.

Keywords: data-driven learning, concordancing, parallel concordancers.

1.   Introduction

Data-Driven Learning (DDL), the use of authentic language samples to examine patterns of language use, is increasingly recognized for its affordances in grammar instruction. In particular, it can draw learners' attention to forms that they may otherwise overlook (Moon & Oh, 2018) and involve a greater cognitive load, which may help learners internalize language items (Herron & Tomasello, 1992; Smart, 2014).

1. Concordia University, Montreal, Canada; june.ruivivar@concordia.ca
2. Concordia University, Montreal, Canada; cynthia.lapierre@concordia.ca

How to cite this article: Ruivivar, J., & Lapierre, C. (2018). Learning outcomes and learners' impressions of parallel and monolingual concordancers. In P. Taalas, J. Jalkanen, L. Bradley & S. Thouësny (Eds), *Future-proof CALL: language learning as exploration and encounters – short papers from EUROCALL 2018* (pp. 278-283). Research-publishing.net. https://doi.org/10.14705/rpnet.2018.26.850

DDL activities are typically carried out using either monolingual or parallel concordancers. Monolingual concordancers draw on samples in one language; for example, a learner may find that *throw*, when used with its common collocate *away*, means *to dispose of*. Parallel concordancers, on the other hand, provide examples from two or more languages and are often used for L1-L2 comparisons. To use the same example, a French-speaking learner might find that *jeter*, when used in the sense *to dispose of*, translates to *throw away*, not *throw*, in English.

Research suggests that both types of concordancers result in learning gains and are well received by learners (e.g. Huang, 2014 for monolingual, and Gao, 2011 for parallel). However, to our knowledge, no published research to date has directly compared these two types. It is not clear, then, whether the documented benefits of monolingual and parallel concordancing are attributable to DDL itself, or to features unique to each type, such as learners' preferences. The present study attempts to address this gap by comparing students' learning gains from, and perceptions of, a monolingual English (Corpus of Contemporary American English, COCA) and parallel French-English concordancer (Tradooit). Specifically, we wanted to compare:

- the effects of a parallel and monolingual concordancer on learners' recognition and productive knowledge of verb-preposition collocations, and

- learners' perceptions of each concordancer's ease of use, usefulness for coursework, and usefulness for general language improvement

Verb-preposition collocations (e.g. *insist on, wait for*) were chosen as a target feature because it was not part of the students' course syllabus, making it possible to isolate the effects of DDL from classroom instruction. Although students may have previously encountered the form, pre-test results suggest that it continues to be a challenge for them.

2. Method

2.1. Participants and context

Participants were 23 students, aged 17 to 40, in an advanced ESL course taught by the second author. The course covered advanced grammar, vocabulary, and source-based writing, and consisted of two 2.5-hour sessions per week over 13 weeks. Students spoke a variety of languages, including Arabic, Chinese, French, Hebrew, and Spanish. These languages were used to assign them to concordancers for the study. Ten proficient or native French speakers were assigned to the parallel concordancer, Tradooit; the remaining 13 were assigned to the monolingual concordancer, COCA.

2.2.   Procedure

2.2.1.   Concordance training

Each group received a 1.5-hour training session on their assigned concordancer. Students were introduced to corpora and concordancing, then provided with instructions on using the concordancer, with focus on collocations. They were then guided through practice activities where they looked up a list of expressions on the concordancer. They also performed a pilot task (not included in the analysis) to ensure that they were familiar with the concordancers before collecting data.

2.2.2.   Treatment

Throughout the semester, students completed three guided induction activities where they corrected a set of sentences by looking up expressions on the concordancer, formulated a hypothesis about the underlying rule, and provided two concordance lines illustrating the rule.

Each assignment included three to four of the 10 target verb-preposition collocations, and three grammar items from the previous unit to serve as distractors. These were given as homework and graded on completion rather than accuracy.

2.2.3.   Instruments

Learning outcomes were measured with pre-, post-, and delayed post-tests measuring recognition (multiple choice) and controlled production (gap-fill). The tests consisted of the ten target items and ten distractors from the previous unit.

Perceptions were measured using an end-of-course questionnaire asking them to rate three items on a ten-point scale: how easy the concordancer was to use, how useful it was for the course, and how useful it was for learning English in general. There was also space for them to write comments.

3. Results and discussion

3.1. Learning outcomes

To compare learning outcomes, paired-samples t-tests were performed between the pre- and post-tests, and between the post- and delayed post-tests. Table 1 shows an increase in mean recognition scores for both groups, which was maintained on the delayed post-test. Pre- to post-test gains were significant for both the COCA, $t(12)=7.63$, $p<.001$, and Tradooit groups, $t(9)=9.22$, $p<.001$, but not significant between post- and delayed post-tests. To compare improvement between groups, we conducted independent-samples t-tests between the mean difference in scores between the pre- and post-tests. We found no significant difference between the students who used COCA ($M=2.92$, $SD=1.38$) and those who used Tradooit ($M=2.90$, $SD=.99$), $t(21)=.04$, $p=.96$, suggesting that they improved to similar degrees.

Table 1. Mean recognition scores

	Mean scores /10 (SD)		
	Pre	Post	Delayed
COCA	6.7 (1.0)	9.6 (.65)	9.8 (.37)
Tradooit	6.6 (.74)	9.5 (.67)	9.6 (.70)

Results for the production test are summarized in Table 2. The differences were again significant for both COCA, $t(12)=6.79$, $p<.001$, and Tradooit, $t(9)=6.00$, $p=.002$. These increases were also maintained in the delayed post-test. The score increase was non-significant between the two groups, $t(21)=0.41$, $p=.69$.

Table 2. Mean production scores

	Mean scores /10 (SD)		
	Pre	Post	Delayed
COCA	7.08 (1.0)	8.54 (.88)	8.78 (1.3)
Tradooit	6.8 (1.0)	8.5 (1.3)	8.5 (1.27)

3.2. Learners' perceptions

Learners' ratings for ease of use, immediate usefulness (for the course), and general usefulness are provided in Table 3. Independent-samples t-tests revealed significant differences between the groups' ratings for ease of use, $t(21)=2.59$, $p=.02$, and general usefulness, $t(21)=2.69$, $p=.01$. There was no significant difference for immediate usefulness, $t(21)=1.62$, $p=.12$. Tradooit users often commented on its simple interface (e.g. "it looks like a dictionary"), while those assigned to COCA seemed intimidated by both the less-intuitive design and technical terms (e.g. *matching strings*). Both groups, however, commented that their concordancer helped with academic writing, an important component of the course.

Table 3. Learners' perceptions

	Ease of use	Immediate Usefulness	General Usefulness
COCA	7.62 (2.26)	6.69 (2.46)	5.69 (3.12)
Tradooit	9.63 (.94)	8.5 (1.84)	8.56 (1.57)

4. Conclusions

We start our discussion with perhaps the most interesting result: the parallel concordancer was easier and more useful, although both types serve the immediate goal of improving academic writing. The interface issues addressed in the comments may have affected perceptions of general versus immediate usefulness: outside of coursework, students may be more inclined to resolve L2 issues by looking up translations or comparing expressions than by analyzing L2 samples. The similarity of immediate usefulness scores may also be due to the course material; during the concordancing assignments, students were likely picking up on features they could use in their writing. In other words, they may find concordancing more useful for features of immediate relevance than for general vocabulary or grammar development.

The comparable learning gains suggest that the two concordancers might nevertheless offer the same benefits, but through different degrees of noticing and cognitive involvement. Tradooit, with direct L1-L2 comparisons, may entail less cognitive work but highlight subtle differences between the L1 and L2 (as is the case with many verb-preposition collocations), as proposed by Moon and Oh (2018). COCA may be more cognitively challenging, as learners had to analyze concordance lines, but consistent with Smart (2014), this may have resulted in awareness and learning of the target features. Of course, because this study was concerned with learning outcomes and perceptions, these possibilities should be tested in future research. Process-focused procedures such as observation, stimulated recall, or mouse-tracking can offer further insight on learners' actual use of the concordancer and what specific features they find useful.

References

Gao, Z.-M. (2011). Exploring the effects and use of a Chinese-English parallel concordancer. *Computer-Assisted Language Learning, 24*(3), 255-275. https://doi.org/10.1080/09588221.2010.540469

Herron, C., & Tomasello, M. (1992). Acquiring grammatical structures by guided induction. *French Review, 65*, 708-718.

Huang, Z. (2014). The effects of paper-based DDL on the acquisition of lexico-grammatical patterns in L2 writing. *ReCALL, 26*(2), 163-183. https://doi.org/10.1017/S0958344014000020

Moon, S., & Oh, S.-Y. (2018). Unlearning overgenerated be through data-driven learning in the secondary EFL classroom. *ReCALL, 30*(1), 48-67. https://doi.org/10.1017/S0958344017000246

Smart, J. (2014). The role of guided induction in paper-based data-driven learning. *ReCALL, 26*(2), 184-201. https://doi.org/10.1017/S0958344014000081

Examining the impact of an automated translation chatbot on online collaborative dialog for incidental L2 learning

Takeshi Sato[1], Masa'aki Ogura[2], Shoma Aota[3], and Tyler Burden[4]

Abstract. This study examines the effectiveness of an automated translation chatbot used in online interactions which consequently could enhance second/foreign language (L2) competence. Based on the sociocultural perspectives of learning, such as communication to recognize the difference from others and to be involved in sense-making processes, this study examines the automated translation chatbot to translate L1 statements into L2 automatically during online interactions by hypothesizing that the chatbot provides a variety of L2 comprehensive input and lowers learners' anxiety to write their L2 posts, which will lead to successful L2 learning. To verify our hypothesis, quantitative and qualitative data was collected by the online interaction, essay writing tasks, and open-ended questionnaire before and after the interaction. The findings of this study will suggest that the efficient use of an online translation bot facilitates collaborative dialog and results in more successful L2 learning.

Keywords: collaborative learning, translation chatbot, online learning community, comprehensive input, incidental learning.

1.   Introduction

Collaborative activities have been acknowledged as being beneficial for L2 learning. This is because of the perspective that these activities serve as communication to recognize the differences from others and establish shared

1. Tokyo University of Agriculture and Technology, Tokyo, Japan; tsato@cc.tuat.ac.jp
2. Osaka Ohtani University, Osaka, Japan; oguramasa@osaka-ohtani.ac.jp
3. University of Tsukuba, Ibaraki, Japan; aota.shoma.fu@u.tsukuba.ac.jp
4. Meisei University, Tokyo, Japan; burden.tyler@meisei-u.ac.jp

How to cite this article: Sato, T., Ogura, M., Aota, S., & Burden, T. (2018). Examining the impact of an automated translation chatbot on online collaborative dialog for incidental L2 learning. In P. Taalas, J. Jalkanen, L. Bradley & S. Thouësny (Eds), *Future-proof CALL: language learning as exploration and encounters – short papers from EUROCALL 2018* (pp. 284-289). Research-publishing.net. https://doi.org/10.14705/rpnet.2018.26.851

meanings (Sharples, 2005). Additionally, such activities could foster learner autonomy particularly when the tasks were conducted via mobile devices (e.g. Reinders, 2011; Sato, Murase, & Burden, 2015). This stems from their nature, which enables prompt access to resources and feedback outside the classroom and consequently facilitates out-of-class learning, which can supplement in-class activities (Kukulska-Hulme, 2015).

However, some challenges are left for mobile-based L2 collaboration. Stockwell and Hubbard (2013) showed that reading and writing L2 texts on small screens could interfere with learning. Writing L2 texts, in particular, would be bothersome for learners who have not often typed the alphabet with their mobile devices. Learners' anxiety for the accuracy of their L2 output can also be another interference. McCarty, Obari, and Sato (2017) reported that Japanese L2 learners' inactivity in an online collaboration results mainly from their perception that their L2 competence is not sufficient enough for their peers to understand their posts. These might prevent their interaction with others and yield unsuccessful L2 learning.

This study aims to tackle these challenges and to facilitate collaborative activities for successful L2 learning. This study utilizes a function in an online communication app: an automated translation chatbot. This bot is offered by LINE, one of the most popular online messenger apps in Japan. It can be used when an online interaction is held using LINE and automatically generates an L2 translation of a statement posted by users. Therefore, the users can see any statement both in L1 and L2 simultaneously on the screen (see Figure 1).

The chatbot can be used during online interactions between peers or among a group, while other machine translation applications like Google Translation cannot be used during the interaction because their L2 output is not provided automatically, interfering the interaction with peers as a result. This is the difference between our study and other studies applying machine translations to L2 learning (e.g. Garcia & Pena, 2011).

The bot offers various types of L2 translation together with the L1 texts, some of which L2 learners could not generate on their own. In that sense, L2 learners are exposed to comprehensive input (Krashen, 1982). Besides, the use of the bot reduces learners' inferiority about their L2 competence. These advantages lead our study to hypothesize that the chatbot will scaffold online interactions, leading to the enhancement of L2 performance and motivation for collaborative learning by the following research questions:

- RQ1: Could L2 learners doing collaborative learning with the translation bot retain the L2 words or expressions found in the automated output?

- RQ2: Could L2 learners produce sophisticated L2 sentences after the collaborative learning with the bot?

- RQ3: Did the experience of the bot change their attitude towards collaborative tasks?

Figure 1.   An example of an online interaction with the chatbot

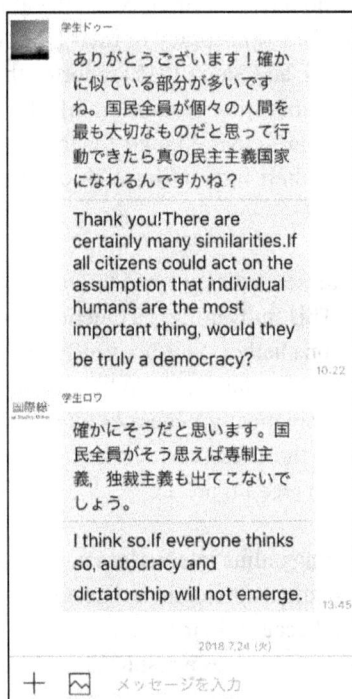

2.   Method

2.1.   Participants and the activity

Three undergraduates at a university in Japan attended the activity; all of them are freshmen but from different departments. They were invited to the research: once a week, they read a book related to political issues and exchanged their opinions in a classroom and then conducted supplemental discussions of the issues via LINE with their mobile devices until the next class.

2.2. Research procedures

After listening to the description of the research project, the participants were asked to answer an open-ended questionnaire regarding the attitude towards collaborative learning. Then they worked on an essay writing task using Criterion®, an essay writing evaluation system by the Test of English as a Foreign Language (TOEFL®). The essay topic we chose from Criterion was a political issue similar to the book they read. Moreover, a questionnaire was conducted which consists of 34 items to measure learners' belief for collaboration in terms of usefulness of cooperation, individual orientation, and inequity (Nagahama, Yasunaga, Sekita, & Kouhara, 2009).

The group discussion via LINE, which was automatically translated into English, was conducted as a supplementary task related to the in-class activities. The participants could freely post their opinions about the materials they read or answer the questions posted by other participants and an author of the present study. After about one month of online interactions, a vocabulary test and follow-up interviews were administered as well as the same questionnaire and writing task. The words for the test were chosen from the L2 sentences the chatbot generated that the participants might not have known before the activity. The follow-up interviews were conducted to confirm the change of their attitude for this activity.

All the data derived from L2 translations, the vocabulary test, two writing tasks, and two questionnaires was collected and then the improvement between the online discussion with the chatbot was observed. However, no statistical analysis was implemented due to the small number of participants.

3. Findings

As a whole, few positive changes were observed: low score of the vocabulary test (RQ1); no improvement of their essay in terms of the evaluation score, and three items of Criterion® (RQ2), but their motivation toward collaborative learning was enhanced according to the questionnaire (RQ3). The follow-up interviews underlay these findings. For example, Student #3, who got the highest score in the vocabulary test and used the expression generated by the chatbot in his/her essay, revealed that the student carefully read the translated output ("a couple of Japanese words with different connotations are translated into the same word in English"). The student also noticed that the exposure to the translation potentially triggered him/her to use some of the words. The interview with Student #3 also indicated that the student evaluated the quality of L2 translation and his/her learning process ("The translation had some mistakes, which I thought I should avoid making").

Meanwhile, Student #2 rarely read analytically the translated output. The student also said that he/she did not remember what words he/she encountered in the chat space and stated that these words need to be encountered many times to be learned. We interpret that the difference between these two students is two-fold. First, Student #3 consciously evaluated his learning, which was not the case with Student #2. The second point is that while Student #3 tried using some of the encountered words, Student #2 did not have such an attempt in the essay. However, it was found that both students shared a recognition that collaborative learning using the translation chatbot can work positively.

4.   Discussion and conclusion

This study aimed to verify the effectiveness of an automated translation chatbot for L2 learning. McCarty et al. (2017) showed that the L2 sentences written by the participants using the chatbot during one month of collaborative tasks became more elaborate than the sentences before the task. The current study, however, showed little improvement of the learners' L2 performance in terms of word recall (RQ1) and writing (RQ2), although their belief towards collaborative learning was positively changed (RQ3). The findings could not support the theoretical advantages of collaborative L2 learning with the automated chatbot in terms of L2 proficiency. However, the chatbot might help the learners to make their belief of collaborative learning more positive.

It should be noted that any generalized conclusion could not be derived from our current study due to the limited number of participants, with no control group available. However, this study might indicate some pedagogical implications to utilizing the chatbot for L2 learning practices: instructors should choose discussion topics for participants to be more involved in the discussion; some tasks can be implemented to examine whether or not the L2 translations by the chatbot could translate L1 statements correctly. To devise pedagogical use of the chatbot, further studies should be conducted.

5.   Acknowledgements

This work is supported by JSPS KAKENHI Grant Number 18K00778.

References

Garcia, I., & Pena, M. I. (2011). Machine translation-assisted language learning: writing for beginners. *Computer Assisted Language Learning, 24*(5), 471-487. https://doi.org/10.1080/09588221.2011.582687

Krashen, S. (1982). *Principles and practice in second language acquisition.* Pergamon.

Kukulska-Hulme, A. (2015). Language as a bridge connecting formal and informal language learning through mobile devices. In L. H. Wong, M. Milrad & M. Specht (Eds), *Seamless learning in the age of mobile connectivity* (pp. 281-294). Springer.

McCarty, S., Obari, H., & Sato, T. (2017). *Implementing mobile language learning technologies in Japan.* Springer.

Nagahama, F., Yasunaga, S., Sekita, K., & Kouhara, S. (2009). Development of a scale to measure belief in cooperation. *Japanese Journal of Educational Psychology, 57*, 24-37. https://doi.org/10.5926/jjep.57.24

Reinders, H. (2011). Learner autonomy and new learning environments. *Language Learning & Technology, 15*(3), 1-3.

Sato, T., Murase, F., & Burden, T. (2015). Is mobile-assisted language learning really useful? An examination of recall automatization and learner autonomy. In F. Helm, L. Bradley, M. Guarda & S. Thouësny (Eds), *Critical CALL – proceedings of the 2015 EUROCALL conference* (pp. 495-501). Research-publishing.net. https://doi.org/10.14705/rpnet.2015.000382

Sharples, M. (2005). Learning as conversation: transforming education in the mobile age. In *Proceedings of Conference on Seeing, Understanding, Learning in the Mobile Age, Budapest, April 28–30, 2005* (pp. 147-152).

Stockwell, G., & Hubbard, P. (2013). Some emerging principles for mobile-assisted language learning. *The International Research Foundation for English Language Education*, 1-15.

Make words click! Learning English vocabulary with clickers

Anne-Marie Sénécal[1], Vanessa Mezzaluna[2], and Walcir Cardoso[3]

Abstract. This study explored the effects of learner response systems (clickers) on the development of vocabulary knowledge in English (L2). Sixty-one Grade 8 learners divided in two groups participated in the experiment, which followed a pretest-posttest-delayed posttest research design. While the experimental group received a clicker-based treatment via PowerPoint presentations, the control group received identical treatment but without the clickers. Although there was no significant interaction between time and group at the time of the posttest, both groups improved over time, but with a trend favoring the Clicker Group.

Keywords: learner response systems, clickers, L2 vocabulary, L2 pedagogy.

1.   Introduction

Research on the pedagogical use of learner response systems (clickers) suggests that their use may contribute to learning (Cardoso, 2011; Cutrim Schmid, 2008), and indicates that students perceive the technology as holding pedagogical benefits (Bruff, 2009; Cardoso, 2011). Most of these studies tend to be in large classrooms and involve adult participants (Cardoso, 2011; Judson & Swada, 2002). Surprisingly, the use of clickers in L2 classrooms has not received careful research consideration (Cardoso, 2011), except for a handful of studies conducted in small language learning environments (McCloskey, 2012).

Clickers are hand-held devices that wirelessly transmit student input to a computer. After creating questions using a presentation software (e.g. PowerPoint), the teacher

---

1. Concordia University, Montréal, Canada; am.senecal@icloud.com
2. Concordia University, Montréal, Canada; vanessamezza@gmail.com
3. Concordia University, Montréal, Canada; walcir.cardoso@concordia.ca

How to cite this article: Sénécal, A.-M., Mezzaluna, V., & Cardoso, W. (2018). Make words click! Learning English vocabulary with clickers. In P. Taalas, J. Jalkanen, L. Bradley & S. Thouësny (Eds), *Future-proof CALL: language learning as exploration and encounters – short papers from EUROCALL 2018* (pp. 290-295). Research-publishing.net. https://doi.org/10.14705/rpnet.2018.26.852

---

projects the questions on a board (see Figure 1-A). The students then respond by pressing the button matching their answer on their clickers (see Figure 1-B), allowing the data to be transmitted to the receiver (see Figure 1-C). When the teacher closes the polling period, the statistical results are displayed on the board (Figure 1-D) (Cardoso, 2011).

Figure 1. Clickers: method of operation (reproduced with permission from *Turning Technologies*)

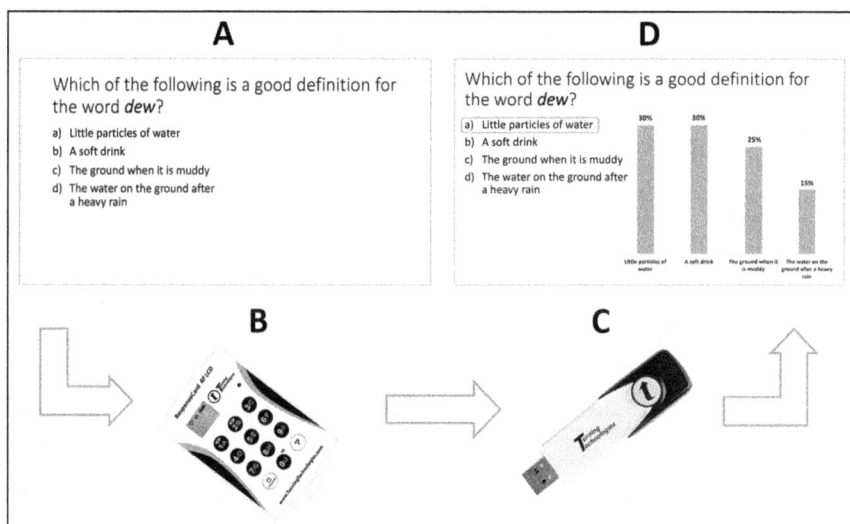

Since previous studies are not definitive as to the extent to which clickers play a role in learning gains and, in addition, they are not in the field of L2 learning, we decided to examine the pedagogical effects of clickers on the acquisition of English vocabulary (L2). Our research question was: Is the pedagogical use of clickers beneficial for the acquisition of L2 English vocabulary for secondary learners? We hypothesized that clickers would positively impact learning. Reasons for implementing clickers include their ability to foster learner interaction and a game-like learning environment (Bruff, 2009), to provide immediate feedback (Draper, Cargill, & Cutts, 2002), and to offer anonymity (Cutrim Schmid, 2008).

2. Method

The participants were 61 high-school students (Grade 8; age range: 13-14) enrolled in an ESL program in Québec (Canada). They were stratified among two groups:

(1) Clicker Group (n=31), wherein participants received a clicker-based treatment through PowerPoint presentations and were asked to vote on questions related to vocabulary; and (2) Non-Clicker Group (n=30), which received the same treatment, but without the clickers; i.e. they selected their answers via hand-raising or orally. Figure 2 illustrates how a sample activity would be conducted in the two groups.

Figure 2.   A sample activity

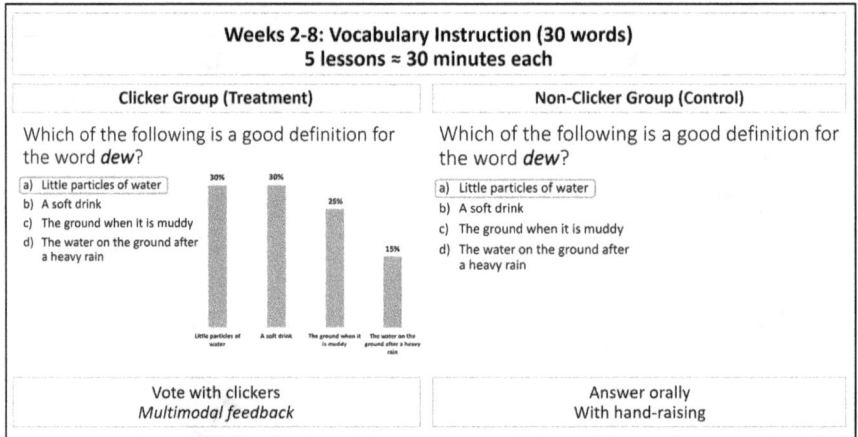

To avoid frequency effects and familiarity with the target words, the vocabulary treatment and testing consisted of 30 low-frequency or off-list words (Nation, 2001). They were extracted from Roald Dahl's novel *James and the Giant Peach*. Participants in both groups were exposed to these words via five treatments lasting approximately 30 minutes each, over a two-month period. The study followed a pretest-posttest-delayed posttest research design where participants were asked to demonstrate their vocabulary knowledge through drawing, translation, or explanation. The pretest assessed their initial knowledge of the target words, and the two posttests assessed the amount of words learned over the duration of the experiment. One posttest was immediate while the other was conducted one month later.

3.   Results

The results in Table 1 show the assessment of the students' ability to recall the 30 target vocabulary items. An independent samples *t*-test confirmed that the Clicker and Non-Clicker groups were comparable at the time of the pretest,

$t(59)=0.87, p=.39$. A mixed ANOVA was run to check for differences between the results of the groups over time (pretest, posttest, delayed-posttest). The analysis revealed a significant difference for time between the pretest and posttest, $F(1.771, 104.5)=159.53, p<.001$. However, there was no significant interaction between time and group, $F(1.771, 104.5)=3.031, p>.05$, and no significant difference for group at the time of the posttest was found, $F(1, 59)=2.78, p=.10$. Thus, the results show that both groups improved in their knowledge of the target vocabulary after intervention, and that there was no significant difference between the two groups.

Table 1.   Descriptive statistics for the vocabulary tests

		Pretest		Posttest		Delayed posttest	
Group	n	M	SD	M	SD	M	SD
Clickers	31	1.29	1.77	6.61	3.81	4.29	3.09
No clickers	30	0.93	1.39	4.97	2.31	3.40	2.08

However, a closer look at the results (Table 1) yield two interesting patterns that seem to favor the Clicker Group: (1) a trend showing its advantage on the two posttests (e.g. $M=6.61$ vs. $M=4.97$; see Figure 3); and (2) a higher SD on both posttests (e.g. $SD=3.81$ vs. $SD=2.31$; see Table 1), indicating high individual differences among the participants in the Clicker Group, thus suggesting that some participants improved more than others.

Figure 3.   Vocabulary development over time

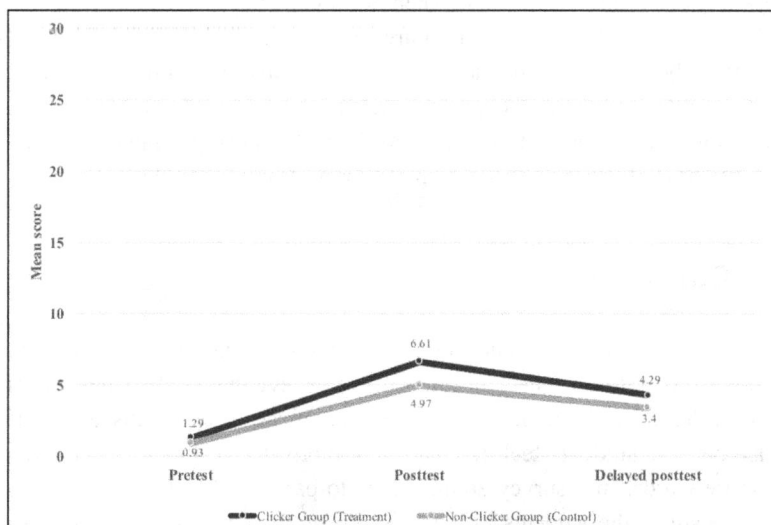

4. Discussion

We hypothesized that the following affordances of clickers would lead to higher vocabulary acquisition: their interactive and game-like approach (Bruff, 2009), immediate and continuing feedback allowing for self-evaluation (Draper et al., 2002), and their anonymity (Cutrim Schmid, 2008). However, our results show that clickers had limited pedagogical value in terms of aiding vocabulary acquisition in comparison with the group not using clickers. We emphasize the term *limited pedagogical value* because we found evidence that clickers may be beneficial for some, possibly due to individual differences and/or learning styles. The disparities in performance suggest that clickers' pedagogical benefits may be affected by individual differences. Finally, we can observe a developmental trend that favored the Clicker Group over the other group, over the two testing periods. Possibly because of higher standard deviations (particularly within the Clicker Group), those differences were not deemed significant by the statistical analyses.

An interesting pattern surfaced in our analysis: a relative decline in the number of acquired words on the delayed posttest, which was observed for both groups. It is possible that this decline (or 'unlearning') is due to the inclusion of rare and off-list words. This may have occurred since the students were not exposed to the words a sufficient number of times, either in or out of class. According to Cobb (2007), six to ten meaningful encounters with a vocabulary item is the minimum necessary for the item to have a potential to be acquired. In our study, the vast majority of the target words were only used in the context of the classroom (e.g. rambunctious, to beckon), thus diminishing their potential to constitute learnable words, as per Cobb's (2007) recommendation. In future studies, we will ensure that participants are sufficiently exposed to the target vocabulary items to optimize their ability to learn the words. Since it is also possible that the use of low-frequency and off-list words compromised the motivation of the students, causing some to question the meaningfulness of the lessons, a different subset of words could be used.

5. Conclusion

Despite the lack of significance observed in clicker-based instruction for the development of L2 vocabulary in English, we believe that clickers have potential for use in the L2 classroom, not only because of the evidence discussed above, but also because students feel they are more motivated to learn and believe they learn more words. In a survey administered to participants in both groups at the end of the study, the students in the Clicker Group significantly outranked their

Non-Clicker counterparts when asked to rate their perceptions of how motivated they were to learn vocabulary and, more importantly, how much they believed they learned. These are very optimistic results that will be addressed in a future study.

Previous research investigating the pedagogical benefits of clickers suggests that their use may contribute to learning (Cardoso, 2011; Cutrim Schmid, 2008). However, most studies are not definitive in their findings. Given that the results of this research follow the trend, more research is needed to ascertain the pedagogical benefits of clickers in second language learning.

6. Acknowledgements

Lots of 'merci' to TurningPoint Canada, Collège Sainte-Anne, Jennifer Lareau (the amazing teacher!) and her students for participating in this research project.

References

Bruff, D. (2009). *Teaching with classroom response systems – Creating active learning environments*. Jossey-Bass.

Cardoso, W. (2011). Learning a foreign language with a learner response system: the students' perspective. *Computer Assisted Language Learning, 24*(5), 1-25. https://doi.org/10.1080/09 588221.2011.567354

Cobb, T. (2007). Computing the vocabulary demands of L2 learning. *Language Learning & Technology, 11*(3), 38-63.

Cutrim Schmid, E. (2008). Using a voting system in conjunction with interactive whiteboard technology to enhance learning in the English language classroom. *Computers and Education, 50*(1), 338-356. https://doi.org/10.1016/j.compedu.2006.07.001

Draper S. W., Cargill J., & Cutts Q. (2002). Electronically enhanced classroom interaction. *Australian Journal of Educational Technology, 18*(1), 13-23. https://doi.org/10.14742/ ajet.1744

Judson, E., & Swada, D. (2002). Learning from past and present: electronic response systems in college lecture halls. *Journal of Computers in Mathematics & Science Teaching, 21*, 167-181.

McCloskey, K. (2012). Using clickers in the second-language classroom: teaching the *passé composé* and the *imparfait* in French. *Journal of Law and Social Sciences, 2*(1), 235-239. https://doi.org/10.5176/2251-3566_L312144

Nation, I. S. P. (2001). *Learning vocabulary in another language*. Cambridge University Press. https://doi.org/10.1017/CBO9781139524759

Exploring visual attentional shifts
of language learners of Japanese

Eline C. Sikkema[1]

Abstract. Familiarity with the television set as a principal news and entertainment medium has allowed for a smooth transition of television programmes into the language classroom (Mishan, 2005). However, in the technology-rich environment we live in today, access to television programmes in foreign languages is not restricted to class. A good understanding of the reception of such authentic material can help inform its appropriate use by learners in different contexts. This study explores the reception of a Japanese variety show that features same-language text on screen by language learners of Japanese and native Japanese speakers through the use of eye-tracking technology and questionnaires (Sikkema, 2017). This paper reports on a section of the findings from the eye-tracking data analysis. Following a brief description of the research project, this paper describes the distribution of visual attention between different stimuli in the video stimulus by taking a closer look at participants' fixation count and total fixation duration.

Keywords: Japanese language learning, visual attention, multimodality, eye-tracking.

1.   Introduction

Recent studies in Synchronous Computer-Mediated Communication (SCMC) have recognised the benefits of using eye-tracking technology to study online language learning behaviour, albeit in combination with qualitative methods and as part of Mixed Methods Research (MMR) designs (O'Rourke, 2012; Stickler & Shi, 2017; Stickler, Smith, & Shi, 2016). Such a combination of methods not only facilitates the triangulation of data sets; it also allows for studies to incorporate participants' own perspectives into the interpretation of the data.

1. Dublin City University, Dublin, Ireland; eline.sikkema2@mail.dcu.ie

How to cite this article: Sikkema, E. C. (2018). Exploring visual attentional shifts of language learners of Japanese. In P. Taalas, J. Jalkanen, L. Bradley & S. Thouësny (Eds), *Future-proof CALL: language learning as exploration and encounters – short papers from EUROCALL 2018* (pp. 296-301). Research-publishing.net. https://doi.org/10.14705/rpnet.2018.26.853

This study employs an MMR design to explore online viewing behaviour of Japanese Language Learners (JLLs) during an experimental task in which participants watch an excerpt of a Japanese variety show that features same-language text on screen (Sikkema, 2017). The main purpose of this research is to examine how JLLs at different stages of their language study receive such multimodal material to inform its appropriate use by learners. It implements eye-tracking technology in order to gain a better understanding of the distribution of subjects' visual attention between stimuli that have the potential to contribute to learners' understanding of the television programme. Questionnaires are used to gain insights into participants' multimodal perception and attitudes towards using such audiovisuals as language learning material.

This paper reports on a section of the findings from the eye-tracking data and discusses what types of stimuli participants visually attend to the most. Results on fixation count and total fixation duration are examined for four participant groups; three consist of JLLs while the fourth group comprises of native Japanese speakers as a point of reference for the analysis of learners' behaviour (Sikkema, 2017, p. 291).

This research is carried out as part of a larger project run at Dublin City University (DCU) that focusses on the reception of the type of same-language text on screen featured in Japanese variety shows (Sikkema, 2017, p. 290).

2.　Method

Data has been analysed from 43 JLLs and five native Japanese speakers who took part in this research on a voluntary basis. For the purposes of this study, the JLLs were organised into three groups based on whether they had been on exchange to Japan at the time of data collection. Seventeen learners who had never been on exchange to Japan formed *Group 1: pre-exchange*. *Group 2: exchange* comprised of 20 participants who were on exchange in Japan for approximately three-and-a-half months at the time of data collection. The remaining six participants were in *Group 3: post-exchange* as they had spent a full year on exchange in Japan prior to their experiment sessions. The native Japanese speakers formed the *Reference Group*. The data sets consist of gaze data recorded with a Tobii X2-60 eye-tracker device, open and closed-ended responses collected through a pre-task and post-task questionnaire, and field notes taken during experiment sessions.

The results have been generated with dynamic Areas Of Interest (AOIs). These were created in the video excerpt and aligned with particular stimuli on the screen in order to extract gaze data associated with these stimuli. The AOIs have been defined with the help of data visualisation tools in the eye-tracking software which showed that faces of people appearing on the show and same-language text on screen that visually represent the dialogue gathered the most visual attention from all participant groups. The charts therefore display the total number and duration of fixations allocated to areas of the screen for *faces*, *same-language text on screen* that show speech, and *other stimuli*. The default settings of the Velocity-Threshold Identification (I-VT) filter[2] were used to generate these numbers.

3.   Results

Figure 1 presents the total number of fixations that landed on faces, same-language text on screen, and other stimuli for each participant group. It illustrates that faces and same-language text on screen gathered the most visual attention for all groups.

Figure 1.   Total number of fixations (sum) per participant group

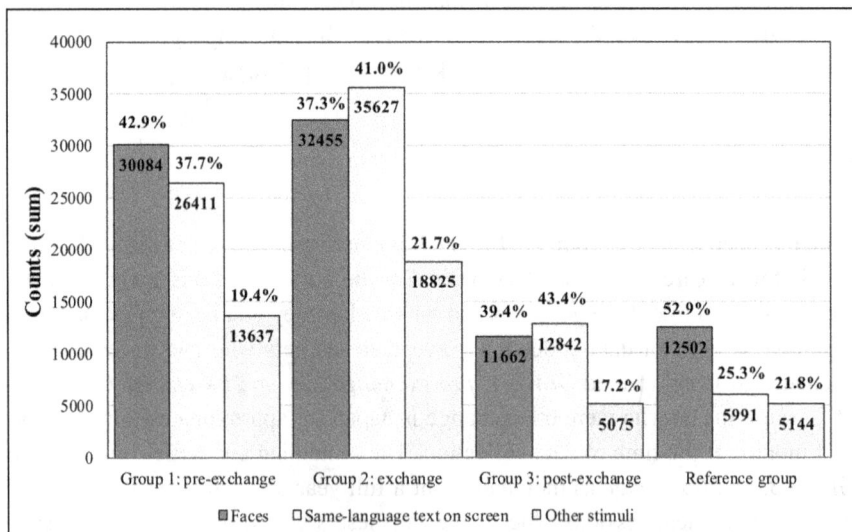

The proportions of the total number of times participants fixated on these particular stimuli were in respective group order: 80.6%, 78.3%, 82.8%, and 78.2%. When

2. https://www.tobiipro.com/siteassets/tobii-pro/learn-and-support/analyze/how-do-we-classify-eye-movements/tobii-pro-i-vt-fixation-filter.pdf

taking a closer look at the proportions for each of the two most attention-grabbing stimuli, it appeared that participants in Group 1 (pre-exchange) and the Reference Group looked more often at faces while Group 2 (exchange) and Group 3 (post-exchange) showed a tendency to look more at same-language text on screen. The proportions for the three learner participant groups seem to be more evenly distributed between faces and same-language text on screen while the Reference Group appeared to have a more even distribution between same-language text on screen and other stimuli.

Figure 2 builds further on these findings and presents the total duration of all fixations combined for faces, same-language text on screen, and other stimuli for each participant group. It shows that the earlier identified attention-grabbers did not only gather the most visual attention, but were also fixated on the longest for all participant groups.

Figure 2.   Total fixation duration (sum) in seconds per participant group

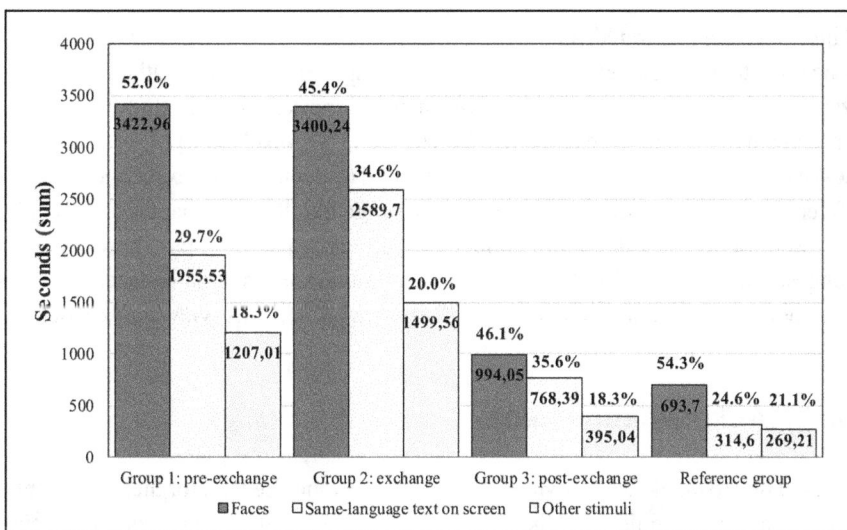

The proportions of the total duration of fixations in seconds that participants spent looking at faces and same-language text on screen are in respective group order: 81.7%, 80%, 81.7%, and 78.9%. As opposed to the previous chart, all participant groups spent most time looking at areas on the screen where faces of people appear on the variety show with the largest ratios for Group 1 (pre-exchange) and the Reference Group.

4.   Discussion

These results are in line with observations of Stickler and Shi (2017) in their study on online communication through a conferencing platform. Their findings showed that learners of the Chinese language looked most (70%) at content areas of the screen in which language teaching content is presented, followed with 20% of fixations directed towards social areas of the screen featuring the presence of participants (Stickler & Shi, 2017, p. 169). In addition, findings from the study of O'Hagan and Sasamoto (2016) on native Japanese speakers' visual attention when watching a Japanese variety show demonstrated that faces attracted the most fixations from participants (pp. 47-50). This relates to the findings of this research, although it is suggested here that JLLs visually attend faces and same-language text on screen in a rather different way from native Japanese speakers.

5.   Conclusion

This paper demonstrated that faces of people appearing on the show and same-language text on screen that represents the spoken dialogue gather the most visual attention from JLLs and native Japanese speakers in this study. Although participants in Group 2 (exchange) and Group 3 (post-exchange) look more often at same-language text on screen when compared to Group 1 (pre-exchange) and the Reference Group, the duration of all fixations together illustrate that faces of people on the show were fixated on the longest for all participant groups. These findings suggest that learners visually attend verbal stimuli more than native speakers and that social, non-verbal stimuli play a large role in participants' viewing experience.

6.   Acknowledgements

I would like to thank Dr Joss Moorkens and Prof. Françoise Blin for their comments on this paper. I would also like to thank the Faculty of Humanities and Social Sciences at DCU for the funding to present my paper at EUROCALL 2018 through the Postgraduate Research Student Journal Publication Scheme.

References

Mishan, F. (2005). Chapter six: the broadcast media. In F. Mishan (Ed.), *Designing authenticity into language learning materials* (pp. 132-153). Intellect.

O'Hagan, M., & Sasamoto, R. (2016). Crazy Japanese subtitles? Shedding light on the impact of impact captions with a focus on research methodology. In S. Hansen-Schirra & S. Grucza (Eds), *Eyetracking and applied linguistics* (pp. 31-58). Language Science Press.

O'Rourke, B. (2012). Using eye-tracking to investigate gaze behaviour in synchronous computer mediated communication for language learning. In M. Dooly & R. O'Dowd (Eds), *Researching online foreign language interaction and exchange: theories, methods and challenges* (pp. 305-341). Peter Lang.

Sikkema, E. C. (2017). Reception of Japanese captions: a comparative study of visual attention between native speakers and language learners of Japanese. In K. Borthwick, L. Bradley & S. Thouësny (Eds), *CALL in a climate of change: adapting to turbulent global conditions – short papers from EUROCALL 2017* (pp. 289-293). Research-publishing.net. https://doi.org/10.14705/rpnet.2017.eurocall2017.728

Stickler, U., & Shi, L. (2017). Eyetracking methodology in SCMC: a tool for empowering learning and teaching. *ReCALL, 29*(2), 160-177. https://doi.org/10.1017/S0958344017000040

Stickler, U., Smith, B., & Shi, L. (2016). Using eye-tracking technology to explore online learner interactions. In C. Caws & M. Hamel (Eds), *Language-learner computer interactions: theory, methodology and CALL applications* (pp. 163-186). John Benjamins Publishing Company. https://doi.org/10.1075/lsse.2.08sti

Stimulating task interest: human partners or chatbots?

Andrew Thompson[1], Andrew Gallacher[2], and Mark Howarth[3]

Abstract. The aim of this research project was to examine the impact of chatbots as conversation partners. First and second year Japanese university students (n=120) from a private university in Southwest Japan were randomly assigned to either conduct a speaking task with an Artificial Intelligence (AI) chatbot or human partner. Preliminary analysis of the data suggests that student interest in interacting with the chatbot conversation partners decreased across the experiment period, whilst interest in performing identical tasks with their peers (human partners) remained relatively stable. The findings suggest that educators and administrators should be cautious about relying entirely on AI conversation partners as a substitute to human partners if they wish to stimulate and maintain student interest levels in conversation tasks. Furthermore, teachers should carefully consider students' language proficiency and communicative ability before designing and implementing speaking tasks that involve the use of AI conversation partners. Using chatbots as an extension of human-human conversation activity practice and not a replacement is recommended in order to maintain student interest and engagement across a language program.

Keywords: CALL, chatbot, student engagement, student interest.

1. Introduction

This study is the first phase in the potential development and integration of using AI chatbots as conversation partners within a Japanese compulsory English language program. Through firstly identifying, understanding, and then exploiting

1. Kyushu Sangyo University, Fukuoka, Japan; andrew@thinkic.com
2. Kyushu Sangyo University, Fukuoka, Japan; gallacher@ip.kyusan-u.ac.jp
3. Sojo University, Kumamoto, Japan; markwhowarth@gmail.com

How to cite this article: Thompson, A., Gallacher, A., & Howarth, M. (2018). Stimulating task interest: human partners or chatbots? In P. Taalas, J. Jalkanen, L. Bradley & S. Thouësny (Eds), *Future-proof CALL: language learning as exploration and encounters – short papers from EUROCALL 2018* (pp. 302-306). Research-publishing.net. https://doi.org/10.14705/rpnet.2018.26.854

the benefits that chatbots offer students, educators and administrators may be better able to increase blended learning task-based opportunities for learners.

1.1. Education and student interest

Research over recent decades has linked student interest levels to vital components of learning, for example: attention, persistence, recall, and the quality of students' learning outcomes (Hidi & Berndorff, 1998). Student interest has been shown to be connected to positive learning outcomes and, more importantly, also influence what learners choose to study in future years (Harackiewicz & Hulleman, 2010). Given the importance that interest plays in learning and its influence on positive academic and future outcomes, it is surprising that little research has been conducted on measuring student interest within the domain of language learning. Research into the development of interest has seen Hidi and Renninger (2006) propose a four-phase model of interest development. This model describes four phases in the development and strengthening of student interest. These phrases are *triggered situational interest, maintained situational interest, emerging individual interest,* and *well-developed individual interest*. It is important for both educators and administrators to be conscious of how student interest is triggered and maintained if we are to truly develop students' long-term interest in English.

1.2. Language learning and chatbots

Today, more and more people are learning English through online technologies. With over 1.7 billion English language learners across the globe, only a small fraction of these learners have access to traditional language learning resources and formal classroom teaching (British Council, 2013). With the explosion of educational technology and the increased accessibility of mobile devices, education providers are actively seeking out ways to utilize chatbots as conversation partners. As Atwell (1999) noted, chatbots provide an opportunity for students to conduct conversational practice outside of the classroom. For an overview of the chatbot used in this study, Cleverbot.com, see Fryer and Carpenter (2006).

Chatbots – also known as 'conversational agents' – are software applications that simulate human speech for the purposes of replicating a conversation or interaction with a human conversation partner. There are two main ways chatbots are offered to language learners. Firstly, through computer applications and also via online apps that can be accessed on mobile devices. This independent learning opportunity has gained interest within computer assisted language learning based research (Goda et al., 2014).

2. Method

This research project had three main focuses: (1) to examine the suitability of chatbots as conversation partners; (2) to compare the levels of students' interest in English language learning: chatbots versus human partners at task, course, and domain levels; and (3) to identify the merits/demerits of chatbots versus human conversation partners.

2.1. Participants

Japanese university students (first year n=91 and second year n=29 students) from a private university in Southwest Japan were requested to complete a spoken conversation task with a chatbot or human partner. Participants were non-English majors and came from five of the university's seven faculties (Engineering, Management, International Studies, Fine Arts, and Economics), with a Common European Framework of Reference for languages (CEFR) basic user level ranging from A1 to B2. Students were allocated into three English levels following a placement test conducted by the university administration. All participants were studying within a coordinated compulsory English as a foreign language program consisting of two 15-week semesters per academic year with one 90-minute Listening and Speaking class per week.

2.2. Procedure

Participants were randomly assigned the same English conversation task with a chatbot or human partner. The task-based conversation took students approximately 10 minutes. Following the task, students self-reported their perceptions of the experience, identifying three advantages and/or disadvantages of speaking with a chatbot or human partner. The final stage of the data collection was an online interest survey. The online measurement was used to capture students' level of interest throughout the course of research. For an overview of the development of the interest measurement, see Thompson et al. (2015). The experiment was conducted four times during one (15-week) academic semester.

2.3. Instrumentation

Following completion of the speaking task, students noted three advantages and/ or disadvantages relating the conversation partner experience (chatbot or human). From the third class of the second semester and each time students completed the task-based conversation component (four times) of this study, students' interest in the conversational task was measured. The survey items were: (Item 1) *this activity was personally meaningful*, (Item 2) *I enjoyed learning English in this activity*, (Item 3) *I liked using English in this activity*, (Item 4) *this activity was interesting*, and (Item 5) *it was fun to review English in this activity*. The items were measured on a six-point Likert scale.

3. Preliminary findings

Preliminary analysis of the quantitative data collected in this study indicates interest levels in English and conversation tasks with a human partner did show a slight increase across the experiment (see Table 1, Table 2, and Table 3).

Table 1. First year students: English interest

Week	Item Mean	Standard Deviation
3	3.85	1.29
15	4.38	1.10

Table 2. Second year students: English interest

Week	Item Mean	Standard Deviation
3	3.53	1.27
15	4.09	1.20

Table 3. First year students: human partner conversation activity interest

Week	Item Mean	Standard Deviation
5	4.37	1.00
12	4.61	1.15

However, there was a slight decline (see Table 4) performing the identical conversation task with a chatbot. This decline in interest may be linked to comments students noted in the qualitative data suggesting that students found the chatbot responses inappropriate and the interaction as being unnatural.

Table 4. First year students: chatbot partner conversation activity interest

Week	Item Mean	Standard Deviation
7	4.18	1.11
12	3.84	1.08

These preliminary findings suggest that educators and administrators should be cautious about relying entirely on chatbot conversation partners as a substitute to human partners if they wish to stimulate and maintain student interest in learning tasks and English more generally.

4. Conclusion

The aim of this research project was to examine the suitability of chatbots as conversation partners and to compare the levels of students' interest in English language learning: chatbots versus human partners at task, course, and domain levels.

The preliminary findings from this study suggest that educators and administrators should be cautious about relying entirely on chatbot conversation partners as a substitute to human partners if they wish to stimulate and maintain student interest in learning tasks and English more generally. As with any study conducted within one university, the external validity of the results awaits further tests both nationally and internationally.

References

Atwell, E. (1999). *The language machine: the impact of speech and language technologies on English language teaching.* British Council.

British Council. (2013). *The English effect: the impact of English, what it's worth to the UK and why it matters to the world.* https://www.britishcouncil.org/sites/default/files/english-effect-report-v2.pdf

Fryer, L., & Carpenter, R. (2006). Emerging technologies. Language in action: from webquests to virtual realities. *Language Learning & Technology, 10*(3), 8-14.

Goda, Y., Yamada, M., Matsukawa, H., Hata, K., & Yasunami, S. (2014). Conversation with a chatbot before an online EFL group discussion and the effects on critical thinking. *Information and Systems in Education, 13*(1), 1-7. https://doi.org/10.12937/ejsise.13.1

Harackiewicz, J. M., & Hulleman, C. S. (2010). The importance of interest: the role of achievement goals and task values in promoting the development of interest. *Social and Personality Psychology Compass, 4*(1), 42-52. https://doi.org/10.1111/j.1751-9004.2009.00207.x

Hidi, S., & Berndorff, D. (1998). Situational interest and learning. In L. Hoffmann, A. Krapp, K. A. Renninger & J. Baumert (Eds), *Interest and learning: proceedings of the Seeon conference on interest and gender* (pp. 74-90). IPN.

Hidi, S., & Renninger, K. A. (2006). The four-phase model of interest development. *Educational Psychologist, 41*(2), 111-127. https://doi.org/10.1207/s15326985ep4102_4

Thompson, A., Ozono, S., Howarth, M., Williams, R. A., & Fryer, K. L. (2015). The development and validation of a measure of student interest in the English learning task. *Kyushu Sangyo University Language Education and Research Center Journal*, No. 10. Fukuoka.

Development of critical thinking skills and intercultural awareness in bilingual telecollaborative projects

Ruby Vurdien[1] and Pasi Puranen[2]

Abstract. This reflective practice will examine and report on students' experiences of three different bilingual (English-Spanish) task-based telecollaborative projects. The observations indicate that throughout these different projects the students were able to develop their intercultural awareness and their critical thinking skills via different online tools and learning contexts like a videoconferencing platform and Facebook. This paper employs both a qualitative and quantitative approach and data were collected from various sources, namely, the questionnaires administered at the beginning and end of the projects. As a conclusion, it is argued that the projects helped students to exchange views about cultural aspects and ask and clarify questions that arose during their interactions, which provided them with the opportunity to develop their critical thinking skills. Sharing thoughts and views on Facebook and videoconferencing has been a meaningful learning experience and students have been able to discover and reflect on useful information about each other's cultural traits.

Keywords: telecollaboration, videoconferencing, intercultural awareness, collaborative learning.

1.   Introduction

Nowadays, different technologies for computer-mediated communication and learning offer ever-growing possibilities for language teaching, learning further skills for intercultural awareness, and for developing students' critical thinking

1. White Rose Language School, Valladolid, Spain; whiterose_va@yahoo.es
2. Aalto University Language Centre, Espoo, Finland; pasi.puranen@aalto.fi

How to cite this article: Vurdien, R., & Puranen, P. (2018). Development of critical thinking skills and intercultural awareness in bilingual telecollaborative projects. In P. Taalas, J. Jalkanen, L. Bradley & S. Thouësny (Eds), *Future-proof CALL: language learning as exploration and encounters – short papers from EUROCALL 2018* (pp. 307-312). Research-publishing.net. https://doi.org/10.14705/rpnet.2018.26.855

capacity. New technologies are valuable ways to interact between different cultures and increase cross-cultural understanding among university students, offering new ways for computer-supported collaborative learning. As Halpern (1999) states:

> "[t]he changing nature of technology has not only provided us with more and better ways to teach in general but has also increased the need for the skills of critical thinking. The easy availability, with just a few keystrokes, of massive amounts of information has made the ability to evaluate and sort information more important than ever" (p. 72).

Computed-mediated communication tools have been found to have great potential for intercultural learning (Basharina, 2009; Belz, 2007), and traditionally this has been asynchronous. Recently, synchronous communication has also become popular and very motivating for students in intercultural exchanges (Helm, 2015). Videoconferencing is able to provide an authentic out-of-classroom learning experience in collaborative international projects (Eaton, 2010).

Critical thinking processes require active argumentation, initiative, reasoning, envisioning, analysing complex alternatives, and making contingency-related value judgements (Simpson & Courtney, 2002). It was hoped that the students would be able to manage such processes while assessing cultural information, with a view to developing their critical thinking skills. Furthermore, they were expected to enhance their "ability to interact effectively with people with different cultures other than one's own" (Byram, 2000, p. 297).

In this reflective practice paper, we aim to examine the following questions:

- How were the students able to develop their skills for critical thinking and intercultural awareness in the telecollaborative projects?

- How were the students able to share their knowledge and views via social networking and videoconferencing?

To examine the questions, qualitative and quantitative data were collated from various sources, namely, videos, Facebook posts, questionnaires administered at the beginning and end of the projects, and individual interviews conducted on completion of each project. To gather more data, a survey in the form of a questionnaire was completed by the students at the end of each project. A five-point Likert scale, ranging from one, strongly disagree, to five, strongly agree, was used.

The content of the students' Facebook posts was examined for quality to provide a better understanding of the participants' learning experiences and development of critical thinking through online interaction. The following points were considered: the way students exchanged views, asked questions to prompt discussions, constructed new meanings, and critically assessed each other's responses. We analysed the video discussions by repeated viewings. The most important features of the interactions and the views exchanged were considered so that there was a pertinent relation to the aforementioned questions.

2.   The projects and tasks

Three different projects involving three different groups of students (19-35) were designed between 2014 and 2016. The first one comprised 19 English as a Foreign Language (EFL) Spanish and 17 Finnish students and Facebook was the platform employed. In the second project (2015), the Adobe Connect videoconferencing tool was used for synchronous oral communication. Seventeen Finnish university students and 12 Spanish EFL students were engaged in the videoconference interactions. In the third project (2016), the 12 Finnish university students and nine Spanish EFL students used both videoconferencing (oral activities) and Facebook (written activities) to perform their tasks. The online tasks in the three projects are displayed in Table 1.

Table 1.   Online tasks

Tasks	Aims
1. Introducing themselves.	Introducing themselves to their foreign partners.
2. Talking about university education.	Thinking about their own culture and environment. Comparing and understanding their university systems.
3. Uploading newspaper articles about current issues and commenting on them.	Comparing attitudes to local issues.
4. Describing traditions, festivals, and gastronomy.	Comparing and contrasting cultural values and life in the different countries.
5. Interviewing each other on an issue (e.g. religion, environment, politics, etc.)	Understanding how members of the different countries experience their own culture.
6. Describing their favourite film, book, poem, place of interest, etc.	Interpreting different cultural traits.

Both the Finns' and Spaniards' levels of English were C1 and C2 – Common European Framework of Reference for languages (CEFR). The latter were native speakers of Spanish, whilst the Finns had a B1/ B2 level of Spanish. Although English was the established lingua franca, in each project Tasks 4, 5, and 6 were performed in Spanish to afford the Finns the opportunity to practise that language.

3. Results and discussion

Based on the results of the questionnaires, the students' evaluation of their learning experience in each project was positive, as shown in Table 2. Although task performance was carried out by different students on different platforms in the three projects, the tools were considered convenient for online engagement. One of the tasks in the projects was to discuss a newspaper article relating to a local issue, the aim being to discover how students could interpret information that is not familiar to them due to their own cultural background. They explained, discussed, and argued their views about the articles and compared their situations with those in their peers' country. Exploring the Facebook posts and videoconference interactions shows how they reflected on their own cultural traits and those of their counterparts, analysed and clarified responses to be successful in critically assessing each other's cultural standpoint, thereby leading to the development of critical thinking skills. These online exchanges also encouraged them to ask for more information and hence widen their cultural knowledge, which helped them to enhance their intercultural awareness. Another task which fostered the development of critical thinking skills and intercultural competence was the debating of stereotypes; this enabled them to explore how people from other countries consider them and their respective culture. As one Spanish student reported in an interview, "[t]his task helped me to gain a better understanding of myself and my peers", which reflected an increase in intercultural knowledge.

Table 2. Students' appraisal of their learning experience (Puranen & Vurdien, 2016, p. 393)

	Mean	Median	Standard deviation
1. I enjoyed exchanging views with my peers via videoconferencing.	4.04	4	0.64
2. I was curious to learn about my peers' culture.	4.25	4	0.70
3. I felt motivated to interact with my peers online.	3.68	3.5	0.86

Task performance via videoconferencing and social networking was deemed beneficial in terms of sharing information with each other. Whilst one Finnish student said that "[s]haring information with someone from a different culture is very useful because you learn a lot about their country, habits, food, etc...", a Spanish student commented that "[i]nteracting on videoconferencing has made me more courageous to speak to people from other countries" (Vurdien & Puranen, 2018, p. 272). They were curious to learn about each other's cultural traits, which motivated them to be fully engaged in their online interactions. In the participants' view, debating the issue on stereotypes encouraged them to modify the image they had of each other's country and people and to build on new knowledge, which suggests the task had a productive effect (Vurdien & Puranen, 2018, p. 275). It is, therefore, crucial to design meaningful tasks that will prompt students to share their thoughts with their peers.

4. Final remarks

This paper has shed some light on how students can experience the development of critical thinking skills and intercultural awareness through task performance with Facebook and videoconferencing as learning tools. Sharing thoughts and views in online interactions has been a significant learning experience, since students have discovered useful information about each other's cultural traits. The projects have clearly afforded the students an opportunity to communicate, exchange, reflect on, and further discuss and analyse their ideas, thereby developing critical thinking skills in order to enhance intercultural learning.

Task performance is of utmost importance to motivate students to exchange views that will give them a full understanding of cultural traits. Both videoconferencing and Facebook seem to be appropriate tools for assisting students in sharing their thoughts, as well as for constructing knowledge together. Notwithstanding, sufficient time should be allotted for task completion for meaningful learning to take place.

Finally, due to the qualitative and reflective nature of the approach, the results cannot be generalised. It is hoped that further research in this area will benefit the learning process.

5. Acknowledgements

We would like to thank all our students in Finland and Spain who participated in the telecollaborative projects.

References

Basharina, O. (2009). Student agency and language-learning processes and outcomes in international online environments. *CALICO Journal, 26*(2), 390-412. https://doi.org/10.1558/cj.v26i2.390-412

Belz, J. A. (2007). The development of intercultural communicative competence in telecollaborative partnerships. In R. O'Dowd (Ed.), *Online intercultural exchange* (pp. 127-166). Multilingual Matters.

Byram, M. (2000). Assessing intercultural competence in language teaching. *Sprogforum, 18*(6), 8-13.

Eaton, S. E. (2010). How to use Skype in the ESL/EFL classroom. *The Internet TESL Journal, 16*(11). http://iteslj.org/Techniques/Eaton-UsingSkype.html

Halpern, D. F. (1999). Teaching for critical thinking: helping college students develop the skills and dispositions of a critical thinker. *New directions for teaching and learning, 1999*(80), 69-74. https://doi.org/10.1002/tl.8005

Helm, F. (2015). The practices and challenges of telecollaboration in higher education in Europe. *Language Learning and Technology, 19*(2), 197-217.

Puranen, P., & Vurdien, R. (2016). A Spanish-Finnish telecollaboration: extending intercultural competence via videoconferencing. In S. Papadima-Sophocleous, L. Bradley & S. Thouësny (Eds), *CALL communities and culture – short papers from EUROCALL 2016* (pp. 391-396). Research-publishing.net. https://doi.org/10.14705/rpnet.2016.eurocall2016.594

Simpson, E., & Courtney, M. (2002). Critical thinking in nursing education: literature review. *International Journal of Nursing Practice, 8*(2), 89 -98. https://doi.org/10.1046/j.1440-172x.2002.00340.x

Vurdien, R., & Puranen, P. (2018). Intercultural learning via videoconferencing: students' attitudes and experiences. In D. Tafazoli, M. Gomez Parra & C. Huertas-Abril (Eds), *Cross-cultural perspectives on technology-enhanced language learning* (pp. 264-282). IGI Global. https://doi.org/10.4018/978-1-5225-5463-9.ch015

Designing English digital stories for global audiences

Yu-Feng (Diana) Yang[1]

Abstract. Viewing digitally-mediated multimodal composing as a new literacy practice, this research investigates how English Language Learners (ELLs) serve as multimodal designers to reach a global audience. Grounded in the perspective of literacy as social practice and the notion of 'designing', it reveals that the two focal groups of this study employ local and global resources for multimodal designing. In addition, their family experience, literacy practices, video experiences, and their interactions with friends, instructors, and peers mediate how they select, expand, and orchestrate the cultural resources at their disposal. In relation to intercultural blending, this study reports that ELLs employ 'authenticating strategies' and 'playful strategies' to reach their global audience. This finding encourages us to reflect upon strategies that can be used to examine the emerging playful or non-traditional multimodal composing that the global youth continues to consume and produce.

Keywords: multimodal composing, new literacies, intercultural blending, learner agency.

1. Introduction

In recent years, a growing number of second/foreign language (L2) educators have started to implement multimodal projects in their classrooms. To understand what L2 learners gain from these projects and how they approach multimodal composing, researchers have investigated multimodal composing as a pedagogical intervention and as a new literacy practice.

Conceptualizing multimodal composing as a new literacy practice, scholars have coined on the notion of *designing* (The New London Group, 1996). Based on

1. National Sun Yat-Sen University, Kaohsiung, Taiwan; dyang@faculty.nsysu.edu.tw

How to cite this article: Yang, Y.-F. (2018). Designing English digital stories for global audiences. In P. Taalas, J. Jalkanen, L. Bradley & S. Thouësny (Eds), *Future-proof CALL: language learning as exploration and encounters – short papers from EUROCALL 2018* (pp. 313-318). Research-publishing.net. https://doi.org/10.14705/rpnet.2018.26.856

Cope and Kalantzis (2009), *designing* is a process that involves the transformation of the 'Available Design' (i.e. available resources in L2 learners' repertoire) to the 'Redesigned' (i.e. appropriating available resources in an unconventional way). For example, in a digital story production, the image of 'parents' and their associated texts can be seen as L2 learners' 'Available Design'. However, when these resources are used repeatedly or assembled in different creative means, they function as the 'Redesigned' for the progressing story (Nelson, 2006).

Notably, during the designing process, designers or learners act on their socio-cultural mediated interests, consider their audience, and reflect their social context for their 'Available Designs' and 'Redesigned' (Cope & Kalantzis, 2009). In relation to audience awareness, Hafner's (2015) notion of *intercultural blending*, the assemblage and the orchestration of multiple cultural resources, can be useful to understand the designing of multimodal ensembles "that is meant for a global audience to create an intercultural blend" (p. 504).

Valuing digitally-mediated multimodal composing as a new literacy practice, this research investigates how ELLs serve as multimodal designers when working on one type of multimodal compositions, digital storytelling, to reach a global audience. In particular, how ELLs negotiate and re-contextualize culturally and linguistically diversified resources in relation to 'designing' (The New London Group, 1996) when performing intercultural blending (Hafner, 2015) is emphasized.

2.   Method

2.1.   The video-based digital storytelling project

This study is conducted in an undergraduate course focusing on multimedia and English communication in a university in Taiwan. To enrich students' multimodal experiences, it requires students to produce a three to five minute collaborative video-based English digital story, with an aim of reaching global audiences. Students work in groups for the project, approach two international students of different regions for peer reviews, and then revise their work before the final presentation.

The topic of the project centers on 'cultural space', a physical site in a local community, a virtual space on the Internet or a metaphorical space that carries personal or collective cultural memories and stories. Students are encouraged to incorporate meaningful scenes, plots, people, social relationships, artifacts, etc., to reflect the aesthetics, cultural values, beliefs, lifestyles, cultural memories etc. of a specific cultural space in their stories (e.g. a renewed building, a historical site, a specific cultural community). In addition, they are advised to think creatively for content development instead of solely presenting the factual information of a cultural space.

2.2. Participants and data collection

Participants of this study consist of 39 ELLs who are in their 20s. Both local students from Taiwan and exchange students from Europe and Southeast Asia participated in this study. This paper analyzes the experiences of eight students who work in two separate groups. The first group includes four English major students who are from Taiwan, and the second group consists of four European exchange students who major either in Business or Computer Science. Data collections include students' digital stories, interviews, journals, questionnaires, and class presentations.

2.3. Data analysis

This study applies Miles, Huberman, and Saldana's (2014) guidelines for data analysis. The researcher first analyzes participants' journals, class presentations, and interviews to locate the vital 'Redesigned' and the 'Available Designs' through provisional coding. She then triangulates the data by examining the final digital story and the video segments the participants produced. Through constant comparison, the identified 'Available Designs' are categorized as local, translocal, and global resources and displayed in a chart. In addition, participants' journals, class presentations, and interviews are re-analyzed again to examine their designing process. Their (re)interpretations, (re)imagination, and recontextualization of cultural resources are identified and compared. Finally, Hafner's (2015) notion of *intercultural blending* is used to identify the 'Redesigned' and the 'Available Design' that purposefully aims at a global audience. Participants' strategies of deploying cultural resources for a global audience, including authenticating strategies and playful strategies, emerge as important themes during the data analysis process in this study.

3. Findings and discussion

This study found that these two groups of ELLs employ local resources, translocal resources, and global resources in their design (see Table 1). Their family, literacy, and video experiences as well as their friends', instructor's and peers' comments mediate how they select, expand, and orchestrate the cultural resources at their disposal.

Table 1. Examples of local, translocal, and global resources

	Group 1: Home is Home	**Group 2: Heart Threat**
Local Resources	-The stubborn father; the daughter who wants to practice filial piety; a gossip neighbor -A Buddhist court; the scooter rider without helmet; the sticky tofu stand; the fruit stand -The local park; an old family photo -Taiwanese soap operas; Taiwanese language; Mandarin Chinese language, etc.	-A taxi driver who cannot speak English -taxi driver's Chinese oral narration -local sceneries along the Love River; local harbor views; tourists' boats -love signs along the Love River
Translocal Resources	-Thai commercials	-A doctor who can speak English "Kaohsiung Daily," a local English newspaper
Global Resources	-English subtitle; English monologue; English songs; English slogan -The concept of home	-The YouTuber style -Foreign exchange students -Love; lovers holding hands together; the color of red; pink flowers -English subtitles; English slogan; marketing videos

However, their performance of intercultural blending demonstrates different orientations. While the first group endeavors to employ 'authenticating strategies', the second group works to incorporate 'playful strategies' for intercultural blending. For example, in the first group's video-based digital story, local images, local languages and local values are incorporated to provide opportunities for global audiences to "experience the local tradition as how one would experience authenticity in a foreign language movie" (Interview). Thus, local images and dialogues emphasizing a stubborn father (i.e. local resource), a gossip neighbor (i.e. local resource), and a caring daughter (i.e. local resource) are designed and orchestrated to present the image of home (i.e. global resource) for global audiences.

In addition, this group struggles to define the role of Taiwanese (i.e. local resources) and English (i.e. global resources) when attempting to imitating the style of a typical Taiwanese soap opera in their story. Experiencing the 'inauthenticity' of a local conversation presented in English, their exploration and negotiation of how to best arrange Taiwanese oral narrations, English oral narrations, and English subtitles to reach global audiences and to uncover the local cultures of family relationships remains salient. This finding manifests that intercultural blending (Hafner, 2015) not only can involve assemblages of multiple cultural artifacts but also orchestration of multiple languages.

Interestingly, the second group works to incorporate 'playful strategies' for intercultural blending. Playful yet illogical designs that resemble the YouTuber style are incorporated. Through the design of the 'taxi driver' who rides a scooter, the taxi driver who wears a mask and sunglasses or the 'shining beautiful lady' besides the river, their digital story attracts global audiences through the humor that global youth can easily follow. Such findings encourage us to further explore the role of genre play (Tardy, 2016) in multimodal composing.

4.   Conclusions

This paper reports ELLs' exploration of intercultural blending in their designing of multimodal composing. How students select and orchestrate local and global cultural resources to reach a global audience is presented. Students' playful multimodal designs challenge us to reflect how to further examine the emerging non-traditional multimodal composing that the global youth may consume and produce. Genre play (Tardy, 2016) or other related frameworks may continue to advance our understanding about non-traditional multimodal compositions.

5.   Acknowledgements

This research is part of a large study funded by the Ministry of Science and Technology in Taiwan, R. O. C. (MOST 106-2410-H-110-038-).

References

Cope, B., & Kalantzis, M. (2009). "Multiliteracies": new literacies, new learning. *Pedagogies: An international journal, 4*(3), 164-195. https://doi.org/10.1080/15544800903076044

Hafner, C. A. (2015). Remix culture and English language teaching: the expression of learner voice in digital multimodal compositions. *TESOL Quarterly, 49*(3), 486-509. https://doi. org/10.1002/tesq.238

Miles, M., Huberman, M., & Saldana, J. (2014). Qualitative data analysis: a method sourcebook (3rd ed.). Sage.

Nelson, M. E. (2006). Mode, meaning, and synaesthesia in multimedia L2 writing. *Language Learning and Technology, 10*(2), 56-76.

Tardy, C. (2016). *Beyond convention: genre innovation in academic writing.* University of Michigan Press. https://doi.org/10.3998/mpub.5173647

The New London Group. (1996). A pedagogy of multiliteracies: designing social futures. *Harvard Educational Review, 66*(1), 60-93. https://doi.org/10.17763/haer.66.1.17370n67v22j160u

JYVÄSKYLÄN YLIOPISTO
UNIVERSITY OF JYVÄSKYLÄ

A flexible online system for curating reduced redundancy language exercises and tests

Torsten Zesch[1], Andrea Horbach[2], Melanie Goggin[3],
and Jennifer Wrede-Jackes[4]

Abstract. We present a tool for the creation and curation of C-tests. C-tests are an established tool in language proficiency testing and language learning. They require examinees to complete a text in which the second half of every second word is replaced by a gap. We support teachers and test designers in creating such tests through a web-based system using Natural Language Processing (NLP) techniques. We provide support both for creating a test from a given text according to guidelines for different languages, as well as for automatically assessing the overall difficulty of the created test.

Keywords: C-tests, exercise generation, difficulty prediction.

1. Introduction

Reduced redundancy exercise formats like C-tests (Grotjahn, 2014) are common and established tools in language learning. C-tests are also frequently used in assessments because they correlate well with general language proficiency (Eckes & Grotjahn, 2006). A C-test consists of a text paragraph with a set of incomplete words containing gaps which the examinee must complete. The prefix of the incomplete word is shown as a hint for the learner. Figure 1 shows an example of an English C-test.

1. Language Technology Lab, University Duisburg-Essen, Germany; torsten.zesch@uni-due.de
2. Language Technology Lab, University Duisburg-Essen, Germany; andrea.horbach@uni-due.de
3. Institut für Optionale Studien, University Duisburg-Essen, Germany; melanie.goggin@uni-due.de
4. Institut für Optionale Studien, University Duisburg-Essen, Germany; jennifer.wrede@uni-due.de

How to cite this article: Zesch, T., Horbach, A., Goggin, M., & Wrede-Jackes, J. (2018). A flexible online system for curating reduced redundancy language exercises and tests. In P. Taalas, J. Jalkanen, L. Bradley & S. Thouësny (Eds), *Future-proof CALL: language learning as exploration and encounters – short papers from EUROCALL 2018* (pp. 319-324). Research-publishing.net. https://doi.org/10.14705/rpnet.2018.26.857

Figure 1.   English C-test with 20 gaps (marked with curly brackets)

Wild boar in Berlin

With their hefty trunks, sharp tusks and adorable striped piglets, wild boars are easy to spot. If y{ou} were stan{ding} in cen{tral} *Berlin's Alexanderplatz* shopping squ{are}, they wo{uld} be ve{ry} hard t{o} miss. Wi{ld} boars a{re} thriving i{n} the ci{ty} and ha{ve} even be{en} spotted roa{ming} through t{he} busiest ar{eas}. The popul{ation} is curr{ently} estimated a{t} 3,000 and th{ere} are three isolated populations in forests of the capital. One person is licensed to cull the pigs in the city, but with restrictions on hunting and no natural predators, the wild boars are here to stay.

According to teachers and test designers (Arras, Eckes, & Grotjahn, 2002), the time-consuming process of designing C-tests is a major hindrance, especially if such tests are used as a type of exercise in language learning instead of summative assessment. Here, it is necessary to create a large number of tests in advance.

In order to decrease the workload of teachers and test creators, we have developed a flexible online tool that allows for the fast and dynamic creation and curation of C-tests. The features of the tool include: (1) automatic application of a general gap scheme, as well as specific gap-schemes for several languages; (2) one-click addition or deletion of gaps for fine-grained manual adjustment; (3) an option to manually adjust the number of deleted characters per gap as well as (4) to specify additional solutions for a gap; and (5) various import and export functionalities.

The tool is freely available at https://github.com/zesch/ctest-builder. We not only host a web-instance, but also give full access to the source code. This allows users to install their own instance, so that it can be adapted to new languages and to ensure that non-free texts do not have to be sent over the Internet.

In the following, we will discuss how C-tests are automatically created using NLP techniques. Subsequently, we will present ongoing and future work regarding how to further automate the C-test creation process.

2.   C-test creation

The core part of our tool is the creation of a C-test from plain text. We provide automatic gap assignment, which the user can adapt later according to their needs.

Incorporated into the tool are both generic and language-specific criteria for C-test creation. Figure 2 shows a screenshot of the tool.

Figure 2.   Screenshot of the C-test tool

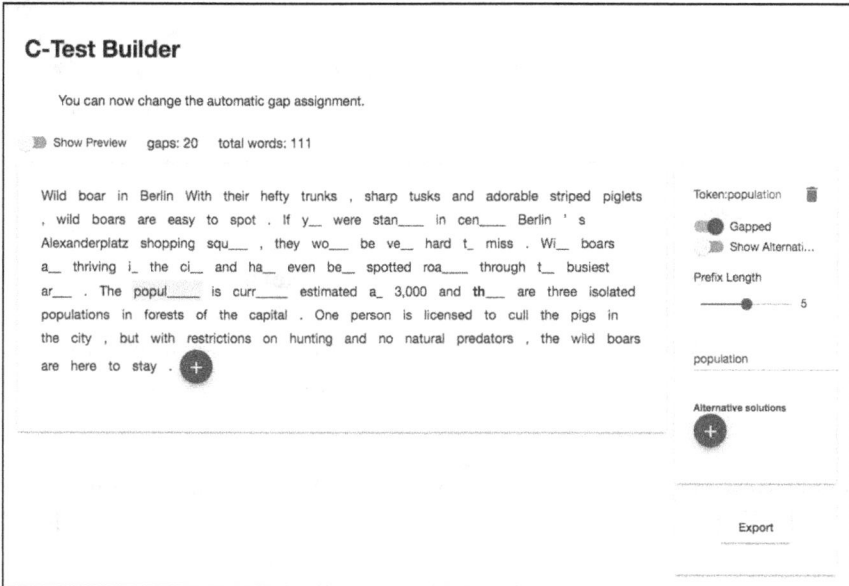

C-Test Builder

You can now change the automatic gap assignment.

▶ Show Preview   gaps: 20   total words: 111

Wild boar in Berlin With their hefty trunks , sharp tusks and adorable striped piglets , wild boars are easy to spot . If y__ were stan____ in cen____ Berlin ' s Alexanderplatz shopping squ___ , they wo__ be ve__ hard t_ miss . Wi__ boars a__ thriving i_ the ci__ and ha__ even be__ spotted roa____ through t__ busiest ar___ . The popul_____ is curr_____ estimated a_ 3,000 and th___ are three isolated populations in forests of the capital . One person is licensed to cull the pigs in the city , but with restrictions on hunting and no natural predators , the wild boars are here to stay . ⊕

Token:population   🗑

◉ Gapped
▶ Show Alternati...

Prefix Length
——————●———— 5

population

Alternative solutions
⊕

Export

While the overall creation rule for C-tests is simple (gap the second half of every second word), there are a number of exceptions that require NLP to ensure a high quality in the automatic gap assignment methods, such as part-of-speech tagging (the identification of word classes like nouns, verbs, or adjectives) and named entity recognition (identifying, e.g. persons, locations, or organizations). We make sure that numbers and dates, abbreviations, punctuation, and named entities are not included in the gapping scheme as they often cannot be predicted or such prediction requires knowledge beyond mere language proficiency.

The process for gap assignment is language independent in its basic version, assuming that a suitable tokenizer (i.e. a tool that automatically identifies word boundaries) for the language in question is available. We currently assume that tokens can be separated by white-spaces and cannot yet deal with languages where this is not the case, such as in Chinese. For a number of languages (English, French, German, Spanish, and Italian), we have already implemented more specific gap assignment methods taking language-specific phenomena into account. However, this requires language-specific NLP tools that are not always available. Thus, we also incorporate simple fallbacks, e.g. counting every capitalized word as a named entity.

An important phenomenon to consider for German, as well as English to some extent, is the frequent occurrence of noun compounds, such as *Haustürschlüssel* (literally 'house door key'). Applying the generic rule to split words in equal halves (*Haustürs_____*) often leads to gaps which are very hard to predict; therefore, compounds in German are usually treated in such a way that only the (right-most) head noun of the compound is gapped. In our example, this leads to the gapped word *Haustürschl_____*. We incorporate this behavior into our tool by employing automatic compound splitting.

In many romance languages, tokens containing clitics like the French *qu'aujourd'hui* need to be properly segmented before adding a gap. In the above example, proper tokenization should split the word into *qu'* and *aujourd'hui,* which would be reduced to *aujou_____*. Therefore, we use dedicated tokenization methods for each language.

In addition to the automatic gap assignment, users always have full control over the C-test and can manually adjust it. For example, users can mark words which should not be gapped, so that these words are not considered for automatic gapping. After the initial gap assignment, users may also modify the C-test by adding or deleting words or modifying the number of deleted characters for a gap.

The system automatically stores the correct solution for a gap based on the input text, so this information can be used later for automatic evaluation of a learner submission for the test. In some cases, however, more than one solution is possible. For example, in the English sentence *They returned to their ho___*, both *house* and *home* could in many contexts be a correct solution for the gap. Our tool gives teachers the option to specify such additional correct solutions for a gap. In the future, we also plan to identify alternative plausible solutions that are potentially unforeseen by the human test creator. One way to do this automatically would be the use of language models, which statistically predict the most likely words for a specific context.

The final C-tests can be exported in various formats to ease the integration with existing computer-assisted language learning systems. We support, for example, export in Moodle format as well as PDFs, which can be used to fill out the test pen-and-paper style. The online system can also be used as a convenient editor to import and adapt existing C-tests.

3.   Outlook and future work

The next steps we take will focus on two aspects related to creating C-Tests: predicting the difficulty of a C-test and searching the web for suitable textual material.

Predicting the difficulty of a C-test is a difficult task for humans (Beinborn, Zesch, & Gurevych, 2014). Therefore, field-tests with real learners are usually necessary before a test can be used to assign test takers to a proficiency level. Automatically assessing the difficulty of a C-test can therefore help to shorten the production cycle for new tests. To this end, we will include in the system a recently developed method (Beinborn et al., 2014) to reliably predict the difficulty of a given gap. This not only helps the exercise designer to adapt the overall difficulty of the test to the appropriate level for a given group of language learners, but also to identify individual problematic gaps.

Identifying suitable texts as input for the C-test tool is another important direction for future work. An appropriated text should be, as far as possible, thematically self-contained within a specific length constraint. It should have adequate complexity and linguistic difficulty. Finding such texts can be time-consuming for humans, while text mining and NLP methods can help by searching the web for good text candidates for a C-test. In the future, we plan to incorporate such a tool into the C-test builder.

4.   Acknowledgements

This work is funded by the German Federal Ministry of Education and Research under grant no. FKZ 01PL16075. We thank our student assistants Mahmoud Hegazi and Marius Hamacher, who contributed to the implementation of the system.

References

Arras, U., Eckes, T., & Grotjahn, R. (2002). C-Tests im Rahmen des „Test Deutsch als Fremdsprache" (TestDaF): Erste Forschungsergebnisse. In R. Grotjahn (Ed.), Der CTest: theoretische Grundlagen und praktische Anwendungen (pp. 175-209). AKSVerlag.

Beinborn, L., Zesch, T., & Gurevych, I. (2014). Predicting the difficulty of language proficiency tests. *Transactions of the association for computational linguistics, 2,* 517-529.

Eckes, T., & Grotjahn, R. (2006). A closer look at the construct validity of C-tests. *Language Testing, 26*(3), 290-325. https://doi.org/10.1191/0265532206lt330oa

Grotjahn, R. (Ed.). (2014). Der C-Test: aktuelle Tendenzen- The C-test: current trends [Bilingual]. Peter Lang GmbH, Internationaler Verlag der Wissenschaften. https://doi.org/10.3726/978-3-653-04578-9

Author index

Z

www.ingramcontent.com/pod-product-compliance
Lightning Source LLC
Chambersburg PA
CBHW061129220326
41599CB00024B/4213